ᴿᴬᴿY, Coventry L

STRATEGIC MANAGEMENT

Cove   Li
Coventry Un

This book is dedicated to my wife, Pamela, and my daughter,
Amanda Kate

STRATEGIC MANAGEMENT

Gordon E. Greenley
University of Birmingham

Prentice Hall
New York   London   Toronto   Sydney   Tokyo

First published 1989 by
Prentice Hall International (UK) Ltd,
66 Wood Lane End, Hemel Hempstead,
Hertfordshire, HP2 4RG
A division of
Simon & Schuster International Group

Printed and bound in Great Britain at
the University Press, Cambridge

British Library Cataloguing in Publication Data

Greenley, Gordon E.
    Strategic management.
    1. Business firms. Management. Long-range
    planning
    I. Title
    658.4'012
    ISBN 0-13-850512-8   Po 3642

1 2 3 4 5   93   92   91   90   89   88

ISBN 0-13-850512-8

CONTENTS

PREFACE

Strategic management is concerned with the overall long-range direction of organizations. The consolidation and study of knowledge pertinent to this discipline is still relatively new, having only comparatively recently been initiated at the Harvard Business School. During the 'early days' this area of study was labelled 'business policy', and this term and 'strategic management' are still often given the same meaning. Like its sources of initiation, the current body of knowledge on strategic management is dominated by publications from the United States.

Although some readers of this book will have already studied strategic management, most will be new to the discipline. However, it is likely that most will have already studied the functional aspects of organizations, such as marketing, finance and personnel. Throughout universities and polytechnics the importance of strategic management as a discipline has been developing. Indeed, current postgraduate programmes in business administration incorporate the teaching of strategic management, while more and more undergraduate programmes include it as a disciplined area of study. In some institutions courses addressing this discipline will have other titles, such as 'business policy', 'business planning', 'corporate planning', 'corporate strategy', and 'organizational policy', but this book is also aimed at these courses.

There are three major features of the treatment of strategic management presented in this book. First, it has been developed as a consolidation of the current body of knowledge that relates to the discipline. The 'early' teaching of the discipline as business policy was based almost entirely on the study of individual company case studies, owing to the lack of a body of knowledge. The current level of knowledge means that such an approach is now no longer necessary.

The second feature is that the company illustrations used throughout the book are set within a European context. Here the aim is to extend the choice in selecting a strategic management book which does not come from the United States, for British educators in particular and European educators in general.

The third feature is that three different types of illustration are used to show the application of concepts to real company situations. These are:

The integrative case study

This case study is first presented in its entirety in Chapter 2. The illustrations of the application of specified strategic management concepts to this case study company appear at the end of each part of the book. Consequently there are five illustrations based on the integrative case study, with each obviously appertaining to the concepts presented in the relevant part. However, the major feature of this approach is that each part is progressively related to a single company, with the aim of integrating concepts into a total understanding. This case is a British company participating throughout Europe and other world markets.

Chapter case study illustrations

These illustrations are based on a different case study for each of Chapters 3–14 inclusive. Here the original case studies are not presented in their entirety. Rather each is a 'free-standing' illustration relating to the respective chapter, having been derived from the original published case study. Rather than reproduce the case studies in full, the approach is to report only those issues of practice that are relevant to the respective chapters. These illustrations are based on well-known companies, located in several European countries.

Chapter exhibits

These are short illustrations of specific concepts and their application to particular companies. They are drawn from reports of company practices which have appeared in the business press. As well as providing illustrations, the aim of these exhibits is to encourage students to extend their reading to cover contemporary company practices, as reported in the business press. Again most are well-known companies, located in several European countries.

The aim of the case studies is to provide a basis for the illustration of strategic management concepts and is not to provide a detailed case-study analysis as would be required of students. However, adoption of the book and the use of these case studies provide the basis for planning a course on strategic management that aims to impart both theory and its application to actual company situations. The case studies used are available through the Case Clearing House of Great Britain, as well as through other European case clearing organizations.

The book is structured into five parts. Part One is an introduction to both the nature of strategic management and the field of study. Part Two is an examination of the total environment in which organizations exist and perform. Part Three looks at the long-range planning of the types of direction that organizations can pursue. Part Four examines the long-range planning of the approaches that are available in order to tackle these alternative directions. Finally, Part Five is concerned with the implementation of the approach which has been selected as being suitable for the direction to be pursued.

The author wishes to acknowledge the help and guidance given to him by the many colleagues with whom he has been associated over his career. They have all provided contributions, either directly or indirectly.

PART ONE
INTRODUCING STRATEGIC MANAGEMENT

OUTLINE OF PART ONE

In introducing the discipline of strategic management, the needs of readers who already have some familiarity with the subject are taken into account, alongside those of readers who are totally new to this area of study. The essence of strategic management is that it addresses the overall long-range direction of organizations. Chapter 1 builds on this premiss in its examination of the nature of strategic management. It also presents the framework on which the treatment of strategic management in this book is based. Chapter 2 presents the integrative case in its entirety, as originally published by its author. Illustrations of the application of the concepts of strategic management, in relation to this case study, appear at the end of each of the five parts of the book. The first of these, that relating to Part One, follows Chapter 2.

CHAPTER 1   THE NATURE OF STRATEGIC MANAGEMENT
CHAPTER 2   THE INTEGRATIVE CASE STUDY

CHAPTER 1

THE NATURE OF STRATEGIC MANAGEMENT

Many important issues will be included in this first chapter. Its overall aims are to introduce the field of study of strategic management and to provide an overview of its nature. Indeed, all the major concepts used throughout the book are progressively introduced as the chapter develops. Each of these concepts is outlined as a prelude to the full expositions that are presented later in the book. This chapter is, therefore, important to readers who are new to the discipline; but it is also important to those who have already studied strategic management as it provides a conceptual framework.

The concept of 'management' is obviously in common usage, although 'strategic management' is not. The chapter starts by simply looking at the concept of management as used in everyday speech, but then goes on to define its nature closely within the context of organizations. This leads on to developing 'what managers do', as a first stage of specifying the component parts of the strategic management process. While management is seen to be practised throughout organizations, different types of management are evident. As a result, the next area of study within this chapter is these different types of management.

Attention is then directed to the type of management which is the subject of this book, providing a focus on the features of strategic management that differentiate it from other forms of management. The next stage of the chapter is concerned with an examination of the model of strategic management that is used in the book. This serves two purposes. The first is that it provides an overview of the nature of each chapter; the second is that it provides the overall framework of the book. Here the chapters are each introduced and their relationship to each other is also established. The major point to emphasize here is that the book framework represents the integration of the component parts of the strategic management process. Finally, attention is given to identifying the value to organizations of utilizing strategic management.

THE NATURE OF MANAGEMENT

The many books that are concerned with principles and practice of management, of which Stoner[1] and Brech[2] are examples, trace the historical development of the understanding of the nature of management. The work of the classical management theorists is explained, and the school of scientific management is recorded as the major development. While full attention to this area of study is considered to be outside the scope of this book, the work of Henri Fayol (1841–1925) seems to be universally accepted as the foundation of scientific management.

Attempts at defining 'management' abound, with each major text presenting its own version. For the purpose of this book management is taken to be a process whereby individuals within an organization are required to anticipate activities likely to be necessary in the future, as well as carrying out such activities, while always attempting to ensure that 'things don't go wrong' with these activities. Such an approach leads to a listing of the functions or elements of management and again the texts addressing management each give a particular version. That given by Ansoff and Brandenburg[3] is based upon three major functions:

- *Planning*. Looking to the future and determining plans of action for the activities that appear to be necessary to pursue certain aims.
- *Implementation*. Communicating the plans to the appropriate individuals, overseeing the execution of the planned activities and providing the necessary motivation and leadership.
- *Control*. Measuring the performance of activities in relation to those that were previously planned.

Indeed, as will be seen later in this chapter, the total process of strategic management is based upon these three fundamental concepts, so that, as a consequence, this book is derived from these three fundamentals.

A feature of all the functions of management is that they require the manager to practise decision-making. Within each of the above three functions a range of decisions will need to be made and it is the tackling of these decisions that will be the subject of Chapters 3–14. In planning, decisions will need to be made on the aims to pursue and on the range of necessary activities likely to be necessary to achieve these aims. During implementation, decisions will need to be made to select the personnel to perform the activities, to direct them in their performance, and to practise motivation and leadership. Similarly, decisions will also be required to achieve control, in order to determine whether actual performance is acceptable and in order to determine the appropriateness of any corrective action. Consequently, attention is now given to decision-making.

In examining decision-making the literature tackles two major aspects. The first is a sequence of logical stages that should be systematically followed in the process of making decisions. The second is a classification of overall approaches that have been observed to be followed by different managers. Here Glueck and Jauch[4] cite the rational-analytical decision-maker who will follow the logical stages, but also

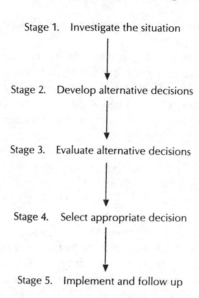

Stage 1. Investigate the situation

Stage 2. Develop alternative decisions

Stage 3. Evaluate alternative decisions

Stage 4. Select appropriate decision

Stage 5. Implement and follow up

Figure 1.1 *Logical stages of decision-making.*

the intuitive-emotional decision-maker, who will not. Additionally, they identify political-behavioural decision-making, an approach which can be affected by numerous influences. The logical stages of decision-making have been adequately presented by Stoner[1]. These have been adapted and are illustrated in Figure 1.1.

Stage 1 is to *investigate the situation*. Here managers must be able to understand the total environment in which they are working and the nature of the aspect of planning, implementation or control that they are tackling. Next they must be able to define the decision to be made, such as the need for a new set of aims or a need for more effective activities.

Stage 2 is to *develop alternative decisions*. In order to ensure that the most appropriate decision is made, managers need to be exhaustive in examining alternative possible courses of action, any one of which could satisfy the definition established in stage 1. Many different types of aim could be considered, but their comparison will help to provide a focus on the most viable course of action.

Stage 3 is to *evaluate alternative decisions*. Each alternative decision must be evaluated in terms of the likely outcome or consequences should that alternative course of action be followed. Much attention is given to this stage throughout this book.

Stage 4 is to *select the appropriate decision*. The potential outcome or consequence provides the basis for selection. However, a major concern is determining which is the 'right' outcome. Although there are approaches that can be taken to establish the value of such outcomes, much selection among alternatives is based on value judgements of either individual or groups of managers.

Stage 5 involves *implementation and follow up*. The selected alternative must be pursued, so the manager must be able to instigate the necessary action from personnel, allocate the necessary resources for its implementation and oversee the actual course of action, so that the resultant suitability of the decision can be assessed.

The final point to be made concerning the nature of management is that, despite the systematic approaches to management presented in the literature, management often fails to be effective. Murdick *et al.*[5] differentiate between failure due to the individual abilities of managers and failure due to the complexity of the business environment in which they work. A common complaint of both managers and writers is that, although managers may study systematic approaches to management, they are often either unable or unwilling to apply the principles to their own organizational situations. Here there are two schools of thought. One is that the literature is not really concerned with management problems, but is mostly concerned with explaining the nature of management; the other is that many managers have developed their own management style and consider that 'theoretical propositions' can do little to enhance their efficiency. Both these schools of thought have been taken into account throughout this book.

The other major cause of failure was given as being the complexity of the business environment. It is likely that readers of this book will be well aware of this, with the overall complexity being rooted in the variability of human behaviour. This complexity is emphasized throughout the book, but the approaches to strategic management that are given are designed for the tackling of this complexity.

TYPES OF MANAGEMENT

Regardless of the size of an organization, or the nature of its business, it is likely that the total number of managers employed will be organized into some type of hierarchical structure. In simple terms, a company may be considered as being a hierarchy with the board of directors at the apex, followed by senior managers, middle managers, junior managers and supervisors. Given the different locations of these managers, it is obvious that their job specifications will be different, in terms of both specific duties and responsibilities. However, the overall nature of the process of management remains the same, in that planning, implementation and control feature at each level of the hierarchy.

Levels of management

Readers who have already studied strategic management will be aware of the many differences in the usage of terminology when designating names to the different types of management at different levels within the hierarchy. As a result, much confusion is apparent in both the literature and in organizations.

Despite such differences there seems to be common agreement on a split between top management, which is concerned with the overall management of the firm in total, and the management of the individual business functions, such as

production, finance and marketing. The former is often labelled 'strategic management' and the latter 'operational management', which is epitomized in major
texts such as those by Pearce and Robinson[6] and Byars[7]. However, writers such as
Pearce and Robinson[6] and Higgins[8] considered that strategic management encom-
passes operational management, to represent the summation of all managerial
activities throughout the hierarchy. However, this approach is not taken in this
book. The functions of these two levels of management are considered to be
different, as previously mentioned, so that they are treated as being separate areas.
The approach taken is that corporate management is labelled as being the summation of all managerial activities throughout the hierarchy. Each of these levels of
management is explained as follows and is illustrated in Figure 1.2.

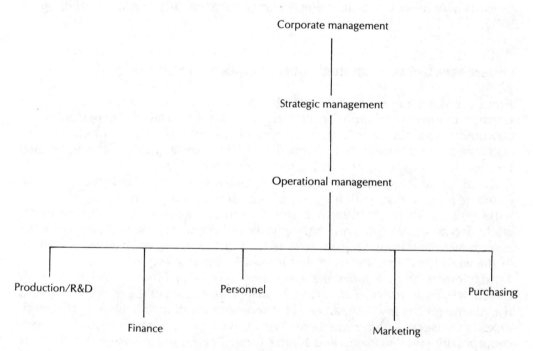

Figure 1.2 *Levels of management.*

- *Corporate management.* The summation of all management throughout the
  organizational hierarchy, incorporating strategic and operational management.
- *Strategic management.* The management of the overall organization in total,
  being particularly concerned with future direction. Consequently, it also provides a framework for operational management.
- *Operational management.* The management of the individual business functions
  or operations, being concerned with the role that each is to play in the total
  organization. Here the operations are taken to be marketing, research and
  development (R&D), production, finance, and personnel.

Companies are also often organized into separate divisions, or even into a number of subsidiary companies, with such splits being based upon variations in the business in which they participate. Within the literature these divisions have been labelled strategic business units (SBUs). In these organizations an additional level of management is likely, although many variations in the organizational structures of these firms are to be found. However the principle is that such a divisionalization will also cause a division within the corporate management of these companies. This additional level of management, which is located at the SBU level within the hierarchy, is illustrated in Figure 1.3. Full details of the differences between strategic management at the organizational level and at the SBU level will be explained throughout the chapters. However, in simple terms, the former is concerned with the total organization, whereas at the SBU level the concern is only with the directional management of that particular division or SBU.

Differences between strategic and operational management

From the above the major difference between strategic management and operational management should be apparent. To recap: strategic management is concerned with the overall management of an organization in total, whereas operational management is concerned with the management of the individual business functions, such as manufacturing and marketing.

At this point it is emphasized that these two major types of management have different roles to play within organizations. However, in recent years the trend within the literature has been to elevate the importance of strategic management, while derivatives of the word 'strategy' have become in vogue throughout the management literature. Indeed, writers such as Carroll[9] have observed the abuse of the word 'strategy', asserting that it has become a 'grandiose synonym for the word "important"'. Similar malapropisms have been observed in firms, with Greenley[10], for example, identifying the inappropriate use of the word 'strategy' in the planning of many companies. The approach taken in this book is that both types of management have equal importance, even though strategic management is conceptually given as being at a higher level. The ramifications of the different roles are featured in the book, although a recent text by Greenley[11] gives equal treatment to both strategic and operational management within the context of marketing.

The other major difference is that strategic management is concerned with the long term, whereas operational management is concerned with the immediate running of companies. Decisions within strategic management will commit the firm to levels of capital investment that can only be exploited over a given period, and will provide manufacturing capacity that is likely to be difficult to replace in the short term. However, operational management is concerned with marketing effectiveness in these selected markets, the effective use of current levels of expenditure and revenue, plus the efficient use of existing production capacity.

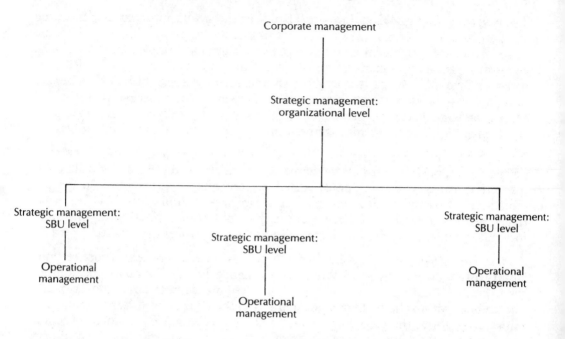

Figure 1.3 *Levels of management: multiple businesses.*

Participation in strategic management

The final aspect in considering the different types of management is to discuss the different types of manager who are likely to participate in the strategic management process.

The first point is that the tremendous variation to be found in organizational structures means that there is also a wide variation in the job titles of managers who are required to participate in strategic management. This includes any split into separate SBUs. Indeed, this issue will be studied in detail in Chapter 9. The second point is that individual differences in managers' abilities and attitudes will affect their willingness to be able to contribute effectively. These effects will be examined in Chapter 8. Therefore, being explicit as to who 'does' strategic management is difficult; all that can be done is to identify individuals, or groups, with the potential to participate.

The board of directors. Where the board consists mostly of executive directors then strategic management may be completed by the directors, although senior managers may also be involved. However, Higgins[8] claims that, for many companies, the board does not perform such functions, which may be particularly prevalent where there are many non-executive directors. Where the company features a number of SBUs it may be that there will be a main board plus a divisional board for each SBU. Here it is likely that the divisional boards would have more involvement than the main board.

The managing director (MD). For small firms, or those without separate SBUs, the chief executive officer may take full responsibility for long-term direction. In some larger firms the office of the chief executive officer may employ personnel who tackle strategic management issues on behalf of the MD. Where each SBU features its own MD, then it may be that the major responsibility of these job functions is to tackle strategic management. However, Mintzberg[12] has identified several tasks that are performed by chief executive officers, so that extensive involvement with strategic management may not be exhibited by many MDs.

Senior managers. For some firms it may be that a particular senior manager is delegated responsibility for strategic management. In many firms this will be the marketing manager, but the point is that responsibility is delegated to a specific job function. A similar situation may be established within each SBU. Alternatively, a committee of senior managers may be constituted to take responsibility for strategic management, which may also include several key executive directors.

A specialized department. In some firms there may be a department whose responsibility it is to be only involved with strategic management, with no responsibilities for operational management. Often called 'planning departments' and normally not 'in line' within the management hierarchy, their function is dependent upon information about the performance of the company, which is provided by senior managers, while the resultant planning of strategic management would be subject to approval by the board.

The consequences of these alternative types of managerial participation are pursued further in Chapters 8, 12 and 13.

THE FOCUS OF STRATEGIC MANAGEMENT

In this section attention is given to the features of strategic management as a prelude to examining the nature of its component parts, which is the subject of the next section. This is approached by first taking a brief look at the historical development of strategic management. Then consideration will be given to attempts at its definition, while the specific features of strategic management are the final area of consideration.

Historical developments

Accounts of the historical development of strategic management are given by writers such as Aaker[13], Gluck *et al.*[14], and Ansoff[15] and interested readers are particularly urged to refer to the latter. Four major stages are commonly recorded as representing the development of strategic management to the current level of understanding.

Budgeting and control

This represents early approaches to systematic management and is associated with the early years of the twentieth century. Based upon the assumption that past conditions will prevail in the future, the approach was simply to establish standard levels of performance in budgets and to compare these with actual levels. Reasons for any variations provided the only learning experiences.

Long-range planning

This is generally associated with the 1950s. The approach was based on the identification of past trends, particularly business growth, as well as methodology to project these trends into the future. Resources would then be planned either to exploit potential growth or to accommodate anticipated contraction.

Strategic planning

This is generally associated with the 1960s–70s. At this stage of development past trends were considered to be inadequate, so that attention was focused on the total, albeit complex, market and business environment in which the firm participates. The focus was also placed upon identifying changes of direction, developing capabilities and creating strategic thrusts for competitive advantage. It was based on planning cycles, with the annual planning cycle being of particular importance.

Strategic management

This is associated with the period from the mid-1970s onwards. Like strategic planning, it is based on the complexities of the total business environment. However, the approach is not to accept current conditions as being restricting. Rather, the approach is led by well-defined aims, well-developed means to achieve them, and by pursuing viable opportunities wherever they can be identified, which may be regardless of the nature of current operations. The approach relies upon a continuous supply of information about the environment and avoids the use of planning cycles in preference to being based upon a continuous process.

Defining strategic management

Many definitions of strategic management have been offered in the literature, although three major approaches are evident across the body of knowledge. These approaches are classified as being:

- The environmental approach.
- The aims and means approach.
- The actions approach.

Environmental approach

An example of the definitions of strategic management taking this approach is taken from Rowe et al.[16]: 'the decision process that conjoins the organization's internal capability with the opportunities and threats it faces in its environment'. The strength of this approach is that the firm becomes orientated to its external environment, so that threats in current markets are likely to lead to the pursuit of other opportunities, some of which may be in markets of which the firm has no previous experience. The other major feature is that internal organizational capabilities may become constraining parameters in business development. Although firms obviously need to be realistic in relation to both resource availability and managerial capability when planning future developments, internal constraints may be detrimental, leading to risk aversion rather than risk evasion. However, this approach is consistent with the explanation of strategic management as given in the description of its historical development.

Aims and means approach

This approach is epitomized by Glueck and Jauch[4]; for them strategic management is 'a stream of decisions and actions which leads to the development of an effective strategy, or strategies, to help achieve corporate objectives'. The use of the word 'stream', in connection with decisions, is to show that strategic management involves a range of decisions each following a logical progression. This concept will arise frequently in the book. The outcome of these decisions is that action throughout the hierarchy will be instigated, as already indicated; and again the detail of this action will be explained where appropriate throughout the book. The word 'objective' is that used for the aims to be established by the firm, while the word 'strategy' is that used to denote their means of achievement. Separate chapters are devoted to both these key areas of strategic management. As with the previous approach to defining strategic management, all the aspects of this definition are consistent with the description of its historical development.

Actions approach

The approach taken by Johnson and Scholes[17] has been selected as being representative of the actions-approach group of definitions. These explain strategic management as being concerned with deciding on strategy and planning how that strategy is to be put into effect. The actions are classified into three broad areas:

- Strategic analysis to understand the current position of the organization.
- Strategic choice, which is concerned with the formulation and evaluation of alternative strategies, followed by strategy selection.
- Strategic implementation, which is directed towards pursuing the selected strategy.

The analysis stage is similar to the environment approach, in that this area of activity is directed towards pursuing an understanding of the full range of variables that are likely to be pertinent to the strategic management of organizations. The stage of choice equates to the logical stages of decision-making, as previously examined. Here the actions are concerned with the establishment of an optimum strategy, or means, for tackling the opportunities identified in the analysis. Finally, actions are needed to execute these stages. Initial actions would be concerned with planning throughout the company as a result of the chosen strategy, followed by its execution over the specified period of time. Actions to complete the stage of implementation involve control, being those actions which have already been discussed. Again this approach is consistent with the explanation of strategic management, as given in the description of its historical development.

Having looked at definitions of strategic management, attention is now given to examining specific features of the process, as a prelude to explaining the model of strategic management used in the book.

Features of strategic management

Aaker[13] identifies 14 features of strategic management. These have been adopted and classified into three groups (Table 1.1). Each is outlined below, and will be developed further in later chapters.

Market orientation. Firms need to be sensitive to market conditions and particularly to the requirements of customers. However, they must also look to the future. It is not enough to project past trends into the future; forecasting needs to be employed, taking into account any new factors which may affect future trends.

Table 1.1   *Features of strategic management.*

External features

- Market orientation
- Market understanding
- Information inputs
- Empirical research
- International business

Systems features

- Decision making
- Entrepreneurial thrusts
- Longer time horizons
- Methodological developments

Internal features

- Proactive strategies
- Multiple strategies
- Interdisciplinary features
- Implementation
- Resource utilization

Market understanding. The potential growth of markets and any changes in their competitive nature is central to strategic management. Such an understanding gives the core assessment of business risk.

Information inputs. The process requires extensive information gathering from all areas of the environment in which the firm participates. A development that has paralleled the development of strategic management has been that of management information systems, which covers not only collection, but also analysis, dissemination, storage and the identification of further information needs.

Empirical research. Although this feature is not directly related to the practical management of firms, the understanding of strategic management within the literature has developed through the 1980s, allowing firms to develop their approach to their business within the context of this body of knowledge.

International business. Strategic management can lead firms to consider exporting their home production, or may even 'force' them to export. However, it can also lead to an international orientation of the firm, with respect to both management thinking and company operations.

Decision-making. Strategic management should be a continuous process of considering the component parts and making necessary decisions, as opposed to being a stop-start planning cycle process.

Entrepreneurial thrusts. Despite the movement towards systematic, logical and information-based management, entrepreneurial flair is still part of business. Opportunities still need to be 'felt to be right', while business risks still need to be taken.

Longer time horizons. While operational management focuses on short periods of time, strategic management focuses on longer periods. However, next year's annual plan represents the first year of the longer term, so that shorter periods still need to be considered.

Methodological developments. While overall systems of this type of management have been developed, methodological systems have also been developed within the individual component parts of strategic management. Many of these methods will be discussed in the relevant chapters.

Proactive strategies. Rather than merely reacting to changes in the environment, strategic management attempts to exert at least a partial influence on future events within the business environment.

Multiple strategies. As already mentioned, a major internal feature is that alternative strategies or means of achieving objectives can be formulated, in order to select that which is anticipated to be the most suitable.

Interdisciplinary features. Despite the establishment of strategic management as a bona fide discipline, and despite the roles of the different functions of a company within operational management, strategic management draws upon the individual disciplines of business. As will be seen throughout this book, methods and philosophical concepts are utilized from, especially, the disciplines of marketing, finance, manufacturing and organizational behaviour.

Implementation. As with all types of management, planned courses of action must be carried out along with necessary control procedures. In particular, links with operational management are needed, which will be addressed in Chapter 12.

Resource utilization. Strategic management provides the overall basis for the allocation of company resources into the long-term future. For some strategies this may involve extensive capital investment, although for many firms it will entail effective utilization of existing capital.

A MODEL OF STRATEGIC MANAGEMENT

This section is concerned with an examination of the component parts that constitute the model of strategic management used in this book. As mentioned in the introduction to this chapter, there are two reasons for this examination. The first is that it provides an overview of the nature of each of the chapters, while the second is that it provides an overall framework for the book. In this examination each of the chapters is introduced and their relationship to each other is established.

As a result of the previous discussion in this chapter, the process of strategic management is first broken down into four major component parts. These have been developed out of the process of management *per se*, plus the nature of decision-making. These four major parts are illustrated in Figure 1.4.

Analysing the environment. This part of strategic management is concerned with research and investigations into the total environment, analysis and understanding of these findings and presentation of the results for subsequent decision-making. The environment is both internal and external. The former not only includes the organization itself, but also the personnel employed. External analysis should ideally include all variables with the potential of affecting the company, although competitors and market structures are of particular importance.

Planning direction. The second part is concerned with determining the future direction to be pursued, by expounding the aims that are seen to be applicable. These aims have already been identified as being objectives for the performance of the company. Also to be considered in this part is the overall philosophy of the company, as well as the different types of business that are considered to be desirable for future participation. Depending upon the organizational structure, this planning may be at two levels: at the organizational level, but also at the SBU level where SBUs are a feature of the structure.

Planning strategy. In simple terms, this part is concerned with designing the means for pursuing the planned direction. It represents 'how' the firm is to tackle its desired levels of performance. By following the principles of decision-making, it is

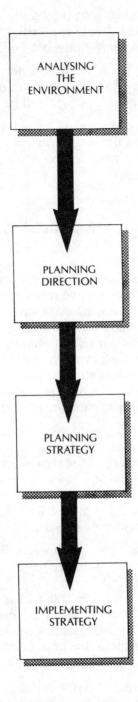

Figure 1.4 *The four major component parts of strategic management.*

concerned with formulating a number of alternative strategies, so that several different approaches can be considered for their individual feasibility. Consequently, the selection of that to be utilized can be subjected to a number of different methods designed to aid in the decision-making process of strategy selection. Again there are likely to be company differences based on organizational structure. Where there are a number of SBUs then it is likely that strategy will be planned at the SBU level, while in a single business firm it will be planned at the organizational level.

Implementing strategy. The final part is the carrying-out of the organizational strategy in the pursuit of organizational objectives. As will be seen later in this book, this is achieved through the individual operations or functions of the company. Operational management requires the formulation and implementation of strategies for each of the operations, such as marketing, manufacturing and finance. The concept of control has already been discussed, but it is emphasized that control is certainly very much the concern of this part of strategic management.

These four major component parts of strategic management have been extended in Figure 1.5. The left-hand side of the figure gives the four major component parts as discussed above. The figure also shows a number of stages for each of these parts, which are connected to each of the four parts. Each of these stages consists of specific decisions within the different stages of the strategic management process, and each is briefly explained as follows:

Strategic audits. The stage of researching and understanding the total business environment, being concerned with methodology for both collecting and analysing data.

Understanding competitors. Also a stage of research and analysis, but devoted to appraisals of the strengths, weaknesses and potential levels of performance of competitive organizations.

Understanding market structures. Again a stage of research and analysis, but concerned with a specific understanding of the nature of both current markets and those for potential participation.

Organizational mission. Here decisions are made about the overall business philosophy of the firm, the broad areas of industry participation and unique features of company *modus operandi*.

Organizational objectives. Determining the specific aims that are to be pursued, which will define the levels of performance to be aimed at. These can be established at both organizational and SBU levels.

Strategy alternatives. Determining a range of strategies, anyone of which could be potentially suitable for pursuing the specified objectives. Again, this can be at either the organizational or SBU level.

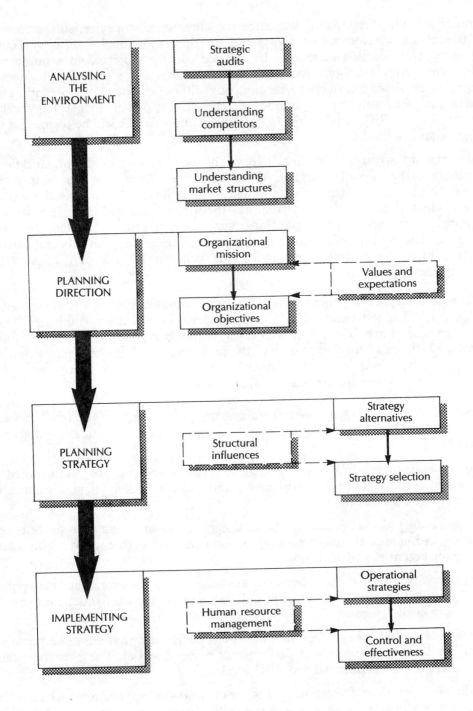

Figure 1.5 *A model of strategic management.*

Strategy selection. A major decision to commit resources to a particular course of action. Once selected, all actions of the total company, or the particular SBU, evolve out of the chosen strategy.

Operational strategies. Just as operational management is obsequious to strategic management, operational strategies are similarly obsequious to organizational strategy. Their performance will contribute to the performance of the superior strategy and will also influence future modifications at this higher level.

Control and effectiveness. Control allows for decisions to modify future plans as a consequence of current performance, as well as allowing for corrective action to be taken in current operational strategies. Assessments of effectiveness allow for longer-term decisions, aimed at improving the value of strategic management.

The remaining features of Figure 1.5 are three boxes labelled 'values and expectations', 'structural influences' and 'human resource management', which relate respectively to planning direction, planning strategy and implementing strategy. These three areas are given as being integral components of the strategic management model, but are not given as stages of its decision-making process. Rather, they are presented as influences which impinge on decision-making within the respective stages. However, as will be appreciated from further study of this book, these areas of the model are as important as those which directly address the decisions of strategic management. Each of these areas is briefly explained as follows:

Values and expectations. Some books on strategic management present the stages of the process as being mechanistic and almost self-generating. However, organizations are only groups of people, albeit several groups with differing interests, so that the values and expectations of both individuals and these groups of people play a major role in the determination of overall direction and specific objectives.

Structural influences. The effects of the organization of companies into separate divisions, subsidiaries or SBUs have already been briefly discussed in this chapter. However, influences due to structure will be evident throughout most of the chapters. Notwithstanding this situation, it is necessary to consolidate these influences into a common area of study, and indeed this is achieved by devoting a single chapter to structural influences.

Human resource management. Once analysis and planning have been completed, many textbooks assume that implementation will merely happen, with little regard to the influences that the people who are required to execute the implementation are likely to have on this stage of strategic management. However, these influences are taken to be a major area of the model used in this book, so that suitable attention is given to these issues.

Framework of the book

The model of strategic management given in Figure 1.5 also serves as a framework for the book. The four major component parts equate to the four parts of the book that follow Part One. Similarly, each of the stages of decision-making attached to each of the component parts in Figure 1.5 is represented by an equivalent chapter within each respective part. Likewise, each of the three areas of influence is represented by a single chapter, where each chapter is located within the relevant part of the book. Consequently, the framework is as that shown in Table 1.2.

Table 1.2 *Framework of the book.*

Part Two Analysing the Environment

Chapter 3	Strategic Audits
Chapter 4	Understanding Competitors
Chapter 5	Understanding Market Structures

Part Three Planning Direction

Chapter 6	Organizational Mission
Chapter 7	Organizational Objectives
Chapter 8	Values and Expectations

Part Four Planning Strategy

Chapter 9	Structural Influences
Chapter 10	Strategy Alternatives
Chapter 11	Strategy Selection

Part Five Implementing Strategy

Chapter 12	Operational Strategies
Chapter 13	Human Resource Management
Chapter 14	Control and Effectiveness

THE VALUE OF STRATEGIC MANAGEMENT

In this last section of the present chapter attention is given to the value or usefulness of strategic management to organizations. Although it can be claimed that this form of management should be endemic within organizations if they are to be effectively managed, researchers have attempted to list the potential values to be gained from the effective utilization of strategic management. Two aspects of the value of strategic management are examined: its likely affect on profits, and other advantages to be gained. Finally, brief consideration is given to the reasons why strategic management should be studied by both practising managers and those taking courses in business administration.

Profits and strategic management

Several researchers have attempted to identify whether or not there is a relationship between high levels of profit and the utilization of strategic management. In a recent article, Greenley[18] has examined those surveys that have investigated this relationship within manufacturing companies. Several surveys do claim that a relationship of improved profits as a result of strategic management was identified, with examples being the research by Ansoff *et al.*[19] and Karger and Malik[20]. However, several other surveys claim that such a relationship cannot be identified, with examples being the research by Kudla[21] and Leontiades and Tezel[22]. After examining the relative reliability of these surveys, it was concluded that current knowledge is insufficient to be able to claim that strategic management either does or does not directly cause an improvement to the profits of manufacturing companies. A similar investigation of research surveys was carried out by Armstrong[23], which also included surveys into non-manufacturing companies. He came to a similar conclusion: that such a relationship cannot be established as a consequence of these results.

Despite this situation, the value of strategic management in relation to profits is still important. Within the total environment in which any company operates there are many factors with the potential of affecting profits, either favourably or adversely. Therefore, to isolate the effect of strategic management within the complexity of these other factors would be almost impossible. Indeed this is the major weakness of all these investigations.

For many writers and managers the a priori case that strategic management will provide a contribution to the earning of profits, as one factor in a complex cause-and-effect relationship, is sufficient. The argument is that the process provides a systematic and logically planned approach to business, which must contribute to performance, even though it may be an indirect effect.

Advantages of strategic management

The major advantages of strategic management will perhaps be evident from the range of issues discussed in this chapter. Study of the other chapters will enhance the importance of these advantages. However, for the sake of clarity, these major advantages are listed below. Consequently, strategic management:

- Forces management to examine the appropriateness and value of current strategies.
- Forces management to look for alternatives in developing their business, so that optimum choices can be made.
- Requires an orientation into the future, which leads to greater consideration of the future ramifications of current decisions.
- Is likely to prevent the occurrence of problems, rather than devoting resources to the solution of an excessive number of problems.

- Allows for a more equitable and effective allocation of resources, as opposed to basing allocations on short-term spontaneous decisions.
- Ensures that both internal and external environments are taken into acount, while providing the means to identify any major changes that are likely to occur.
- Leads to management which is based on a systematic and logical process of thinking, while developing methodology to aid in decision-making, which will contribute to more effective management.
- Can be used as a vehicle to develop co-ordination, communication and control procedures throughout the organizational structure.
- Helps to stimulate the motivation and enthusiasm of employees, through both participation in the process and through the formalization of company direction.
- Also helps to reduce employees' resistence to change, again through participation and formalization.

Studying strategic management

In looking at reasons why strategic management should be studied it is perhaps meaningful to take two perspectives: that of practising managers and that of students preparing for a career in business.

For those managers who have already been involved in strategic management, this book will provide a structured framework of the process as an aid to conceptual understanding. For those executives who are more formally involved and bear major responsibilities, again the structured framework is offered as an aid to conceptual understanding. In addition, methodology is included in the book which may not have been previously used, so that inspiration to try some of these may be achieved. Also, the book provides a broader framework and greater depth of understanding of many concepts than is probably featured in many organizations. Here the book would hopefully stimulate both breadth and depth of thinking.

For managers who only get involved with operational management there are still benefits to be gained from studying this book. It is likely that managers will perform better at the operational level if they understand the process of management in the higher levels of the managerial hierarchy. Leading on from this, it is also likely that decisions will become less spontaneous and less reactive, while significant changes in the business environment, pertinent to the long term, will be more easily identified. Another benefit to operational managers is that their study may lead to suggestions within any of the stages of strategic management, resulting in their employment being of more value to their organizations. Leading on from this point, career advancement could follow such a level of contribution. Indeed, managers aspiring to develop their careers into senior management would certainly need to understand the strategic management process.

For students preparing for a career in business there are also benefits to be gained from studying this book. First, it is about organizational behaviour, allowing for an increased understanding of the nature of organizations *per se*. Second, this discipline is now offered in most taught business programmes, with the emphasis being particularly important at the Masters degree level. This book is orientated to this type of study. Third, an understanding of strategic management also provides an understanding of 'how firms work', which is often difficult to appreciate when employed in a first job at a low level in the hierarchy. Finally, knowledge of strategic management will prove to be invaluable as part of the range of knowledge and experience needed for career advancement.

SUMMARY

This chapter introduced the field of study of strategic management. This was done by examining its nature, by discussing its focus, and by presenting the model of strategic management to be used in this book.

The chapter commenced with an examination of the nature of management *per se*, and then considered the different levels of management found in an organization. This section also examined the differences between strategic and operational management, as well as the participation of different management levels in strategic management.

Attention was then directed to the focus of strategic management. This commenced with a description of its historical development, which was followed by an examination of definitions of strategic management. Three major approaches were identified in the literature, which were classified as the environment approach, the aims and means approach and the actions approach. Finally in this section, major features were presented, which were classified as external, internal and systems features.

The major thrust of the chapter was contained in the next section, which presented the model of strategic management to be used in this book. This consists of four major parts: analysing the environment; planning direction; planning strategy; and implementing strategy. Within these parts are nine major decision-making stages and three major areas of influence. This model also represents the framework of the book, while the designation of the components of the model to the chapters of the book was outlined.

The final section addressed the potential values of strategic management to organizations. These were related to profits and other advantages.

REFERENCES

1. Stoner, J. A. F., *Management*, Prentice Hall, Englewood Cliffs, NJ, 1982.
2. Brech, E. F. L., *The Principles and Practice of Management*, Longman, London, 1975.
3. Ansoff, H. I. and Brandenburg, R. G., 'The Design of Optimal Business Planning Systems', *Kommunikation*, **3**, 4, 1967, 163–188.
4. Glueck, W. F. and Jauch, L. R., *Business Policy and Strategic Management*, McGraw-Hill, New York, 1984.

5. Murdick, R. G., Moor, R. C., Eckhouse, R. H. and Zimmerer, T. W., *Business Policy: A Framework for Analysis*, Wiley, New York, 1984.
6. Pearce, J. A. and Robinson, R. B., *Strategic Management*, Irwin, Homewood, IL, 1985.
7. Byars, L. L., *Strategic Management*, Harper and Row, New York, 1984.
8. Higgins, J. M., *Organizational Policy and Strategic Management*, Dryden, New York, 1983.
9. Carrol, P. J., 'The Link between Performance and Strategy', *Journal of Business Strategy*, **2**, 4, 1982, 3–20.
10. Greenley, G. E., 'The Relationship of Strategic and Marketing Plans', *European Journal of Operational Research*, **27**, 1, 1986, 17–24.
11. Greenley, G. E., *The Strategic and Operational Planning of Marketing*, McGraw-Hill, Maidenhead, 1986.
12. Mintzberg, H., *The Nature of Managerial Work*, Harper and Row, New York, 1973.
13. Aaker, D. A., *Strategic Market Management*, Wiley, New York, 1984.
14. Gluck, F., Kaufman, S. and Walleck, A. S., 'The Four Phases of Strategic Management', *Journal of Business Strategy*, **2**, 3, 1982, 9–21.
15. Ansoff, H. I., *Implanting Strategic Management*, Prentice Hall, Englewood Cliffs, NJ, 1984.
16. Rowe, A. J., Mason, R. O. and Dickel, K. E., *Strategic Management*, Addison-Wesley, Reading, MA, 1986.
17. Johnson, G. and Scholes, K., *Exploring Corporate Strategy*, Prentice Hall, London, 1984.
18. Greenley, G. E., 'Does Strategic Planning Improve Company Performance?', *Long Range Planning*, **19**, 2, 1986, 101–9.
19. Ansoff, H. I. *et al.*, 'Does Planning Pay?', *Long Range Planning*, **3**, 2, 1970, 2–7.
20. Karger, D. W. and Malik, Z. A., 'Long Range Planning and Organizational Performance', *Long Range Planning*, **8**, 6, 1975, 60–4.
21. Kudla, R. J., 'The Effects of Strategic Planning on Common Stock Returns', *Academy of Management Journal*, **23**, 1, 1980, 5–20.
22. Leontiades, M. and Tezel, A., 'Planning Perceptions and Planning Results', *Strategic Management Journal*, **1**, 1, 1980, 65–75.
23. Armstrong, J. S., 'The Value of Formal Planning for Strategic Decisions: A Review of Empirical Research', *Strategic Management Journal*, **3**, 1982, 197–211.

CHAPTER 2
THE INTEGRATIVE CASE STUDY

The integrative case study is presented in its entirety after this introduction. It is presented in full and as originally published by the author, Professor Eric Newbigging. Plessey is a major Britain-based firm, although nearly 42 per cent of its sales are in world-wide markets. The study follows the development of the utilization of strategic management by Plessey over the period 1971–84. Plessey is a multiple business company, and the case study shows the complexities involved with such an organizational structure. However, the full value of this case study lies in the fact that it tackles many issues and concepts of strategic management.

The major aims of including an integrative case study are twofold. It allows for the illustration of each of the five parts of the book as entities, but giving progressive illustrations as the concepts of each chapter, of each of the five parts, are gradually introduced. As each of the five illustrations relates to the same company, all five illustrations integrate and consolidate the total strategic management process as presented in this book. This gives a total of five illustrations of the strategic management of Plessey, showing their application within the complexities of an organizational context. The approach also allows readers progressively to follow the total process of strategic management, to get a fuller understanding of and 'feel' for the utilization of the process.

The first task of the reader is obviously to read the full Plessey case material before looking at any of the five illustrations. Although each of the latter should be self-explanatory, the real understanding comes from a full and committed study of the case. As with all case-study work, for whatever purpose, 'the more you put into it the more you get out of it'. In addition, readers will also find that they will need to refer back to the detail in the total case study when examining each of the five illustrations.

The final point concerns the other case-study illustrations that are used throughout the book, as already mentioned in the Introduction. These are separate from the Plessey case study. This other approach features a single illustration for each of the chapters, where each is based on a different case study. Here the original case studies are not presented in their entirety. Rather, each illustration is a 'free-standing' and self-explanatory exhibit, although each was derived from an original published case study. All the full versions of these original publications are available through the Case Clearing House of Great Britain, so that they are also available through other European and world-wide case clearing organizations.

CASE STUDY
THE PLESSEY COMPANY PLC

In 1983, Plessey sales broke the £1,000 million barrier. Pre-tax profits, at £146.4 million, were up 31% on the previous year (see Exhibits 1–3 for Plessey's ten-year financial record). In this annual review, Chairman and Chief Executive, Sir John Clark, stated that 'increased attention to world-wide marketing now plays a major part in ... improving performance and profitability ... the total technology approach requires the product development engineer to consider in parallel the needs of product design and manufacturing to ensure optimum performance ... a development capability vital to our future in high technology identifying ever more closely with our customers' needs is a major task, but with our professionalism in technology, new product development and manufacturing capability, we have the essential experience and skills to respond even more competitively'.

In 1984, Parry Rogers, Personnel Director of Plessey, commented on the Company's evolution: 'Ten years ago we were broadly in the same three product areas (telecommunications, defence electronics and solid-state physics), but the telephone exchanges we made ... involved machine shops removing and shaping metal, making components to be built into electromechanical exchanges. The defence electronics side was perhaps more advanced, but still involved a good deal of mechanical and electrical equipment. On the components side, we had an extremely wide range of activities, from sheet metalwork and sub-contracting ... through to passive components like capacitors and resistors ... Telephone exchanges today ... are program controlled, ... computers in specialised applications ... this ties in with developments in the semi-conductor solid-state field, ... no longer a manufacturer of large-volume electro-mechanical components, we are essentially a system house producing large, complex, digital systems.' (See Exhibit 4 for Plessey's sales and profits by market 1974–83.)

COMPANY BACKGROUND

Founded in 1917, Plessey began making pianoforte actions and later jigs and tools. The grandfather of the present chairman put money into the company and his son Allen joined. With the beginning of radio broadcasting, Plessey manufactured first components, then complete radio receivers, under contract. In 1925, the present company was set up with a share capital of

This case study was prepared by Professor Eric Newbigging, Visiting Professor in Business Policy at the Cranfield School of Management, with the assistance of Sharon Tanser. Copyright © 1985 Eric Newbigging.

£20,000, and moved to Ilford, a London suburb. Prior to the Second World War, Plessey added aircraft components to its operations. In 1937, when turnover exceeded £1 million, Plessey became a public company. During the war Plessey produced shell and bomb cases, breeze connectors, wiring harnesses, engine cartridges and aircraft fuel pumps, including the fuel pump for the first jet engine. In the 1950s Plessey grew rapidly, mainly as a subcontractor, in telecommunications. Sir Allen Clark, by then Chairman, doubled the size of the company. With the acquisition of Automatic Telephone and Electric, and Ericsson Telephones, Plessey joined the telecommunications industry's leaders. Following Sir Allen Clark's death in 1962, John Clark became Chief Executive and his brother, Michael, his deputy. City observers evaluating the early years of the Clark brothers' stewardship considered that they had not maintained their father's entrepreneurial achievement.

The 1960s saw a steady annual increase of around 18% in Post Office orders for telecommunications equipment. Through a bulk supply agreement with the Post Office, Plessey, GEC and Standard Telephones and Cables (STC) shared orders on a strict 40:40:20 basis. When this agreement was dropped, Plessey's market share increased to 44% and telecommunications were at the core of Plessey's success in the 1960s. Plessey's other major area was defence. Its only UK customer was the government, with the Ministry of Defence the industry's largest single purchaser.

In 1970, Plessey bought Alloys Unlimited for £38 million to gain a manufacturing foothold in the USA. After 18 months, profits of £6 million had slumped to a loss of £6 million as the US semi-conductor market collapsed. This experience prompted critical self-analysis. In spring 1971, the five top managers – the Clark brothers, Geoffrey Gaut (for 37 years Technical Director), Eric Frye (Financial Director) and Tom Hudson (Non-executive Director) – met in the South of France to find out where Plessey had gone wrong and work out how to put things right.

The main weakness had been lack of foresight in strategic thinking: 'Too much brawn, not enough brain', as one critic commented. With a strong product and multinational base, the company was entering the 1970s with the wrong product mix, inadequate acquisitions criteria, and with the McKinsey organization structure unsuited to Plessey's management style. The nature of the Company had changed with a £250 million annual turnover in 1971 and multinational ambitions. New problems arose which needed different responses. Previously a sub-contractor and even, in 1971, with half of its business from the Government, Plessey had developed strengths in quality production and cost control. With respect to marketing, Michael Clark admitted, it 'used to be all seat of the pants stuff. I used to spend once a week in London going round all the Ministries.'

1971 reorganization

With Alloys Unlimited, the emphasis had been on acquiring US production facilities, without due consideration of the market. With the 1971 reorganization, Eric Frye was placed in charge of long-range planning. Looking back to Plessey's early planning experiences, Parry Rogers remembers: 'We produced an annual strategic plan. Strategic planning was seen to be a part of the Finance Department, what they produced was numbers, numbers which met an objective. Produced by the planners and not by the operating management, it gave the Board what it was seeking in terms of a progression from today to the objective five years on ... The concept that one's immediate operating budget is year one of a five year plan is a sophistication that we hadn't got to even by 1975.'

Plessey was recentralized, in order to 'get the top of the company more identified and closer to the action in order to deal with these difficult conditions' (see Chart 1 for Plessey's organizational structure in July 1972). Plessey's non-telecommunications activities split into 23 businesses, self-contained profit centres, each with a manager bearing full profit responsibility. The business manager reported to a divisional managing director who acted as a buffer between the business and the head office. Michael Clark and Stan Williams, Director of Management Services, conducted monthly control meetings with every business manager. John Clark chaired a monthly product board meeting, attended by Michael Clark and Eric Frye, as well as the business managers, at which strategy and forward plans were reviewed. Company accounting was simplified from four levels to two accounting units, the business and the company. The new structure clarified individual management accountability at divisional level by eliminating the 'group' level. Divisions, described as a philosophical concept, were the vehicle on which a divisional managing director travelled, since he had no staff of his own, and needed to call upon corporate staff in matters involving more than one business.

Between 1960 and 1973, Plessey's turnover increased annually by 19%, profit by 16% and eps at 5.5%. However, important pressures which demanded changes included the problem, with the greater proliferation of products, of concentrating on central issues. The pace of technological change was now threatening the 'breadwinning' products of the 1960s. The company's increasing size and complexity brought a need for changes in management style and organization structure, as well as in the product portfolio which was not generating enough cash to invest in potential growth products. The strategic planning department was formed in 1973 to deal with the above pressures. In 1974, annual planning reviews were introduced, beginning with the issue of plan instructions in August, and ending nominally in May with the corporate consolidation of individual business plans. All aspects of the overall planning were examined first by each business, then by corporate staff, and on the basis of the examination, five-year programmes were drawn up.

PLESSEY PERFORMANCE 1974–9

Plessey products 1974

The nine major product divisions, each with subsidiaries, were:

- *Telecommunications*. Four product divisions covered every aspect of public and private line switching and communication.
- *Radar*. Two divisions combined all major capability in ground radar systems for air defence and traffic control, and for many other civil and defence uses.

- *Communications and marine.* Plessey's major defence capability in radio communications and underwater weapons and systems, with facilities for contract manufacture and assembly of electronic equipment.
- *Industrial electronics.* Applied electronic engineering to handling data for instrumentation, telemetry and the control of items as diverse as road traffic, documents and machine-tools.
- *Dynamics.* Offered highly specialized capability in aeronautical, mechanical, electrical and hydraulic engineering for the aerospace, transportation and industrial markets.
- *Electronic sub-systems.* Computer memory and other data-storage systems now increasingly related to microcircuits and semiconductors.
- *Contract and supply.* Four divisions handled several contract activities for both in-house and general industry demands.
- *Electrical components.* Included the manufacture of electronic and electrical components for entertainment and professional equipment.
- *Consumer electronics.* Made and sold electronic equipment and systems for entertainment and other consumer purposes, through Garrard Engineering Ltd.

Environment

In 1974, Sir John Clark was concerned about a number of aspects of Plessey's hostile operating environment, including high inflation; recession; punitive taxation; the high cost of borrowing and the consequent erosion of UK competitiveness abroad which, in turn, were aggravated by fears of imminent public spending cuts and, worse, the threat of nationalisation. The oil crisis, the three-day week, the 1974–5 recession, double-figure inflation, Post Office expenditure cuts and a squeeze on profit margins now shifted the focus towards short-term activities.

The POST programme

In 1975 the POST programme (Plessey Objectives, Strategy and Tactics) and the supporting STAMP (Strategic and Tactical Asset Management Programme) were introduced. The purpose was to effect fundamental changes in corporate behaviour. This would enable the company to get to grips with the impact of inflation on profit, the tendency of Plessey's random management approach to create a gulf between immediate decisions and longer-term objectives, the threat of competition, and the failure of investment decisions and resource allocation to reflect the company's strategic intentions.

POST operated in two stages. First, portfolio analysis was used to segment Plessey's products and markets, compare them with the competition and identify threats and opportunities for leadership. In the second stage, marketing analysis was integrated into the business planning cycle enabling management to set long-term objectives, agree strategies, define investment priorities, allocate resources and establish operating tactics. POST identifed 160 market segments covering 90% of the company's activities, and a large number of 'dead dogs'. To avoid the imbalance of cash flows and the stunting of growth, investment priorities were reviewed and tighter resource controls instituted. In retrospect, the benefits of POST were a better appreciation of the importance of market share, competition and segmentation, as the company streamlined its product range. The organizational impact of POST was the allocation of product responsibilities among members of the Chief Executive Office and the formation of product subsidiaries.

Corporate staff

The Corporate Service Department could advise general management to change a given practice: if general management would not, the corporate staff could try to persuade the Board of Directors' General Purposes Committee of the need for change. This Committee would then give instructions to general management. By 1975, corporate staff numbered 1,400, the majority involved in management services; rather than playing a typical corporate staff role they were available to help to solve problems arising in the company's businesses. One executive commented: 'The idea that you can give the managing director of a subsidiary or profit centre a management job to do, and then, when he looks as though he is having difficulty, go and interfere, is a contradiction to what I believe management is all about, and one of our main problems arose from interference called "help".'

International business

In 1975, Plessey was trading in 136 countries (see Exhibits 4 and 5 for Plessey's sales and profits by market and region).

The Australian government imposed tariff barriers and, in Portugal, the political and economic situation forced closure of Plessey's memories business in 1976. However, the promise of the opening of EEC markets was symbolized for Plessey in 1974 by a planned Anglo-French joint venture to manufacture and market an electronic telecommunications system for the British, French and export markets. By October 1978, the *Financial Times* was to comment that this was another deal which never quite came off for Plessey. Resistance from both the British Post Office and its French counterpart prevented the launch of the venture. 'The disquiet voiced about Plessey centres on how decisively its top management operates. . . . It has failed to demonstrate a sharp enough edge in finding and seizing the new opportunities which its technological excellence should enable it to exploit.'

By 1977, the Middle Eastern markets were beginning to invest their oil revenues and Plessey was penetrating those countries 'on the basis of selective specialization' with telecommunications and electronic systems. In the United States, Alloys Limited had by 1974 overcome its earlier troubles, and US sales and profits had increased substantially. However, the US recession was particularly harsh, and by 1975, Plessey's activities had made a net loss. In the same year, Plessey acquired under licence from the ROLM Corporation advanced technology for the manufacture and marketing of a new range of digital private communications systems, including development of the PDX (private digital exchange) which attracted £8 million of domestic and export orders.

UK public sector markets

The purchasing policy of the UK Post Office (now British Telecom) constrained Plessey's internationalization. With narrow Post Office specifications, markets often found Plessey's products unacceptable. Subsequent government intervention ensured that the Post Office, and the Defence Ministry, only ordered products immediately available for sales elsewhere. Plessey now had to create products suitable for world markets. With public spending cuts, profits in Plessey's telecommunications declined from 63% in 1975 to 56% by 1978, on a 3% decrease in turnover. For the UK market, telecommunications represented 18% of sales but a lower share of profits. The work-force was reduced from 66,456 to 53,528 by 1979, with 50% of the redundancies in telecommunications.

System X

The United Kingdom telecommunications modernization programme was based on the digital System X, to be manufactured by GEC, STC and Plessey, and marketed by a separate joint organisation, British Telecom Systems. System X is a 'comprehensive family of digital exchanges, built from modular sub-subjects covering both hardware and software. It caters for easy growth, adapability for different regional requirements and in-service flexibility, while providing full compatability with previously installed analogue equipment. It will form part of an Integrated Services Digital network to handle voice, data, telex, facsimile and video services.' Much Plessey effort went into converting production from labour-intensive electromechanical switching systems to capital-intensive electronics. System X was to be introduced early in the 1980s. Meanwhile, the Post Office had selected Plessey's TXE4 semi-electronic system to be manufactured at Huyton, Lancashire, to replace the analogue Strowger system currently in use.

Other UK activities

While Plessey's profits were down in 1976, a rights issue raised £27 million, aiding cash flows. Plessey increased its shareholding in ICI. Plessey's diversification into consumer electronics through Garrard proved a loss-maker. Despite drastic attempts to streamline, with the work-force reduced from 1,830 to 580 in 1978, Garrard was eventually sold to a Brazilian company for £1 million in 1979.

Plessey appeared to have been bypassed when the National Enterprise Board set up a £50 million new venture in semiconductors (later to become Inmos). GEC planned a link-up with the US firm Fairchild, though this collapsed in 1980. In 1978, with the possible sale of Plessey's semiconductor business to GEC, *The Times* commented: 'With capital spending of £28 million Plessey continues to consume cash after last year's outflow of £20.7 million. ... Plessey is simply not generating enough cash at a time when it is urgently needed in several major areas of technological development.'

Chief Executive Office established

Plessey had organizational studies carried out every four years, though top management made no commitment to their outcome. However, in 1975–6, the chairman and top managers were persuaded to devote considerable time to the study. In January 1976 the Chief Executive Office (CEO) was established as Plessey's sole executive committee. It consisted of Sir John Clark, Michael Clark and three deputy chief executives: Eric Frye, Bill Willetts and the American Warren Sinsheimer. Responsibility for major product and geographic areas was split among the five members of the CEO with dual responsibilities in each division. The purpose was to ensure much closer liaison between divisions and more direct responsibilities at the top, and was a concrete acknowledgement that one man could not bear the entire responsibility for managing Plessey. Divisional general managers henceforth reported directly to the CEO.

Control procedures in Plessey were horizontal and vertical. The main board reviewed all results in some detail each month. The Chief Executive Office and its members reviewed business results frequently and in detail. Individual members of the CEO were also concerned with problems and opportunities of tactical or short-term nature. Divisional managing directors held monthly control meetings with each business and business general managers held similar meetings with their staff. By April 1976, a strategic planning exercise was completed, followed by vital decisions on the products and markets which would decide Plessey's development over the next few years. The Corporate objectives published in Plessey's 1975–6 annual report to shareholders were:

- To maximize earnings per share.
- To become a world-wide enterprise.
- To invest in selected products and markets on a planned basis, choosing opportunities which optimize the use of resources within prescribed fields of business, e.g. telecommunications, electronic systems and components.
- To sustain an efficient and productive organization, competitive in world markets in management technology, manufacturing and market skills.

From divisions to subsidiaries

In March 1976 a management reshuffle led to some 17 new appointments. The most significant was Bill Willetts as the Chairman of the Telecommunications Division. Later in 1976, Sir Francis Sandilands, Chairman of Commercial Union Assurance, and Mr Parry Rogers, who came as Personnel Director from IBM (UK), joined the board. Still later in the same year, a new subsidiary, Plessey Electronics Systems Limited (PESL), setting a pattern described below, was established under the chairmanship of Michael Clark. This was followed by the establishment of Plessey Hydraulics, a new business. Plessey now consisted of eight main product divisions, plus a management services division, and five regional responsibility centres. Each product or regional division reported to a specific member of the CEO (see Chart II for Plessey Organization in 1976).

From 1976, Plessey's organizational strategy was to form a number of major product subsidiaries with world-wide product management responsibility. Overseas interest would be grouped as regional subsidiaries constituted as statutory bodies with their own boards of directors, financial structure and management resources. Parry Rogers commented: 'Managing directors of our subsidiary companies know that they are on their own ... and if they get it wrong, there isn't a fire brigade to come in and rescue them ... Since we moved into that mode of operating, we haven't had the same sort of catastrophic problems that arose under the old system.'

Planning changes

In 1977, the main weakness of the POST system became increasingly apparent. The absence of corporate objectives in a form which could be effectively transcribed into business strategies resulted in problems over the determination of priorities and resource allocation, and the failure to incorporate tactical planning into the routine management process. The corporate strategy formulated in 1977 aimed to:

- Compete in world markets where there were opportunities for dominance (electronic systems, main exchanges, overseas transmission, data communication).
- Provide key technological and components support internationally to systems activities through, e.g., electronic components, memories, semiconductors.
- Avoid portfolio imbalance through excessive dependence on systems, public sector or high-technology, e.g. through aerospace, hydraulics and Garrard.
- Invest selectively to maintain portfolio balance. In the inflationary environment of 1977, the corporate objective was to finance routine operations internally and reserve debt capacity for acquisition and investment opportunities.

It was considered vital to make regions and divisions appreciate that business planning was an essential tool of business management. POST aimed to create a routine link between objectives, the management review and the decision process, and tactical and functional plans. Divisional chief executives reviewed marketing plans, prepared according to corporate guidelines to include a business's or division's competitive position, market analysis, market-share objective, product strategy, resources and action plan.

In 1978, the planning process was revised to avoid fragmenting effort through attempts to serve too many markets with too few resources. The approach was to identify and adopt selective strategies at various organizations, prior to formulating business plans. The result was to give priority to high-technology activities and led to some 18 divestments. Corporate centre defined the overall direction of company development, choosing between business areas as recipients for resources, and communicated its strategic plans by the issue of planning guidelines to management boards or direct to the trading companies. If authority was delegated to the trading company, the management defined its direction of development, choosing between trading subsidiaries as recipients for resources, and passed on similar planning guidelines to each trading company. CHRONOS, an asset management system and an extension of STAMP, now required operations managers to manage trading company assets on the basis of targets and performance measurement.

Contracts won by Plessey 1974–9

Significant contracts included a £17 million UK defence contract for the Ptarmigan military communications system, offering soldiers in battle access to STD-type facilities. Other developments were the microwave aircraft landing system, in co-operation with the Government, though the United Kingdom Civil Aviation Authority did not finally adopt Plessey's system. The first orders came for a new naval radar system. Plessey led the UK market in urban traffic control systems, and the City of São Paolo, Brazil, ordered a new traffic control system worth £14 million. Plessey contributed to a US Army radio communications system worth £7 million. Smaller PABXs with less than 100 lines were to be replaced by the Monarch digital system, for which orders in 1979 topped £14 million. In 1979, Plessey entered joint ventures with Marconi and Hughes to develop the UK Air Defence Ground Environment (UKADGE) data-processing and display system, and with ITT for the NATO radar-replacement programme.

1979 results

Plessey's 1978–9 report showed a stronger balance sheet, with total debt reduced by £20.4 million by regulating trading company borrowings. However, Plessey's return on capital employed (ROCE) of 22% was below industry norms of 25–27%. Losses in the Liverpool factory making the absolescent Strowger exchanges doubled to £7.8 million. Plessey sold its ICL stake, which raised £33.5 million cash, as well as Garrard (Plessey's mechanical engineering subsidiary), and the numerical control machine-tool shop. Abroad, the printer division of its US subsidiary, and its Portuguese subsidiary, were sold. Investments for 1980 were budgeted at a high of £40 million, and, following the launch at the 1979 Geneva Telecom fair, production began on System X.

PLESSEY'S COMPETITORS

Plessey's four main competitors were Ferranti and Racal who competed mainly in the defence markets, STC in telecommunications, and GEC who covered parts of both areas. In 1977 with rationalization in the electronics industry and talk of takeover bids Plessey's market capitalization was approximately £175 million, though the company seemed well protected by a share yield of 8.5% compared with 5% for the average blue chip. Financial commentators criticized Plessey for being slower than its major competitors, GEC or STC, in adapting to new technology. The star performer, Racal, was reportedly building up a shareholding in Plessey, which in 1977 was revealed as no more than 0.4%. The *Financial Times* of 11 October 1978 commented: 'Plessey did not use the 1960s profits to develop the products to give it standing in world markets. Electronics systems have grown fastest, from 5% to 30% of profits in 5 years. But this is a growth industry and Racal, in the military sector, has far outperformed Plessey. If Plessey had been better managed, it would have had much more of the business and profits which went to Racal.' In May 1979, Racal's capitalization was £563 million, compared with £233 million for Plessey, but Racal sold its shareholding in Plessey just before Plessey announced its 1979 results.

GEC

GEC's turnover was £3.3 billion, profits £378 million and cash balances £730 million. Of GEC's six autonomous divisions, telecommunications, electronics and automation were the fastest-growing, contributing 30% of overall profits, with sales of £862 million and profits of £101 million. Product areas included avionics, TV cameras, satellite communications, radar, torpedo and tank-gunnery control equipment, computers, telephone equipment and industrial controls. Profits were down, however, in Power Engineering, Industrial and Components, and Cable and Wire divisions, and slightly ahead in the Overseas and Consumer Products divisions. The previous five years had not seen real volume growth in sales, but the balance sheet was exceptionally strong and profit margins had increased.

Racal

Racal, the outstanding performer in the electronics and electrical sector, had an excellent record of sales and a profit growth in the 1970s. Racal's product profile had changed considerably, as its data-communications turnover approached the same level as radio turnover. New developments in computer-aided design, safety helmets and communications security were adding to profitability. Borrowings had, however, reached 50% of equity. Growth had been largely internally generated through the successful exploitation of a limited product range. Racal's acquisitions also performed well, including recently acquired Decca, whose low-frequency and microwave communications for marine and aviation uses complemented Racal's HF, VHF and UHF radio bands for land-based military markets.

By 1979, Racal's product portfolio consisted of radio communications (44%), data communications (32%) with the remainder in acoustics, antennas, automatic test and diagnostic equipment, computer-aided design, communications security, health and safety, instrumentation, magnetic recording media, microwave radar and intruder protection, recorders and others.

Ferranti

Of Ferranti's turnover, 45% came from defence contracts, but profit margins were higher. Ferranti had come to the market in 1978, with the National Enterprise Board owning 50% of shares. Ferranti had a technological lead in such essential defence areas as inertial navigation systems. Civil instruments and systems were often spin-offs from military work. Ferranti had aimed to balance military and civil sales but the attraction of high margins and stable growth pattern in military markets halted this policy.

The *Tornado* and other such orders would ensure sales for years ahead. Low profit- and loss-makers had been sold or rationalized in an attempt to improve an erratic financial record prior to 1976. Since then, Ferranti had shown consistently strong profit growth as the company became more successfully established in vital areas of defence where technology was more important than price and comparatively long production runs had been established. Ferranti's main product divisions were Computer Systems (military and civilian), Scottish Group (military), Instrumentation, Electronics and Engineering.

STC

STC was a subsidiary of ITT, which held 85% of shares until 1984, when its holding was cut to 35%. STC, involved in the strong growth areas of the UK electronics industry, telecommunications and component distribution, had access to ITT's entire research and development facilities. Since 1974, sales had increased by 55% to £374 million, but profits had fallen by 5% to £27 million. The UK market accounted for 80% of sales. STC's two main product areas, telecommunications and electronics, represented 60% of the sales and most of the profit. STC was a major supplier to the Post Office and other UK governmental and commercial organizations. Its other area was component manufacturing and distribution. STC was world leader in submarine, cable technology and supply. STC's poor profit record in 1974–8 was attributable to the costs of rationalization and the changeover to electronic technology, but it did seem set to move ahead, though it would need to remain responsive to the rapid technological progress of the industry. Hopes were pinned on System X for profit growth, but in October 1979 STC withdrew.

PLESSEY PERFORMANCE, 1980–3

By the end of 1980, the tide had turned. Sales increased by 15.8% on the previous year and profits by 29.9%, with barely any increase in capital employed, and with improvements in profit margins, ROCE and gearing. Capital expenditure totalled £35 million, with £42 million budgeted for 1981. The results boosted Plessey's share price to a ten-year high of 181p. Policies of rationalization, improved efficiency and the disposal of loss-makers enabled Plessey to shed its image as the 'sleeping giant'.

Exhibit 6 shows Plessey's position in relation to major electronics competitors in 1981 and 1982. Plessey's 1980 results must be seen against a background of a disastrous engineering strike, escalating inflation and interest rates, the continued strength of the pound, deepening recession throughout the West and a highly volatile international situation. Sir John Clark saw the 1980 results as the successful outcome of Plessey's strategy over the previous five years, the key elements of which were:

- Establishment of the Chief Executive Office.
- Introduction of product and regional subsidiaries.

- The rebalancing of the portfolio, emphasis on marketing and improved responsiveness to competition.
- Extension of programmes for new product development in the field of solid-state digital technology.
- Divestment of loss-making operations. Eighteen businesses had been sold over a period of thirty months.

1981 performance

Record profits were again reported in 1981 — an increase of 40.7% despite the recession, on a sales increase of 12.5%. Total debt was down to £54 million. Plessey was now organized into three divisions, reflecting its major areas of logically integrated activities — Plessey Telecommunications and Office Systems, Plessey Electronics Systems, and Plessey Engineering Components, whose many activities offered vertical integration with the first two areas. A new subsidiary was set up for new and existing display technologies.

1982 results

A 36.2% increase in profits pleased the market but it was noted that half the profits came from a build-up of cash generated by mature products. In four years, Plessey had eliminated low-technology businesses, slashed the workforce by 25%, and doubled profits, dividends, sales per employee and R&D expenditure.

Current cost accounts indicated that dividends had been stable, but profits before extraordinary items had quadrupled. Short-term deposits, investments and bank balances had increased from £62.3 million to £237.7 million resulting in net interest receivable of £6.9 million, compared with net payable of £4.6 million in 1981.

UK telecommunications

British Telecom, stripped of its monopoly powers and due to be privatized in 1984, was getting tougher with its traditional suppliers. Since no export orders had been won since 1979, the Government pressed for improvements in the marketing of System X, against a background of production delays and rising costs. By October 1979, STC had withdrawn from System X. With Plessey emerging as prime contractor and GEC as subcontractor the Government then released £16 million in grants.

The *Investors Chronicle* noted that: 'Plessey has managed to get itself into peak condition for the big race of the next two decades — the gathering revolution in communications.' The *Financial Times* pinpointed as key signs of this revolution the proliferation of new transmission methods and services, including high-power communications, direct broadcasting satellites, optical fibre circuits, cellular mobile radio communications and cable-borne computerized information systems. The convergence of telecommunications and data processing meant growing competition between companies formerly in separate markets, with IBM moving into telecommunications and AT&T (American Telephone & Telegraph) towards data-processing and office systems. In April 1983, Plessey held discussions with Burroughs Business Machines on technology exchange, though without an equity link. Increasingly, industrial alliances were forming across international boundaries as manufacturers shared costs in order to expand into new geographic markets.

The rate of technological change led to shorter product life cycles, which required higher development and capital investment. Costs as high as £1 billion could not be recovered through sales to a single market, even the USA, hence the increase in exports, local manufacturing, joint ventures and licensing. National governments were tending to use telecommunications modernization programmes as a platform for developing national high-technology industries. The growing impact of telecommunications as a competitive factor in many businesses meant the spread of sophisticated private corporate networks for voice and data transmission.

The US market

Under US anti-trust legislation, 1982 saw the break-up of AT&T. By September that year, Plessey was preparing to make AT&T products under licence. Through the purchase of Stromberg Carlson, Plessey became the first UK company to enter the US public exchange market, for £33 million cash. In the first year, Plessey reduced Stromberg Carlson's £9 million loss to £1.9 million.

The following year, Plessey formed a joint venture with Scientific Atlanta to exploit international markets in satellite and cable communications equipment. Plessey bought 0.2% of its collaborator's shares, with options to increase its holding up to 30%. Sir John Clark explained the USA focus: 'We needed 5–6% of the world telecommunications market to secure our long-term future.' Also moving into the USA were the Japanese Nippon Electric and the Swedish L. M. Ericsson. At the same time, AT&T sought markets abroad for the first time. Stockbroker Laurie, Millbank had forecast a world telecommunications market of £30 billion by the late 1980s, and, though critical of the UK industry's growth rate compared with a rate of 12% internationally, predicted that Plessey had the products and potential to achieve growth.

Contracts 1980–3

Plessey won the £250 million UK payphones renovation contract but lost a £400 million Iraqi electronic contract to a French company, prompting Sir John Clark to comment: 'Britain is going on playing cricket while the rest of the world is playing karate.' The Plessey–Marconi consortium won a £100 million NATO contract for UKADGE, and beat a Government moratorium on defence spending to win a £150 million contract for the Ptarmigan battlefield communications system. Plessey also won a share of the Trident nuclear missile system contract to supply sonar, communications and submarine-guidance equipment. Plessey won contracts for the London Transport public address system, and as a main contractor for the new Abidjan airport in the Ivory Coast.

Contracts won in 1983 included electronics and communications equipment for the new airport in the Falklands and a £500 million Navy contract for air surveillance radar. Also, British Telecom placed orders for System X worth £500 million. The UK government commitment to NATO to increase defence spending in real terms by 3% per annum would end in 1985/86, and was not likely to be renewed.

PLESSEY'S PRODUCT RANGE, 1983

By 1983, Plessey operated in three major and two minor product areas.

Telecommunications and Office Systems

With seven operating subsidiaries this major product subsidiary acted as systems designer and private contractor supplying digital exchanges for public networks, including System X. Digital transmission systems had largely replaced analogue services. New-technology products included fibre optic systems, cable TV and direct broadcast satellite systems. Ancillary and peripheral products included microprocessor-controlled payphones, and Plessey's joint venture with Scientific Atlanta offered the planning, supply and installation of coaxial cable TV systems for franchised cable operators. Launched in 1983, the IDX Plessey's digital private automatic branch exchange (PABX), captured two-thirds of the UK market for large digital PABXs. The core of the electronic office, this system allowed link-up with word processing, mainframe or desktop computing, telex, viewdata and other electronic services.

Packet-switching technology met demands for faster, cleaner and more cost-effective data traffic between terminals and computers, and between computer systems. Among Plessey Controls's major telex projects was the design and installation of the UK's largest computer-controlled telex exchange, increasing overseas telex capacity by 30%. Plessey aids to traffic control included pedestrian-controlled crossings, motorway signalling, automated toll systems, breakdown and accident-reporting systems. Other control technique applications included industrial material handling, postal mechanization, nuclear reactor monitoring and protection and radiation detection and measurement.

Plessey Electronic Systems

In this area there were ten subsidiaries dedicated to meeting a country's land, sea and air defence needs. Plessey's special capability was as a prime contractor in defence projects. For naval use, Plessey designed and integrated electronic and radar shipborne systems, and complete action information and underwater defence systems. Plessey was the Royal Navy's major sonar contractor and supplied underwater defence systems to navies around the world. Army battlefield communications, command, control and intelligence systems included Ptarmigan and Project Raven. The British Army Wavell project was a system for handling battlefield data. A large range of strategic air defence and airborne systems were also offered.

Plessey also worked in high-security sectors such as (electronic countermeasures (ECM), (electronic counter-countermeasures (ECCM)), surveillance, cryptography and information-system security. Air traffic control radar systems, both civil and military, were supplied to 83 countries. Plessey was a leading supplier of turnkey civil airport projects, involved in fund sourcing, systems engineering and civil and building works disciplines.

Plessey engineering and components

This product area encompassed nine operating subsidiaries, offering high-technology back-up for other Plessey operations and new projects; it achieved a high degree of market orientation, with the majority of its business with outside customers. Technologies such as fluidics, pneumatics and electrics were used in turbojets pressure ratio transducers, thrust reversal and aircraft components. A full range of aircraft fuel-management systems was supplied. Anti-ship missile decoy systems included SHIELD.

Plessey Connectors products met interconnection needs at every level of electrical, electronic and fibre optical systems. A range of specialized switches and wire-wound devices is made and supplied to its major international markets in defence communications, public telephone networks, office equipment and domestic appliances. Plessey Optoelectronics manufactured light-emitting diodes used in optical fibre systems and sunlight-visible displays. Plessey Microwave products included solid-state microwave components and Plessey Materials developed radar-absorbent, radar-transparent and microwave-conducting materials. Plessey Semiconductors claimed in 1983 to be Britain's largest indigenous producer of integrated circuits, designed to match specific customer needs, enabling customers to lease software or delegate the design task to Plessey.

Increasingly, industrial and consumer products were being engineered in plastics materials. These were functionally and aesthetically more satisfactory; and overall energy costs favoured plastics over metal. Plessey's Birkbys Plastics were leading subcontractors to passenger and commercial vehicle, domestic appliances, telecommunications and business machines industries. Plessey Microsystems produced processing and memory systems for commercial, telecommunications and military data-processing applications. Plessey Peripheral Systems offered a product range of DEC-compatible computers, memories, mass storage subsystems, peripherals and software.

RESEARCH AND DEVELOPMENT IN PLESSEY

About 75% of R & D funding, which increased from £35.6 million in 1974 to £166.8 million in 1983, was provided by customers, and the rest by Plessey. In 1978, the Allen Clark Research Centre, near Northampton, was involved in such technological breakthroughs as electrochromic displays, holographic memory, aircraft-collision avoidance systems, infra-red detectors and new lasers.

The Economist commented on the optical electronics industry which had started as a project in the central laboratory: 'For once the accountants were not allowed to stifle it and now it is making good profits on a £3 million a year turnover, with plans to grow 4- or 5-fold with Department of Industry backing. It has worked because the accountants have kept out of the technologists' hair — and for once it paid.'

By 1980, with Plessey's slimmer product range and an excellent R & D record in solid-state devices, the dominance of electronics gave R & D a sharper focus and the company now appeared strong enough to make the large investments necessary for leadership in advanced microtechnology. In 1982, £13 million of the £134 million total spent on R & D went in supporting research at Caswell. With 530 scientists, 45% of Caswell's work was for British Telecom and the British Ministry of Defence. Half of the remaining 55% was for Plessey's corporate headquarters and half for its operating divisions, a £10 million interactive Computer-Aided Design system linking Caswell scientists with designers in the operating divisions. A key Plessey breakthrough was the development of gallium arsenide, an alternative to silicon for use in semiconductors. Although far more expensive and difficult to handle than silicon, its performance was twice as rapid.

JOINT VENTURES

Joint ventures, as a means of acquiring new skills and technologies, were seen as an increasingly important development for Plessey and its competitors in the 1980s. There was a link-up with Andersen Laboratories, Connecticut for the research, development and manufacture of advanced signal-processing devices for defence and of telecommunications technology for data-processing expertise. Another joint venture was with Scientific Atlanta Inc. Parry Rogers commented: 'We recognized ... that [with] the nature of competition changing ... we had to be prepared to cope with competition from multinational giants and of course it is the American and Japanese that we watch most closely. We saw ... that in many parts of the world, joint ventures are the only way that we will succeed on the scale that we wish to succeed.'

REORGANIZATION, 1983

By 1983, Plessey had about 70 active subsidiaries around the world. Sir John Clark had established as the principal criteria for the size of an operating subsidiary in his 1975–6 review 'that it shall be big enough to attract and retain a calibre of management at least equal to international competition. This requires a size which will enable it to operate at a high level of organizational independence and to be seen as a company of standing in its own right. It is therefore likely to have potential annual sales of approximately £100 million on the basis of a logical grouping of technology and product interests.'

By 1983, reorganization resulted in the structure shown in Chart III. Each of the British national and regional subsidiaries was responsible to the Chief Executive Office through a management board or individual director. There were three main product divisions: Electronic Systems; Components and Engineering; and Telecommunications and Office Systems. The Chief Executive Office controlled the policy of the subsidiaries within overall group policies and objectives, including major tenders and non-budgeted investment proposals, product and commercial policy, review of subsidiaries objectives, business plans and performances, acquisitions and divestments, and business organization and structure. Not illustrated were three committees which reported to the main board: Industrial Relations; Renumerations; and Finance. The Finance Committee comprised the chairman, the Finance Corporate Staff, Mr Sinsheimer, and three outside directors. Corporate staff retained their advisory role, but needing the CEO's intervention to change a subsidiary's management practice.

PLANNING CHANGES

The trading companies defined selective product/market strategies and appropriate resourcing as the basis of detailed planning to achieve the objectives stated in the planning guidelines. By the end of 1983, Plessey faced new challenges from the increasingly competitive markets and technology/market convergence. Effective strategic planning was seen as the key to survival for those businesses which had thrived by exploiting protected markets. Plessey undertook an audit of its planning activities, the objectives of which were to investigate ways of improving the quality of analysis and creative thinking about customer needs, emphasizing line management's responsibility to formulate high-quality strategies, and of developing a clearer sense of the direction in order to sustain long-term competitiveness. The revisions to the strategic planning system were viewed as a substantial evolution of POST, 'providing a better understanding of the market place and the necessary strategies to provide a bedrock for developing realistic business strategic plans'. It would enable developing rolling plans to be updated with company views and changes in the marketplace. These changes did not mean the relaxation of POST disciplines. The 'business' five-year financial plans will still be taken as a management commitment to likely future performance in general and to budget objectives in particular.

PLESSEY MANAGEMENT AND PERSONNEL

The Clark brothers

John and Michael Clark took over the management of Plessey in 1962 on the death of their father. Sir John Clark, born in 1926 and educated at Harrow and Cambridge, received his early industrial training with Metropolitan Vickers and the Ford Motor Company in the USA, where he spent a year studying the electronics industry. After service as a naval officer in the Second World War, he joined Plessey in 1949 as Assistant to the General Manager of Plessey International Ltd and became a member of the main board in 1953. He succeeded Lord Harding as Chairman in 1970.

Shamoon[1] said of Sir John Clark that 'he thinks as a proprietor' and is 'possessive' and 'paternalistic' about Plessey. 'He thinks big. He thinks about the world market and Plessey's place in it.' Among his plans are those for doubling Plessey's 3 per cent share of the world public telephone switching market in the next five years. He was described as 'demanding of senior staff' but, by his account, 'stays close to the shop floor'. According to Sir John, it took some ten years to transform Plessey from a highly centralized and paternalistic business — under 'the old man', Sir Allen — to a modern industrial company. Each of the managing directors of the 27 operating companies can earn up to a 50 per cent performance bonus on their salaries. Among the managing directors is his son Nigel, a lawyer, who recently joined the coil-winding division at the Ilford works. 'I shall find out,' says Sir John, 'if he can make a profit before I decide whether he will make a "successor".'

Michael Clark, born in 1927 and educated at Harrow, was from 1945 to 1948 a subaltern in the 1st Foot Guards. After a year at Ford, he joined Plessey in 1950 and the main board in 1953. In 1971, a *Financial Times* article described the Clarks as running Plessey as owner-managers. 'The Clark brothers, like their legendary father before them, belong to the "drive 'em" school of management. "The thing to do is drive it," says Michael Clark, "to make it happen ... I don't think I'm a universally easy person to work for." John Clark was a more reserved and quieter man than Michael, who "worked himself to the bone" and employed a direct, if not blunt, management style, reminiscent of his father.'

Senior management

Top-management instability was a recurring problem for Plessey through-out the period of the case study. In 1977 Peter Marshall joined Plessey as Financial Director, enabling Eric Frye to concentrate fully on his role as Deputy Chief Executive. A year later, Eric Frye left after 12 years with Plessey, reportedly due to ill-health, though stories circulated about a personality clash between him and Sir John Clark. The same year, Bill Willetts, who had also been in the Chief Executive Office, left after ten years with Plessey and joined Vickers. Following Willetts's departure, Sir John took over the chairmanship of Telecommunications. The gaps in the Chief Executive Office were filled by Peter Marshall and Bill Dalziel. In 1979, Derek Roberts left Plessey Microelectronics to join GEC and Desmond Pitcher, Managing Director of Plessey Telecommunications, joined the main board having come from British Leyland in 1978.

In 1980, Frank Chorley, who had joined Plessey six years earlier, became Deputy Chairman and Managing Director of Plessey Electronic Systems Ltd, as well as Chairman of Plessey Research, thus controlling 35–40% of Plessey's annual turnover. Professor Gosling of Bath University also joined Plessey Electronic Systems as Technical Director. The appointment streng-thened the image Plessey was developing as a technological leader.

In 1981, the functions of Technology and Strategic Planning were combined, and Dr K. Warren was appointed Director. In 1982, as rumours flew about Desmond Pitcher's future with Plessey, the Managing Director of Plessey Avionics, Martin Richardson, resigned to join Racal. In September, John Whyte joined Plessey as Chairman of Plessey Telecommunications International. In November, after a second approach by an outside company, Desmond Pitcher left Plessey to become Chief Executive of the Littlewoods Group. Despite being known in the industry as 'Mr Telecommunications' and credited with a major role in Plessey's recovery after a poor financial performance in the 1970's, and with being a moving force behind Plessey's expansion internationally in telecommunications, Pitcher never became a member of the Chief Executive Office. Peter Marshall is seen inside Plessey as 'effectively number two', and 'must be favourite for the top job'. Shamoon[1] reports Clark as merely saying: 'I have not chosen any successor yet, although I know that is a prime responsibility'.

Personnel

In ten years Plessey's work-force decreased from 75,000 to 40,000; staff costs rose from £213.3 million in 1976 to £376.9 million in 1983. Over the same period turnover rose from £400 million to £1,074.8 million. The skills mix of employees changed considerably over this period. Large numbers of semi-skilled female employees, described as 'women with soldering irons', were replaced by 1983 with graduates in electronic engineering, physics, mathematics and computer science. This change in skills mix led in Liverpool, for example, to simultaneous heavy recruitment and redundancy with which, according to Sir John Clark, the trade unions offered full co-operation. The average cost per employee in 1973 was £1,900; in 1984 it was £9,900. This partly reflected a general scarcity of highly skilled personnel.

The increase in sales per employee from £5,300 (1973) to £32,000 (1983) came largely from technology, rather than from mere efficiency drives and reductions in manning. For example, Post Office public spending cuts in 1976 jolted what Plessey had foreseen as a phased, gradual changeover from electromechanical to digital switching technologies, and immediately resulted in a cut of about 4,800 jobs in that year. Labour-force reductions which had included closures, rationalizations and disposals, had heavy costs. Recorded as extraordinary items these were never less than £1 million annually between 1975 and 1983, reaching a peak of £10,015,000 in 1978. A significant part of Plessey's full range of management-development programmes for graduate induction, functional and general management is the Management Development Programme (MDP) sponsored by Plessey's Chief Executive Office, the aims of which are to provide the managers needed for growth and innovation for the coming 10–15 years. The programme supports Plessey's strategic thrust of concentrating on satisfying customer requirements.

REFERENCE

Shamoon, S. 'The Proprietor of Plessey', *Observer*, 12 August 1984.

Exhibit 1 *Plessey: Consolidated profit and loss accounts, 1974–83 (£ millions)*

	1983	1982	1981	1980	1979	1978	1977	1976	1975	1974
Turnover	1,074.8	963.1	844.5	751.0	648.3	611.1	568.8	490.1	318.9	399.5
Operating profit										
Associated companies	119.0	100.1	86.0	66.3	44.6	41.3	39.2	34.5	28.8	40.3
Interest receivable	6.7	4.4	3.1	3.5	10.5	10.2	8.4	6.0	3.3	4.2
Interest payable	33.4	22.3	7.9	2.6	2.2	1.7	1.5	1.2	0.8	2.2
	(12.7)	(15.4)	(12.5)	(12.3)	(11.0)	(10.3)	(8.8)	(6.9)	(5.6)	(6.4)
Profit before tax	146.4	111.4	84.5	60.1	46.3	42.9	40.3	34.8	27.3	40.3
Taxation	(60.5)	(38.5)	(29.0)	(19.0)	(14.2)	(14.7)	(12.9)	(11.0)	(9.3)	(11.2)
Profit after tax	85.9	72.9	55.5	41.1	32.1	28.2	27.4	23.8	18.0	29.1
Minority interests	(3.1)	(2.0)	(1.6)	(1.5)	(1.2)	(0.9)	(1.0)	(1.1)	(0.7)	(0.1)
Profit before extraordinary items	82.8	70.9	53.9	39.6	30.9	27.3	26.4	22.7	17.3	29.0
Extraordinary items less tax	(1.4)	(2.9)	(1.5)	(4.7)	(2.9)	(9.9)	(14.6)	(1.4)	(5.4)	(4.0)
Profit attributable to members of holding company	81.4	73.8	52.4	34.9	28.0	17.4	11.8	21.3	11.9	25.0
Dividends	(24.4)	(21.0)	(18.5)	(16.5)	(15.0)	(12.8)	(11.5)	(9.9)	(5.5)	(6.9)
Retained profit for year	57.0	52.8	33.9	18.4	13.0	4.6	0.3	11.4	6.2	18.1
Earnings per share (pence)										
Before extraordinary items	34.0	29.3	22.5	16.7	13.1	11.6	11.2	11.5	9.3	15.5
After extraordinary items	33.4	30.5	21.9	14.7	11.8	7.4	5.0	10.8	6.3	13.4
Dividends per share (pence)	9.9	8.6	7.6	6.9	6.3	5.4	4.8	4.99	3.6	3.7

Source: Plessey Annual Reports

Exhibit 2 *Plessey: Consolidated balance sheets, 1974–83 (£ millions)*

	1983	1982	1981	1980	1979	1978	1977	1976	1975	1974
Fixed assets										
Tangible assets	171.8	143.6	141.0	133.0	133.5	135.4	139.8	126.4	104.4	84.4
Asset investments	18.6	10.7	11.8	12.5	11.5	32.2	28.4	24.1	20.1	18.8
Deferred taxation	46.5	26.1	3.7	1.6						
Current assets										
Cash and short-term investments	271.5	237.7	62.3	21.0	19.1					
Other current assets	482.1	400.8	428.6	397.3	362.5					
Current liabilities										
Loans and overdrafts	(57.3)	(55.8)	(54.1)	(62.3)	(71.7)					
Other creditors	(418.1)	(330.0)	(255.3)	(225.8)	(199.5)					
Provisions for liabilities	(97.1)	(65.4)	(33.1)	(22.5)	(13.8)					
Net current assets	181.1	187.3	148.4	107.7	96.6	115.2	125.7	144.8	121.8	128.6
Net assets employed	418.0	367.7	304.9	254.8	241.6	282.8	293.9	295.3	246.3	231.8
Share capital	122.1	121.3	120.3	119.1	118.5	118.1	117.7	117.5	93.6	93.5
Reserves	285.7	238.3	177.5	128.7	116.6	109.5	111.6	115.5	91.0	75.8
Shareholders' funds	407.8	359.6	297.8	247.8	235.1	227.6	229.3	233.0	184.6	169.3
Minority interests	10.2	8.1	7.1	7.0	6.5	6.3	6.5	6.2	6.3	5.6
Loans and long-term debt						43.7	52.8	48.5	47.2	47.1
Liability to pension fund						2.8	3.3	3.8	4.2	1.4
Deferred credits						1.9	2.1	1.9	1.7	1.9
Deferred taxation						0.5	(0.1)	1.3	(0.2)	–
Corporation tax						–	–	0.6	2.5	6.5
Capital employed	418.0	367.7	304.9	254.8	241.6	282.8	293.9	295.3	246.3	231.8

Source: Plessey Annual Reports

Exhibit 3 Plessey: Sales and profit by product, as a percentage of total sales/profit

Year	Telecommunications and Transmissions[1]		Electronic Systems and Equipment[2]		Microelectronics and Components[3]		Aerospace Engineering[4]		Computer Peripherals[5]		Profit from group services
	Sales	Profit	Sales	Profit	Sales	Profit	Sales	Profit	Sales	Profit	
1973–4	42	57	26	20	22	14	10	9	–	–	
1974–5	46	63	26	22	18	8	10	7	–	–	
1975–6	43	56	29	35	17	–	11	9	–	–	
1976–7	37	46	33	44	19	4	11	6	–	–	
1977–8	39.6	58.3	26	30.2	17.6	11.0	13.3	12.9	–	–	
1978–9	39.9	38.6	27.6	35.6	16.3	14.1	14.3	18.1	3.5	(12.4)	
1980	39.9	45.3	27.9	19.6	16.3	17.1	15.1	19.2	2.9	(6.4)	
1981	41.9	46.5	30.9	26.3	12.5	3.7	14.7	17.5	0.8	(1.2)	
1982	43.5	54.5	28.9	21.9	11.8	6.3	12.9	15.3	0	0	6.0
1983	47.2	56.8	30.3	24.4	9	9.5	11.2	7.2	2.9	(1.8)	3.8
									2.3	(2.1)	4.2

[1]Public and private systems, sales and rental
[2]Up to 1977: radar, radio and electronics
[3]Prior to 1980: electronics and mechanical components
[4]Up to 1981: aerospace and hydraulics
[5]Up to 1981: consumer electronics

Source: Plessey Annual Reports

Exhibit 4 *Plessey: Sales and profit by market as a percentage of total sales*

Year	UK sales				UK	Overseas	
	British Telecom	Other governmental	Industry/Commerce	Exports from UK	Profit (total)	Sales	Profit
1974	24	11	17	13	68	35	32
1975	27	12	17	13	67	31	33
1976	24	13	17	14	69	32	31
1977	19	14	16	17	49.5	34	50.5
1978	16	15	16	–	57	53	43
1979	18	16	17	–	56	49	44
1980	21	18	20	–	65	41	35
1981	28	21	14	–	80	37	20
1982	30	21	10	–	78	39	22
1983	28.8	20.1	9.6	–	na	41.5	na

Source: Plessey Annual Reports

Exhibit 5 *Plessey: Overseas sales by market as a percentage of total company sales*

Year	Europe	Australia	Africa	N. America	Latin America	Asia
1978	13	5	8	15	2	9
1979	12	5	6	14	3	9
1980	11	3	5	13	2	7
1981	9	4	6	11	11	6
1982	8	4	9	11	2	5
1983	6.8	4.5	9.4	12	0.4	7.4

Source: Plessey Annual Reports

Exhibit 6 *Comparison of major electronics companies, 1981 and 1982*

	Sales (£ millions)		Pre-tax profit (£ millions)		Profit margin (%)		Tangible net assets (£ millions)	
	1981	*1982*	*1981*	*1982*	*1981*	*1982*	*1981*	*1982*
GEC	4190	4626	584.3	670.4	13.9	14.5	2323	2622.8
Thorn EMI	2435.9	2716	105.4	122	4.33	4.5	809	875.6
BICC	1604.3	1799.1	101.9	98.6	6.3	5.5	446.4	469
IBM-UK	1001.8	1240.1	160.8	224.7	16.1	18.1	409.5	532.7
Plessey[1]	963.1	1074.8	111.4	146.3	11.6	13.7	367.7	418
Racal	643.9	763.6	102.6	114.3	15.9	15	357.2	466
STC	567.5	628.5	50.6	64.3	8.9	3.3	213.4	225.8
Ferranti	306.9	372.2	23.8	31.5	7.8	8.4	106.8	129.5

[1]1981 and 1982 represent Plessey financial years ending 31 March 1982 and 31 March 1983, respectively

Source: Jordans Survey of the Electronics Industry, 1983

50

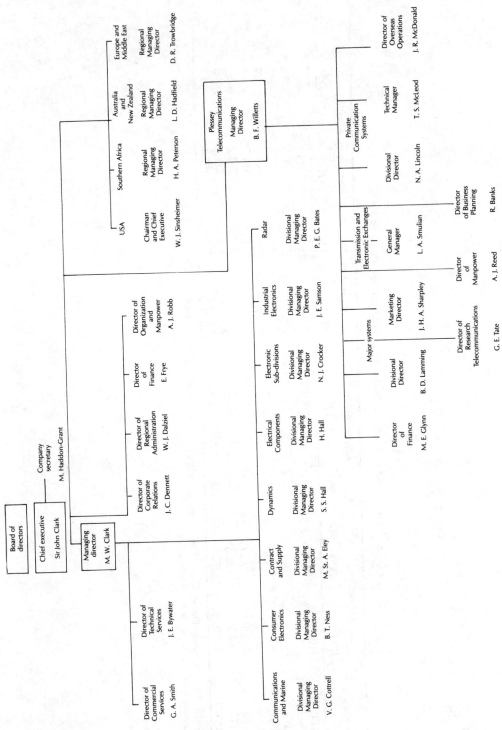

Chart I *The Plessey Company Limited main organization July 1972.*

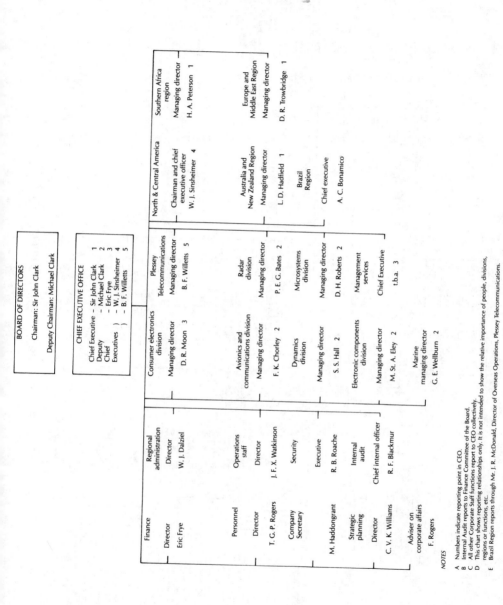

BOARD OF DIRECTORS

Chairman: Sir John Clark

Deputy Chairman: Michael Clark

CHIEF EXECUTIVE OFFICE

Chief Executive	–	Sir John Clark	1
Deputy	–	Michael Clark	2
Chief	–	Eric Frye	3
Executives)	–	W. J. Sinsheimer	4
)	–	B. F. Willetts	5

Corporate staff:

- Finance — Director — Eric Frye
- Regional administration — Director — W. J. Dalziel
- Personnel — Director — T. G. P. Rogers
- Operations staff — Director — J. F. X. Watkinson
- Company Secretary — M. Haddongrant
- Security — Executive — R. B. Roache
- Strategic planning — Director — C. V. K. Williams
- Internal audit — Chief internal officer — R. F. Blackmur
- Adviser on corporate affairs — F. Rogers

Consumer electronics division — Managing director — D. R. Moon 3
- Avionics and communications division — Managing director — F. K. Chorley 2
- Dynamics division — Managing director — S. S. Hall 2
- Electronic components division — Managing director — M. St. A. Eley 2
- Marine — managing director — G. E. Wellburn 2

Plessey Telecommunications — Managing director — B. F. Willetts 5
- Radar division — Managing director — P. E. G. Bates 2
- Microsystems division — Managing director — D. H. Roberts 2
- Management services — Chief Executive — t.b.a. 3

North & Central America — Chairman and chief executive officer — W. J. Sinsheimer 4
- Australia and New Zealand Region — Managing director — L. D. Hadfield 1
- Brazil Region — Chief executive — A. C. Bonamico

Southern Africa region — Managing director — H. A. Peterson 1
- Europe and Middle East Region — Managing director — D. R. Trowbridge 1

NOTES

A Numbers indicate reporting point in CEO.
B Internal Audit reports to Finance Committee of the Board.
C All other Corporate Staff functions report to CEO collectively.
D This chart shows reporting relationships only. It is not intended to show the relative importance of people, divisions, regions or functions, etc.
E Brazil Region reports through Mr. J. R. McDonald, Director of Overseas Operations, Plessey Telecommunications.

Chart II *The Plessey Company Limited main organization January 1976.*

52

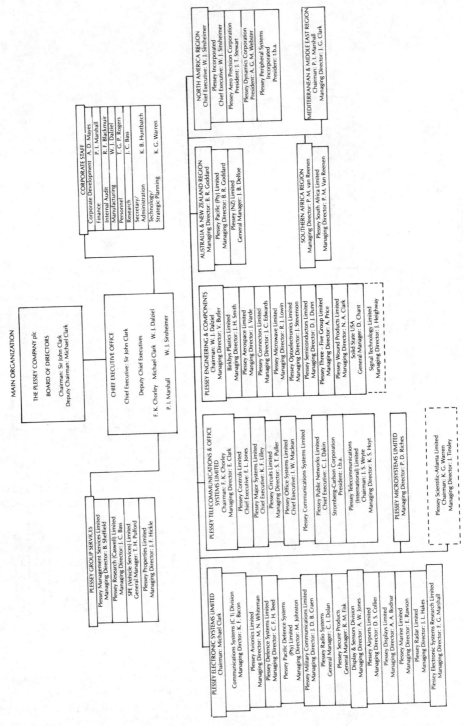

MAIN ORGANIZATION

THE PLESSEY COMPANY plc
BOARD OF DIRECTORS
Chairman: Sir John Clark
Deputy Chairman: Michael Clark

CORPORATE STAFF

Corporate Development	A. D. Mayes
Finance	P. I. Marshall
Internal Audit	R. F. Blackmuir
Manufacturing	W. J. Dalziel
Personnel	T. G. P. Rogers
Research	J. C. Bass
Secretary/ Administration	K. B. Huntbatch
Technology/ Strategic Planning	K. G. Warren

CHIEF EXECUTIVE OFFICE
Chief Executive: Sir John Clark
Deputy Chief Executives
F. K. Chorley   Michael Clark   W. J. Dalziel
P. I. Marshall   W. J. Sinsheimer

NORTH AMERICA REGION
Chief Executive: W. J. Sinsheimer
Plessey Incorporated
Chief Executive: W. J. Sinsheimer
Plessey Aero Precision Corporation
President: J. T. Stewart
Plessey Dynamics Corporation
President: A. G. M. Webster
Plessey Peripheral Systems
Incorporated
President: t.b.a.

MEDITERRANEAN & MIDDLE EAST REGION
Chairman: P. I. Marshall
Managing Director: J. G. Clark

AUSTRALIA & NEW ZEALAND REGION
Managing Director: B. R. Goddard
Plessey Pacific (Pty) Limited
Managing Director: B. R. Goddard
Plessey (NZ) Limited
General Manager: J. B. Deltoe

SOUTHERN AFRICA REGION
Managing Director: P. M. van Reenen
Plessey South Africa Limited
Managing Director: P. M. Van Reenen

PLESSEY GROUP SERVICES
Plessey Management Services Limited
Managing Director: B. Sheffield
Plessey Research (Caswell) Limited
Managing Director: J. C. Bass
SPE (Vehicle Services) Limited
General Manager: T. H. Pulford
Plessey Properties Limited
Managing Director: J. F. Hickle

PLESSEY ENGINEERING & COMPONENTS
Chairman: W. J. Dalziel
Managing Director: V. Butler
Birkbys Plastics Limited
Managing Director: J. H. Smith
Plessey Aerospace Limited
Managing Director: J. Varde
Plessey Connectors Limited
Managing Director: J. C. Edwards
Plessey Microwave Limited
Managing Director: R. J. Lowin
Plessey Optoelectronics Limited
Managing Director: J. Stevenson
Plessey Semiconductors Limited
Managing Director: D. J. Dunn
Plessey Three – Five Group Limited
Managing Director: A. Price
Plessey Wound Products Limited
Managing Director: N. A. Clark
Solid State USA
General Manager: D. Chant
Signal Technology Limited
Managing Director: J. Heighway

PLESSEY TELECOMMUNICATIONS & OFFICE SYSTEMS LIMITED
Chairman: F. K. Chorley
Managing Director: E. Clark
Plessey Controls Limited
Chief Executive: E. L. Jones
Plessey Major Systems Limited
Chief Executive: K. F. Lilley
Plessey Circuits Limited
Managing Director: S. T. Puller
Plessey Office Systems Limited
Chief Executive: I. W. Maclean
Plessey Communications Systems Limited
Plessey Public Networks Limited
Chief Executive: C. J. Dakin
Stromberg-Carlson Corporation
President: t.b.a.
Plessey Telecommunications
(International) Limited
Chairman: J. S. Wyrte
Managing Director: K. S. Hoyt

PLESSEY MICROSYSTEMS LIMITED
Managing Director: P. D. Riches

Plessey Scientific-Atlanta Limited
Chairman: K. G. Warren
Managing Director: J. Tinsley

PLESSEY ELECTRONIC SYSTEMS LIMITED
Chairman: Michael Clark
Communications Systems (C 1) Division
Managing Director: K. F. Bacon
Plessey Avionics Limited
Managing Director: M. N. Whiteman
Plessey Defence Systems Limited
Managing Director: C. F. H. Teed
Plessey Pacific Defence Systems
(Pty) Limited
Managing Director: M. Johnston
Plessey Military Communications Limited
Managing Director: J. D. B. Craen
Plessey Radio Systems
General Manager: C. I. Dolan
Plessey Secure Products
General Manager: R. M. Fisk
Display & Sensors Division
Managing Director: A. W. Jones
Plessey Displays Limited
Managing Director: D. S. Collier
Plessey Marine Limited
Managing Director: A. A. Bodnar
Plessey Radar Limited
Managing Director: E. Rawson
Plessey Radar Limited
Managing Director: I. L. Hakes
Plessey Electronic Systems Research Limited
Managing Director: F. G. Marshall

Chart III   *The Plessey Company Limited June 1984.*

INTEGRATIVE CASE ILLUSTRATION: PART ONE

The integrative case study traces the development of the utilization of strategic management by Plessey from 1971 to 1984. Particular attention is given to major changes that were made in their planning at the strategic management level. This illustration is based upon these changes, within three major time periods.

1971–3

At the beginning of this period several weaknesses were reported in Plessey's strategic management. One major weakness was a lack of foresight in strategic thinking. The philosophy was orientated to production and cost control with little concern for the needs and requirements of the markets served. Consequently, in 1971 Plessey was seen to have the wrong product mix and an organizational structure that was unsuited to the style of management that featured within the hierarchy.

Strategic planning was not well developed and was merely an adjunct of the financial function. It was based almost entirely on quantitative financial measures, representing levels of performance that the board wanted to see, rather than being systematic and logically planned company developments. This planning of Plessey's strategic management was done by managers employed only to do the planning and was not the responsibility of managers in the managerial hierarchy.

The organizational structure in 1972 is shown in Chart I, which featured a telecommunications SBU; 23 other SBUs; group commercial and technical services; and overseas subsidiaries. Each SBU was accountable for its own profits and each had a managing director.

In 1973 a strategic planning department was established for the systematic strategic management of Plessey. Five-year plans were to be the basis, which would be revised on an annual cycle. This would start with each of the SBUs formulating its own long-range plans, to be consolidated for the total organization by the planning department.

1974–9

At the beginning of this period the Chief Executive was concerned about Plessey's 'hostile environment', which featured high inflation, a recession, punitive taxation, high interest rates, a general erosion of the competitiveness of UK firms abroad, imminent cuts in public spending, and the threat of nationalization. As part of its approach to this environment a new planning system was developed, which was called POST (Plessey Objectives,

Strategy and Tactics) and STAMP (Strategic and Tactical Asset Management Programme). The purpose was not only to tackle the hostilities of the environment, but also to overcome some basic but major management weaknesses, not least of which was its poor ability to identify and exploit business opportunities.

By 1976 it is reported that the directors were fully committed to the system; regular and detailed reviews were carried out by the directors of the SBUs for which they were responsible, while the planning cycle was being adhered to. At this time comprehensive objectives for the Plessey organization had been established, which were reported to the shareholders.

The organizational structure established in 1976 is given in Chart II. The major features of this structure were:

- Eight main product divisions or SBUs.
- An established Chief Executive Office, which was to be directly responsible to the board.
- A director of strategic planning to reflect Plessey's commitment to strategic management.
- Five overseas divisions.

At the same time the organizational strategy of Plessey was outlined as involving the formation of a number of product subsidiaries or SBUs, each of which would manage its respective products on a world-wide basis.

However, by 1977 several weaknesses were apparent within the POST system. These were:

- Weak objectives that were not easily translated into meaningful strategies.
- Problems in determining resource allocations to the SBUs.
- Failure to incorporate planning into operational management.
- A general problem of getting managers to appreciate the value of planning.

Consequently, changes were made to POST in 1978. Rather than starting within the SBUs, the group senior management was to identify potential strategies for each of the SBUs and would allocate resources to those for development, having determined a range of priorities. The group senior management would also communicate the overall strategic plans for the Plessey Group as a whole, which would provide guidelines for subsequent planning within each SBU.

1980–3

At the beginning of this period Plessey was again faced with a difficult environment in which to pursue its businesses. This involved a deepening recession, escalating inflation and interest rates, a disastrous engineering strike, and a strong pound. In 1980 its organizational strategy was based on:

- An organizational structure based upon product and geographic SBUs.
- The rebalancing of products and the extension of new product development.
- An emphasis on marketing and improved responsiveness to competition.
- Divestment of loss-making operations.

The organizational structure of Plessey in 1983 is given in Chart III. Its major features were:

- Five SBUs based upon products, with each incorporating a number of subsidiary companies.
- Four overseas divisions.
- Retention of the Chief Executive Office.
- Corporate staff to concentrate on the management of group activities, being responsible to the Chief Executive Office.
- The establishment of strategic planning as a major responsibility of the corporate staff.

By the end of 1983 Plessey's environment featured a more intense level of competition than had been the case in previous years. At this time it was stated that the board considered that effective strategic planning of the SBUs was to be central to the future succes of Plessey's strategic management. A major audit of the company was undertaken, with the aim of improving its analysis of markets, formulating higher-quality strategies, sustaining its competitiveness, and increasing the participation of line managers in long-range planning. This commitment was intended to enhance the POST system for the effective strategic management of Plessey in the future.

Analysing the Environment

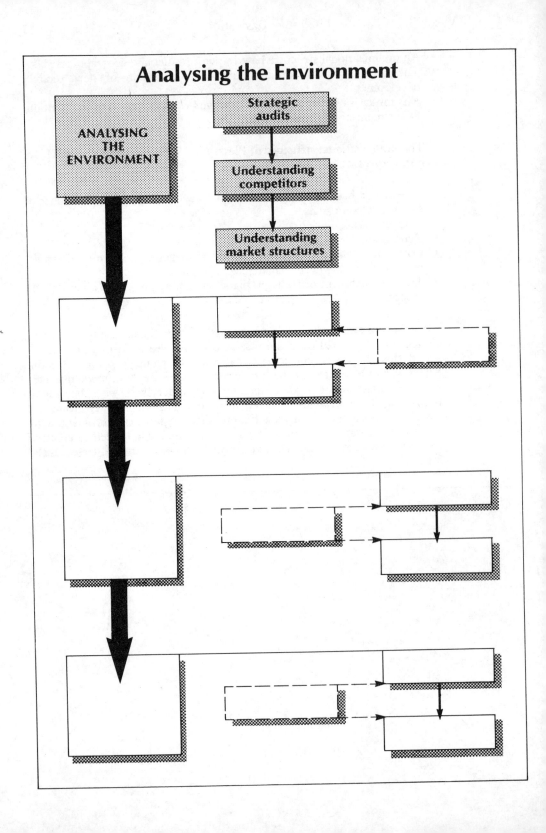

PART TWO

ANALYSING THE ENVIRONMENT

OUTLINE OF PART TWO

This part of the book is concerned with an examination of the overall environment in which organizations exist and perform. Given that the essence of strategic management is to address the overall long-range direction of organizations, understanding the environment provides a basis for decision-making to plan this direction. This need for an understanding is pertinent to all strategic management decision-making, and to all SBUs, and, indeed, analysis of the environment relates to decision-making throughout the rest of the book. The treatment of the environment is based on three areas of understanding, each presented in a separate chapter. In Chapter 3 the general external and internal environments are examined. Chapter 4 is concerned with understanding competitive organizations, focusing on their strategies, weaknesses and potential levels of performance. Finally, Chapter 5 addresses the understanding of market structures, focusing on detailed knowledge of current and potential markets rather than on a general environmental understanding.

CHAPTER 3   STRATEGIC AUDITS
CHAPTER 4   UNDERSTANDING COMPETITORS
CHAPTER 5   UNDERSTANDING MARKET STRUCTURES

CHAPTER 3
STRATEGIC AUDITS

This chapter addresses the general internal and external environments of organizations. It gives full attention to the internal environment, but only partial attention to the external environment. Internally, the audits or examinations are concerned with several aspects of the capabilities of organizations, which include the capabilities of managers. Externally, the audits or examinations discussed in this chapter are concerned with the broad and general environment, although the specific environments relating to competitors and markets are set in context as a prelude to Chapters 4 and 5. An overall feature of the chapter is the complexity of the many variables that need to be understood in order to tackle strategic management decision-making.

In this chapter a broad approach is taken to the understanding of the environments in which organizations are located and in which they pursue the fulfilment of their mission and objectives. This understanding is achieved through the collection of information pertaining to the many areas of the organizational environment and through the analysis of this information. This represents the first of the logical stages of decision-making that were presented in Chapter 1 and illustrated in Figure 1.1.

The achievement of such understanding, within the many areas of the environment, will allow for decision-making in all the component parts of strategic management. The need for this information and a subsequent understanding is simply based on the principle of the reduction of risk in decision-making. However, in practice the complexities of the environment mean that risk reduction is far from simple.

Audits have been well described in the literature and well used in companies as a method of providing a searching examination or exhaustive investigation of specified aspects of business. The strategic audit is concerned with an exhaustive investigation of all the areas of company environments. Although this chapter initially addresses all these areas, two are given fuller treatment in Chapters 4 and 5 – competitors and market structures, respectively.

As the total environment conveniently divides into internal and external environments, this approach is taken in this treatment of strategic audits. However, the first section of this chapter addresses more fully the need for the collection of information. This is followed by consideration, first, of the internal environment, and then of the external environment. As companies generally have little control over the many and complex variables that comprise the various external areas, particular attention to these investigations is necessary. The final section looks at methods of forecasting that can be used in relation to the external environment, given the general problem of lack of control over the environmental variables.

THE NEED TO COLLECT INFORMATION

Although generally needed for strategic management decision-making, information collected internally and that collected externally provide different inputs. External information is collected to provide an understanding of the likelihood that organizational objectives will be realized, but must also allow for the identification of opportunities for setting additional objectives as well as potential threats to the achievement of objectives. Internal information should highlight the strengths and weaknesses of the organization, providing guidance, along with the external understanding, for the process of strategic management. While many of the factors of the internal environment may be controllable, most firms will find that most external factors are likely to be uncontrollable. Consequently, part of the strategic audit requires decisions on those factors to which the firm should react, those which it should try to influence and those which it should ignore. Such judgements are inevitably influenced by the personal values and expectations of the executives making these decisions, as well as the intrinsic nature of the variables. This issue will be part of the internal appraisal itself, but is also tackled in detail in Chapter 8. In addition, the dynamic nature of both environments means that the relative influence of identifiable factors will change with time. New technological advances may have had a recent effect on competitive strengths, but are likely to have less influence as competitors gradually adopt these advances. Consequently, establishing cause-and-effect relationships remains a difficult problem, especially when a major thrust of strategic management is that of long-range direction.

Action and reaction

As the role of strategic management is forward direction, the onus is on taking action within the total environment to promote future success. Such action may necessitate changes to the internal environment, but may also require the firm to attempt to influence external factors. Customers and competitors are obvious areas of planned influence, but attempts may also be made to influence industry trends or the development of technology. Here the principle is that firms need to collect information for the purpose of taking action to reduce internal weaknesses and build on strengths, as well as taking action to pursue selected opportunities and to overcome threats. Several writers have suggested that a major weakness of many firms is that, although they may collect information, they do not use it fully in their decision-making. Rhyne[1] has emphasized that the integration of information into planning processes is as important as the acquisition of information. Indeed firms that are able to apply sophisticated information systems may be able to convert the application into a competitive advantage. Similarly, Houlden[2] has pointed out that weaknesses are often created in the misuse of information, where strategic management decisions that are made without reference to information are a major misuse.

Given the complexity of the environment it is unlikely that all conditions will be accurately identified. Many situations will arise where the effects brought about by changing factors will have a greater impact than anticipated. A new competitive product may achieve a higher market share, or an industrial relations dispute may affect corporate image. In such situations the firm will need to react as a result of its understanding of the environment. In some cases adjustments to tactics at the operational management level may be adequate, but in others decisions may be necessary which require a modification to the strategic plan. A new product launch may need to be accelerated or major changes to personnel policy may be essential.

The internal requirements

An audit of the internal environment is concerned with an assessment of the total capability of the organization through an appraisal of its strengths and weaknesses. This capability includes the resources of the company, but also includes

---

EXHIBIT 3.1

Europe Heads for the Open Market

The EEC consists of 320 million people, with a GDP equivalent to £1,639 billion. As a market it is second in size only to the United States. By 1992 it will be a completely open market. All goods, people, services and capital will be able to move freely between the member states. For companies in member states the EEC will become a single domestic market of great size. Opportunities for these firms will be greater potential for growth, for economies of scale, for product standardization, and for collaboration with companies in other member states. At the beginning of 1988 it was claimed that few British companies were aware of the implications of the single European market, whereas, in general, companies in other member states were aware and were making detailed plans to take advantage of the opportunities. For example, a recent survey by the Paris Chamber of Commerce indicated a high level of preparedness on the part of companies in its area.

Adapted from *The Director*, February 1988

the proficiency of all functions within the company, as well as the competence of individual managers. Although the internal requirements will include factual information about actual performance against specific measures, observation and opinions and attitudes are also likely to be included in the internal appraisal. Here the main aim will be to provide a basis for matching internal capabilities with the external environment, which could be indicative of either inadequate resources or a surfeit of resources to pursue further opportunities.

The external requirements

The requirement of the strategic audit with regard to the external environment is that of understanding all those factors that are likely to impinge upon the organization. Although this is a simple tenet, the many areas of the external environment and their respective complexities mean that this area of understanding is far from simple. Several approaches to understanding the external environment have been developed, with Lenz and Engledow[3], for example, suggesting five major approaches. These will be discussed later in this chapter.

Finally, the major thrust of the need for information collection is that of providing a balance between the internal and external environments. Shipper and White[4] have advised that it is the linking of both sets of information, to provide a *Gestalt* strategic audit, that will provide maximum benefit for strategic management decision-making.

INTERNAL AUDITS

To recap from the last section, the requirement of audits of the internal environment is an understanding of the total capability of the organization, which includes resources, the proficiency of the individual company functions or operations, and the competence of individual managers. The focus of this understanding is the identification of organizational strengths and weaknesses.

In this section attention is given to the specific areas that need to be considered for this audit. Although it has already been recognized that opinions, values and expectations of managers will inevitably be included along with factual information, this approach of listing areas to be considered is based upon the assumption that managers will be willing to participate in the internal audit and that such participation will not influence the validity of the results. As this is not likely to be the case in many situations, consideration of this complication is tackled later in this section, but is also examined in Chapter 13 on human resource management. Variations are to be found in the literature with respect to approaches that are advocated for the internal audit. However, those taken by Glueck and Jauch[5] and David[6] have been found to be of particular value.

The rest of this section is concerned with the three areas of organizational capability, which are taken to be:

- *Resource capability*. An appraisal of the current position and potential for future expansion.
- *Operations capability*. An appraisal of the contribution of each of the functions or operations to total corporate performance.
- *Managerial capability*. An appraisal of the strengths and weaknesses of individual managers.

Resource capability

Resources that are employed range from capital, through plant and machinery, people, and distribution channels, to various types of intangible asset such as corporate image. While many of these resources are conveniently considered within the appraisal of operations, an overview of internal resources is still of value. However, the approach will depend upon the organizational structure. Where there are a number of subsidiaries, divisions or SBUs, it is likely to be more meaningful to constitute a separate appraisal for each entity.

At this stage the total resources can be classified into a number of different types, prior to the detailed appraisal of each of the operations. These classifications could be:

- *Financial structure*. The current structure of capital employed and the potential availability of future funds. The major items of asset utilization, profitability, income growth and other sources of funds would be included here, as would an overview of capital budgeting for the allocation of resources to long-term projects.
- *Physical resources*. The overall stock of land, buildings, plant and machinery. Here capability needs to be assessed in relation not only to the range available, but also to current conditions, geographical spread, special replacement needs and current technology.
- *Human resources*. Organizations evolve around people and their capabilities will only be as good as the capabilities possessed by those people. Perhaps a split into managerial decision-makers and non-managerial operatives is applicable here, with overall changes in each group being of central importance.
- *Administrative systems*. The systems which are used to implement both strategic and operational plans can be either strengths or weaknesses. The internal organization of work and delegation of duties need to be effectively administered as a major capability.
- *Intangible resources*. Regardless of the size or type of organization, it will have an image or images in the perception of stakeholders which may result in either strengths or weaknesses. Other intangible resources include goodwill (which has traditionally been calculated by accountants), concessions, and patents. Of particular importance are brand or product images, including brand or product names, trade marks, reputation, consumer loyalty, and relationships developed within distribution channels.

When identifying strengths and weaknesses from these classifications it is necessary to compare the current situation with trends in recent years. However, the prevailing external environment is also of importance, so that results from the external audit need to be included here. Also, whether the resource capability is a strength or weakness will depend upon aspirations for future direction, which will be defined in the organizational objectives (see Chapter 7). For example, little predicted growth in size may be consistent with the prevailing financial structure and additional funds may not be necessary. Finally, the appraisal of strengths and weaknesses is also carried out in comparison with similar organizations. These could be direct competitors, other firms operating in the same industry, or non-related firms of a similar size or structure or at a similar stage of development.

Operations capability

As mentioned earlier, this appraisal is concerned with the contribution of each of the operations to the total corporate performance, through the identification of strengths and weaknesses. Although each of the operations merits its own audit, there are, of course, many interrelationships among the operations. Although part of each of these audits should address these interrelationships, likely ramifications should be given full consideration in the selection of organizational strategies (see Chapter 11). Appraisals included in the internal audit also link into the strategic management stage of control and effectiveness, which is the subject of Chapter 14. The measurements which are used for control purposes also provide an input to this part of the strategic audit, and readers are urged to examine Chapter 14 at this juncture in the book.

We now look individually at the major operations which should be examined.

Marketing

As this is the function which has direct involvement with the marketplace, strengths can be gained by being more effective at marketing than competitors. Marketing strategy needs to be examined in relation to market segmentation and positioning, as well as the utilization of the elements of the marketing mix. Marketing research needs to be examined in relation to the success of identifying customer requirements and the effectiveness of the mix elements. The latter should be examined as follows:

- Suitability of current products in relation to market needs, as well as the development and implementation of product modifications.
- Price structures relative to profitability and market price levels.
- Appropriateness and effectiveness of selling and distribution, including the total service provided.
- The role of promotional communications within the mix in relation to expenditure and effectiveness.

Also to be included is the use made of marketing expertise in strategic management decision-making. As was outlined in Chapter 1, much of the thinking needed for strategic management requires a marketing orientation, so that marketing personnel represent a valuable asset for this process. For further reading the texts by Kotler[7] and Greenley[8] are recommended.

Research and development

The importance of R&D varies from industry to industry so that the very nature of the industry in which the organization participates will influence the level of capability required. This level will also be influenced by the availability of external R&D institutions in relation to a business policy decision to invest heavily in R&D.

Strengths can be developed from R&D that can provide competitive advantages. Given the level of expenditure needed for R&D the major appraisal is to determine its value in relation to such competitive advantages. These advantages can be either intrinsic developments of the technical aspects of products, or advantages through improved efficiency of manufacturing. For some firms these competitive advantages will be pursued as an offensive approach to tackle competitors and in such cases the audit will need to assess the success of such an approach. For other firms R&D will be pursued only as a defensive approach, in that they will merely imitate and follow the technical developments that are initiated by competitors. For these firms the appraisal will be to determine whether or not this approach is still appropriate, or whether R&D should provide more of a contribution to competitive advantages. The total approach to competitive advantage is given fuller consideration in its role within organizational strategy, which is discussed in Chapter 10. For further reading the book by Wissema[9] is recommended.

Production

Although there are again obvious differences in the production facilities required from industry to industry, the principle of building strengths in capability to develop competitive advantages is common. Internal strengths come from improved efficiency leading to cost reductions, while external strengths would be improved product quality and reliability, with improved efficiency giving greater margins for price stability or reduction.

Schroeder[10] has identified five major functions of production operations, all of which need to be examined as part of the internal audit. These can be examined as follows:

- The design and appropriateness of the production process in relation to current technology and the processes adopted by competitors.
- The relationship of current capacity in relation to current and potential market demands plus economies of scale to be achieved at different levels of output.
- The effectiveness of the management of raw materials and components, work in progress, and finished products within the production process.

- The organization of all levels of people employed in production, with particular attention to work motivation and the utilization of skills.
- The maintenance of quality control throughout the production process and an appraisal of current standards in relation to market requirements.

Perhaps the major contemporary issue in production is the rapid development of robotics and computerized work stations. International competitiveness is now very much dependent on the adoption of computer-aided manufacturing and flexible manufacturing systems. Here the appraisal needs to include not only the current adoption of these systems but also potential adoption. Although advantages to be gained in terms of efficiency and cost savings are great, capital investment can be extensive, so that long lead times may be needed for many companies. For further reading the book by Hill[11] is recommended.

Finance

In conjunction with the examination of financial structure, which was part of the resource capability, this aspect of the internal audit is concerned with a company's financial strength in comparison with that of competitors and in relation to the identification of strengths and weaknesses throughout the organization. A major way of determining such strengths and weaknesses is through financial ratio analysis. Several ratios can be calculated and many classification systems of ratio analysis have been established. For example, that of Holmes and Sugden[12] consists of the following:

- Operating ratios which are concerned with the company's performance, but which do not include the financing of that performance.
- Financial ratios which measure the financial structure.
- Investment ratios which relate share ownership and the market price of shares to profits, dividends and assets.

Here again the internal audit relates very closely to the stage of control in the total strategic management process. These ratios need to be calculated and interpreted for control purposes and therefore provide an input to the internal audit. Consequently, a fuller treatment of ratio analysis is given in Chapter 14. However, it needs to be emphasized again that the interpretation of these ratios needs to take place against a background of previous company trends, prevailing external conditions and appropriate company comparisons.

The financial audit should also include three major areas of appraisal, as proposed by David[6]. The first of these is investment decisions or capital budgeting. Here the audit needs to consider the allocation of capital to SBUs, products, functions or special projects. The second area is that concerned with the attainment of finance and the financing mix of the capital structure. Thus the appraisal would include an examination of retained profits, current and future borrowing, the selling of assets and the raising of share capital. The other area is that of dividend decisions. This appraisal is concerned with the balancing of dividend payments to shareholders and the retention of funds for internal development. Previous trends need to be considered as well as the shareholders' expectations as a major stakeholder group. All these aspects of financial capability have a major bearing on the organizational strategy that can be adopted, so that further consideration is given in Chapter 11.

Personnel

As previously established the overall capability of an organization will be constrained by the capabilities of its personnel. As the capability of managers is of particular importance the next section is devoted to this issue.

For non-managerial personnel several considerations are necessary in order to appraise strengths and weaknesses. The first is an analysis of the range of employment skills that are needed, in relation to the production and administrative systems that are used. Following on from this is an analysis of the range of skills that are currently employed, as well as the number of people employed within each skill classification. Work-force strengths and weaknesses can thus be identified. Second is the ability of the company to be able to attract and retain skilled employees. A history of low attainment in certain areas and high employee turnover represent major weaknesses for many firms. Another major consideration is that of the importance of the unionization of employees. High levels of unionization can be either a strength or a weakness. Close industrial relations can mean harmony within the work-force and can provide a vehicle for introducing changes that may be necessary as a result of strategic management decision-making. In opposition, weak industrial relations can mean little harmony with consequential disruption in the work-place. For further reading the book by Torrington and Chapman[13] is recommended.

Managerial capability

This area of the organizational capability audit was initially explained as being an appraisal of the strengths and weaknesses of individual managers. Although texts on general management have given approaches to be used for managerial performance appraisal, the work of Ansoff[14] has developed the concept of management capability within the context of strategic management. Here the implication is that performance appraisal, which is to be found in texts on general and personnel management, is applicable to functional managers within the operations, whereas management capability is concerned with an appraisal of the endeavours of the managers who participate in strategic management.

For this particular aspect of the internal audit both performance appraisal and management capability are appropriate. The former would be used to identify strengths and weaknesses in the operations as such knowledge is necessary to anticipate potential influences on the implementation of strategic management decisions. However, management capability tackles, in the words of Ansoff's definition, 'managements' propensity and ability to engage in behaviour which will optimize the attainment of the firms' objectives'. In this book, *Strategic Management*, management capability relates to all those managers who participate in strategic management decision-making. While both performance appraisals and management capability are also considered in Chapter 13 on human resource management, management capability is outlined here in its role as a major part of the internal audit.

From his definition of management capability, Ansoff goes on to explain that it should be examined in two ways:

- Resultant company responsiveness to anticipate and react to changes in the environment.
- An assessment of certain managerial attributes which will give resultant capability profiles.

He goes on to recommend that assessing resultant company responsiveness can be based upon three features of the managerial ethos of the company:

- The responsiveness climate, which is the propensity of management to react in a particular way to changes that are required through strategic management decision-making. Managers may be prepared to welcome, control or reject change.
- The competence of managers to respond to change. This is the ability of managers to cope with change and is particularly concerned with managerial systems that have been established to handle change, including the total strategic management process.
- The capacity of managers to absorb and carry out the volume of work that would be needed to achieve these changes.

Again the point is that strengths and weaknesses are likely to be identified within current management capability. This could result in the need to train certain managers, the identification of a need for additional managers with specified skills or experience, or perhaps a realization that certain parts of the organizational structure would benefit from reorganization. The whole issue of the role of organizational structure in strategic management is tackled in Chapter 9.

The second way in which management capability can be examined is through a range of managerial attributes to give a resultant capability profile. This consists of several attributes which have been adapted and summarized from Ansoff[14] in Table 3.1. In the first group of attributes specific strengths and weaknesses of individual managers are to be identified. As will be seen from Table 3.1, these consist of their mentality to handle their managerial roles, personal power to enforce their managerial skills, individual competences and their capacity to carry out the work demanded of their managerial roles. The second group of attributes is concerned with the climate or ambience that the managers have created within the organization in which decision-making is carried out. Here weaknesses and strengths would be identified as a result of the internal atmosphere in which the managers operate, where conditions which are either favourable or unfavourable

Table 3.1 *Adaptation of Ansoff's management capability profile
(H. I. Ansoff,* Implanting Strategic Management, © *1984 Adapted by
permission of Prentice Hall Ltd.)*

Managerial attributes

- Mentality
- Power
- Competence
- Capacity

Climatic attributes

- Culture
- Power

Procedural attributes

- Information systems
- Problem-solving procedures
- Rewards and incentive schemes

---

to strategic management decision-making are of central importance. The final group of attributes addresses the general competences that prevail within the managerial procedures that the company uses, as opposed to individual managerial competence. Here any systems of management could be identified as strengths or weaknesses, ranging from general information and problem-solving systems, to systems for rewarding and providing incentives for managers.

EXTERNAL AUDITS See pg 62 for start.

Several comments about the importance of external audits have been made in the earlier sections of this chapter. The major role of external audits is to provide an understanding of the likelihood that the organizational objectives will be achieved. However, knowledge about trends in the external environment is required for all the subsequent stages of strategic management, as will become evident in later chapters.

Of similar importance is the need to identify business opportunities that have the potential for exploitation, representing potential changes to future direction and objectives. These could range from the identification of new export markets to poor performance by competitors. Similarly, there is a need to identify threats to the achievement of current organizational objectives, as well as to the total performance of the company. Such threats could range from the decline of specific markets or industries to the ramifications of a country's poor economic growth and performance.

Although the principle of external auditing is that it should seek to identify any external variable that is likely to impinge upon the company, the practical reality of identification is far from simple. Complexity is caused by the sheer range of

EXHIBIT 3.2

Russia's Hard-cash Shopping Spree

A combination of economic, technical and political factors have resulted in Russian markets becoming more accessible to companies in Western Europe. The Soviet economy is said to have been growing by about 3% per annum over recent years, although the aim for future years is said to be over 4% per annum. Western Europe is needed by Russia both to provide inputs and to purchase products. Technology from Western Europe is also needed to modernize ageing factories and to build modern efficient plants. In recent years purchases of machinery have rapidly increased from France, Italy, Britain and West Germany. In the future European firms should obtain even higher levels of sales, with the chemical, plastics and steel industries likely to be the most important. Western Europe is a huge customer for Russian oil and gas, and countries such as France have threatened to consume less unless Russia imports more French goods and services. Finance for purchasing Western goods comes largely from this exporting of oil and gas, reflecting its importance, and from borrowing from Western banks. Increased purchases of European products also means increased business potential for European financial institutions. Finally, in the early 1980s Russia suffered from low grain harvests, forcing it to purchase high volumes from the West. These purchases should decline in the late 1980s, as Soviet agriculture becomes more efficient, releasing additional finance to import more Western goods.

Adapted from *Fortune*, 20 January 1986

areas to be considered (as specified presently), the complex relationships of the many variables within each area, the practical difficulty of carrying out adequate research to provide an understanding of each area, and the subsequent difficulty of identifying cause-and-effect relationships.

Given this complexity it is perhaps not surprising that different writers, and indeed different disciplines within management studies, have developed different ways of explaining the external environment. Lenz and Engledow[3] have claimed that these different approaches can be classified into five different models. Within these different models they have identified different assumptions about the nature of the environment, about the ways in which environmental changes occur, and about the ways firms tackle the identification of and their reaction to these changes. While the detail of these five models is outside the scope of this book, it is important to realize that environmental complexities have led to these variations in the explanation of the external environment.

Writers of books on strategic management have tended to adopt a two-way conceptualization of the external environment: a general and wide environment in which all organizations operate, and a specific environment which can be considered to be unique to a particular firm. A number of labels are used to identify these two environments, but those used by Pearce and Robinson[15] have been adopted for this book. These labels are the 'operating environment' for that specific to each company and the 'remote environment' for that which is common to all firms. The constitution of both the operating and remote environments is given in Figure 3.1, although they are not fully consistent with that given by Pearce and Robinson.

The four areas of the operating environment are obviously central to all aspects of strategic management, representing fundamental and essential knowledge for decision-making. However, all are closely related in that customers and their buying behaviour constitute markets, while a number of markets represent the structure of a particular industry. Competitors, in simple terms, are other firms contending for the same markets and customers.

The five areas of the remote environment are related in that variables within each can influence the others, but effects caused by each area on the organization are wide and various. Indeed all are major disciplines of study in their own right, so that treatment given to each of these areas in a strategic management book is limited to an exposition of central issues.

The operating environment

Knowledge of all these areas is generally treated as being within the scope of marketing research. Therefore responsibility for the collection and analysis of information is likely to be located in the marketing department, so that this aspect of operational management will provide an input to strategic management. However, it must be realized that the information needs are different at the two levels of management. At the operational level the need is orientated to decision-making about current products in current markets, with decisions being particularly focused on tactical changes concerned with elements of the marketing mix. At the strategic level the need is particularly oriented to identifying long-term trends, where trends and probable turbulance in markets and industries are of particular importance. Consequently, although the marketing research function is able to provide inputs to the external audit, it may be that, for some firms, the traditional terms of reference need to be extended to include these information requirements, or it may be necessary to establish a separate research function. This issue will be pursued further in Chapter 9, which is concerned with organizational structures per se.

The paramount importance of all these areas of the operating environment is perhaps obvious, particularly as their understanding is an essential stage for the pursuance of marketing orientation. However, readers will be familiar with many case studies and histories of companies which have not followed such a business philosophy, despite the common-sense argument for adoption, and have suffered as a consequence. Given the importance of these areas, fuller treatment than could be given in this chapter is deemed to be of importance and is presented in Chapters 4 and 5. Chapter 4 is devoted to competitors, while Chapter 5 is devoted to customers, markets and industries.

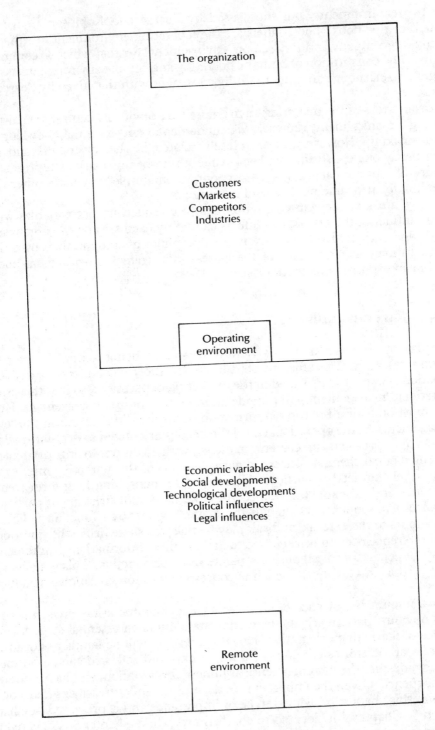

The organization

Customers
Markets
Competitors
Industries

Operating
environment

Economic variables
Social developments
Technological developments
Political influences
Legal influences

Remote
environment

Figure 3.1 *External environments.*

The remote environment

The approach taken in this section is to address each of the areas of the remote environment in turn, following the sequence presented in Figure 3.1.

Economic variables

In so far as the discipline of economics is concerned with the creation and distribution of wealth, an understanding of both these phenomena provides the overall framework of the opulence available in the countries in which a firm participates. This overall appraisal requires an understanding of trends in the growth of GNP and its distribution both demographically and geographically. Included in this understanding of trends would be a classification of the current state of the economy, with depression, recession, recovery and prosperity being classificatory stages of the economic cycle.

As a consequence of the economic situation prevailing in a given country, government will adopt fiscal and monetary policies in order to pursue economic objectives. Interest rates are likely to have some influence on the acquisition of funds that the company may need to pursue growth, while the availability of credit and borrowing to the general public will affect their purchasing power and propensity to consume. Levels of income tax will affect levels of disposable income, while indirect taxes will have a direct affect on market price levels.

Attempts at controlling other economic objectives, such as inflation and the balance of payments, are also central issues to be monitored. For the former, measures to control wage increases or to stabilize aggregate demand may result in a decline in demand in some markets but not in others. Attempts at controlling the balance of payments may stimulate a favourable environment in the home market through the control of imports, but such measures in countries where the firm exports are obviously indicative of an unfavourable environment.

Social developments

Pearce and Robinson[15] state that 'social considerations involve the beliefs, values, attitudes, opinions and lifestyles of those [people] in a firm's external environment, as developed from their cultural, ecological, demographic, religious, educational, and ethnic conditioning'. Thus the way people are and behave, within the society of each of the countries in which the firm participates, is based on an extremely complex set of conditioning variables. Social attitudes related to the consumption of certain products may change very quickly, such as clothing styles, books and popular music. For other products associated attitude changes may occur over a long period of time, such as 'healthy' eating, energy conservation and road safety.

As standards of living increase so do people's expectations, although the nature of these expectations shows obvious variation within different societies, with dramatic differences between some countries. In Europe these expectations are particularly reflected in beliefs, values and attitudes towards consumer durables. Although these expectations have led to new opportunities in the case of products such as video recorders and compact disc players, threats to growth have occurred in the case of products such as vacuum cleaners, washing machines and home computers, where markets have matured.

Complexity is a major concern for organizations as, although many trends develop over a relatively long period of time and can be identified, their influence tends to be situation-specific to industries and markets. Research into social trends is likely to be instigated through marketing research, in that all these issues influence buyer behaviour, with writers such as Chisnall[16] adequately addressing these issues. However, again the point to be made is that, for strategic management, the focus is on long-term trends as well as current patterns of buyer behaviour.

Technological developments

These developments in the external environment obviously need to be monitored in relation to internal research and development, as discussed in the section on internal audits. There are two major aspects to this audit: the technical developments that are being achieved by competitors, and those that represent advancements in specific areas in the world at large. As with R&D these developments may relate to benefit improvements in competitors' products, or to improved efficiency of competitors' production processes. Both are likely to represent threats. However, technical advancements developed by research institutions or individual inventors are likely to be available as opportunities for all companies.

Although the impact of technology varies from industry to industry, current developments in computer-aided systems and microprocessor-based equipment means that most organizations can receive some benefits; indeed, if the latter are not taken, such lethargy could become a threat. Frohman[17] has suggested that, for many companies, a major problem has been the integration of technology into strategic management, given that market, competitive, and resource forces have traditionally been given overriding importance. Therefore, a change in managerial attitudes towards technology is advocated, which will be pursued further in the selection of strategic alternatives in Chapter 11.

Political influences

The range of policies that a government develops to influence various sectors of the economy is unavoidably couched within the political philosophy of that particular government, which will be between the extremes of a free market economy and a centrally controlled economy. Governments which are biased towards either extreme will implement policies with the potential of affecting strategic management decision-making. In the free market economy the encouragement of enterprise, relatively low taxation and scant control of wages, for example, are likely to present opportunities, although encouragement of competition may mean threats, especially from foreign companies. A more centrally controlled economy may give more protection to domestic companies, although the domination of the government in many large industries may mean fewer business opportunities for firms from the private sector.

When a new government is elected the first part of this aspect of the external audit is to examine the published programme of intended actions, in order to identify policies which are likely to pose either an opportunity or a threat. Subsequent monitoring is to follow the progress of the instigation of such actions. However, in the long term the problem can be a change of government to an administration with a different political philosophy, resulting in the implementation of different policies. For example, increases in taxation may subdue market size, while the privatization of key industries will provide opportunities for many organizations.

Legal influences

As a result of the government's policies legislation will eventually be passed. In most developed countries, there is a massive body of legislation within which companies must operate. Indeed, at the operational level there is much legislation, covering such areas as health and safety at work, employment protection and consumer protection. Although such legislation is obviously of vital importance, its consideration is more appropriate at the operational level.

For strategic management there are two reasons for the need to monitor legal influences. First, the company must ensure that all legal requirements are being met at the operational level. Second, the ramifications of potentially new legislation should be anticipated in advance of their coming into force, in case it should represent an opportunity or a threat. This could be legislation applicable to companies in general, such as changes to regulations governing consumer credit, or legislation which is specific to a particular industry, such as that aimed at controlling the pharmaceutical industry.

However, given that the focus of strategic management is on direction, legislation concerned with fair trading, competition and consumer protection are of central importance. Here again the central need is to anticipate change and the potential ramifications of such change. While there is probably little need for the managers who participate in strategic management to have expert knowledge of the complexities of legislation, it will be necessary to seek guidance from the legal profession, especially in relation to overseas markets.

Appraisal of opportunities and threats

The final stage of the audit is to take the information generated from the examination of the operating and remote environments and to appraise the identified opportunities and threats in relation to internal capabilities. Such an appraisal can then be used for decision-making. Although this can be done intuitively, several writers have suggested systematic approaches to this appraisal. Although none of the methods can be considered totally satisfactory, in that they are unlikely to provide categoric listings, the aim is to provide systematic thinking to the appraisal system. Indeed the complexities of the combined internal and external environments are indicative of the problems of such methodology.

Consequently, the discussion which follows in the rest of this section is sugges-
tive of the type of thinking to be followed in arriving at an appraisal of opportunities and threats. It has been developed from ideas that have been suggested by
Rowe et al.[18], Aaker and Mascarenhas[19], Shah and La Placa[20], and Hoch[21]. This
approach is based on four stages.

Identification

From the examination of both the operating and remote external environments a
list is made of the identified opportunities and a separate list is made of the
identified threats. (At this point it should be repeated that the operating environment, as explained earlier in this chapter, is examined in detail in Chapters 4 and
5.) Although this may appear to be a stage of merely listing, it involves identification within the environmental complexities as already described. At this stage the
identification will be based on research carried out into each of the environments,
including the latest trends.

Relevant capabilities

It is then necessary to assess the likely impact of each listed opportunity or threat
on the organization and the internal capabilities that are available to tackle these
consequences. For each of the opportunities it is likely that an assessment of the

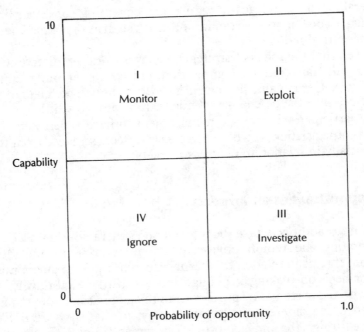

Figure 3.2 *Classification of opportunities.*

highest probable level of potential should be compared with the lowest probable level of potential, with the chosen level being ultimately based on value judgement. At this stage the assessment will also need to include a forecast into the future; for example, a forecast of the trend in market size will be necessary in assessing the opportunity to exploit a new geographical market. Methods of forecasting are outlined in the final section of this chapter.

From here a judgement is made of the capability of the firm to exploit each opportunity, which would be based on the internal audit. Although weaknesses may be identified within specific aspects of capability, the predicted impact of the respective opportunities will be indicative of the need to compensate for these weaknesses, which will also be addressed in the selection of organizational strategy in Chapter 11. An overall score is given to the assessed capability to exploit each opportunity, where 0 represents no capability and 10 represents total capability.

A similar exercise is then completed for each of the identified threats. A forecast is made of the maximum detrimental effect on the firm, as well as the minimum effect. Again the capabilities of the firm to tackle a threat from, say, major new competitive products is assessed and again a score is given to the overall capability to tackle each threat. Here 0 represents no capability to overcome the particular threat, while 10 represents sufficient capability to conquer the threat. These scores will be used later in the approach.

Assessment of probabilities

The next stage is to take each of the opportunities and threats in turn and make a judgement as to the probability that each will occur. Again forecasting will be necessary to allow for these judgements to be made, but developed from research into the external environment. Probabilities would be assigned from 0, which would represent no chance of occurrence, to 1, which would represent certainty of occurrance. These probabilities can then be compared to the respective capability scores for each opportunity and threat identified.

Classification of opportunities and threats

Each of the identified opportunities and threats can then be classified in a matrix, using the measures of probability of occurrence and degree of relevant capability. A matrix for opportunities is exhibited in Figure 3.2, while that for threats is given in Figure 3.3.

Opportunities classified into quadrant II are obviously of maximum interest and would almost certainly need to be pursued further with the view of exploitation. Those in quadrant III represent considerable potential for the company, although current analysis indicates a low capability for exploitation. Further investigations of internal capabilities would be needed. The first quadrant is indicative of a lesser opportunity but a high ability to pursue it; consequently, further monitoring of the environment would be needed over the next period of time. Finally, opportunities with little chance of occurrence which are

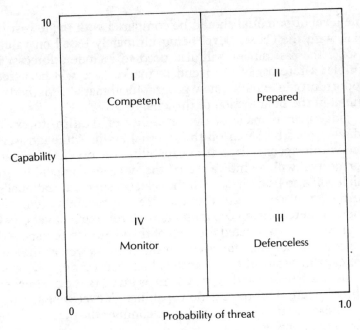

Figure 3.3   *Classification of threats.*

accompanied by weak internal capabilities (classified into quadrant IV) are likely to be ignored.

The major threats are patently those which are classified into quadrant III of Figure 3.3, where there is a high probability of occurrence and where the company has little capability to respond. These situations represent the main impediments to the company's future success, requiring remedial action if they are to be overcome. Threats appearing in quadrant II are of major concern, but here the analysis is indicative of a higher level of capability; the firm is prepared to challenge such threats, but they need to be given attention in the subsequent decision-making. Quadrant I represents those threats with a low probability of occurrence, although the capabilities of the firm are deemed to be such that they are competent to tackle these situations should they arise. Finally, quadrant IV represents low-probability threats, although little capability to tackle them is predicted. These potential threats are difficult in that they need to be closely monitored because, should they become real, then it is likely that the firm will need to improve its capabilities.

FORECASTING EXTERNAL TRENDS

Although a full treatment of forecasting techniques is considered to be outside the scope of this book, the aim of this section is to give an overview of methods which are applicable to the external environment. Particular attention has been given to forecasting in the marketing literature, developed out of the need for sales forecasting. Here the need is to project past trends into the future, despite the likelihood that the relative influence of future environmental variables will be different to that of historical influences. Tull and Hawkins[22], for example, group forecasting techniques into judgemental methods, time-series analysis and projection, and causal methods. The major techniques advocated by Tull and Hawkins are described later. Alternatively, techniques can be grouped as either quantitative or qualitative methods. In the former, regression analysis, trend extrapolation, and econometric models represent major approaches. Major methods for qualitative forecasting include expert judgement, market research surveys, and scenario and Delphi techniques.

The use of these methods within the context of strategic management has been tackled by Higgins[23]. His approach is to present methods to be used for three classifications of the external environment: economic forecasting, technological forecasting, and social and political forecasting. The following discussions in this section have been developed from this work by Higgins, but start with methods given by Tull and Hawkins[22] for sales forecasting. This range of forecasting techniques is listed in Table 3.2.

Table 3.2 *Major forecasting methods.*

Sales/economic forecasting	Technological forecasting	Social and political forecasting
Sales representatives' estimates	Scenario writing	Historical analogy
Expert opinions	Quantitative extrapolation	Scenario writing
Delphi method	Relevance trees	Delphi method
'Naive' method	Morphological analysis	Cross-impact analysis
Moving averages	Delphi method	Quantitative extrapolation
Exponential smoothing	Cross-impact analysis	Surveys
Regression analysis		Value profiles
Causal regression models		Probability diffusion matrix
Econometric models		
Surveys		
Input–output models		
Barometric forecasting		

Sales forecasting

These forecasts relate to the external operating environment, combining the influences of customers, markets, competitors, and industries on the sales volume to be achieved. As previously indicated, this forecasting would probably be the responsibility of the marketing department and would probably include specific forecasts for specific products and markets.

Judgemental methods

These include estimates made by sales representatives, which are aggregated to give an overall forecast. Short-term accuracy may be good, while long-term accuracy is likely to be poor, and bias needs to be carefully assessed. Selected experts can also be asked to give estimates, which would include internal executives and external experts. These estimates may be discussed by the experts to give a consensus, or they may be merely aggregated to give an overall view. The Delphi method also uses a number of experts, but each provides an anonymous estimate which is sent to each expert. Further estimates are then requested from each expert and they are again exchanged until a consensus is reached.

Time-series analysis and projection

This group of techniques is based on observations of a variable in time, and the assumption that patterns of change in the variable, over previous periods of time, can be used for future prediction of the variable. The four major methods in this group are based on a 'naive' model, moving averages, exponential smoothing, and regression analysis. However, caution needs to be exercised in the interpretation of these results, in that such forecasts are developed from the historical relationships of variables, which are unlikely to be exactly repeated in the future.

Causal methods

These methods are based on identified factors that influence the level of sales. The latter is the dependent variable while the influencing factors are independent variables which have an effect on the volume of sales. The methods require the identification of independent variables, measurements of changes in their value, and the establishment of their relationship with the dependent variable. Known or predicted changes in the independent variables can then be used to forecast changes in the dependent variable through this causal relationship. Major methods include causal regression models, econometric models, surveys of buyers' intentions, input–output models, and barometric forecasting. Again caution is needed in the interpretation of these forecasts, in that the method is also based upon historical relationships of variables, which are likely to change in the future.

Economic forecasting

According to Higgins[23] most of the above methods are also applicable to economic forecasting. However econometric model-building is perhaps the most widely used method for forecasting economic variables. Many forecasts are produced by specialist organizations, so that, in all but the largest companies with resources to complete their own forecasts, these are readily available for the appropriate purchase fee. However, the problem faced by purchasers is that of variations in the models used, which are likely to produce different results in their forecasts of the same phenomena. Purchasers will thus be faced with alternative sets of possible future occurrences and the problem of reconciling these differences.

Technological forecasting

Although common techniques are available for forecasting technological developments, the pace and magnitude of change can obviously differ quite drastically from industry to industry. Six major methods of forecasting are given by Higgins, which are also featured in Table 3.2.

Scenario writing starts with the current technology and predicts a range of alternative ways in which the technology could develop. This could be limited to three scenarios of pessimistic, likely and optimistic, to cover a wider range. Such a range could be developed through internal brainstorming sessions with managers, or by the use of the Delphi method (as outlined previously). Where quantitative measures are appropriate, it may be possible to use regression analysis or moving averages to provide alternative scenarios. This leads on to quantitative extrapolation as a major method, using the quantitative techniques previously given. Here the caution is that, although a forecast may be possible, economic viability needs also to be addressed.

Relevance trees are similar to decision trees, and provide guidance through several alternative situations that would be needed to satisfy a particular objective. Morphological analysis is a specialized method of anticipating alternative technologies for given products or production processes, by listing and combining alternative approaches to each feature of the product or each stage of the production process. The Delphi technique is as already outlined. Cross-impact analysis takes specific major advances in technology and attempts to identify their impact or influence on specified products or production processes. The Delphi method can also be incorporated with this approach.

Social and political forecasting

Again many of the previous techniques of forecasting have been applied to the social and political environment. Although many external organizations also produce these forecasts, but with again different predictions, the aim here is to highlight the techniques which can be used.

Those that are suggested by Higgins[23] have been listed in Table 3.2. Historical analogy has been a traditional approach in the social sciences and still has its place in forecasting. However, scenario writing, the Delphi method, and cross-impact analysis have become important approaches. Quantitative extrapolation has also been used where appropriate, while market-research surveys can also be important in understanding these trends.

Another method, which has been labelled 'value profiles', attempts to assess changes in values within the society. Yet another method has been labelled the 'probability diffusion matrix'. Here certain social or political events are taken and their associated probability of occurrence is estimated, along with the likely period of time over which the event will diffuse throughout society.

SUMMARY

Strategic audits provide investigations of the total environment in which organizations exist and perform; this environment is comprised of an internal environment and an external environment.

The first section of the chapter discussed the need for the collection of information during these investigations. The second section addressed internal audits, where the internal strengths and weaknesses of an organization are investigated. This was based on three areas of organizational capability — resource capability, operations capability, and managerial capability. All three areas are of equal importance for strategic management decision-making, although overall internal capability is related to the external audit later in the chapter.

The external audit was focused on the opportunities and threats which are to be identified in organizations' external environments. This total environment was presented as an operating environment and as a remote environment. Although some attention was given to the former in this chapter, the major presentation of this material occurs in Chapters 4 and 5. Discussions on the remote environment covered economic variables, social developments, technological developments, political influences, and legal influences. The final topic of this section was the appraisal of opportunities and threats in relation to internal capabilities.

The final section of this chapter considered forecasting. However, the aim of the section was merely to provide an overview of techniques that can be used to forecast external trends.

CHAPTER CASE STUDY ILLUSTRATION:
FORD OF EUROPE AND LOCAL CONTENT REGULATIONS*

At the time of the case study (1983), Ford of Europe was the eighth largest producer of motor cars in the world. Although Europe represented con-

---

*Derived from the original case study by H. Landis Gabel and Anthony E. Hall. Copyright © 1984 by INSEAD.

tinued opportunities, the major threat was the growing Japanese presence in the European industry. The full case study presents the many and complex issues pertaining to this threat.

Aspects of both the internal and external environments of Ford are treated. In the case of the latter these relate to the operating and remote environments, with the major threat of the rapidly expanding rivalry from Japanese manufacturers dominating management thinking. This threat was perceived as taking several forms:

- As already mentioned, the Japanese were obtaining a rapidly expanding market share, achieved with imported products.
- Although the manufacture of Japanese cars in Europe had only just started and was at a low level of output, the probability was that this would expand dramatically.
- New Japanese factories in Europe would incorporate the most advanced technology and work methods, which would represent severe competitive forces.
- As well as threatening market share, European production of Japanese cars would expand industry capacity, which was already suffering from an excess volume of 20%.
- The Japanese manufacturer Honda already had a collaborative agreement with British Leyland (now the Rover Group), with BL assembling the Honda Ballade under licence in the UK as the BL Acclaim.
- Japanese components were already being sold in Europe direct to car manufacturers, with, for example, General Motors using a Japanese gearbox for the Cavalier/Rekord.

Ford of Europe could also look to the experience of Ford in the United States of America. Japanese imports had incrementally achieved higher market shares until a voluntary limit had been agreed between the two governments. However, it was now likely that this limit would be raised. During the period Ford's share of the US car market had fallen from 26% in 1976 to 16% in 1982.

During 1983 it seemed that the continued marketing of Japanese cars in Europe would continue to pose a threat to Ford, and indeed other European manufacturers. Although increased imports were a threat, perhaps a greater threat would be the establishment of major factories by Japanese car companies in Europe.

EXTERNAL ENVIRONMENT

Other issues from the external environment were also pertinent to this major threat. A major issue of the operating environment was that Ford was currently competing very successfully against other European manufacturers. Indeed in 1983 it had achieved, for the first time, leadership in terms of market share. However Ford's forecasts predicted slow market growth for the future, so that increased sales of Japanese cars in Europe could only be to the detriment of Ford's existing market share. Increased rivalry was therefore an immediate threat to Ford's dominant position in European markets. To exacerbate the situation it also perceived a threat from manufacturers in Eastern Europe. Although not an immediate problem, its perception was one of potential additional competitive rivalry within the marketplace.

As part of the remote environment of Ford, there were in existence a number of bilateral trade agreements between some individual European countries and Japan. For example, Japan's shares of the French and British markets were informally limited to 3% and 11% respectively. In Italy imports were restricted to 2,000 cars a year. Action by the Government in the USA also had an effect in Europe. Imports of cars into the USA had been restricted, with the result that Japanese manufacturers were more attracted to Europe in order to achieve their world sales growth objectives.

Another alternative for regulating the influence of Japanese companies was for European governments to stipulate that a certain proportion of the content of Japanese cars sold in Europe should have been produced in Europe. This is known as a 'local content regulations'. These did not, at the time, exist in EFTA or the EEC, except for Portugal and Eire. While the principles of the EEC did not really favour bilateral agreements between member countries and other countries, EEC Regulation 916 allowed for the protection of specific industries.

INTERNAL ENVIRONMENT

Although the Ford Motor Company in the USA had previously favoured unrestricted international trade, during the 1980s the company had adopted the value of fair trade with an element of protectionism. Therefore Ford of Europe were at liberty to lobby governments and the EEC for the introduction of local content regulations in relation to all non-European manufacturers. Indeed Ford claimed that 95% of the content of their European cars was made in Europe, from their 25 plants located in six European countries.

To combat this threat Ford had started to turn its internal weaknesses, vis-à-vis the Japanese competition, into strengths. It had studied and installed Japanese manufacturing and management techniques, including robotics, in its factories. However, it considered itself still five or ten years behind the Japanese in catching up on their cost advantages. Meanwhile, in the USA, protectionism from the Japanese was being challenged. It was being suggested that poor competitiveness on the part of US companies was largely a result of their own weak management.

Another aspect of Ford's lobbying for European local content regulations would weaken internal operations. This was related to Ford's development as a global organization, when standard parts would be manufactured in many countries, each where the best advantages would be gained. Cars would then be built for specific markets with world components, with European-built Fords also having world components. Therefore, local content regulations for protection against Japanese manufacturers would also be detrimental to Ford's developing long-term strengths in globalization.

REFERENCES

1. Rhyne, L. C., 'The Relationship of Information Usage Characteristics to Planning System Sophistication', *Strategic Management Journal*, **6**, 1985, 319–37.
2. Houlden, B. T., 'Data and Effective Corporate Planning', *Long Range Planning*, **13**, 1980, 106–11.
3. Lenz, R. T. and Engledow, J. L., 'Environmental Analysis: the Application of Current Theory', *Strategic Management Journal*, **7**, 1986, 329–46.
4. Shipper, F. and White, C. S., 'Linking Organizational Effectiveness and Environmental Change', *Long Range Planning*, **16**, 3, 1983, 99–106.
5. Glueck, W. F. and Jauch, L. F., *Business Policy and Strategic Management*, 4th edn, McGraw-Hill, New York, 1984.
6. David, F. R., *Fundamentals of Strategic Management*, Merill, Columbus, OH, 1986.
7. Kotler, P., *Marketing Management: Analysis, Planning and Control*, 5th edn, Prentice Hall, Englewood Cliffs, NJ, 1984.
8. Greenley, G. E., *The Strategic and Operational Planning of Marketing*, McGraw-Hill, Maidenhead, 1986.
9. Wissema, J. G., *R&D Strategic Management*, Pinter, London, 1985.
10. Schroeder, R., *Operations Management*, McGraw-Hill, New York, 1981.
11. Hill, T., *Production/Operations Management*, Prentice Hall, London, 1983.
12. Holmes, G. and Sugden, A., *Interpreting Company Reports and Accounts*, 3rd edn, Woodhead-Faulkner, Cambridge, 1986.
13. Torrington, D. and Chapman, J. *Personnel Management*, Prentice Hall, London, 1983.
14. Ansoff, H. I., *Implanting Strategic Management*, Prentice Hall, Englewood Cliffs, NJ, 1984.
15. Pearce, J. A. and Robinson, R. B., *Strategic Management*, 2nd edn, Irwin, Homewood, IL, 1985.
16. Chisnall, P. M., *Marketing: A Behavioural Analysis*, 2nd edn, McGraw-Hill, Maidenhead, 1985.
17. Frohman, A. L., 'Putting Technology into Strategy', *Journal of Business Strategy*, **5**, 4, 1985, 54–65.
18. Rowe, A. J., Mason, R. O. and Dickel, K. E., *Strategic Management*, Addison-Wesley, Reading, MA, 1986.
19. Aaker, D. A. and Mascarenhas, B., 'The Need for Strategic Flexibility', *Journal of Business Strategy*, **5**, 2, 1984, 74–82.
20. Shah, K. and La Placa, P. J., 'Assessing Risk in Strategic Planning', *Industrial Marketing Management*, **10**, 2, 1981, 77–91.
21. Hoch, S. H., 'Integrating Social, Economic, Political and Technical Forecasts into Business Strategy', *Research Management*, November 1981, 8–12.
22. Tull, D. S. and Hawkins, D. I., *Marketing Research*, 3rd edn, Macmillan, New York, 1984.
23. Higgins, J. C., *Strategic and Operational Planning Systems*, Prentice Hall, London, 1980.

CHAPTER 4
UNDERSTANDING COMPETITORS

In this, the second chapter concerned with analysing the environment, attention is given to competitive organizations. This understanding of competitors develops out of the strategic audit, expanding issues which were initially raised in Chapter 3. Although companies logically should have as much knowledge about their competitors as they do about themselves, in practice this is difficult to achieve. However the chapter is concerned with improving this situation. Like all the knowledge which is gained from the analysis of the environment, that concerning competitors is used in the later stages of strategic management decision-making.

In the introduction to Part Two it was said that this chapter focuses on the strengths, weaknesses and potential performance levels of competitive organizations. In attempting to understand the nature and behaviour of competitors, these strengths and weaknesses become manifest as threats or opportunities from the external environment. For single business firms these will cover the total environment, but where a firm is organized into several SBUs then they are likely to be specific to each respective SBU.

In Chapter 3 several competitive issues were raised within the context of the external environment, of which the importance of identifying and understanding these opportunities and threats was central. Competitive analysis was identified as being part of the operating environment, along with customers, markets and industries. Although all areas are closely related, treatment of these other three areas is combined in Chapter 5. The attainment of knowledge about competitors was given as being generally treated as part of marketing research, although the need for such knowledge at the strategic management level is different from that at the operational management level, being orientated to identifying long-term trends.

The need to understand competitors traverses all areas of strategic management, so that frequent reference to their activities is a feature of almost all the chapters of this book. Indeed this is the approach which has been taken by most of the writers of books on strategic management. Consolidation of the understanding of competitors within the context of strategic management was led by the work of Porter[1] which has had an important impact on the majority of writers and researchers in this area. This previous fragmented approach to competitors was recorded by Rothschild[2] in 1979 as a major weakness of many organizations, although th subsequent books by Porter have provided the means for overcoming such a lack of understanding.

The approach taken in this chapter to the understanding of competitors commences with an examination of the meaning of competition. The next area of attention is the identification of competitors, and this is followed by a look at the analysis of the nature of those identified, their strategies, and the different types of competitive environment.

THE MEANING OF COMPETITION

The concept of competition is one encountered every day; it involves individuals challenging, contesting or fighting other individuals for a specific reason. In business competition may be restricted to the number of companies that supply alternative products to those of a particular company. Alternatively, it could be a measure of the way a particular market is divided between several companies, as a measure of relative market share. At the operational level competition is heavily entrenched in the marketing tactics of firms. Here competitive actions are taken to make products more attractive in the eyes of consumers than those of competitors, while prices are adjusted to reflect these attractions. Selling activities are manipulated to gain sales volume and share, while advertising and sales promotion tactics are manipulated to persuade consumers of product differentiation and superiority. However, the meaning of competition can be more comprehensive and can include a full understanding of the make-up of competitive organizations and the product offerings which they supply to the marketplace.

In explaining the meaning of competition, Jain[3] examines two broad approaches, one based on economic theory and the other on the industrial organization perspective.

Economic theory

Traditional economic theory includes several models that provide explanations of the nature of competition in specified market structures. These models incorporate the nature of demand within the market structures, and the relative degree of elasticity of demand. Additionally, the market structures include a number of assumptions about the homogeneity of products that firms supply to the marketplace, the knowledge that firms have about the nature of the market, and the mobility of resources for entry and exit to the market. Four major models of monopoly, oligopoly, monopolistic competition, and pure competition provide a competitive continuum of market structure. These are summarized in Table 4.1.

Although these models are useful for broad conceptualizations of types of competitive structure, the respective assumptions reduce their usefulness for strategic management. Also, they do little for a company in its endeavour to understand the nature of its competitors, while predictions about competitive behaviour are also

Table 4.1 *Economic theory: competitive continuum of market structure.*

Assumptions	Monopoly	Oligopoly	Monopolistic competition	Perfect competition
1. Number of firms	One	Few	Many	Infinite
2. Consumer behaviour	Accepts price	Responds to offers	Responds to price and non-price variables	Responds only to price
3. Demand curve	Inelastic	'Kinked' demand curve	Relatively inelastic	Perfectly elastic
4. Product homogeneity	Unique	Considerable differentiation	Some differentiation	Complete homogeneity
5. Firms' knowledge	Perfect	Imperfect	Imperfect	Perfect
6. Resource mobility	No mobility	Some barriers	Relatively few barriers	Complete mobility

limited. Current treatment of economic models owes much to the work of Chamberlin[4], but readers wishing to pursue these models further should refer to texts such as those by Call and Holahan[5] and Wilson[6].

Industrial organization perspective

This approach is based on the principle that it is the characteristics of the industry environment in which a firm competes which dictate its competitive standing, which has been succinctly explained by Porter[7]. In this approach these characteristics of the environment which influence the meaning of competition are based upon the industry structure, the conduct of competing firms, and the performance of these firms.

Industry structure

Industries are, overall, affected by the total environment in which they are placed, that is, the compilation of all those variables that were designated as the remote environment in Chapter 3. In addition the nature of competition is dictated to by the structure of the markets which make up the particular industry. Full consideration will be given to these aspects in Chapter 5. Also a number of competitive forces can be identified which influence the intensity of competition within an industry. Central to these forces is the concept of rivalry between companies vying for the same business. Scherer[8] sees rivalry as the pursuit, by firms, of positions within a market which are incompatible, in that each seeks market share to the detriment of the others, but with each company aware of the ramifications of such incompatibility. Porter[1] includes within these competitive forces the concept of extended rivalry, where potential competitors, suppliers of substitute products, suppliers of inputs, and buyers in the industry contribute to the total meaning to be given to competition. He lists a number of competitive forces:

- The threat of new entrants into the industry, which will depend on barriers to entry which may exist and the likely reaction from existing competitors to such entry.
- The intensity of rivalry among existing competitors, with particular attention to the reactions of competitors following a change in the strategy or tactics of a competitor.
- Potential changes in the intensity of rivalry, such as industry maturity causing intensification of rivalry.
- Pressure from substitute products, which means the ability of products to perform the same function as the product of the industry, resulting in extended competitive forces beyond direct competition.
- Buying power which can be exercised by consumers, distributors, retailers and other buying groups and which results in the pursuit of their interests to the detriment of those of competitors.
- The bargaining power of suppliers of component parts and raw materials to the industry, resulting in, for example, higher input costs and higher final product prices.

In addition to these general competitive forces further forces are to be found in specific types of industry structure, the nature of which will be examined in the last section of this chapter.

Conduct of competing companies

As a result of the industry structure, the remote environment and the operating environment, each competitor will develop an organizational strategy. Although this development can be described as being within the strategic management framework, as presented in Chapter 1, variations will be found from company to company in the sophistication of strategy development and in the utilization of strategic management. The identification of competitive strategies and advantages will be examined later in the chapter.

Performance of competing companies

Perhaps the true meaning of competition to a company is the resultant performance of each of its competitors and the end results that they achieve. Although market share will be a major criterion for assessment in most industries, several other measures can be used, including profitability, sales growth, product innovation and social responsibility. Further attention is given to the analysis of competitors' performance later in this chapter.

EXHIBIT 4.1

A Dutch Challenge to the King of Stout

Despite the dominance of Guinness and its near-monopoly situation in the supply of stout, a major competitor has entered the market – Heineken, the Dutch producer of light European beers. Heineken obviously recognize that in Europe and the United States little stout is consumed, but they are prepared to market the product, with the aim of increasing consumption, despite the competitive rivalry of Guinness. Entry to this business was through the acquisition of the Irish brewery James J. Murphy. They aim to be competitive by acquiring some of Guinness's market share in traditional markets, but also by participating in new countries where stout has not been traditionally consumed.

Adapted from *Fortune,* 3 February 1986

IDENTIFYING COMPETITORS

Given the industrial organization perspective on the meaning of competition, the process of identifying competitors obviously extends beyond those organizations which currently offer similar products. However, before approaching identification, firms need to consider the extent of rivalry and define that which will be used as the framework for their competitive situation. For single-business companies this analysis will include the total environment, whereas for companies with a number of SBUs it will be more meaningful to complete the analysis for each SBU. Table 4.2 illustrates an approach to the conceptualization of competition, by giving general levels of classification. At the simplest level the firm is only concerned with direct competitors, or those which produce similar products, whereas at level II potential changes are also included. However, at level IV competition is classified as being both current and future rivalry from both similar and substitute products, while level VI incorporates the concept of extended rivalry given in the last section.

The rest of this chapter is concerned with levels I to IV inclusive, concentrating on product competition and excluding the power of buyers and sellers. This approach is merely an organizational arrangement in the presentation of the book; the power of sellers was included in strategic audits (Chapter 3), whereas the power of buyers is considered in Chapter 5. However, the concept of extended rivalry is maintained as an important concept within the understanding of competition.

Therefore this section is concerned with the identification of organizations that will be in the business of supplying either similar or substitute products. Four different orientations of competitor classification are discussed. Three of these

Table 4.2 *Levels of competitive rivalry.*

Level I	Existing rivalry intensity from similar products.
Level II	Extension of level I to include future potential changes in intensity.
Level III	Extension of level II to include existing rivalry intensity from substitute products.
Level IV	Extension of level III to include future potential changes in rivalry intensity from substitute products.
Level V	Extension of level IV to include power of buyers and sellers to influence the intensity of competitive rivalry.
Level VI	Extension of level V to include future potential changes due to buyer and seller power.

orientations are based on those advocated by Aaker[9], while the other is based on industry profiles as developed by Rothschild[2]. One of these, the strategic group orientation, has gained recent prominence in the literature, claiming in particular to be useful for strategic management purposes.

Customer base

This orientation focuses on customer needs and then directs attention to the companies that seek to satisfy these needs. The discipline of marketing has provided the concept of markets to explain groups of people who share common needs. These can be conceived in different ways and Kotler[10], for example, specifies the following:

- Need markets such as entertainment or transport.
- Product markets such as shoes, televisions or watches.
- Demographic markets such as the youth market.
- Geographic markets such as Eastern Europe or Australia.

Although competitors in a product market may be relatively easy to identify, the others are more complex. Entertainment can range from television through hi-fi to magazines or cinema. Some of the discretionary income of the youth market may be diverted from the purchase of clothes and records to the purchase of alcoholic drinks, while bank services may provide little attraction. Geographic markets require careful consideration in that variation is likely to be found in both consumer needs and in the supplying companies. However in all these situations the point is that the nature of consumer needs within each market type will dictate the range of products that are able to satisfy the respective needs, which in turn will indicate the range of competitors to be identified.

Within each of these markets several states of consumer demand may be identified. Existing demand occurs when a product is purchased to satisfy a recognized need, whereas latent demand is where a particular need has been recognized, although products have not been developed to satisfy this need. Alternatively, incipient demand is where it is anticipated that a particular need is likely to emerge, although it has not yet been recognized by a significant number of consumers. While the identification of competitors in the case of existing demand is through the classification of a market type, latent and incipient demand represent greater problems for the identification of competitors. While firms may modify and improve existing products to meet such demands, the development of a 'breakthrough' product, which offers a totally different benefit package, can provide a major competitive advantage for that company.

Industry profile

This orientation provides a focus on the types of organization that are to be found in the industry and the geographical spread of their business, an approach which has been suggested by Rothschild[2]. First, the organizations are classified as being either single-industry, multi-industry or conglomerate companies. Here the need is to identify commitment to the industry, where those involved in several industries may have the option of using income generated in one industry to subsidize others and thus enhancing rivalry in these weaker industries. Alternatively, they may have the option of withdrawing from an industry, which would have the effect of reducing rivalry.

Second, the organizations are classified on the basis of the geographical spread of their business. Here the classifications are that of either domestic concentration, selective export concentration, or multinational spread. Again the classification can be indicative of the type of competitive action that may be taken. Firms concentrating on domestic markets have no option but to protect their business if they are not to change their approach. Selective export concentration provides some possibilities of selective competitive action, while multinational operations obviously offer additional flexibility.

These two classifications can be used to form a matrix in which each competitor can be located, as in Figure 4.1. In this hypothetical example all four organizations have been concentrated domestically, with only organization D participating in several industries. However the forecasts show that A is to spread geographically but is likely to remain in the same industry. Organization B is to develop into other industries, but is also to pursue selective export markets. Meanwhile, C is to consolidate its business in domestic markets through entry into other industries. Finally, Organization D is aiming not only to become a multinational organization but also to participate in a much broader spread of industries.

Strategic groups

This orientation provides an extension to the industry profile approach. This is by developing an understanding of the competitive structure of an industry through

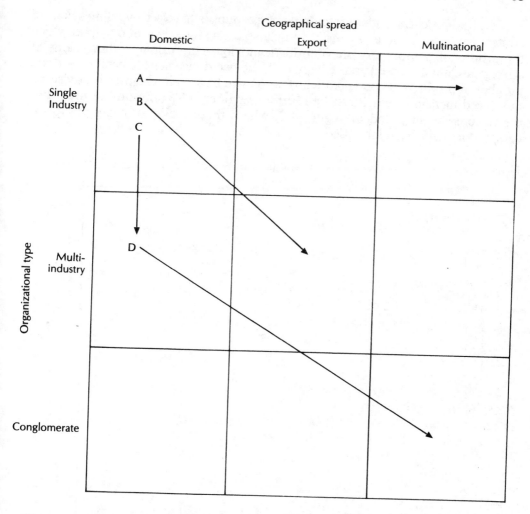

Figure 4.1 *A competitive industry profile. (Reprinted, by permission of the publisher, from 'Competitor Analysis' by Rothschild,* Management Review, *July 1979 © 1979 American Management Association, New York.)*

the classification of firms by the type of strategy which they pursue. A particular strategic group will feature all competitors following one particular strategy type, while another group will feature only those firms following another strategy type. This concept is relatively new to the literature, and McGee[11] has identified several differences, or refinements, that have been offered, although the thrust of the approach is the behaviour of firms in relation to their markets through their strategy formulation. The strength of the approach is that it aims to identify the different and major competitive thrusts of competition at one level of understanding, as well as the number of firms and intensity of rivalry that are a feature of each group.

A useful approach to identifying strategic groups is to select two dimensions of strategy and to use these dimensions to construct a strategic group map in which the groups of competitors are identified and located. Although dimensions of strategy are not discussed until Chapter 10, the two dimensions to be used here are number of products and corporate image. As will be seen in Chapter 10, these are but two dimensions which can be central to strategy. Mapping using these two dimensions is illustrated in Figure 4.2, where three major strategic groups of competitors have been identified.

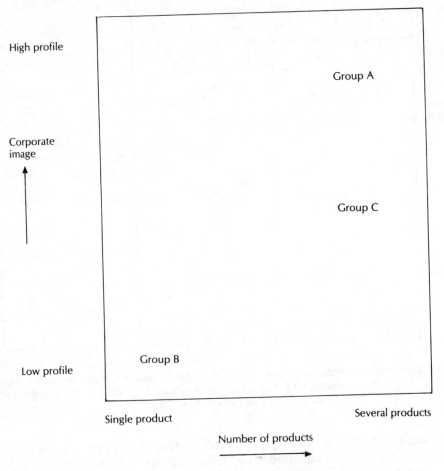

Figure 4.2 *Strategic group mapping.*

The organizational strategy of firms falling within group A is based on the development of many products, probably in pursuit of the satisfaction of the majority of consumer needs. These firms have also decided that an important part of 'how' they will pursue their business is through the projection of a higher-profile corporate image, in order to enhance recognition and reputation as perceived by consumers.

Competitors falling within group B have a strategy based on one or a few products, aiming to satisfy a selected type of consumer need. This targeting of only a specific number of consumers is compatible with little requirement for a high-profile image, so that this is not a main feature of their strategy.

Although companies in group C have a strategy based on several products, less attention is given to corporate image. As with group A, the aim is to satisfy a wide range of consumer needs, but it is likely that more emphasis will be placed on marketing tactics than on corporate image projection.

Porter[1] has suggested a number of important analytical steps from such mapping. The first is to identify the ability of firms to be able to move into another strategy group, or new firms to enter any group, which can be avoided by mobility barriers such as economies of scale, product differentiation, technology and capital. Indeed McGee[11] sees barriers to mobility as being central not only to the classification of strategic groups, but also to increased rivalry. The second analytical step is the identification of firms that are marginal participants of specific groups. Where the mapping does not produce realistic homogenous groups, then judgemental decisions on location may mean arbitrary groups, or the wrong classification for certain firms. The third analytical step is to use the map as a basis for charting changes to firms' strategies and as an input for forecasting potential changes to competitors' strategies.

Potential competitors

Aaker[9] includes potential competitors as one of the orientations for the identification of competitors. However, several directions in the identification of potential as opposed to current competitors have already been given, so that this section will consolidate these as well as giving Aaker's recommendation.

Directions for identifying competitors that have already been given started with the levels of competitive rivalry shown in Table 4.2. The orientation based on the customer base included the concepts of latent and incipient demand, which include a requirement to consider potential competitors. The use of industry profiles also included a consideration of potential rivalry in that shifts in the nature of firms are anticipated. Similarly, strategic group mapping can also be used to predict the nature of future rivalry.

Aaker[9] has also suggested that potential competitors can be identified by searching for potential entrants who are wanting to extend their market spread or product range. This can include firms looking for additional markets for existing products, such as geographic or demographic spread. Extending the product range may include the introduction of additional products into existing markets, resulting in increased product competition but from the same number of firms. Alternatively some firms may pursue diversification, with their new products and market participation representing increased rivalry from new market entry.

EXHIBIT 4.2

Jaguar's German Test

The British manufacturer of luxury cars, Jaguar, faces considerable competitive rivalry from Mercedes Benz and BMW. In the late 1970s and early 1980s Jaguar had a reputation for unreliability. At the time it was part of the state-owned British Leyland Group. However this began to change in 1980 with the appointment of Sir John Egan, and the improvement continued following privatization in 1984. A first stage to regaining competitiveness was an order from Egan to acquire several Mercedes cars and for Jaguar engineers to dismantle and rebuild them several times. Here the aim was to impress upon them the detailed precision and quality of competitive products. Similarly a newly developed engineering centre was to be modelled on that of Porsche. Despite the reputation of unreliability, Jaguar's competitive strength has been its ability to project an image of foreign exclusivity in its export markets, combining an appeal to nostalgia with electronic sophistication. However a major competitive disadvantage is Jaguar's smallness. Although they have had major increases in capital investment, R & D expenditure, and advertising expenditure, these are still at very low levels compared to those of Mercedes Benz and BMW.

Adapted from *Business*, January 1987

UNDERSTANDING COMPETITORS

Having identified competitors, the next stage is to understand the nature of each of these organizations, particularly their strengths and weaknesses. In simple terms a company should acquire knowledge about its competitors which is similar to its own internal knowledge as collected in the strategic audit (see Chapter 3). However, in reality this is unlikely to be achieved by many firms, although the nature of this knowledge still needs to be identified and striven for. This section is concerned with the identification of this knowledge to give an understanding of competitors, although knowledge about competitive strategies is given fuller consideration in the next section.

Major areas of knowledge about competitors have been suggested by Aaker[9]; these are listed in Table 4.3.

Table 4.3 *Major areas of competitive knowledge.*

Size, growth and profitability
Objectives and assumptions
Current and past strategies
Organization and culture
Cost structure and exit barriers
Strengths and weaknesses

Size, growth and profitability

These are quantitative measures of each competitor, with the focus on trends. Size and growth can be measured in terms of assets, sales volume, production output, number of employees and organizational structure. Profitability can be measured by relating profits to a base such as capital employed. These measures are based on calculations that would also be carried out internally for the company as already indicated in Chapter 3, but which are detailed in Chapter 14. This knowledge will provide competitive norms so that the company can compare its relative standing with these norms and with each individual competitor.

Objectives and assumptions

A knowledge of the objectives of competitors serves two purposes. First, it identifies the direction and aspirations that are to be pursued following recent growth and profitability trends. Relating these to the potential that is likely to be available from respective markets will give another indication of future rivalry. Second, strategy follows from objectives, so that knowledge of the latter can allow for an appraisal of strategies that could be adopted in the future. Alternatives can be identified from the approaches to be discussed in Chapters 10 and 11, while a likely change of strategy by a major competitor may be an important consideration in the firm's selection of its future organizational strategy. Where competitors have several SBUs then it may be necessary to identify both total company and respective SBU objectives.

As will already be apparent to the reader, assumptions need to be made in all areas of strategic management decision-making. Competitors will, therefore, be making assumptions about their business environments and about their own future in these environments. Knowledge of these assumptions will also help the understanding of competitors.

Current and past strategies

Attention to the understanding of competitors' strategies is to be found in the next section of this chapter. This depth of treatment reflects the importance of understanding competitive strategies. However, it logically follows the appraisal of objectives and assumptions.

Organization and culture

This area of knowledge is concerned with the way the managers of each competitor are organized and their behaviour within that structure. Parallel understandings for the firm are tackled in Chapters 8 and 9 and again the knowledge to be acquired follows that recommended in these chapters.

Cost structures and exist barriers

Knowledge about operating costs again allows for the establishment of competitive norms. Trends would need to be identified in costs related to labour, raw materials and components, plant and equipment, marketing and distribution.

Commitment to a particular business may be enforced by factors such as the possession of fixed assets, contractual obligations, or marketing commitments to customers. Here the appraisal is that of the ability of competitors to cease participation in a particular business, probably in relation to their respective cost structures.

Strengths and weaknesses

In Chapter 3 attention was given to assessing strengths and weaknesses in the form of capabilities related to resources, operations and managers; such an assessment is also applicable in gaining knowledge about individual competitor's strengths and weaknesses.

As a result of the collection of this knowledge about competitors the understanding can be expanded by classifying the strength of each competitor and by assessing how each competitor is likely to behave over the next period of time. An approach to the former has been cited by Kotler[10] which has been developed by the Arthur D. Little organization[12]. The classificatory system places each competitor in one of six positions, as shown in Table 4.4. Such a classification gives the relative strength of each competitor and focuses on those to which the greatest attention will need to be given in the later stages of strategic management decision-making.

Likely behaviour can also be assessed from the competitive analysis, as well as from the classification of strengths. The major deduction is whether or not each

Table 4.4 *Classifying competitive strengths.*

Classifications	Features
1. Dominant	Firm controls behaviour of other competitors.
2. Strong	Can take independent action without endangering long-term position.
3. Favourable	Competitors have certain strengths in the pursuit of particular strategies.
4. Tenable	Satisfactory performance but is strongly influenced by major competitors.
5. Weak	Unsatisfactory performance but potential is available for improvement.
6. Non-viable	Unsatisfactory performance and no potential for improvement.

competitor is satisfied with its current performance and whe̦
respective organizational strategies are likely to result. Porter
'offensive move' to indicate a change in strategy as a result of su̦
As already indicated, this assessment of strategies is to be consid̖
section, but of equal importance are the likely ramifications of change̦
tive strategies. Where changes in strategy are not anticipated attention
to the defensive capabilities of competitors to be able to retain their mark̖
Here assessments are recommended of the ability of each competitor to reta̦
changes in the strategies of other competitors, or indeed of their vulnerability to
any changes in the business environment.

COMPETITORS' STRATEGIES

As already established, identifying the strategies of competitors is central to the
overall understanding of these organizations. In Chapter 1, it was explained that
strategies may be developed at several levels within the organizational structure.
At the apex of the hierarchical structure would be the organizational strategy,
appertaining to the total corporate body. Where there are several SBUs or divisions then there may also be organizational strategies for each of the SBUs. At the
operational level there will be strategies for each of the functions, such as marketing and manufacturing, although again each SBU is likely to feature its own set of
operational strategies. Consequently identification of competitors' strategies is
necessary at these three different levels.

The features that are to be investigated in these strategies are outlined later in
this section. Prior to this examination attention is given to a broader and initial
approach to understanding strategies, as developed by Porter[1]. In the last section it
was said that, over the next period of time, competitors will take either an overall
offensive or defensive approach to their strategies. Porter[1] suggests that these
approaches will be based upon three broad generic strategies, which can be used as
a basis for pursuing their business and for building the additional features of its
organizational and operational strategies.

Porter's generic strategies

These three broad generic strategies are based on cost leadership, differentiation,
and focus. The pursuit of one of these generic strategies is intended to provide the
basis for outperforming competitors, although the pursuit of only one is
recommended.

Cost leadership

Here the strategy is simply to achieve lower costs than competitors, but without
reducing comparable product or service quality and benefit offerings. In practice,

 not be quite so simple in that significant reductions in both variable and
costs, as well as considerable attention to subsequent cost control, need to be
ved. There are a number of major advantages to achieving such a strategy:

- The achievement of returns in excess of industry averages despite competitors.
- Defence against rivalry with greater flexibility than competitors to increase costs and overcome competitive forces.
- More flexibility to absorb input costs and retain profit margins or price levels.
- Lower than average costs can also provide a barrier to entry.

However, achieving this strategy may necessitate the attainment of high market shares in order to achieve economies of scale as a necessity for cost reduction. Also, customer benefits may be lost if products need to be modified or degraded in order to reduce manufacturing costs, while high initial capital investment may also be essential.

Differentiation

Where the generic approach on which strategies are based is that of product or service differentiation, industry-wide recognition of uniqueness is the extreme achievement. Differentiation can take many forms, many of which are marketing-related. These could include, for example, superior tangible benefits in the core product, intangible features in design or brand image, superior customer service, or superior dealer networks. The major advantages of achieving this generic strategy are as follows:

- The achievement of returns in excess of industry averages due to a strong competitive advantage in the marketplace.
- Insulation against competitive rivalry because of customer brand loyalty.
- A barrier to entry because of brand loyalty.
- Brand loyalty should also be effective against market-share encroachment by substitute products.

However, achieving this generic strategy may also result in some disadvantages. Product differentiation and specialism in product offerings may result in limited customer appeal, which places a constraint on potential market share to be gained. Economies of scale may not be achieved so that costs may be higher than industry norms. Where differentiation requires a selling price higher than that of competitors, due to either higher costs or as dictated by the exclusiveness of the brand image, then the higher price may also result in limited customer appeal and reduced market-share potential.

Focus

Although it is given as a separate generic strategy, Porter recognizes that this approach is developed out of the other two generic strategies. Rather than attempting to satisfy all customer requirements for a particular need, the firm's strategy is to concentrate or focus on a particular market segment, geographical area, or product type. The aim is to achieve competitive advantage by serving well the selected area of business, which necessitates a higher commitment on the part of the operational functions. Indeed, as will be seen later, marketing strategy has much in common with this approach. The closeness to the other two generic strategies is that focusing also leads to differentiation of products or services, or can also result in cost reductions, or both.

Attention has been given to these generic strategies by several researchers, with results being generally supportive of the claims of Porter. Readers wishing to pursue this area of study further should examine the articles by Hambrick[13], Galbraith and Schendel[14], Karnani[15] and White[16].

Organizational and operational strategies

An outline of these strategies is given here – the full explanations are given in Chapters 10 and 12. In these chapters the presentation is given for the subject company, but the features of these strategies are equally applicable to its competitors.

Although there are several features and approaches that can be used in formulating oganizational strategy, four major components are outlined here which can be central to identifying and understanding competitors' organizational strategies. The first is to identify the number of businesses in which each competitor participates, which is generally labeled the product-market scope component of strategy. The second component is concerned with each competitor's intention to pursue growth in each product-market scope, or to pursue stability without growth, or to defend its current share of the business in each sector. The third component is an understanding of advantages that each competitor has in relation to all competitors, which can arise from the nature of the organization itself, such as size or financial structure, or from operational features such as well-established brand images or advanced production technology.

Fahey[17] differentiates between competitive advantages and distinctive competences. The former are any features of the firm which favourably distinguish it from competitors in the perception of customers. Well-respected brand images or unique product features would be classified as such. However, distinctive competences could be production efficiency, which is not perceived by customers, or improved product technology, which is not detected by customers as providing additional benefits over other products. The final major component of organizational strategy is that which has been labeled 'synergy'. For each competitor this is the amalgamation of strengths into combined capabilities, where the resultant *force majeure* of these capabilities is greater than each strength working independently. As already mentioned, an extended explanation of this and the other major components is given in Chapter 10.

Details of operational strategies are given in Chapter 12 and again these details are applicable in both identifying and understanding these strategies as developed by competitors. Presentation of these details in this chapter would be mere replication, but operational strategies are applicable for the functions of finance, marketing, production, research and development, and personnel.

COMPETITIVE ENVIRONMENTS

In this final section attention is given to a number of different types of competitive environment. These competitive environments are featured in fragmented industries, emerging industries, industry maturity, declining industries and global industries. These types of competitive environment are labelled 'generic industry environments' by Porter[1], who gives considerable attention to each environment by devoting a chapter to it. The aim of this detailed treatment is to show the implications for the development of strategy, by the subject company, given these particular industry environments. However, the aim in this chapter, which is devoted to the understanding of competitors within the context of analysing the total business environment, is different to that of Porter. Here the aim is to show that the competitive environment is different in each of these types of environment and to illustrate that companies need to understand these differences as part of their total understanding of competitors. Consequently, all the knowledge on competitors will move through the strategic management process, but it is particularly prevalent throughout the planning of organizational strategy as discussed in Part Four.

Fragmented industries

This type of competitive environment is to be found in industries where the business is divided among several firms, none of which have a large market share. This fragmentation and spread of business means that none of the competitors has a significantly large enough market share to be able to exercise power to influence conditions within the environment. Each firm is thus faced with similar competitors, none of which is able to achieve market leadership. Some of these industries may feature many small and medium-sized companies, and conditions may equate to the market structure model of perfect competition.

Several causes of fragmentation within this type of competitive environment have been cited by Porter[1]. Therefore, in attempting to understand this type of environment the firm needs to identify probable causes and to assess the perpetuation of their influence in the industry. There are several major causes of fragmentation:

- Low barriers of entry to the industry allowing for the continuation of spread of market share despite the actions of established competitors.
- Little opportunity to develop economies of scale or experience curve savings.

This could be because of the nature of the type of industry which is fragmented, such as non-advanced manufacturing, or, because of low market share, little need for long production runs.

- High transport costs in relation to a single plant location can limit the geographical spread of sales, resulting in little company growth.
- Small firms often face difficulty in carrying large stocks of finished products, which can be exacerbated if the industry features erratic fluctuations in sales. Costs of holding stocks may mean lost sales when demand increases, or diverting production capacity to specific customer needs.
- Diseconomies of scale are often a cause of fragmentation, particularly where frequent product modifications are needed or where many products are manufactured to customer specifications.
- Where there is fragmentation of customer needs, resulting in much segmentation of markets, then demand for specific products may be small, restricting the ability of small companies to expand their market shares.
- Exit barriers, due to lack of ability to diversify and/or managerial resistance to change, can lead to many companies featuring little in the way of structural changes over a long period of time, thus perpetuating fragmentation.

Emerging industries

These are new industries which have emerged as a result of new customer needs, technological innovations or other changes in the business environment that provide potential for new business. Porter cites some recent emerging industries such as video games, word processing, personal computers and solar heating. Emerging industries also include those that have been in decline, but are now showing a sustained growth. The problem with emerging industries is not only the lack of previous knowledge about markets and, in particular, customer requirements, but also the identification of the organizations which are likely to participate in the industry. Consequently, the competitive environment will be difficult to predict, with the issues that have been presented in this chapter also being difficult to utilize.

However Porter[1] has given several features of emerging industries, which, it is claimed, appear to typify an industry at this stage of development. The first of these is uncertainty about the technology to be used and the strategies to be developed to exploit the new potential. Customer needs will not be fully understood, demand will be difficult to predict, so that the 'best' product technology and the 'best' strategy to pursue market potential will be shrouded in much uncertainty. High costs are also likely to be a feature, comprising of initial capital investment and high variable costs due to low volume production and low experience of production.

Externally companies are faced with developing the learning experience of customers to recognize these new needs and to associate satisfaction with its product. At the initial stage most customers will, of course, be first-time buyers. Mobility barriers for both exit and entry are different to those for established industries,

with barriers such as brand loyalty and economies of scale being of little importance. Barriers in new industries normally include the availability of risk capital,
access to raw materials and components, efficient use of distribution channels,
availability of industry-specific technology, and acquisition of suitable personnel.
Finally, new industries are often typified in that the participating competitors are
often new and embryonic in nature. Some new industries may be developed by
small companies with limited resources, or the majority of competitors may be
comprised of new-venture companies that have been established by larger organizations to exploit potential from the emerging industry.

Industry maturity

The concept of a life cycle can be applied to industries. After the stage of emergence that of growth can be expected, but there will be a maximum to this growth,
when all customers have reached their optimum levels of consumption. The stage
of little growth with a sustained level of demand is indicative of maturity in the life
cycle of an industry.

At this stage of maturity the competitive environment changes in that companies can no longer achieve significant growth of sales through the expansion of
market size, but can only achieve it by increasing market share to the detriment of
their competitors. Porter[1] highlights one major problem that companies often
experience in this type of environment. The changing environment will almost
certainly require major strategy changes, with probable consequential changes to
organizational structure. However, the recognition of change by managers and
their acceptance that maturity requires a consequential change in established management practices can itself constitute a major problem.

Major features of the competitive environment in mature industries are as
follows:

- Competition is now for market share only and not for the 'natural' growth of the
  market.
- Customers are predominantly those with experience of purchasing in this
  market, experience of product benefits, and subsequent purchases are repeat
  purchases.
- Competitors often seek advantages through cost reductions and increased customer services as potential for developing other advantages is often exhausted.
- Following on from this last feature, product modification and innovation
  become more difficult. Not only will most of the alternatives have been already
  considered, but a maturing industry represents greatly increased risks for a new
  product launch.
- Maturity is often linked with excess production capacity in the industry. This
  can lead to excess supply and falling prices, but can also lead to 'forced' exit
  from the industry on the part of some competitors and a resulting change in the
  competitive structure.
- Increased competition normally leads to a necessity to improve the efficiency of

operational management. Production processes are examined for reductions in unit costs, personnel may be made redundant, product lines may be rationalized and distribution networks may be consolidated.

- The resultant competitive situation and enforced decisions are likely to lead to falling profit margins. This puts greater pressure on firms participating in the industry, exacerbating the competitive environment as they seek to retain profit margins.

Declining industries

Following maturity the next stage in the development of the life cycle of an industry is a decline in the total volume of sales that all competitors are able to achieve. This decline would be over a sustained period of time and would not be caused by a short-term fluctuation in trends. Competitive features are a consolidation of those experienced in the maturity stage, although contracting profit margins, product-line contractions, pressure on costs, elimination of investment, and maximizing cash flow become more acute.

Porter[1] has referred to three major issues which determine the nature of competition in declining industries. The first of these is a decline in demand. Here uncertainty is a feature of competitive actions, reflected in the difficulty of forecasting rates of decline and resultant volume sales. Slow rates of decline obviously give firms more opportunity to adjust their strategies and to plan the product offerings with which they will continue, or to plan their eventual withdrawal. However, decline may be at a different rate in different market segments. Some geographical segments may still exhibit maturity rather than decline, while some overseas markets may even feature growth. Here an assessment of competitors' intentions towards such segments is of obvious importance.

The second major issue determining the nature of competition during decline is that of barriers to exit from the industry. A major barrier is that of the fixed and working capital that has been acquired for participation in the industry. If a company is to withdraw totally then assets must be sold, although their market value is likely to be extremely low if they are specific to the declining industry. There may be other exit costs. These could range from redundancy payments to personnel, through costs of maintaining services for consumers who have recently purchased products, to the intangible cost of lost confidence on the part of customers and other external institutions. Another barrier can be the reluctance of managers to move out of an industry of which they have extensive knowledge, and which will require major changes to strategy, the disappearance of a particular SBU, or even complete closure and personal redundancy. Other barriers to exit can include pressures from the government or other stakeholder groups. The latter are discussed in Chapter 6.

The final major issue concerning the nature of competition during decline is the volatility of rivalry. As sales decline rivalry obviously increases as firms strive to increase or retain market share, while also striving to retain profit margins. As competitors plan their exits from the industry it may be that rivalry will reduce, although the resultant volatility effect is the balance of this rate of decrease with the rate of decline of sales and associated increase in rivalry.

Global industries

International business and the behaviour of multinational organizations are areas of study which have developed their own literature in recent years, albeit within the context of strategic management and marketing management. Readers interested in expanding their understanding are urged to refer to Doz[18], Rugman *et al.*[19], and Wortzel and Wortzel[20] on the former, and Gilligan and Hird[21], Keegan[22], and Paliwoda[23] on the latter.

Organizations participating in global industries perceive of their markets as being world-wide in nature, but also conduct their strategic management decision-making within the context of these international markets. Although global industries obviously provide the advantage of greater potential business than that available in a limited number of countries, as well as allowing the firm to balance declines in certain countries against growth in others, there are also potential problems. A major concern is that, even within the same need market, different countries will feature different consumer requirements. Additionally, cultural and social factors will necessitate differences in the presentation of products and in the way they are marketed. Methods of manufacture are likely to be different, as are the payment and treatment of personnel, while the availability of capital will also show major differences. However, the approach to analysing the environment in global industries is the same as that presented in this part of the book; strategic audits as in Chapter 3, competitors as in this chapter, and market structures as in Chapter 5.

SUMMARY

Although reference to competitors traverses all the chapters of the book, the aim of this chapter is to consolidate major issues in the understanding of competitors.

The first section was concerned with the meaning of competition and rivalry. Two major approaches were examined: that from economic theory, and that based on the industrial organization perspective; the latter was seen to be more important within the context of strategic management.

The second section approached the identification of competitors, developed from the concept of extended rivalry. Four approaches to identifying competitors were examined, from the point of view of customer base, the industry profile, strategic groups, and potential competitors.

The third section was devoted to understanding the nature of each of the identified competitors. Six major areas of knowledge about competitors were examined: size, growth and profitability; objectives and assumptions; current and past strategies; organization and culture; cost structure and exit barriers; and strengths and weaknesses.

The penultimate section examined competitors' strategies. A broad approach to understanding competitors' strategies was tackled first, based on Porter's generic strategies of cost leadership, differentiation, and focus. An outline of the organizational and operational strategies of competitors was then given, although the major issues here are discussed in Chapters 10 and 12, respectively.

In the final section attention was given to a number of different types of competitive environment, with the aim of showing how different environments can influence competitive conditions. Those competitive environments were based on fragmented industries; emerging industries; industry maturity; declining industries; and global industries.

CHAPTER CASE STUDY ILLUSTRATION:

TISSOT—COMPETING IN THE GLOBAL WATCH INDUSTRY*

This case study is concerned with the Swiss watch consortium ASUAG-SSIH, of which Tissot is a major brand. In 1970 the global watch industry had been dominated by Swiss watch manufacturers, but increased world competition had reduced Swiss volume share from 42% in 1970 to just 9% in 1983. This meant that Switzerland was now ranked third in the world, behind Hong Kong and Japan. At the time the case study was written (1985), the competitive environment had recently seen radical changes, with rapid entry and exit of many new competitors, as well as the exit of some established competitors. Innovation in products, production and marketing had also been a feature of this period.

The full case study contains information about the competitors of ASUAG-SSIH, of the type discussed in this chapter. Some of the major competitors over the period of this case study are described below.

HONG KONG COMPANIES

Hong Kong watchmakers (sales of 325 million units in 1984) did not supply their products under their own company or brand names, but produced private-label products for other companies. This was part of the strategy of these companies, which also included restricting their business to inexpensive electronic and mechanical watches. Objectives were geared to high volume sales, low input costs, and low unit profit margins.

Their major strengths were twofold. First, many of the companies were very small and production featured very low start-up costs and minimum overheads. Second, production was limited to assembly only, producing copies of other world manufacturers' products. This meant that inexpensive components were purchased in bulk on world markets, while product design and development costs were minimum or non-existent.

SEIKO

Seiko (sales of 55 million units in 1984) is a Japanese company with several product lines based on consumer and industrial electronic products. Within ten years of entering the world watch industry the company had achieved the phenomenal objective of becoming the market volume leader. Its strategy was based on both electronic and mechanical watches over a wide range of prices. Within this strategy it offered over 2,300 product models world-wide, which included analogue, digital and multifunctional watches. At the time it was also planning to broaden its price range. A major advantage of Seiko was its strengths in manufacturing. Mechanical watches had been produced on factory assembly lines since the 1950s, and the company was one of the first to initiate large-scale production of electronic watches. Another strength was that it owned sales subsidiaries in all its major markets, including service centres for the direct repair of its products. Finally, a major strength was a strong brand image which had been created by its quartz technology and reputation for accuracy, and which was promoted by world-wide advertising.

CASIO

Casio Computer Company (sales of 30 million units in 1985) is a Japanese computer company which entered the market with only digital watches. They achieved the objectives of doubling sales annually during the period 1974–80 and achieved 12% of all Japanese watch sales. Its strategy was based on low prices, but it offered multi-functional watches, of which timekeeping was but one function. The strategy was also to offer watches as technical products, rather than focusing on their aesthetic appeal. Channels of distribution were also innovative, in that watches were sold with consumer durables such as cameras, stereos and calculators, rather than in the traditional jewellery store outlets. A major strength of Casio was high automation in its factories, based on the production of electronic products, rather than the traditional labour-intensive production of mechanical watches.

SWISS MANUFACTURERS

At the time of the case study the majority of the Swiss companies were producing traditional watches based on reputation and fine craftsmanship. They were mostly mechanical, mostly high-priced, and included luxury and exclusive products. However, the influence of world competition resulted in a major contraction of the Swiss industry, with a reduction from 1,618 manufacturing companies in 1970, to just 634 in 1984. Major companies and their brands were Longines, Rolex, Omega, Rado, Piaget, Ebel, Audemaro-Piguet and Patek-Philippe.

A major innovation by ASUAG-SSIH was the introduction of the Swatch brand, a plastic quartz analogue watch with a low retail price. Here the strategy was to attempt to capture some of world market for cheaper watches, which had been developed and captured by the Hong Kong and Japanese companies.

REFERENCES

1. Porter, M. E., *Competitive Strategy; Techniques for Analyzing Industries and Competitors*, The Free Press, New York, 1980.
2. Rothschild, W. E., 'Competitor Analysis: The Missing Link in Strategy', *McKinsey Quarterly*, Autumn 1979, 42–53.
3. Jain, S. C., *Marketing Planning and Strategy*, 2nd edn, South-Western, Cincinnati, OH, 1985.
4. Chamberlin, E. H., *The Theory of Monopolistic Competition*, Harvard University Press, Boston, 1933.
5. Call, S. T. and Holahan, W. L., *Microeconomics*, 2nd edn, Wadsworth, Belmont, CA, 1983.
6. Wilson, J. H., *Microeconomics: Concepts and Applications*, Harper and Row, New York, 1981.
7. Porter, M. E., 'The Contributions of Industrial Organization to Strategic Management', *Academy of Management Review*, 4, 1981, 609–20.
8. Scherer, F. M., *Industrial Market Structure and Economic Performance*, Rand McNally, Chicago, 1970.
9. Aaker, D. A., *Strategic Market Management*, Wiley, New York, 1984.
10. Kotler, P., *Marketing Management: Analysis, Planning and Control*, 5th edn, Prentice Hall, Englewood Cliffs, NJ, 1984.
11. McGee, J., 'Strategic Groups: A Bridge between Industry Structure and Strategic Management' in H. Thomas and D. Gardner, (eds), *Strategic Marketing and Management*, Wiley, Chichester, 1985.
12. Wright, R. V. L., *A System for Managing Diversity*, Arthur D. Little, Cambridge, MA, 1974.
13. Hambrick, D. C., 'Operationalizing the Concept of Business-level Strategy in Research', *Academy of Management Review*, 5, 1980, 567–75.
14. Galbraith, C. and Schendel, D., 'An Empirical Analysis of Strategy Types', *Strategic Management Journal*, 4, 1983, 153–73.
15. Karnani, A., 'Generic Competitive Strategies — An Analytical Approach', *Strategic Management Journal*, 5, 4, 1984, 367–80.

16. White, R. E., 'Generic Business Strategies, Organizational Context and Performance: An Empirical Investigation', *Strategic Management Journal*, **7**, 1986, 217–31.
17. Fahey, L., 'Marketing and Competitive Advantage', *Irish Marketing Review*, **1**, 1986, 103–8.
18. Doz, Y., *Strategic Management in Multinational Companies*, Pergamon, Oxford, 1986.
19. Rugman, A. M., Lecraw, D. J. and Booth, L. D., *International Business*, McGraw Hill, Singapore, 1986.
20. Wortzel, H. I. and Wortzel, L. H., *Strategic Management of Multinational Corporations*, Wiley, New York, 1985.
21. Gilligan, C. and Hird, M., *International Marketing: Strategy and Management*, Croom Helm, Beckenham, 1986.
22. Keegan, W. J., *Multinational Marketing Management*, 2nd edn, Prentice Hall, Englewood Cliffs, NJ, 1980.
23. Paliwoda, S. J., *International Marketing*, Heinemann, London, 1986.

CHAPTER 5
UNDERSTANDING MARKET STRUCTURES

This final chapter of Part Two is concerned with market structures; it completes the analysis of the environment in which organizations are located. This area of study is vital to strategic management decision-making, while it builds on and enhances the material presented in Chapters 3 and 4. Of central importance is the interface between industries and markets. Difficulties exist in defining both industries and markets, although the chapter suggests parameters or boundaries that can be used to aid these definitions. For strategic management purposes the central issue is long-range trends in both industries and markets. Although the understanding of markets has developed as part of the discipline of marketing, the focus here is on its role at the strategic management level as opposed to the operational management level.

In the examination of the total environment that was presented as the strategic audit in Chapter 3, the operating environment was seen to be unique to each organization. It was seen to consist of customers, markets, industries and competitors. While competitors were the subject of Chapter 4, the other three areas are discussed in this chapter. Although this split into chapters has been necessary for presentation purposes, it must be emphasized that all these environmental variables are interrelated, an issue which is perhaps already apparent to readers.

While all the chapters of Part Two are concerned with generating information for the planning of direction and strategy, there are two orientations that are central to understanding market structures. The first is the identification of trends and the prediction of change in the markets of current participation, in that they have a direct effect on the company. The second orientation is the attractiveness of current markets for continued participation as well as the attractiveness of other markets for potential participation.

This chapter starts by addressing the nature of industries; this is followed by an examination of industry life cycles. The rest of the chapter is then devoted to an understanding of customers and markets. The first section addresses the interface of industries and markets. The subsequent sections address demand and market size, buyer behaviour, and market segmentation.

THE NATURE OF INDUSTRIES

The term 'industry', in its everyday usage, has perhaps an obvious meaning. People will talk about the pharmaceutical industry, for example, and also use the term to refer to the agricultural industry and the coalmining industry. Indeed classifying business activities by the types of action performed to generate similar types of product is one way of explaining the nature of industries. In common with many countries the United Kingdom uses Standard Industrial Classifications (SIC), which give the range of industries to be found in the country, based on business activities. Examples from SIC are given in Table 5.1, which illustrates the widespread and diversity of industries in which organizations can be located. This classification is important in that, for the UK, much of the information that is produced by the government's Statistical Service is collected and presented within these classifications.

However, writers such as Bates and Eldredge[1] have pointed out that such an approach is not adequate for strategic management purposes on two counts. The first is that such classifications are, generally speaking, production- and company-orientated as opposed to being defined in terms of serving the requirements of closely defined groups of people or organizations. The second inadequacy is that such standard classifications are general in nature, lacking the clarity and precise-ness of definition which is needed for strategic management purposes. In order to be more precise three approaches to defining the nature of industries are suggested below. That to be adopted is less important than ensuring that consistency is maintained both over time and when comparing own performance with that of competitors.

Porter's definition of industry

Porter[2] has defined an industry as a group of firms producing products or services that are close substitutes for each other. Here an industry is defined in terms of competition, through the use of the concept of extended rivalry as introduced in Chapter 4. The attractiveness of a particular industry to a particular firm can be measured in terms of long-term return on investment, where the degree of extended rivalry will have a major impact on the return that participating firms can achieve.

The boundaries or parameters of an industry are laid down in terms of the following variables, which were originally introduced in Chapter 4:

- Competition from existing firms.
- Threats of entry from other firms.
- Competition from substitute products or services.
- Bargaining power of suppliers.
- Bargaining power of customers.

Table 5.1 *Examples of Standard Industrial Classifications.*

Agriculture, forestry, fishing
001 Agriculture and horticulture
002 Forestry
003 Fishing

Mining and quarrying
101 Coalmining
102 Stone and slate quarrying and mining
103 Chalk, clay, sand and gravel extraction
104 Petroleum and natural gas
109 Other mining and quarrying

Food, drink and tobacco
211 Grain milling
212 Bread and flour confectionery
213 Biscuits
214 Bacon curing, meat and fish products
215 Milk and milk products
216 Sugar
217 Cocoa, chocolate and sugar confectionery
218 Fruit and vegetable products
219 Animal and poultry foods
221 Vegetable and animal oils and fats
229 Food industries not elsewhere specified
231 Brewing and malting
232 Soft drinks
239 Other drink industries
240 Tobacco

Coal and petroleum products
261 Coke ovens and manufactured fuel
262 Mineral oil refining
263 Lubricating oils and greases

Chemicals and allied industries
271 General chemicals
272 Pharmaceutical chemicals and preparations
273 Toilet preparations
274 Paint
275 Soap and detergents
276 Synthetic resins, plastic materials and synthetic rubber
277 Dyestuffs and pigments
278 Fertilizers
279 Other chemical industries

Metal manufacture
311 Iron and steel (general)
312 Steel tubes
313 Iron castings, etc.
321 Aluminium and aluminium alloys
322 Copper, brass and other copper alloys
323 Other base metals

Porter goes on to highlight the current debate about what an industry is. The debate centres around the need to perceive of an industry as extending beyond current products or technology, beyond existing competitors, and beyond geographical boundaries. Too limited a definition can lead to the failure to identify emerging trends which are outside of the current scope of operation but are likely to affect business in the future. However, Porter suggests that by taking the above variables firms should be able to orientate their thinking towards such emerging trends.

Porter also suggests a range of generic industry environments in which the industry-defining variables will be different. This provides an additional focus in that the industry can be seen to be fragmented, global, or at a particular stage in the industry life cycle. Features of these generic industry environments were also examined in Chapter 4, but further attention will be given to industry life cycles later in this chapter.

Ansoff's approach

The approach taken by Ansoff[3] is focused on areas of the total environment in which the firm aspires to participate, with particular emphasis being placed upon demand and current plus potential technology to be used to serve that demand. The analysis is based on a full understanding of environmental variables, as discussed in Chapter 3, with the emphasis being on identifying trends and their underlying opportunities and threats. Those that are selected for participation become the firm's 'industries', although Ansoff uses the term 'strategic business area' (SBA). An SBA is defined as 'a distinctive segment of the environment in which the firm does (or may want to do) business'. Therefore the approach is that the areas of involvement are defined in terms of environmental variables rather than in terms of the firms that participate in the environment. Internally the firm then organizes its structure and resources into strategic business units (SBUs), a concept which has already been well discussed, which are based on the exploitation of the selected SBAs. The strength of this approach is that it avoids the perpetuation of a historical projection by the firm and its products, through the exploitation of opportunities and the advancement of technology to make historical approaches obsolete.

The mission approach

Here the industries are defined through the formulation of the organizational mission, which, as explained in Chapter 1, is the first stage in the strategic management component of planning direction. In Chapter 1 the organizational mission was said to be concerned with, *inter alia*, the broad areas of industry participation.

A full treatment of organizational mission is given in Chapter 6. At this stage it is sufficient to say that several criteria need to be considered in the formulation of the mission, many of which are concerned with specifying boundaries to the industries in which the firm will or may be involved. For example, decisions need to be made about the specification of market domains, market orientation, basic product or service definitions, customers and market definitions, and opportunities and threats.

Three outcomes of these decisions within the context of defining the nature of industries need to be considered:

- The broad specification of market domains provides the possible range to be selected, although participation for the next planning period will be specified in the organizational strategy. The latter is examined in Chapter 10.
- The range of potential markets can then be subjected to investigation and understanding, details of which constitute the latter sections of this chapter.
- Where several industries are identified then there may be a need to establish several SBUs. This being the case then market investigations will be separate, in that consumer requirements will vary across the SBUs.

THE INDUSTRY LIFE CYCLE

Readers will be aware that the process of change is endemic in business; witness the development of the concepts of evolution and life cycles which pertain to the business environment. Readers will probably be most familiar with the product life-cycle model, which has been given considerable attention in the marketing literature. Reviews of parts of the literature concerning the product life cycle have been given by writers such as Rink and Swan[4]. The hypothesis is, quite simply, that, after the launch of a new product, its sales will tend to follow a pattern or cycle that features phases of introduction, growth, maturity and decline, resulting in the ultimate death or withdrawal of the product from the marketplace. The product life cycle is not given major treatment in this book, as the basics are adequately described in texts such as those by Baker[5] and Oliver[6].

Several criticisms have been directed at this model, not least of which is that it is product-based and is not consistent with firms orientating their decision-making to the external environment. However, the life-cycle concept has also been applied to the external environment, partly because of the need to overcome product-based thinking, but partly based also on empirical evidence and observation. The concept has been discussed in the literature in terms of: long-term cycles in general economic activity; life cycles as a feature of industry evolution; market life cycles; and product life cycles, as mentioned above. While the cycle of economic activity provides a separate explanation, writers such as Primeaux[7] have highlighted the controversy as to whether the others are different phenomena or are indeed explanations of the same phenomenon. The approach taken in this book is that each of these views is worthy of consideration. As a result the first two are considered in this section, while the concept of market life cycles is addressed later in the chapter.

Regardless of the level of analysis the aim is the same, that is, to identify and forecast trends of evolution and to anticipate the likely influence that a particular stage of the cycle, or cycle transition, is likely to have on the future performance of the firm. Additionally, such predictions will contribute to the attractiveness of continued participation in current industries as well as future entry into new industries.

Economic cycles

Although changes in the economic activity of a country over time obviously represent a complex of relationships, economists have identified cycles of activity with distinct phases, though some simplification of reality is necessary to achieve this. However, the depression of the 1930s, the repression of output caused by increases in the price of crude oil in the early 1970s, and the recession of the 1980s, are pointed to as examples of inflection points in the cycle of economic activity.

A major work which has consolidated the debate and evidence on economic cycles is that by Van Duijn[8]. The general hypothesis, analogous to the product life cycle, is depicted in Figure 5.1. It is shown that, with time, although expansion of the economy can be achieved in the short term, there will be a ceiling to that growth, which is likely to be followed by a recession and a depression of output. However, again with time, further expansion will be achieved. For strategic management purposes the central issues are identifying the phase that a country is currently in, the length of time that the phase will continue before the onset of the next phase, and the causes of potential change in the cycle.

As a guide to this dilemma, Van Duijn[8] has identified four different types of cycle, based principally on time periods:

- The Kitchin or inventory cycle of three to five years.
- The Juglar or investment cycle of seven to eleven years.
- The Kuznets or building cycle of 15–25 years.
- The Kondratieff or long-wave cycle of 45–60 years.

These classifications provide bases for forecasting cycles, although the causes of inflection are obviously central to the forecasting. However, as with the discussions of forecasting given in Chapter 3, the longer the time period the greater the obvious difficulty in producing meaningful forecasts.

Industry life cycles

The work of Porter[2] is again central to another area of understanding the environment. He supports the hypothesis that an industry is likely to exhibit a life cycle of four phases, similar to the product life cycle, as shown in Figure 5.2. Here the principle is that sales increase gradually during the introduction phase, but will show a rapid increase over the growth period. Once maturity is reached the model

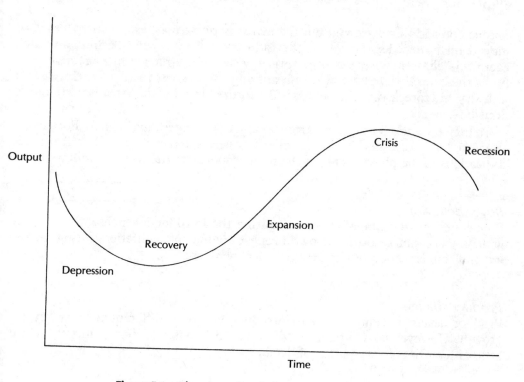

Figure 5.1 *The generalized phases of an economic cycle.*

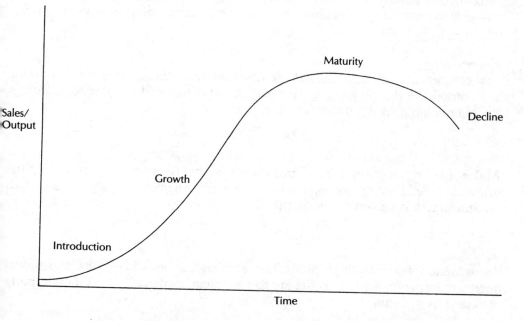

Figure 5.2 *The generalized phases of the industry life cycle*

predicts no additional growth, but the maturity phase may last for many years, or indeed many decades. However, the industry will eventually decline, although again this phase may spread over several years. For strategic management purposes the central issues are again identifying the current phase of each relevant industry and forecasting changes over the future period of time that is pertinent to decision-making.

To help try and identify the current phase or an impending change, Porter[2] has suggested several criteria to be examined, where the nature of each will provide indications of the phase. Some of the more important criteria are as follows:

Buyer behaviour
Buyer inertia would be experienced during the introduction phase, followed by widening acceptance during growth; repeat buying and saturation during maturity; and sophistication of buying at the decline phase.

Product change
Product design is central during introduction, while differentiation is key for growth. However, less product differentiation is possible during maturity, and little differentiation is a feature of decline.

Manufacturing
Introduction features overcapacity, while growth often features undercapacity, maturity some overcapacity, although decline will feature substantial overcapacity.

Competition
Few competitors will be found during introduction, although rivalry will develop and consolidate during growth. However, competitors will exit during maturity, leading to falling rivalry during decline.

Risk
Major risk is a feature of introduction, while further risks can be taken during the growth phase. During maturity and decline the original risk is past, although additional risk is unlikely to be justifiable.

Profits
Introduction features little profit but accelerating growth means substantial increases in profit. Lower profits are to be earned in maturity, and these rapidly reduce during decline.

Ansoff's life cycle models

While the last section gave some indications within the basic four-phase model, Ansoff[3] has given some modifications based on the work introduced earlier in this chapter. Two models have been presented which are pertinent to the understanding of industry life cycles. The first is the demand–technology life cycle, and the other is an extension of this model through the inclusion of relevant product life cycles. The former is illustrated in Figure 5.3.

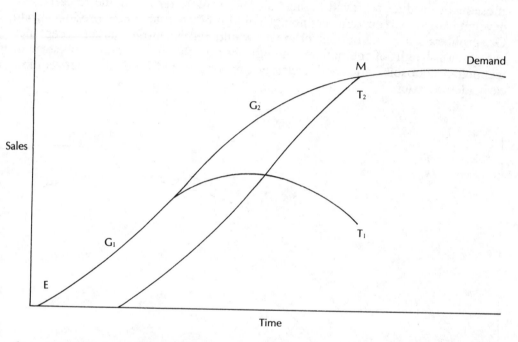

Figure 5.3 *The demand-technology life cycle (H. I. Ansoff,* Implanting Strategic Management, *© 1984. Reproduced by permission of Prentice Hall Ltd.)*

The demand curve for the typical industry is illustrated in four distinct phases. E represents the emergence of the industry, while G_1 is the stage of accelerating growth, followed by a slowing down of growth at G_2. The final stage, that of maturity, is given at M, although a stage of decline is not depicted. Within this overall life cycle T_1 and T_2 represent the satisfaction of industry demand with two distinct technologies. This illustration shows that the emergence and initial growth were based on the initial technology T_1, and although the new technology T_2 was introduced during the growth phase, its full impact was not felt until the maturity phase of the industry life cycle. Thus, in this example, the industry life cycle has been compounded of two demand–technology life cycles.

This demand–technology life cycle can be extended by the inclusion of product life cycles for specific products as launched by a particular company over a period of time. This type of extension is illustrated in Figure 5.4. Here the industry life cycle from Figure 5.3 is reproduced, but only up to G_2, while only the satisfaction of demand attributed to technology T_1 is included. P_1, P_2, and P_3 represent the life cycles of three different products, all based on the same technology. For this particular firm P_1 satisfied the majority of demand during the emergence of the industry. However, as the industry grew the company lost market share to companies who entered the industry, although, with the growth of the industry, each subsequent product achieved higher sales in absolute terms. While research and development within current technology could produce viable new products up to G_1, proliferation of additional products would receive little market acceptance with the onslaught of the new technology. For T_1 this is, therefore, the stage of technological obsolescence and is clearly a major point of inflection that requires early identification.

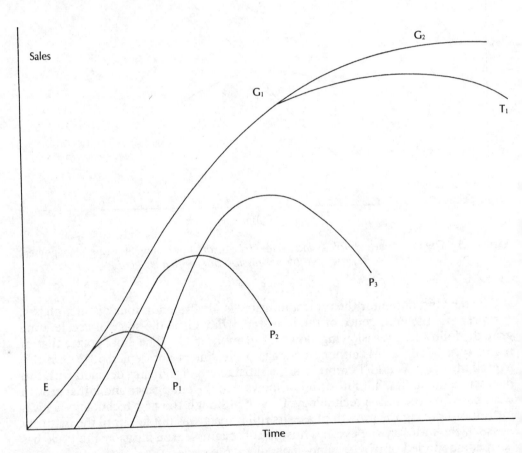

Figure 5.4 *Extended demand-technology life cycle.* (H. I. Ansoff, Implanting Strategic Management, © 1984. Reproduced by permission of Prentice Hall Ltd.)

Criticisms of life-cycle models

Perhaps the major criticism is that these models attempt a commonality of explanation when in reality there are obviously many differences between the structures of industries, the technologies that are utilized and the successes of products. Therefore, although it can be claimed that there is a tendency for most industries to follow a similar type of pattern as illustrated, for a particular industry which is evolving the cycle cannot be easily predicted.

More specific criticisms of life-cycle models have been documented by writers such as Greenley[9], Porter[2] and Primeaux[7]. The first of these is that, when plotting the actual progression of the life cycle over a period of time, it is not often clear which phase the cycle is currently in. Although growth may have been a feature of the preceding period, forecasting and prediction are needed to assess whether the growth will be perpetuated. The second criticism is that some cycles may not feature all the phases and can go from growth into decline. Also, although in some situations it may appear that decline has started, revitalization may occur, resulting in further growth and then maturity.

Another criticism is that, although life-cycle models are intended to be tools for prediction and decision-making, life cycles may not be totally independent of the actions of companies. Developments of new technologies can influence the industry life cycle, while product innovations and modifications as well as marketing activities can influence the shape and duration of both demand–technology and product life cycles. The final common criticism is that the nature of competition within the stages can vary for different industries. Some may have few competitors during emergence, although they experience a build-up during growth. Others may be faced with many competitors throughout, while others will operate in an oligopoly-type structure. Again this causes difficulties in planning and decision-making, as differences in competition are an indication that the life-cycle stages have different meanings in these different competitive environments.

EXHIBIT 5.1

Geest's Fresher Fruits

Fresh foods group Geest participates in British fruit and vegetable markets in which consumption is static, if not declining. Indeed the volume of their imports of bananas has hardly changed in 20 years. However, the market for exotic fruit and vegetables with high retail prices is expanding, although it is still only small, representing only 4% of Geest's total turnover. Also, the demands of the retail multiples have changed. Distribution is moving from direct to the stores, to a limited number of major sites for further distribution to individual stores. As a result of these changes in customer requirements, Geest has had to inject £20 million of capital investment into its distribution operations.

Adapted from *Management Today*, April 1987

FROM INDUSTRIES TO MARKETS

This chapter has so far concerned itself with the industry component of a company's operating environment. The rest of this chapter is concerned with an understanding of markets and customers. These areas have traditionally been the preserve of the marketing literature, so that the following sections draw heavily on this source material.

Just as different approaches and difficulties exist in understanding industries, so do they also exist in defining markets. For some firms it will be difficult to draw the line between where the industry ends and where the individual markets that constitute the industry begin. Baker[5] has emphasized that, while these difficulties exist, each firm needs to define the boundaries of specific markets, even though such parameters may be selected on an arbitrary basis. Orientation for these definitions can be developed from the definitions of industries that were discussed earlier in the chapter.

Standard Industrial Classification

Where SIC proves to be of value in defining the industry, it may also be of value in setting the boundaries for markets to be found in the industry. For example, the classification '240 Tobacco', as given in Table 5.1, may be taken to consist of markets for cigarettes, cigars, snuff, and pipe tobacco. Similarly, classification '274 Paint', may be taken to be made up of markets relating to the general public, the decorating trade, industrial and marine applications. In both cases the industry is based on common or similar raw materials and related production, although final products will feature some differences. However, within each market the requirements of customers will differ, while the future growth of volume sales to be pursued and the extent of competition for these volumes in the different markets are likely to vary widely. A method for developing such definitions has been given by Hlavacek and Reddy[10].

Competitive definitions

Here the industry is defined in terms of the firms that produce products which are close substitutes for each other, while markets are explained in terms of the buyers of those products. Consequently, the industry is explained in terms of rivalry between competitors, while markets are explained in terms of the buying behaviour exhibited by customers. Here the skills needed to understand an industry relate to the theories of organizational behaviour, whereas the skills needed to understand markets relate to the theories of psychology and sociology which explain human behaviour. While the former were discussed in Chapter 4, the latter are discussed later in this chapter.

Environment definitions

Discussed here are Ansoff's SBA approach and that related to the organizational mission. From each of these approaches boundaries need to be established to explain each of the relevant markets. Such boundaries can perhaps be best developed from the starting point of a simple definition of a market, such as that proposed by Kotler[11]: 'A market consists of all the potential customers sharing a particular need or want who might be willing and able to engage in exchange to satisfy that need or want.' This definition suggests overall criteria that can be established as the boundaries in defining a market. First there is the total number of people who share the need or want, which can be explained as the concept of demand. From here the actual purchases that take place will represent the size of the market. Another criterion is that of the buying behaviour of customers in converting from 'might buy' to 'will buy', while any variations in customer requirements in relation to the basic need would represent another criterion. Consequently boundaries such as the following are suggested for defining markets:

- Demand and market size giving the explanation of those people who 'might buy' and those who 'will buy'.
- Buyer behaviour as the explanation of the process which leads people to buy within the market.
- Market segmentation which provides the explanation for variations in requirements within the common overall need.

The rest of this chapter is organized around the above, with major sections being devoted to each of these boundaries.

Finally, before moving on to each of these sections attention is diverted to a major issue in the understanding of markets, which has been well discussed in an article by Day[12]. This is that the perspective of defining markets in relation to serving customer requirements may be in conflict with the needs of the organization. His suggestion is that a dual approach is necessary to balance the 'bottom-up' needs of customers with the 'top-down' needs of the company. However, while recognizing that this issue is of major importance to companies, it is argued that the balancing can be achieved through systematic strategic management and particularly at the stage of organizational strategy selection.

DEMAND AND MARKET SIZE

While the discipline of microeconomics provides a conceptual understanding of the quantities of product that consumers are likely to buy, the marketing literature has wrestled with the practical limitations of economic theories. Some writers have retained the concepts from economics, others have abandoned them in favour of measurements of factual but historical sales volumes, while writers such as

Watkins[13] have presented treatises that combine both schools of thought. The approach taken in this book is that the economists' concept of demand provides an overall and useful framework of understanding, but that the concept of actual behaviour provides a more meaningful base for decision-making pertinent to the future.

An outline of demand

The concept of demand has been defined by Wilson[14] as: 'The quantity of a good or service that consumers are willing and able to purchase at various prices during a given time period, *ceteris paribus*.' As this definition stands, for the given product or service, the quantity demanded will be dependent on price, and the other variables which could also influence quantity are taken to be constant. This gives rise to the traditional demand curve which simply shows that, for most products, higher quantities will be demanded at lower price levels, as illustrated by the curve D_1 in Figure 5.5. However, with time other variables outside the relationship are likely to change, such as consumers' income, tastes or the prices of competitive products. D_2 in Figure 5.5 shows such a shift in demand, caused by, say, increased consumer income. Economists also present demand at different levels. A market demand curve would represent the price-quantity relationship for all consumers that are willing and able to purchase the particular product. However, the company demand curve refers only to those consumers whose intentions are directed towards a particular organization, while economists are also concerned with individual consumer demand curves.

There are several practical limitations to this theory, three of which are mentioned below. As pointed out by Greenley[15], the fact that consumers are 'willing' does not mean that they will actually purchase the quantities that are indicated by

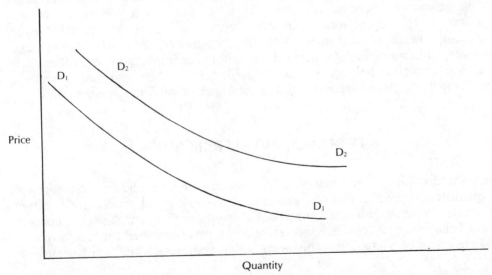

Figure 5.5   *Traditional demand curve.*

the levels of demand for each price. Lancaster[16] considers that demand relates to 'planned' quantities of purchase, at various prices, in that actual quantities purchased may not always be equal to the quantities that were initially 'planned' to be purchased. Consequently, the buyer behaviour of consumers also needs to be studied; this will be discussed later.

Another limitation is that most firms will be unable to construct a demand curve for a particular product. At a particular point in time they will charge a particular price, given the competitive conditions to be found in the marketplace, and their experience of the price–quantity relationship will be within a band around that price. Even where firms participate in experiments of modifying their price to assess elasticity of demand, this will be within a relatively narrow band. Figure 5.6 shows this type of knowledge. P_0 is taken to be the market price level, which we assume the company adopts, which allows it to sell quantity Q_0. Prices P_1 and P_2 represent levels that could be experimented with under test marketing conditions, with the results indicating that quantities Q_1 and Q_2 would be achieved. Therefore this type of research would indicate a demand schedule given by the curve BAC, although outside these parameters the firm's knowledge would be lacking. Indeed, even the curve BAC is subject to uncertainty over time, given the weaknesses of experimentation as a method of marketing research.

Another limitation is that there is likely to be variation in the requirements of consumers for the same product need, so that lack of homogeneity means that

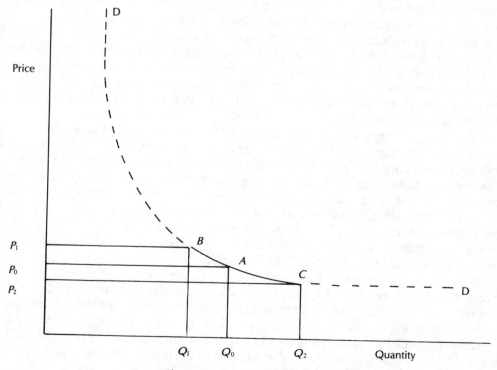

Figure 5.6 *Demand curve knowledge.*

these different aspects of buying requirements must be understood. As already mentioned above, this is the concept of market segmentation and is given fuller attention later in this chapter.

Market size

To avoid such limitations the concept of 'market size' can be used. This can be defined as the actual volume of sales achieved historically. However, in defining 'market size' by volume sales achieved, boundaries need to be given which define the market in terms of:

- The product, product class or product lines to which the market relates.
- The units of measurement of size as either physical units, volume or weight, or unit of currency.
- The country or geographical area to which the volume of sales relates.
- The time period over which the volume was achieved.
- The relevant shares of the market size that were achieved by competitors.
- A breakdown of the total market by the different market segments that have been identified (see below).

Assuming that the company is able adequately to define each of these and determine the sales of competitors, then factual information is obtained rather than a hypothetical demand curve. These results of market behaviour have been caused as a result of all the environmental variables that were discussed in Chapter 3 in the strategic audit, including competitive rivalry and buyer behaviour. In addition the trend in market size and changes in the share achieved by competitors can be established over a number of years, assuming that the definitions of each of the boundaries are not changed over the period. This gives important knowledge about the growth of the market, as well as changes in the relative market domination of each of the competitors.

From here the next stage is obviously the forecasting of the future trend in market size and changes in the market shares of competitors. Here the forecasting methods that were given in Table 3.2 in Chapter 3 can be utilized. However, where this historical trend is to be extrapolated forward then the resultant forecast will be uncertain, in that the environmental conditions from previous years are likely to change in the future. However, as will be already apparent to the reader, all methods of forecasting include weaknesses which mean that their results will feature uncertainty; until the art of forecasting becomes an exact science such weaknesses are part of the 'normal' business risk.

The final consideration in this section is that of the concept of the market life cycle, which was mentioned earlier in the chapter in the section devoted to the industry life cycle. Despite the controversy as to whether or not the market life cycle is merely a reflection of industry or product life cycles, it is suggested that the concept of a cycle in market trends can be useful to their understanding. Kotler[11] has suggested five stages in a generalized model of the market life cycle, as follows:

Market-crystallization stage

This is the stage prior to market development and is often considered as a latent market. A sufficient number of people may share a common need to constitute a viable market, but either companies are not supplying products to satisfy the need or those products that are available give little consumer satisfaction.

Market-expansion stage

Companies enter the market, consumers become aware of the alternative products and the growth occurs as additional consumers enter the market. With growth and the entry of new consumers the increasing variation in requirements will lead to the development of market segmentation, with some companies beginning to specialize in supplying specific segments.

Market-fragmentation stage

At this stage market segmentation is well developed and this aspect of buyer behaviour is having a major influence on the marketing strategies of the competing firms. Many divisions of the market may be applicable and many approaches to segmentation (which will be discussed below) may be possible to give several aspects to market fragmentation. Competition will also have intensified as the competing firms select their segments for participation, enhance the efficiency of their marketing activities, and aim to increase their market share.

EXHIBIT 5.2

How Heineken Stays on Top

The Dutch company Heineken is the world's largest privately owned brewery. During the 1980s it has grown rapidly, in terms of output, sales, profits and return on capital employed. One reason given for its success is its understanding of the world-wide buyer behaviour of the people who constitute the market segments in which Heineken lagers are purchased. These consumers prefer an exclusive brand and buy Heineken because it is expensive and has snob appeal, which differentiates it from the many cheaper brands which are available to these consumers. Millions of Dutch guilders are spent annually to reinforce the image required by these consumers. In the United States in 1985 the falling value of the dollar meant that imported lager beers were becoming more expensive, relative to domestic brands. Although other importers lowered their prices Heineken retained its premium prices, while increasing advertising expenditure to stimulate consumer demand in its market segments. However, the company is realizing that world markets are becoming more segmented, so that attention will need to be given to understanding the needs of these new segments.

Adapted from *Business*, July 1986

Market-reconsolidation stage
As the market reaches maturity in its growth, decline may result in the erosion of segments with the market contracting into a small number of consolidated segments. Also a radical product innovation by one company is often followed by other companies in order not to lose competitive advantage. This can lead to a commonality of requirement on the part of consumers, leading to a reconsolidation of the market.

Market-termination stage
For all markets it is predicted that there will be eventual termination as consumer requirements change or as new technology leads to different products and a new market, in the sense that the definitions of boundaries have changed.

BUYER BEHAVIOUR

All books on marketing management include chapters on buyer behaviour, which are usually split between consumer buying and that carried out by organizations. In addition a separate literature has developed but as the requirement of this book is for only a cursory treatment of buyer behaviour, interested readers are directed to the books by Chisnall[17], Foxall[18] and Williams[19]. In line with books on marketing in general, this section gives attention to both consumer and organizational buyer behaviour.

Consumer buyer behaviour

The book by Murphy and Enis[20] presents the fundamentals of understanding consumers in a way which is typical of marketing texts. They present a range of variables that affect the consumer's purchases but which are internal to the consumer's personal make-up. In addition they give a range of variables which are external to this make-up, but which nevertheless also influence purchasing decisions. The final part of their presentation is concerned with a number of stages which the consumer goes through in the decision-making process to complete a purchase. These are summarized in Table 5.2.

Internal variables
Homo sapiens, by nature, features a complexity of needs and wants for which he pursues satisfaction. Motivation, given as the first internal variable in Table 5.2, describes the inner drive that prompts individuals to pursue the satisfaction of needs and wants. Perhaps the most famous and most quoted classification of needs is that by Maslow[21], a hierarchy rising from basic physiological needs to the more complex needs of self-actualization. The products and services which a company

Table 5.2 *Summary of consumer buyer behaviour.*

Internal variables
- Motivation
- Perception
- Learning
- Personality
- Attitudes

External variables
- Culture
- Social class
- Reference groups
- Family

Decision-making process
- Need recognition
- Search
- Evaluation of alternatives
- Purchase
- Post-purchase evaluation

supplies can simply be seen as means of satisfying selected needs, so that motivation must be instigated in the direction of the company's own products. Perception is concerned with the process of taking in and understanding the stimuli that will suggest that certain products have the potential for satisfying certain needs. Stimuli from advertising, selling and the products themselves are related to past experiences and knowledge, although individuals are selective about that which is acceptable.

If an individual's behaviour towards consumption in relation to a particular need is modified, then learning has taken place, with the anticipation that the learning is to associate the company's product with satisfaction. Although personality, which represents the unique characteristics of an individual, plays a part in both the reaction to stimuli and subsequent learning, recent research by Engel and Blackwell[22] has suggested that it is of less importance than other variables. Finally, attitudes are learned predispositions to respond to particular stimuli in certain ways. In buyer behaviour the aim is that individuals should form attitudes towards the company's product such that subsequent product stimuli should trigger the association of satisfaction with the product, leading to repeat purchases.

External variables

Although individuals ultimately select their own purchases, they are very much influenced by the society in which they live, with much of this influence being at the subconscious level. Culture has been described as the intellectual and social heritage of a specific society, representing a range of behavioural norms which are expected of individuals living in the particular society. This behaviour is passed on from generation to generation through learning processes, although norms change with time. Also, subcultures are to be found in most cultures, where there are variations in the behavioural norms. Social class represents a breakdown of the society into different groups based on social prestige, occupation and income. The principle is that these groups will feature individuals with shared attitudes and values which may be different from, or modifications of, the norms of the overall culture. For companies it is important to identify the influence that these norms, values and attitudes, which are endemic within the society, are likely to have on the purchase of products of immediate commercial interest.

Reference groups and an individual's family are also likely to influence an individual's buying behaviour. Of all the smaller groups of people that an individual interfaces with in day-to-day living the reference group is that which is of major importance. Similarly the obvious importance of the family group in Western Europe represents another important source of influence. Again, for the particular product group, firms need to identify the reliance placed on reference group advice and the role of the family group in both the selection and consumption of these products.

Decision-making process

The stages that are given in Table 5.2 represent a process that consumers will undergo, although in every day purchasing it is unlikely that the majority of people will be aware of this process for the majority of their purchases. For companies the point is that they need to provide incentives to convert the 'willingness' to purchase into actual purchases which are understood to be need-satisfying. Research into consumer buyer behaviour has resulted in the development of models which attempt to explain this process, of which those by Engel et al.[23], Howard and Ostlund[24], Nicosia[25], and Andreason[26] have been documented by many writers.

Organizational buyer behaviour

While the buyer behaviour that takes place in organizations is ultimately carried out by people and is therefore subjected to the same influences as consumer buyer behaviour, the commercial requirements and group behaviour characteristics of organizations provide additional variables in buyer behaviour within the context of organizations. Major influences on organizational buyer behaviour have been given by Hutt and Speh[27], as illustrated in Figure 5.7.

Individual forces

These are based on those variables that relate to the individual as discussed in the last subsection on consumer buyer behaviour. In addition there are variables that affect the individual in his buying capacity due to his position in the organization, the most important of which are now outlined. First, there are the rewards that are received as a result of purchasing decisions, being either intrinsic, such as self-fulfilment, or extrinsic, such as salary or job status. Another force is that generated

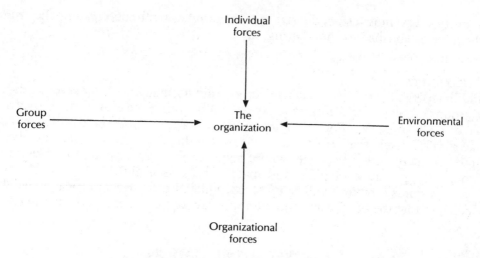

Figure 5.7 *Organizational buyer behaviour.*

by the information systems within the company and how the dissemination of relevant information can aid the buying process. Additionally there is the ability of the individual to make buying decisions through delegated authority, or the necessity to refer decisions to a higher authority or a buying committee. The final consideration here is the level of risk that the individual needs to take, his personal ability to accept risk, and the likely consequences of decisions that are perceived to be possibly incorrect.

Environmental forces

The environmental forces that were discussed in Chapter 3 on the strategic audit are also applicable here. These variables can influence the purchasing decisions of organizations, as well as their long-range planning decisions, so that these decisions also need to be based on an understanding of the ramifications of such environmental variables.

Organizational forces

This group of influences is described by Hutt and Spey[27] as evolving around those that can be classified as being part of the behaviour theory of the firm and those which can be classified as being part of the organizational climate. In the former are forces such as organizational conflict and the avoidance of uncertainty. The former arise from the variation in and opposing nature of the objectives of individuals and departments, which can impinge on buying decisions, while the latter are concerned with the importance attached to the avoidance of uncertainty such as retaining known suppliers and products.

The organizational climate refers to the total ambiance which pertains in companies and which, in the case of purchasing, relates to features such as innovativeness, motivation, the status of the purchasing function, and policy rules which are established for purchasing.

Group forces

Within an organization purchasing decisions are normally made by several people or groups of people, while others may have some influence even though they are not directly involved. For straightforward repeat purchases of components or materials it is likely that only those in the purchasing department will be involved. However, at the other extreme, where major capital investment is to take place through the purchase of plant and machinery, it is likely that personnel from several business functions will be involved, while director-level ratification will be needed, so that the purchasing function will only represent one of many interests.

MARKET SEGMENTATION

Given the many influences on buyer behaviour it is not surprising that most markets will feature variations in customer requirements developed from the same core need. This heterogeneity of buyers' requirements means that firms are faced with investigations in order to understand these variations, but they are also faced with decision-making to select the groups of people or market segments that they will serve. For many companies it may not be possible to serve all customer requirements, while selectivity of and concentration on certain market segments can give competitive advantages and become part of the strategy selection process. This section is concerned with the nature of segmentation as part of the process of understanding, while the selection of segments is tackled in Chapter 12 as part of the marketing operational strategy.

Understanding market segmentation is based on identifying several bases into which the variations of customer requirements can be grouped or clustered. Again the approach taken in the marketing literature is to give separate attention to both consumer and industrial markets.

Segmenting consumer markets

The approach taken by Kotler[11] is that four major bases can be used for consumer markets, all of which include variables that can be used to explain customer variations.

Geographical segmentation

Many firms find that there are variations in consumer requirements in different continents, countries, regions, cities and towns, and even neighbourhoods. Geographical spread of business is an obvious concern for all firms, although resource restrictions may limit increased participation in further segments. Although extreme variations in customer requirements may also limit spread, similarity in certain segments may necessitate little product modification, allowing for increased participation.

Demographic segmentation

Variables related to this base are commonly used as they exhibit strong clusters of similarity which are relatively easy to measure. Some of these demographic variables are concerned with the individual, such as age, sex, income, occupation and education. Within each of these variables consumers can be classified into further subgroups, based on, for example, income or job type. Another approach is to base segmentation on the family group, with the variable of size being one approach and that of the family life cycle being another. Other groups within society have also been found to display similar buying requirements and have been used for segmentation purposes. These include nationality, race and religion, which again reflect a tendency towards a clustering of consumer requirements.

Psychographic segmentation

Three major divisions are given by Kotler within this base for segmentation —social class, lifestyle and personality. The former is derived from arbitrary classifications of people into different classes, where levels of income and behavioural norms influence purchasing requirements. Lifestyle classifications are based on patterns of living which reflect people's activities, interests and opinions, with classifications such as the 'plain woman', the 'fashionable woman', and the 'manly woman'. Personality segmentation is based on the selection of a particular personality trait as the common variable linking people's purchasing requirements, such as conservatism, aggression, confidence, independence and impulsiveness.

Behavioural segmentation

This base of segmentation traverses individuals and groups in society by taking the type of buying situation as opposed to variables which are endemic within the population. One approach is to use the occasion for which the product is used; here Kotler gives the example of air travel which, on this basis, can be occasion-segmented as holiday, business, or visiting friends and relations. Another approach is to segment people by the major benefit they seek from a particular product. Such benefits could range from price, through image or economy of use, to quality. Other approaches can be based on the frequency of use, quantified perhaps as high, medium, or low; or on user status, such as non-users, ex-users, potential users, first-time users, and regular users.

Segmenting industrial markets

Cravens and Woodruff[28] have suggested four major bases for segmenting industrial markets, which will be discussed below. However, Hutt and Speh[27] give a more extensive range of variables that can be used for classificatory purposes; interested readers are directed to this text.

Geographical segmentation
The approach here is similar to that in consumer markets, where customers can be broken down by continents, countries, regions, or even towns and cities.

Industry segmentation
Where industrial products are needed across a range of different industries it is likely that there will be a variation of requirements within each industry. Such differences may merely require modifications to tolerances and quality of components, or variations in the chemical composition of raw materials. However, in some cases different products may be required for each industry, as in the case of computer software.

Usage or volume-purchased segmentation
Companies supplying industrial products often segment their markets by customer size, where the latter is based on volume of purchase. Many firms find that a large proportion of their business is achieved with a relatively small number of customer firms. This segment is obviously of major importance so that considerable effort is devoted to understanding customers' requirements. Segments can also be 'created' by classifying customers into arbitrary groups based on a descending scale of volume of purchase.

Benefit segmentation
Again similar to consumer segmentation, where industrial buyers are often found to lend themselves to classification based on particular benefits which are deemed to be of particular importance. These benefits could include quantity discounts, delivery, quality and tolerances, technological developments and reliability in use.

SUMMARY

This chapter completes the treatment of Part Two, which was concerned with analysing the environment. The understanding of market structures was split between a treatment of the broader issue of industries and a more specific treatment of markets.

The first section was concerned with the nature of industries, where different methods of defining industries were examined. The next section tackled the concept of the industry life cycle. The concept was underpinned by the phenomenon of economic cycles, as a prelude to the general industry life cycle. Extensions to this model were also discussed, which incorporate technology and product life cycles. However, several criticisms of life cycle models are pertinent, based on limitations of the models, and these were also discussed.

The next major section was concerned with the interface between industries and markets and the problem of defining the boundaries of markets. Attention was then directed to comparing the concepts of demand and market size. While the former is seen to be useful as a basis for a conceptual understanding, it is limited for strategic management decision-making purposes. Market size is based upon factual measurements of historical sales, but within specified boundaries. Although based on factual data, projections of trends into the future are subject to uncertainty because of possible changes in environmental conditions. The final discussion here was the application of the life-cycle concept to the development of markets.

The penultimate section examined the nature of the buyer behaviour of the people who constitute markets. This was split into that of consumers and that applicable to organizations as buyers. The former was seen to be influenced by personal variables as well as variables within the society. Similar variables are also important in organizational buyer behaviour, but forces within the organization also have a major influence.

The final section considered another major feature of markets, that of market segmentation. This concern for variation in customer requirements, developed from the same core need, was also examined in relation to consumers and organizations as buyers. For each set of buyers four bases were given for segmentation purposes, although several variables within each give alternatives for segmenting specific markets.

CHAPTER CASE STUDY ILLUSTRATION:
THE CHOCOLATE DIVISION, NESTLÉ PRODUCTS LTD*

Although the subject of this case study is Nestlé Products Ltd, information is given about the chocolate industry and its constituent markets. Although the study is centred on Switzerland, the trends discussed were endemic to

*This case study illustration is based on the original case. 'The Chocolate Division, Nestlé Products Ltd M 24', prepared by Research Associate, Stephen R. Wilkinson, under the direction of Professor John R. Kennedy as a basis for class discussion. Copyright 1977 by IMEDE, Lausanne, Switzerland. All rights reserved. Summarized by permission. IMEDE declines all responsibility for errors or inaccuracies in the summary.

other countries in Western Europe. Although the industry had historically featured growth, at the time of the case study it was in decline.

The information in the case study allows for a discussion of the chocolate industry life cycle in Switzerland, an examination of the range of markets that were defined within the industry, as well as a discussion of the market for tablets or chocolate bars.

THE INDUSTRY

When the case study was written the industry life cycle was well established. It had grown substantially from its beginnings early in the nineteenth century, and this growth had continued into the twentieth century. However, early in the twentieth century two major factors arrested this growth, resulting in a plateau in the life-cycle curve. The first was the establishment of high customs tariffs and strict currency control by foreign governments, which had the obvious effect of reducing the export of Swiss chocolate. The second was as a result of the Second World War, during which raw materials for chocolate manufacture became difficult to obtain, while their costs rose accordingly. Both consequences had drastic effects on the industry life cycle.

Growth continued during the 1950s and 1960s until the life cycle peaked with maximum sales of 58,000 tonnes in 1972, representing a per-capita consumption of 9.9 kg. The ten-year period of the life cycle to this maximum started from a base of sales of 42,000 tonnes in 1962, which represented a per-capita consumption of only 8.2 kg. However, the period to 1975 experienced another depression in the life cycle as annual sales fell to a level of only 49,000 tonnes in 1975, representing a per capita consumption of only 8.6 kg, not much higher than 1962 levels. A number of causes were perceived as responsible for this industry decline:

- The upward valuation of the Swiss franc which caused a reduction in foreign visitors who generally purchased Swiss chocolate.
- The economic recession of the mid-1970s which supressed retail spending generally in Switzerland.
- A decline in the number of foreigners living or working in Switzerland, causing a significant reduction in population.
- A recent decline in exports despite a previous trend of increasing exports.

THE MARKETS

The total Swiss chocolate industry was defined in the case study as consisting of five markets:

- Tablets or chocolate bars, where market size per annum had grown to a peak in 1972 but had declined up to 1976.
- *Confiserie* or candy chocolate, where market size per annum had grown to a peak in 1973 but had declined up to 1976.

- Special chocolate, such as Easter eggs, where market size had remained almost constant.
- *Couvertures* for *pâtisserie* shops, where market size per annum had peaked during 1972 and 1973 but had declined up to 1976.
- Powdered cocoa and chocolate, where again market size had grown to a peak in 1972 although subsequent declines to 1976 were not substantial.

An indication of market shares is given in the case study, although a breakdown for each market is not given. About half the total sales in 1975 were achieved by the four largest companies, Lindt, Nestlé, Suchard and Tobler. About 25% of sales were achieved by Migros, a Swiss chain-store company with its own manufacturer. The remaining 25% were spread among other companies. These market shares had been more or less constant over the previous ten years.

THE TABLET MARKET

Some information, albeit limited, is given about the segmentation of the tablet market, and about buyer behaviour. The major approach to segmentation was based upon age groups, following a pattern as follows:

- 3–12: high per-capita consumption from both own purchases and those of parents.
- 12–24: decline of per-capita consumption.
- 24 onwards: per-capita consumption increases because as parents they buy chocolate for their children, which leads to increases in their own consumption.
- Once children become teenagers, parental consumption declines as their children's consumption declines.

Additional segmentation was based on tourism and exports. In the former sales were particularly important, with tourists from Germany, France, Britain, and the United States being of major significance. Exports were also important to the industry in that they represented about 17% of sales, although the case study does not give a breakdown by country, so that geographical segmentation cannot be specified.

The four indications about buyer behaviour relate to both retailers and consumers. Swiss grocery chain retailers allocated considerably more shelf space to chocolate products than did retailers in other countries. As these stores were, at the time of the case study, gaining an increasing proportion of retail sales to the detriment of small retailers, this resulted in increased promotion of chocolate products. In return retailers expected a 20% margin as well as quantity discounts. Retailer buyer behaviour was also now looking to develop private brands to be sold in competition with manufacturers' brands. Consumer buyer behaviour was geared to 20 brands presented under the Cailler and Nestlé family brand names and sold in several sizes. Although retail prices of the four largest manufacturers (including Nestlé) were significantly higher than those of Migros, the previously given market share figures suggest that price is perhaps less important than other marketing variables in the buying decisions, or at least for certain other segments of the tablet market.

INTEGRATIVE CASE ILLUSTRATION: PART TWO

The integrative case study features many of the environmental issues that have been faced by Plessey. These are presented as historical issues for the two major periods of 1974–9 and 1980–3, as well as issues that were pertinent to the current strategic management decision-making. The following illustration combines strategic audits and market structures as given in Chapters 3 and 5, which is labelled general environment, but gives separate treatment to competitors.

GENERAL ENVIRONMENT

During the 1960s Plessey participated in two major industries, that of telecommunications and that of defence. In the case of the latter we are told that the Government was the only British customer, while buyer behaviour was exercised through the Ministry of Defence as the purchaser within the defence policies established by the Government. During the 1960s Plessey's markets in telecommunications were dominated by the Post Office (now British Telecom), although annual growth in market size averaged 18%. Supplies agreements had existed whereby the Government shared its orders between Plessey and its major competitors GEC and STC on a 40:40:20 basis, respectively. However when this agreement was dropped, Plessey achieved a market share of 44%.

Internally the Plessey environment in the 1960s had featured a lack of foresight in strategic planning which, it is reported, resulted in the wrong product mix for the next decade, an orientation towards products as opposed to markets, an inappropriate organizational structure in relation to management style, and the establishment of inadequate criteria for the acquisition of companies. By 1973 this weakness in strategic planning was exacerbated by two further environmental issues. Externally rapid changes in technology were taking place which were making Plessey's products obsolete. Internally, and as a result of the latter, the product portfolio was not generating sufficient cash to invest in new product development, while the increasing size and complexity of the organization meant that changes in management style and organizational structure were needed. By 1974 there were nine major product divisions: telecommunications; radar; communications and marine; industrial electronics; dynamics; electronic subsystems; contract and supply; electrical components; and consumer electronics. However telecommunications represented the largest generator of sales and profits.

In 1974 the remote environment of Plessey featured high inflation, recession, punitive taxation, high interest rates, the erosion of British competitiveness abroad, and the oil crisis. In addition major threats from the operating environment were imminent public spending cuts, cuts in Post Office expenditure, reduced profit margins, and the possibility of the nationalization of Plessey's activities.

Export sales in 1974 accounted for 35% of total sales, while profits achieved from these sales accounted for 32% of total profits. However, in the telecommunications industry the influence of the buyer behaviour of the Post Office had a detrimental effect on export sales. Product specifications required by the Post Office were often not acceptable in export markets and Plessey was forced into developing new products to satisfy the requirements of world markets.

Market potential for telecommunications in the 1980s was instigated through a programme for the modernization of British telecommunications. This was to be named System X and was to be manufactured by Plessey, GEC and STC. This new computerized system would be more efficient than existing equipment, although it would be compatible with it. System X would also feature benefits of adaptability to regional requirements, in-service flexibility, and would allow for easy growth.

By 1980 the remote environment was exacerbated by escalating inflation, a major engineering strike, escalating interest rates, a strengthening pound, and a deepening recession throughout the Western economies.

COMPETITORS

The case study reports that Plessey competed with four major organizations. In the telecommunications industry there was STC and GEC, while in defence there was Ferranti, Racal and GEC. At the time Plessey could be ranked as the second largest organization after GEC, as indicated by the measures for 1982 shown in Table 5.3. Several criticisms were made concerning the competitiveness of Plessey:

- It was slower than its competitors in adapting new technology to its products.
- Profits earned in the 1960s had not been used to develop products to meet the needs of world markets.
- It had not fully exploited market growth but had merely been influenced by market trends.
- If the company had been 'managed better' then it could have achieved more business and greater profits, which instead had been achieved by competitors.

The case study gives some information, albeit limited, on these competitors.

GEC

The major strength of GEC is obviously its size relative to other competitors. It was structured into six autonomous divisions or SBUs, but featured many product-market scopes from computers, through TV cameras and avionics, to telecommunications. Although little growth in sales volume

Table 5.3 *Sales and assets of Plessey and its competitors, 1982.*

	Sales (£m)	Tangible net assets (£m)
GEC	4,626	2,623
Plessey	1,074	418
Racal	764	466
STC	629	226
Ferranti	372	129

over the five years up to the case study had been achieved, profit margins had been increased.

STC

As a subsidiary of ITT, this competitor had access to ITT's R&D operations. Although sales volume had expanded since 1974 profits had marginally declined, while it relied on British markets for 80% of its business. Although initially involved with System X, it withdrew at the end of 1979.

Ferranti

Almost half of Ferranti's business was achieved in the defence industry. It had achieved a competitive advantage from technological leads over competitors. Indeed this had resulted in sustained profit growth as the firm began to dominate markets where technology was more important than price. Long production runs were also established, which had contributed to this trend.

Racal

This organization was recorded as being the 'outstanding performer in the electronics and electrical sector' and had achieved 'an excellent record of sales and profit growth'. Racal had concentrated on a limited product range, but successful marketing had achieved this growth. However, additional products were being developed, which were also contributing to growth.

Plessey and its competitors compared

Indications of Plessey's performance in comparison to these firms are available from the case study. However, these are limited to profit margins for 1982 and a 'crude' measure of profitability by relating pre-tax profits to tangible net assets. These comparisons are shown in Table 5.4. Plessey's profit margin compares favourably with that of its competitors, and this particular measure of profitability is superior to the others. However, the case study reports that half the profits came from a build-up of cash generated by mature products. Also, low-technology business with low profits had been eliminated and the work-force had been reduced by a quarter, which had also boosted profits. Despite this situation profits for 1982 showed a significant increase on previous years. Although these figures do give a comparison they are inadequate on two grounds. First, they are only for a single year and the trend over several years would clearly be more meaningful. Second, this measure of profitability is limited as more concise measures can be made. These measures will be examined in Chapter 14.

Table 5.4 *Profitability of Plessey and its competitors, 1982.*

	Profit margin (%)	Profitability (%)
GEC	14.5	25.6
Plessey	13.7	35.0
Racal	15.0	24.5
STC	3.3	28.5
Ferranti	8.4	24.3

A final point on competition comes from one of the senior directors of Plessey during the mid-1980s. According to him, Plessey had perceived that the nature of global competition was changing, in that it was now competing with several large multinational corporations. A reaction to this change in rivalry was to consider joint ventures to acquire new skills and technologies for further competitive action.

REFERENCES

1. Bates, D. L. and Eldredge, D. L., *Strategy and Policy*, 2nd edn, Wm. C. Brown, Dubuque, OH, 1984.
2. Porter, M. E., *Competitive Strategy: Techniques for Analyzing Industries and Competitors*, The Free Press, New York, 1980.
3. Ansoff, H. I., *Implanting Strategic Management*, Prentice Hall, Englewood Cliffs, NJ, 1984.
4. Rink, D. R. and Swan, J. E., 'Product Life Cycle Research: A Literature Review', *Journal of Business Research*, September 1979, 219–42.
5. Baker, M. J., *Marketing Strategy and Management*, Macmillan, London, 1985.
6. Oliver, G., *Marketing Today*, 2nd edn, Prentice Hall, London, 1986.
7. Primeaux, W. J., 'A Method for Determining Strategic Groups and Life Cycle Stages of an Industry' in H. Thomas and D. Gardner (eds), *Strategic Marketing Management*, Wiley, Chichester, 1985.
8. Van Duijn, J. J., *The Long Wave in Economic Life*, Allen and Unwin, 1983.
9. Greenley, G. E., 'An Understanding of Marketing Strategy', *European Journal of Marketing*, **18**, 6/7, 90–103.
10. Hlavacek, J. D. and Reddy, N. M., 'Identifying and Qualifying Industrial Market Segments', *European Journal of Marketing*, **20**, 2, 1986, 8–21.

11. Kotler, P., *Marketing Management: Analysis, Planning and Control*, Prentice Hall, Englewood Cliffs, NJ, 1984.
12. Day, G. S., 'Strategic Market Analysis and Definition: An Integrated Approach', *Strategic Management Journal*, 2, 1981, 281–99.
13. Watkins, T., *The Economics of the Brand*, McGraw-Hill, Maidenhead, 1981.
14. Wilson, J. H., *Microeconomics: Concepts and Applications*, Harper and Row, New York, 1981.
15. Greenley, G. E., 'The Company and Its Customers: A Marketing Model', *Quarterly Review of Marketing*, 8, 1, 1982, 13–18.
16. Lancaster, K., *Introduction to Modern Microeconomics*, Rand McNally, Chicago, 1969.
17. Chisnall, P. M., *Marketing: A Behavioural Analysis*, 2nd edn, McGraw-Hill, Maidenhead, 1985.
18. Foxall, G. R., *Consumer Choice*, Macmillan, London, 1983.
19. Williams, T. G., *Consumer Behaviour: Fundamentals and Strategies*, West, St Paul, MN, 1982.
20. Murphy, P. E. and Enis, B. M., *Marketing*, Scott, Foresman and Company, Glenview, IL, 1985.
21. Maslow, A. J., *Motivation and Personality*, Harper and Row, New York, 1954.
22. Engel, J. F. and Blackwell, R. D., *Consumer Behaviour*, 4th edn, Dryden, Hinsdale, NY, 1982.
23. Engel, J. F., Kollat, D. F. and Blackwell, R. D., *Consumer Behaviour*, Dryden, Hinsdale, New York, 1978.
24. Howard, J. A. and Ostlund, L., *Buyer Behaviour: Theoretical and Empirical Foundations*, Knopf, New York, 1973.
25. Nicosia, F. M., *Consumer Processes: Marketing and Advertising Implications*, Prentice Hall, Englewood Cliffs, NJ, 1969.
26. Andreason, A. R., 'Attitudes and Consumer Behaviour: A Decision Model' in L. E. Preston (ed.), *New Research in Marketing*, Institute of Business and Economic Research, Berkeley, CA, 1965.
27. Hutt, M. D. and Speh, T. W., *Industrial Marketing Management: A Strategic View of Business Markets*, 2nd edn, Dryden, New York, 1984.
28. Cravens, D. W. and Woodruff, R. B., *Marketing*, Addison-Wesley, Reading, MA, 1986.

Planning Direction

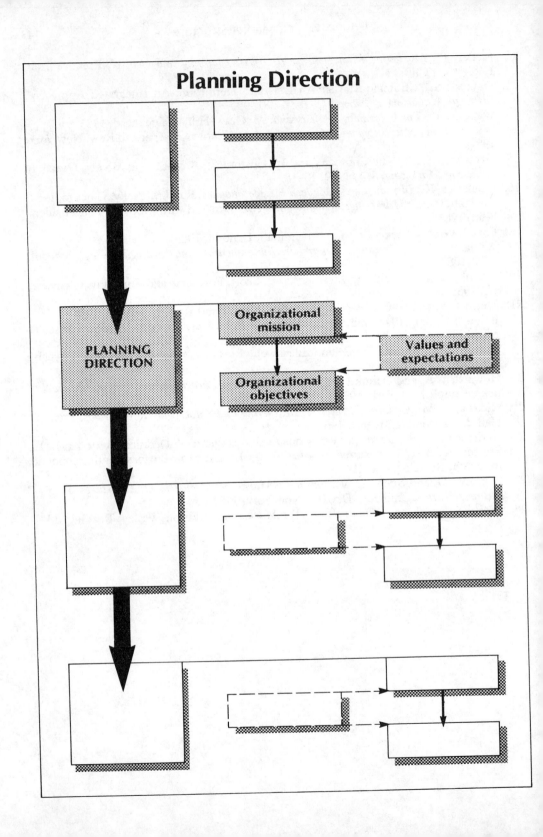

PLANNING DIRECTION

Organizational mission

Values and expectations

Organizational objectives

PART THREE

PLANNING DIRECTION

OUTLINE OF PART THREE

Part Three is concerned with the nature of the direction to be pursued rather than means of achievement. The future direction needs to be determined from the multiplicity of variables to be found in the environment, by expounding aims to be pursued. In simple terms the outcome of this part of strategic management should be that levels of performance to be achieved over the long term should be specified. This not only serves to give vision and definition to company direction but also provides a basis for strategy selection and subsequent implementation (to be addressed in Parts Four and Five, respectively). Broad indications of direction are initially considered in Chapter 6, where the organizational mission is established. This provides the overall purpose and philosophy of the company, plus broad areas of industry participation. From the mission detailed organizational objectives are determined, which is the subject of Chapter 7. It is here that levels of performance to be pursued are specified. Like all aspects of strategic management the values and expectations of managers are a central influence in determining direction, and these are addressed in Chapter 8.

CHAPTER 6   ORGANIZATIONAL MISSION
CHAPTER 7   ORGANIZATIONAL OBJECTIVES
CHAPTER 8   VALUES AND EXPECTATIONS

CHAPTER 6
ORGANIZATIONAL MISSION

The organizational mission represents the first stage in planning direction, as established in the model of strategic management presented in Chapter 1. The overall aim of the organizational mission is to encapsulate the whole purpose and philosophy of the organization, as well as to provide broad indications of direction. This chapter examines an approach to be taken in formulating the mission, but also discusses the major internal and external influences on its formulation. The overall aim of this chapter is to not only discuss the nature of the mission but to also prepare the reader for the other stages of the strategic management process.

The organizational mission can be considered to be a statement or formal explanation of the nature of the business in which a firm participates. For some firms it may be a simple sentence such as to make money or maximize profits, as based on the traditional reason that the discipline of economics has given for firms being in business. For other firms it will be a more comprehensive explanation.

The complexities associated with business environments have led to a need for a more comprehensive and meaningful reason, which has resulted in the utilization of mission statements. As will be seen later in this chapter, several features can be incorporated into the mission statement to make it comprehensive and meaningful. However, the major aims of the mission should be that it gives overall purpose and direction to the company; it should thus distinguish it from other firms and outline the range of businesses or SBUs for potential participation. The first section of this chapter looks at how an organizational mission can be formulated.

The mission statement should encompass the core of the firm's reason for being in existence. As such many groups of people associated with the firm will have a vested interest in the nature of its business, its future direction, the areas of business or SBUs into which it is likely to develop, and its competitive standing. These groups of people have come to be known as 'stakeholders', so that the second section of this chapter looks at the various stakeholder groups. One other area of consideration is also of importance. This is the firm's responsibility to society as a whole, which needs to be reflected in the mission statement. Therefore social responsibility is examined in the final section.

FORMULATING THE MISSION STATEMENT

In this section it is necessary to differentiate between the reasons why an organizational mission is needed and the criteria that can be used for writing and formulating the mission statement. Both are essential. As will be already evident, the mission is the logical starting point of strategic management, so that careful attention needs to be given to the core of the firm's reason for being in business, as it affects the other stages of strategic management. Although the statement does not include detailed specifications that feature in the other component parts of strategic management, the lack of detail is intentional. Although broad, implied and all-encompassing statements may be criticized for their lack of clarity and directness, attention to the criteria of formulation (to be discussed later in this section) will contribute to a meaningful statement that becomes an essential part of the process.

David[1] has suggested two main reasons why the mission statement needs to be broad. The first is that it allows for greater scope and flexibility to develop alternative strategies and objectives and particularly to allow for several alternative growth opportunities. The other reason is that it will allow for the satisfaction of the needs of the many groups of people who are involved with an organization —an issue that will be addressed later in this chapter. However, statements which are too broad with little focus will be of little use, but attention to the criteria of formulation should overcome such weaknesses.

EXHIBIT 6.1

Moët Vuitton's Joint Vintage

The press recently reported the merger of two famous French companies, Louis Vuitton and Moët Hennessy. The new company's products are champagne, cognac, luggage, roses, and perfume. Its brand names are Dom Perignon, Veuve Clicquot, Moët et Chandon, Mercier, Hennessy, Hine, Vuitton, Dior and Givenchy. Its business is world-wide participation in top-of-the-line luxury goods, which are French in origin and nature. Its target is people who aspire for increasing materialism and who wish to demonstrate their own acquired materialism with expensive brands featuring expensive images. The new group will aim to create power to dominate the businesses in which it participates.

Adapted from *Management Today*, November 1987

A main feature, which was developed in the early writings on business policy, is that the statement should be a vehicle to help focus the total organization on the requirements of customers, rather than being in the business of manufacturing to a particular technology. Levitt[2], for example, stressed that business success is based on the ability to define the business in terms of customer needs rather than on manufacturing or servicing capability. Although this approach is simple in its conception, history is replete with examples of companies having foundered because of a failure to take such an approach.

Reasons for the organizational mission

King and Cleland[3] have listed reasons for establishing a mission statement. Similarly, Greenley[4] has discussed the aims of having a mission, although this was to show how marketing orientation is applicable to strategic planning. These aims are listed in Table 6.1.

Table 6.1 *Reasons for the organizational mission.*

Unanimity of purpose
Resource utilization
Company climate and philosophy
Long-range vision
Business domain specification
Market-base orientation
Motivation of personnel

Unanimity of purpose
The first aim is specification of the broad industries that are currently seen to be those in which the firm will participate, even if they are not current ventures. This gives direction by the nature of the business and, although for some firms it may mean no change from a single industry, for others it may mean business potential in other sectors. This aspect means that all executives can be made aware of such intentions.

Resource utilization
As a consequence of purpose the mission also allows for an initial overview of the directions in which resources are to be utilized. It may provide the impetus to consolidate use in certain sectors, or it may provide the motivation to acquire additional resources to pursue business potential in other sectors.

Company climate and philosophy
The mission provides a starting point for the whole ethos of the running of the company. It needs to epitomize the values, beliefs and guidelines that are to be the business culture and which will regulate the behaviour of the company. Social responsibility and business policy, which represent the overall approach to external and internal environments, respectively, should be included. Further attention is given to both these issues later in this chapter.

Long-range vision

A major reason for having a mission is to provide a starting point for thinking beyond current business involvement, allowing for the development of a scenario that will provide future aspirations. Such a feature goes beyond forecasts from current data bases, requiring inspirational thinking, entrepreneurial flair and 'gut feeling' for long-range opportunities.

Business domain specification

Abell[5] has suggested that the organizational mission can be more effective if it is specific rather than consisting merely of broad statements; customer groups to be served and customer needs to be met should be included. The objection to such detail at this early stage of strategic management is that it becomes too restrictive and can immediately mean that some business opportunities may be lost. Rather, the business domain should be broad in nature to avoid the restriction of opportunities. This issue will be examined further in relation to formulation criteria.

Market-base orientation

As mentioned in the introduction to this section, this feature of the mission is to provide an initial and overall focus on customers. Customers should be put at the centre of the business, so that the total organization can develop an orientation towards satisfying their requirements. This is also the concept of marketing orientation, which needs to provide an overall philosophy to the company, as well as a basis for the marketing operations.

Motivation of personnel

Here the principle is that the mission statement should be able to encompass the nature of the company's business in a format which is readily available to and is easily understood by personnel. Motivation is encouraged in that such a situation should allow personnel to understand the direction in which the company is going, as well as the way in which their roles relate to this overall direction.

Formulation criteria

In this section attention is given to the writing of mission statements. The aim of this section is to feature those criteria that should be considered in formulating the statement. These criteria should provide guidance in formulation, but without causing rigid constraints on the statement, as the latter have been seen to run the risk of stifling creativity in business enterprise. However, this range of criteria should provide guidelines within which creative thinking and entrepreneurial flair can be accommodated, allowing for richness in organizational development.

Two types of criterion are pertinent. The first are those to be included in the statement, while the other criteria are those which are likely to influence the formulation. Criteria to be included in the mission have been given by Pearce and

Robinson[6] which were developed from an earlier work by Pearce[7]. Both types are given in Table 6.2. The case-study illustration for this chapter discusses some of these criteria.

Table 6.2 *Formulation criteria.*

Criteria to be included in the organizational mission
- Basic product/service definition
- Definition of customers and markets
- Technology
- Growth and profitability
- Company philosophy
- Social responsibility and public image

Criteria influencing organizational mission
- Company history
- Distinctive competences
- Opportunities and threats
- Resource availability

Criteria to be included in the organizational mission

Basic product/service definition. The mission statement needs to reflect the broad product base which is likely to encompass the customer base to be pursued. At this stage of strategic management it should merely represent the broad business or industries in which the company desires to participate over the long term. These considerations obviously relate closely to markets to be served, and, indeed, markets should perhaps be given first consideration. However, organizations start the next period of their history from experience of past and current technology, which must influence future business development.

Definition of customers and markets. This reinforces a basic tenet of strategic management, which is defining the total organization in terms of customer requirements rather than of the product or service itself. A statement in terms of the transportation business gives orientation to customer requirements to satisfy such needs, which would not be achieved if the company were defined in terms of car manufacture. This criterion may seem to be in conflict with that of product/service definition. However, as will be seen in the development of organizational strategy in Chapter 10, these two concepts are combined to form the concept of product-market scope, which is a major consideration in strategy development.

Technology. While current technology may dominate the overall nature of an organization, over the long term new developments are likely to make existing technology obsolete. This may be either the technology associated with product performance or that which determines the nature of the manufacturing process. Here the point is that the mission should not necessarily constrain the future to current technology, while orientation to customers and markets reinforces this point.

Growth and profitability. The mission needs to reflect aspirations for growth and profitability. Growth can be measured in several ways, including market share, sales volume, production output and product range. At this stage of strategic management it is likely that only one or two measures will be used. Here the requirement is to give direction on the general rate of growth and the ultimate size seen to be valid for the future. For some firms only modest rates of growth may be applicable, or stability may be the preferred future posture. Specific rates of growth will be defined in organizational objectives (see Chapter 7), while further attention follows in planning organizational strategy (see Chapter 10).

Similarly, broad and general attention to profitability may be given in the mission, while specific levels will be given in the objectives. It is likely that profitability will vary across the product range, and the potential for profitability improvement is likely to be different in each of the SBUs served. However, given the obvious importance of profitability, it is recommended that it should be considered in the mission to provide overall direction.

Company philosophy. Although philosophy was given as a reason for needing a mission, a reflection of the managerial culture and ethos needs to be included in the statement. This aspect will provide a basis for developing guidelines for the way that the company is to be run internally and can reflect the attitudes and beliefs of senior managers as the official *modus operandi*.

Social responsibility and public image. Part of the statement should demonstrate the acceptance of responsibility for all actions that are taken and decisions that are made. Such responsibility includes product reliability, efficiency of operations and general relationships within the societies in which the company operates. Fuller consideration is given to these responsibilities later in this chapter.

Public image is concerned with the communication of the acceptance of these responsibilities to the general public. Here the emphasis in the statement would be a commitment that such communications will be forthcoming. Such a commitment often leads to corporate advertising, to be used in conjunction with product advertising, the latter being part of the marketing operations.

Criteria likely to influence the organizational mission

Company history. Where there is a long history of involvement in a particular industry changing direction may be problematic, with two major ramifications. Physical resources will have been established for participation in that industry so that any modifications to direction may not be compatible with current resources. Also, the expertise and capabilities of managers will be imbued with knowledge, norms and practices within that industry. Here the implication is that it may be difficult to instigate and implement any changes in direction where there is such a company culture. This is not to say that the organizational mission should cause a change in direction, but that an introverted approach may lead to lost opportunities.

Distinctive competences. This influence develops out of special strengths or abilities that the company has acquired which differentiate it from its competitors. Full consideration of the understanding of competitors was given in Chapter 4 and the issues that were discussed there are applicable here. Competences can range from being ahead in product technology, through efficiency in production processes, to marketing strengths such as high market shares or high brand loyalty. The premiss is that such competences should be exploited, to gain competitive advantage, so that they should logically influence the direction to be outlined in the mission statement. However, the exploitation of such advantages also needs to be related to orientation towards market and customer needs. Efficient production processes will be of little value in a market where consumer demand for the products that it produces has declined.

Opportunities and threats. Analysis of the total environment in which organizations are located was the subject of Part Two. In simple terms, the mission will need to give direction for the pursuit of pertinent opportunities, or may need to instigate a change in direction to avoid the threat of, say, declining markets in a particular SBU. Like competences, opportunities and threats can be identified in several areas. Marketing opportunities and threats from competitive actions are obvious examples, but others can range from a skilled labour force, or, conversely, chronic industrial relations problems, to availability of capital investment from a parent company or a lack of capital to introduce new production plant.

Resource availability. There is probably little point in attempting to broaden the market base if there is little chance of obtaining the necessary resources. Consequently, analysis of the financial structure in the strategic audit (see Chapter 3) will give guidance on such decisions. However for some companies it may be realistic to establish a broad market base in the mission, as the detailed costing of strategy selection needed to pursue such an extension is completed later in the strategic management process (see Chapter 11).

STAKEHOLDER INFLUENCE

In Part Two attention was given to the environment in which organizations operate. There the emphasis was on the collection and analysis of information pertaining to all aspects of the environment, with the aim of providing understanding for effective decision-making in strategic management. Another way of understanding the total environment is to perceive it as being constituted of many groups of people. Several of these groups will be able to influence the behaviour of organizations, while some groups can be influenced by particular organizations. Taylor[8] cites the viewpoint expressed in the 1970s by the Stanford Research Institute: organizations have many obligations to many groups of people beyond their shareholders and customers. The consequence is that firms need also to focus their attention on groups that have an interest in them, have a claim to the way they operate or are able to influence their behaviour. Such groups of people have been labelled 'stakeholders', with Freeman[9] defining a stakeholder as being any group or individual who can affect or is affected by the achievement of an organization's purpose. Some stakeholders may therefore influence organizational mission, but may also be influenced by its resultant utilization. Similarly, some stakeholders will be able to influence other stages of strategic management, while others will be influenced by their resultant utilization. However, an important concept for firms is the establishment of the legitimacy of any stake or influence that specific groups may claim to have. Where legitimacy is identified then satisfaction of stakes or claims needs to be pursued, just as the needs of customers are pursued, while legitimate influences on performance must also be accommodated.

Classifying stakeholders

Several writers have attempted to classify stakeholders by merely listing different groups that have the potential to affect, or be affected by, organizations. An approach taken by Greenley[4] was to classify stakeholders into several groups within three broad assemblages (see Figure 6.1).

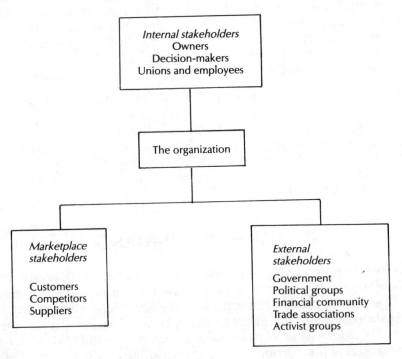

Figure 6.1 *Classification of stakeholders (G. E. Greenley,* The Strategic and Operational Planning of Marketing, © *1986. Adapted by permission of McGraw-Hill Ltd.)*

Internal stakeholders
A major influence here is the split of power between the owners of a company and the executives who are responsible for major strategic management decisions. Where ownership is widely dispersed among many shareholders then decision-making power is likely to lie with company executives. However, in situations where ownership is concentrated, for example family-owned businesses or owner-

ship by a parent company, then this concentration can influence the internal decision-making process.

In addition to the influence caused by the split of ownership, the personal values and expectations of decision-makers constitute another stakeholder influence. Personal aspirations for career enhancement, job security and family quality of life are all part of the make-up of managers and such traits are likely to have an influence on strategic management decisions. The importance of these influences is reflected in the fuller attention given to values and expectations in Chapter 8.

Similarly, the values and expectations of other employees, and any unions or associations which represent their interests, represent another stake which needs to be accommodated. There is obviously wide variation among companies in the power that such groups have been able to achieve to influence strategic management decisions, as well as the degree of power that companies allow such groups. Further attention is given to these issues in Chapter 13.

Marketplace stakeholders

This assemblage consists of groups that both affect and are affected by an organization. The expectations and behaviour of both customers and competitors are obviously of central importance to the total *modus operandi*, but are particularly central in developing the company to serving the requirements of the markets to be served. Marketing orientation is also of particular importance here; this will be examined further in Chapter 12.

The influence of suppliers can be conceptualized as being twofold. The organizational aspirations and expectations of suppliers are obviously central in negotiations for components and materials, but the quality and reliability of these will also affect the final product and, in turn, the ability of these final products to satisfy customer requirements.

External stakeholders

This assemblage, for a particular organization, is meant to include any groups that have the potential to cause some effect on that company. Indeed the range of potential groups could exceed those given in Figure 6.1. While the general economic and political policies of governments will affect companies in general, specific policies relating to specific industries or consumer interests will have direct effects on certain companies. However, the overall principle is that of a general and continuous appraisal of the external environment, as discussed in Chapter 3.

Analysis of stakeholder influences

Owing to the diversity of stakeholder groups, as shown in Figure 6.1, the methodologies for the analysis of the potential influence of stakeholder groups is equally diverse. Some of the groups have been tackled in the literature. Customers have obviously received the greatest attention, with the whole of the marketing literature being devoted to their dispositions. Research into buyer behaviour is of particular importance, with major texts such as that by Chisnall[10] contributing to this understanding. The consequences of buyer behaviour have already been tackled in Chapter 5, where the understanding of market structures was examined. Methodology devoted to understanding the potential influences of competitors has been given recent attention. Porter[11] has proposed a methodology for identifying the major forces exhibited by competitive organizations as well as the likely impact of these forces. The work of Porter and others who have developed the literature on competitors was discussed in Chapter 4.

A general methodology for the understanding of stakeholder groups *per se* has been prescribed by Rowe *et al.*[12]. This approach is based on an assumption that the current organization is the resultant outcome of previous supporting and resisting forces of the various stakeholder groups, while its future posture will be the result of the cumulative effect of potential supporting and resisting forces of stakeholders. Consequently, the validity of strategic management for the next period of time will be dependent on assumptions which the organization makes about the potential influences of its stakeholders.

The method which they give★ is generic in nature, but is aimed at developing assumptions about stakeholder groups, which will become part of the data base for decision making. The method is comprised of the following:

Stakeholder identification
An exhaustive search to identify stakeholder groups, both the obvious and those which may be likely to become prominent. Checklists can be referred to, such as that given in Figure 6.1 or those given in other strategic management books.

Surfacing assumptions
Here it is suggested that assumptions should be developed for each stakeholder group, within the context of either a proposed strategy for the coming period or as an input to a new strategy where this has not been planned. Although the principle on which both these situations should be assessed is simple in concept, assessments in practice are likely to be complex, although information for these assessments can be drawn from the strategic audit data base as discussed in Chapter 3.

Where a strategy has been proposed assumptions about each stakeholder group are surfaced by asking what are the most plausible assumptions that must be made about each stakeholder in order for the strategy to be successful. Where a strategy has not been proposed the question to be asked is what are the most plausible assumptions to make about each stakeholder. All assumptions should then be classified as either supporting/driving forces or resisting/constraining forces.

Assumption rating
This stage is concerned with determining the relative degree of importance of each

★Rowe, Mason, Dickel, *Strategic Management: A Methodological Approach*, © 1986. Addison-Wesley Publishing Co. Inc., Reading, MA, pages 107–9 – reproduced with permission.

of the assumptions. Two numerical scores are given to each assumption, one for importance on a scale from 0 (unimportant) to 9 (very important), and the other for certainty or reliability of the assumption on a scale from 0 (very uncertain) to 9 (very certain). Such quantification is obviously subjective and relies on the information obtained about each stakeholder group. However, the aim is to focus attention on those forces or influences that are likely to be extremely beneficial or detrimental.

Implications of influences

If the supporting forces outweigh the resisting forces then the resultant influence is likely to be beneficial. However such a simple balancing of forces is unlikely to be of great value in itself; subsequent strategic management decisions must seek to take advantage of supporting forces and seek to overcome the resisting forces.

Managing stakeholders

Having followed the analysis of the potential influences of stakeholders, companies then need to assess how they are to react to or manage these forces. The management of stakeholder groups has been addressed by MacMillan and Jones[13], who classify all groups as being either internal or external stakeholders. At this juncture of the book attention is given only to external groups as internal stakeholder management is discussed in Chapter 13.

The basis of an organization's management of external stakeholders is the power and influence that it is able to create and sustain with respect to the groups that it needs to react to or manage. In tackling this management MacMillan and Jones suggest four dimensions as options to be taken in reacting to external stakeholder groups.

Target of action

Depending upon the number of forces that are identified in the analysis of stakeholders, decisions must be made concerning those on which action must be directed. This will depend upon both the magnitude of each group's influence and the number of such groups which have been identified. While essential action may be necessary to counteract resisting forces of, say, an imminent new product launch by a major competitor, action may also need to be targeted towards exploiting supporting forces of, say, increased support from a trade association to exploit export markets. However, limited resources, including time and effort, may preclude action towards certain groups.

Direct or indirect actions

The company may act directly by introducing new competitive products or by negotiating with agents to develop new distribution channels. Where resisting forces are important from, say, activist groups, it may be necessary to operate indirectly through a public relations campaign, or by encouraging retailers or distributors to improve their communications skills with final customers.

Manipulative or accommodative action

Manipulation is concerned with the use of political power to coerce the resisting forces of a stakeholder group. Suppliers may be 'forced' to improve deliveries through threats of alternative suppliers, while competitors may be 'forced' into a premature new product launch by competitive product benefit enhancement. Accommodative action can be either by joint agreement with the threatening group, by co-optation, such as including unions in decision-making, or by coalescence, such as a merger by two competitors.

Action by structural changes

If the organization is unable to overcome competitors then it may decide to cease its business in that particular SBU. Similarly, chronic problems with unions may lead to a decision to abandon traditional work practices and to establish new, union-free operations. These are examples of attempts to manage detrimental influences of particular stakeholder groups by changing a basic structure.

Stakeholder responses to management

The final consideration of stakeholder influence is how they are likely to react to any attempts to manage their influence. Stakeholder responses that are likely to be experienced have also been given by MacMillan and Jones[13], developed from the earlier work by MacMillan et al.[14]. In assessing likely responses they suggest that the following should be considered:

- Previous objectives of the stakeholder organization and the form that they are likely to take in the future; aggressive growth, for example, would allow for little control of their influences.
- Likely deployment of resources with levels of commitment that are likely to be pursued in the future.
- Stakeholders' satisfaction with the status quo and any likely shift in the company's organizational mission.
- Appraisals of strengths and weaknesses, with a resultant appraisal of stakeholders' ability to counterattack attempts at managing their influence.
- The possibility of major retalitary action leading to battles of attrition.
- Potential inhibitions to retalitary action, such as other major problems, perception of little threat, or attention being directed towards new and major opportunities.
- The likely internal political turmoil that could ensue as a result of tackling influences from other organizations.

SOCIAL RESPONSIBILITY

Earlier in this chapter, when attention was given to formulating the organizational mission, social responsibility was given as a criterion which can be included in the mission statement. Here the implication was that part of the mission statement should demonstrate the acceptance of responsibility for actions taken and decisions made, such as product liability, efficiency of operations, and general relationships within the societies in which the firm operates.

Defining social responsibility

Davis and Blomstrom[15] have defined social responsibility as 'the obligation of decision makers to take actions which protect and improve the welfare of society as a whole, along with their own interests'. Here the emphasis can be seen as an extension of the stakeholder concept in that the firm needs to address itself to the well-being of society as a whole, as well as to specific and identifiable groups of people. However, the definition strongly points to a balance between the interests of the firm and the interests of society. In theory these should be compatible. Detrimental company actions, such as poor product reliability, are likely to be unacceptable to the society, which will lead to unacceptable company performance. Similarly, short-term costs associated with public relations and advertising activities may be an initial burden, but accurate communication of concern for the general public is likely to enhance the general business environment through an improved corporate image, leading to improved company performance.

EXHIBIT 6.2

Fiat's Italian Job

Despite near bankruptcy in the 1970s, the Italian car company Fiat is again successful in the late 1980s. To demonstrate its social responsibility, Fiat is financing the restoration of historic buildings in northern Italy. The first was the building in Turin which had previously housed their Lingotto plant, and which had been closed in 1982. This was developed into a complex of apartments with gardens and courtyards, Turin's foremost exhibition centre and the national museum of Italian radio and television. In Turin Fiat have also financed the restoration of the former palace of the House of Savoy and the Royal hunting lodge at Stupinigi. In Venice they have restored the Palazzo Grassi, a neo-classical building by the Grand Canal. The most ambitious project is to transform the dreary Novoli area near Florence, where it has a components factory employing 1,000 people, into a vibrant satellite town.

Adapted from *Business*, February 1987

In addition to any concern for the balancing of interests there is also the moral issue of decision-making. Here the implication is that decisions which enhance the interests of the firm but which are detrimental to the interests of the society, such as product degradation or reduced after-sales service, are perhaps immoral. However, determining what is right and what is wrong is subjective and likely to be situation-specific, as well as being relative to the interests of specific groups of people. Further attention will be given to this issue later in this section.

Ackerman[16] has identified certain managerial deterrents to the adequate consideration of social responsibility in strategic management decision-making. Of major concern is that social responsibility may be perceived as something additional to organizational management, so that only the interests of formidable stakeholder groups may be taken into account. Such a deterrent can be overcome by ensuring that the strategic audit (see Chapter 3) includes a broad survey of society, while specific organizational objectives addressing social responsibility are established (see Chapter 7) and by ensuring that decisions on strategy selection also include a consideration of social responsibility (see Chapter 11).

The other major deterrent is the managerial opinion that costs must be incurred in order to be socially responsible, leading to a reduction in profits. However, as already mentioned above, although the satisfying of such interests may mean initial costs, actions taken are likely to result in benefits. Indeed lack of action towards public interest may not only result in lost benefits, but may result in a detrimental corporate image which could lead to reduced performance.

Reacting to public interests

Chang and Campo-Flores[17] have discussed the problem of identifying the many and complex interests in society and those to which an organization should react. Given the obvious vast differences that exist among the products and services offered in Western Europe, the interests that a given firm needs to identify and react to are likely to be unique to that firm. However, these writers have suggested three broad areas of social responsibility in general:

- *Quality of life.* Concerned with the degree of harmony that people are able to achieve in their living environments. The major issues are health, safety, ecology and standards of living.
- *Human resource management.* Concerned with human dignity in all aspects of company practices. Internally this would include all relations with personnel, from conditions of employment to interpersonnel relationships. Externally this would include respect for and understanding of all individuals who come into contact with the firm.
- *Corporate power.* Although society is able, to a certain extent, to control the power of organizations, primarily through market forces and legislation, self-control of corporate power represents a socially responsible mode of operation on the part of organizations.

The extent to which organizations will react and assume responsibility within these broad areas and within their unique set of social interests will obviously vary. Johnson and Scholes[18] have identified four broad ways in which firms react to social responsibility, developed from research carried out by the European Foundation for Management Development and the European Institute for Advanced Studies in Management[19].

The first way is not to react or not to accept their social responsibility. This developed from the work of Friedman[20], who states that firms are only responsible for maximizing profits by developing their economic efficiency, while social responsibility is seen to lie with the government.

The second way is to select carefully only those aspects of social responsibility which are seen to be of direct long-term benefit. This could be to avoid potential legal conflicts or to achieve image advantages over competitors. The real reason to react is for personal gain.

The third way is that used by 'progressive' companies, which consider that a wide range of social issues are of central importance to their strategic management. Although this type of company would be prepared to forgo some profits in its acceptance of social responsibility, conflicts are likely to arise in this type of trade-off.

The fourth way is that of organizations whose sole purpose is to serve society and where the achievement of profits is only of secondary importance. Public services, charities and some nationalized industries take this approach, which is obviously of paramount importance to their organizational mission. Other firms that seek to take such an approach are, however, faced with the basic issue of balancing their own commercial interests with those of the society.

Major considerations

Following their discussion on the many interests of social responsibility, Chang and Campo-Flores[17] go on to suggest major considerations for strategic management.

Profit maximization

The requirement for organizations to be seen to be striving to achieve maximum profits is obviously entrenched within the foundations of the Western capitalist system. Reference has already been made to the work of Friedman[20] and his claim that profit maximization is the major responsibility of firms. Indeed the performance of companies and the executives who work in them is largely judged by the level of profits achieved.

However, this aim of maximization is easily challenged in that, at the end of a particular period, it is difficult, if not impossible, to know whether or not profits were actually maximized. Perhaps some costs could have been reduced or perhaps greater efforts would have yielded increased revenue. The reality is that performance is probably judged on a satisfactory level of profits, where satisfaction is set within the context of expectations which were developed from the previous year's performance, that of competitors, and current trading conditions. If adaptation to interests of society incurs additional costs then profits will not be maximized. However, such reductions may fall within expectations, particularly if the firm has addressed itself to social responsibility in the past.

Also to be considered is the level of profits to be pursued in relation to the products and services to be offered to consumers. For many organizations it will be market forces which will achieve the balance between the acceptability of product offerings, acceptable price levels, and profit margins to be achieved. However, where firms have sufficient power to reduce product quality, or to increase price, or to do both, then the issue of reacting responsibly is again prevalent.

Social values

Here the basic principle is that organizations are run by people, with the social values which companies adopt being reflective of those of the people who participate in the decision-making process. Values held by executives will be given full examination in Chapter 8. At this juncture in the book it is sufficient to say that differences in individuals' values will be discussed, values formed by coalitions will be promulgated, while compromises will be exercised to give the resultant set of values to be adopted by the organization. The relationship of these resultant values with the dominant values within the societies in which the organization operates is based upon two issues. First, the personal values of the company executives will have been influenced by the society in which the company is located, in that they, too, are part of the society. However, the second issue is that conflicts of values may develop, in that other values are developed which are specific to aspirations that will be included in the organizational objectives (see Chapter 7). Where such conflicts are imminent then judgements need to be made to pursue either these aspirations or the goal of social responsibility. Therefore the major consideration is potential conflict between values adopted by the organization and those of the societies in which it operates.

Ethics

Developing from the establishment of values is behaviour which has been influenced and directed by these values. Here the consideration is the rules of conduct practised by individuals and the firm as a whole. This moral behaviour needs to reflect that expected by the society, so that the firm is seen to be carrying-out its business properly and efficiently, while discharging the power that it is able to exert over the society in a responsible way. The pursuit of ethical behaviour stems not only from the values held in the company, but also from norms of behaviour that are established in the culture. Here the firm needs to consider differences in these norms that are to be found in the different countries in which it operates, as well as differences which may occur in subcultures that are a feature of each country.

Despite this perhaps self-evident need to ensure that business behaviour is couched in the ethical norms of society, little research appears to have attempted to investigate the relationship between attention to social responsibility and company performance. However, research in the United States by Aupperle et al.[21] found both profitable and marginally profitable companies that were both socially responsible and socially irresponsible.

SUMMARY

This chapter addressed the organizational mission as a statement or formal explanation of the nature of the business in which a firm participates. However, this was presented within the context of stakeholder expectations, and the external requirements of social responsibility.

In discussing the formulation of the mission statement two major areas were presented. The first considered the reasons why such a statement is needed, while the second tackled the criteria to be considered when actually formulating the mission. These criteria consist of issues that can be included in the actual statement, plus criteria that are likely to influence the formulation but which do not become part of the statement.

The next section of the chapter discussed the role of stakeholder and how they are able to influence not only the organizational mission, but also the other decision-making stages of strategic management. This section was comprised of a classification of the different groups of stakeholders, which was followed by an analysis of their potential influences. The final consideration was approaches that can be taken with the aim of managing these influences.

Attention was then directed to the pursuit of social responsibility. This entails identifying those issues to which a firm should react from the many complex interests to be found in society. This was followed by the major considerations of social responsibility that should be common to all organizations.

CHAPTER CASE STUDY ILLUSTRATION:
INTERNATIONAL COMPUTERS PLC (ICL) (A)*

In 1981 International Computers (ICL) was the third largest European computer manufacturing company in Europe, and the fourth largest in the

*Derived from the original case study by E. C. Lea and B. Kenny. Copyright © 1982.

world. However, the world market was dominated by IBM, which had a 52% market share in 1981, when this case study was written. The full case study traces the major strategic management decisions that were made as a result of trends in the world computer market, the needs of the British Government and the competitive strategies of IBM.

At the beginning of the case study the basis of ICL's organizational mission in 1968 is outlined with respect to purpose and resource utilization. The company had been created, in that year, by an amalgamation of several divisions of a number of firms, through the auspices of the British Government. The latter had established the mission of ICL to become a 'national champion' of sufficient size to compete with American multinational computer companies, especially IBM. This was underpinned by the provision of financial resources by the Government, in the form of both grants and the purchase of equity in ICL. These resources represented nearly 40% of its working capital at that time.

As a consequence of this purpose other features of the mission of the new company were established.

- *Definition of customers and markets.* ICL was to concentrate on specific industry/market sectors, especially central and local government, retailing, distribution and manufacturing.
- *Growth and profitability.* Here the mission was to double sales by 1978 with exports accounting for 50% of sales volume. Also, profitability was to be substantially improved.
- *Basic product/service definition.* This was defined as mass data storage with remote access, but with scope for future communications development. Additionally, the mission specified ICL's determination to 'provide in all aspects a service of the highest standard'.
- *Company philosophy.* It was decided that ICL would seek to meet all the data-processing needs of its customers by providing a total systems approach to its products and services. However, it would pursue selective improvements in the design of its computer systems, allowing for adaptations to and developments in the use of computers by its customers. This was consistent with the adoption of a new marketing orientation, following the appointment of a new managing director in 1972.
- *Technology.* The mission also included the goal of improved economies, through improvements in technology, which would be of mutual benefit to ICL and its customers.
- *Social responsibility and public image.* The major implication here is directed towards its customers. This mission criterion was couched in terms of the conservation of the investment that individual customers had made in the purchase of ICL computer systems. Such responsibility was also extended to allow them to upgrade, develop and extend these existing systems.

Despite the success of ICL during the 1970s, environmental variables led to the near-collapse of the company in 1980. Although the company was now in private ownership, the Government decided to guarantee loans up to a level of 63% of working capital at that time. These guarantees also allowed the Government to make senior management changes and a new managing director was appointed in 1981. Again the future mission was to be influenced by the availability of resources, while the ascendancy of the government as a major stakeholder is evident.

The new managing director introduced several modifications to the mission criteria which had already been established. He re-emphasized the requirement to safeguard customers' investments in ICL products. Internally the major mission criterion was to restore profitability by establishing it as being more important than growth. Product and service offerings were to be improved, which would include collaborative ventures. However, he identified the need to improve competence in reducing the time needed to develop new products and to launch them into the marketplace. Although this could introduce increased risk, the company was still to offer reliability in its products. Similarly, competence in greater speed to introduce technological developments would be needed, although increased risk could again be introduced. Indeed, the concept of 'managed risk' was to become part of the mission philosophy. Finally, the definition of customers and markets was epitomized in the selection of a business domain of 'information technology dependent on distributed computing and the convergence of telecommunications with information processing systems'.

REFERENCES

1. David, F. R., *Fundamentals of Strategic Management*, Merrill, Columbus, OH, 1986.
2. Levitt, T., 'Marketing Myopia', *Harvard Business Review*, **38**, 1960, 24–47.
3. King, W. R. and Cleland, D. I., *Strategic Planning*, Van Nostrand Reinhold, New York, 1979.
4. Greenley, G. E., *The Strategic and Operational Planning of Marketing*, McGraw-Hill, Maidenhead, 1986.
5. Abell, D. F., *Defining the Business: The Starting Point of Strategic Planning*, Prentice Hall, Englewood Cliffs, NJ, 1980.
6. Pearce, J. A. and Robinson, R. B., *Strategic Management: Strategy Formulation and Implementation*, Irwin, Homewood, IL, 1985.
7. Pearce, J. A., 'The Company Mission as a Strategic Tool', *Sloan Management Review*, Spring 1982, 15–24.
8. Taylor, B., 'Managing the Process of Corporate Development' in B. Taylor and J. R. Sparks (eds), *Corporate Strategy and Planning*, Heinemann, London, 1979.
9. Freeman, R. E., *Strategic Management*, Pitman, Boston, 1984.
10. Chisnall, P. M., *Marketing: A Behavioural Analysis*, McGraw-Hill, Maidenhead, 1985.
11. Porter, M. E., *Competitive Strategy: Techniques for Analyzing Industries and Competitors*, Free Press, New York, 1980.
12. Rowe, A. J., Mason, R. O. and Dickel, K. E., *Strategic Management: A Methodological Approach*, Addison-Wesley, Reading, MA, 1986.
13. MacMillan, I. C. and Jones, P. E., *Strategy Formulation: Power and Politics*, West, St Paul, MN, 1986.

14. MacMillan, I. C., McCaffery, M. L. and Van Wijk, G. L., 'Competitive Responses to Easily Initiate New Products', *Strategic Management Journal*, **6**, 1, 1985, 75–86.
15. Davis, K. and Blomstrom, R. L., *Business Society: Environment and Responsibility*, McGraw-Hill, New York, 1975.
16. Ackerman, R. W., 'How Companies Respond to Social Demands', *Harvard Business Review*, **51**, 4, 1973, 88–98.
17. Chang, Y. N. and Campo-Flores, F., *Business Policy and Strategy*, Goodyear Publishing, Santa Monica, CA, 1980.
18. Johnson, G. and Scholes, K., *Exploring Corporate Strategy*, Prentice Hall, London, 1984.
19. *Facing Realities — The European Societal Strategy Project — Summary Report*, European Foundation for Management Development and the European Institute for Advanced Studies in Management, 1981.
20. Friedman, M., 'The Social Responsibility of Business is to Increase Its Profits', *New York Times Magazine*, 30 September, 1970.
21. Aupperle, K. E., Carroll, A. B. and Hatfield, J. D., 'An Empirical Examination of the Relationship between Corporate Social Responsibility and Profitability', *Academy of Management Journal*, **28**, 2, 1985, 446–63.

CHAPTER 7

ORGANIZATIONAL OBJECTIVES

Establishing organizational objectives is the second stage in planning direction, as established in the model of strategic management. There is a logical progression from mission to objectives, with the focus in this chapter being on organizational and business objectives. The core of the chapter is a range of alternatives from which objectives can be selected. These are applicable to both organizational and business objectives, although companies tend to be selective in those to be adopted. As will be seen in the chapter, objectives play many roles in strategic management. Although the role of planning direction has been established as being of major importance, these specific roles of objectives are also essential.

In this chapter specific indications of direction are examined, which are developed out of the broad directions given in the organizational mission. As organizational objectives are the objectives of strategic management they relate to total organizational performance, being superior to objectives which are established for only part of the company in the form of operational objectives for particular business functions.

In establishing organizational objectives for companies with several business domains an immediate concern is the definition of the total organization. Where the range of business domains results in a company structure consisting of several SBUs, then it is likely that there will be an overall set of organizational objectives, as well as a set of objectives for each of the SBUs. Attention is given to the development of such hierarchies of objectives in the first section of this chapter.

The establishment of the objectives to be pursued is the result of several considerations. The second section of this chapter examines these considerations. The first is the types of objective which can be established, providing a range for potential selection. The second relates to the periods of time to which objectives should apply, while the other consideration relates to determining the magnitude of objectives. This section is sequenced to allow the reader an early appreciation of the types of organizational objectives.

The next section looks at the nature of objectives, with particular attention to their role and importance within strategic management. In simple terms the objectives represent 'what' the company is aiming to achieve, whereas strategy represents 'how' they are to be achieved. This section expands on features which explain the nature of objectives.

The penultimate section addresses the processes involved in the establishment of organizational objectives. Managerial participation is a central theme here, with concern for the necessity to involve different levels of managers in this process. The final section looks forward into strategic management to provide an overview of how organizational objectives relate to the subsequent stages.

HIERARCHY OF OBJECTIVES

Classical economic theory is based on the assumption that the objective of firms is to maximize profits. Managers are seen to be rational decision-makers who make their decisions in order to attain this. Errors in decision-making lead to suboptimization, with the theory predicting the measurement of such errors as costs, where the latter is the difference between the profits that should have been achieved and those which were actually achieved.

The reality of modern organizations is a complexity of multiple objectives, with many variables affecting maximization, and where the ability and personal preferences of managers not only influence the setting of objectives but where their personal objectives are part of the system. As already indicated, objectives are also established at other levels in a company, while the larger and the more complex the structure the greater the potential for a wide range of objectives, in order to accommodate the aims of the many business domains. Additionally, largeness and complexity are normally associated with larger numbers of managers and executives, all of whom will have personal objectives. Given the occurrence of this 'natural' hierarchy the major issue becomes one of a purposely designed hierarchy of objectives where the objectives of the organization (at various levels in the structure) can be integrated with those of managers. An early but important contribution to the purposeful design of objectives into a hierarchy was the article by Granger[1], which has done much to influence subsequent work in this area.

This need to integrate the variety of interests into a structured hierarchy is perhaps obvious, although in practice inconsistencies and conflicts occur. An early writer on objectives, Urwick[2], stated that unless purposes (objectives) are specified then individuals find difficulty in co-operating. Through a carefully designed hierarchy many interests can be accommodated, giving common purposes to allow for the co-operation of individuals. Nevertheless, inconsistencies and conflicts are still likely to exist, which is an issue which will be explored in the section concerned with the process of setting organizational objectives.

A simple hierarchy

A simple way of depicting the hierarchy is merely to list objectives which are established at various levels within the organizational structure of a firm. Such an approach has been depicted by Rue and Holland[3], which is similar to that given in Figure 7.1.

At the apex of the hierarchy is the broadest aim for the total company, regard-

Figure 7.1 *A simple hierarchy of objectives.*

less of structural divisions, represented by the mission as discussed in Chapter 6. At the next level are the detailed objectives pertaining to the company as a whole, the nature of which will be examined in the next section. The next level is a set of overall objectives for each of the SBUs or divisions, applicable to companies where such a structure has been adopted. The type of objectives to be set at this level would probably be selected from the range labelled 'organizational objectives', as given in the next section. The operational objectives are specific to each of the business functions, such as manufacturing, marketing, purchasing and personnel. Subunit objectives appertain to specific activities within each of the operations; for example, advertising objectives would fall into this classification. Finally, the bottom of the hierarchy represents the personal objectives of individuals, where each set is obviously unique to each particular manager.

Comprehensive hierarchies

Other writers have presented hierarchies which are more comprehensive than that given in Figure 7.1. Rowe *et al.*[4] have integrated the various types of objective with levels of strategy. This hybrid of objectives and strategies has been labelled the 'hierarchy of values', although the weakness is that the 'what' and 'how' have been combined, rather than identifying and linking the different needs for objectives at different levels in the organization.

Richards[5] has presented the concept of a hierarchy of objectives in conjunction with other hierarchies that are to be found in companies. This explanation relates levels of objectives to levels within the organizational structure, particular managerial job titles, and the strategies which are established at different levels in the structure. While such a framework is more comprehensive, the many differences to be found in both the structure of companies and in the job titles that are used detract from the requirement to establish an integrated and coherent arrangement of objectives that reflect both company and individual interests.

The hierarchy of objectives established for this book is illustrated in Figure 7.2. This presentation attempts to show the objectives at various levels in the company, along with those of individuals employed throughout the structure. Each particular level of objectives for the company has associated objectives for a particular group of people, with the right-hand side of Figure 7.2 showing types of objective for each. Some of the company objectives are compatible with individual objectives, such as company performance, although specific features of these and other personal objectives may result in conflict. Company rate of growth may be in conflict with personal aspirations, for example, while career advancement may not be compatible with company structuring.

Conflicts can also occur within the objectives of the company. Aims to increase market share or to extend the product line may lead to reduced profitability, although an important issue can be that of timing. In both these cases the reduction may be only in the short-term, whereas the achievement of higher market share and a longer product line may lead to greater profitability in the long term. The issue will be pursued further in the next section. Conflicts and inconsistencies may also occur between the SBUs. For example, while the overall organizational objectives will establish a particular rate of growth, it is likely that some SBUs will achieve this rate and some may not. Conflicts here could be between the senior managers responsible for individual SBUs as well as between directors where the concern would be for the relative mix of SBU performance in the future.

The treatment of these different types of objective is given in several chapters in the book. Those of the owners, as stakeholders, and the organizational mission have already been examined in Chapter 6. Organizational objectives, including those at the SBU level, are tackled in this chapter, whereas reference to operational objectives is made in Chapter 12. Personal objectives of all individuals, excluding the owners, are discussed in Chapter 8.

Hierarchy characteristics

For this type of hierarchy Granger[1] has suggested some important characteristics:

- The full range is distressingly broad so that the structure of the hierarchy needs to be carefully planned, especially as each manager is likely to relate only to those within his immediate vicinity.

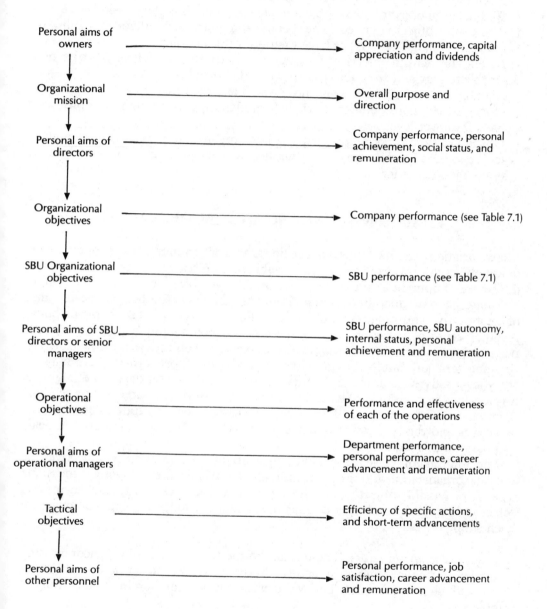

Figure 7.2 *Adopted hierarchy of objectives.*

- The higher level objectives relate to longer periods of time while progression down the hierarchy leads to progressively shorter periods of time.
- With time all objectives are subject to change, including the mission.
- While some objectives need to be specific and quantified, others are qualitative in nature, though both types have important roles to play.
- Ascendancy within objectives is difficult to establish as each level has a particular role to play and superiority is only based on level.
- The higher-level objectives are those which are often less clear and which have often had less consideration in their formulation, even though they provide a basis for lower levels.
- Objectives should not be restricted to large organizations and even the higher-level and broader aims are equally applicable to small companies; only the scale of operation is different.

ESTABLISHING ORGANIZATIONAL OBJECTIVES

Many variations are to be found in the literature concerning the range of organizational objectives that companies can establish. One reason for the variation is a difference of opinion about the value of qualitative objectives, with some writers claiming that only quantitative aims should be set, whereas others advocate a mix of quantitative and qualitative objectives. The latter view is taken in this book. Another cause of variation is the time-scales which should be associated with particular types of objective. Should all organizational objectives be only related to the long term or should they also be related to the short term? There may be specific periods in a company's history when the latter is essential even though the former may be the norm. Attention will be given to timing later in this section. Another cause of variation is the advice given about the magnitude of quantitative objectives and the severity of qualitative objectives. This issue will also be dealt with later in this section.

The other major cause is the advice given about the split between objectives for the total organization and those for individual SBUs. In the following discussions a range of possible objectives is given as a common stock from which firms can select and establish both types of objective, where the following explanations have been adopted:

- *Organizational objectives.* These relate to the total organization, encompassing total performance from all structural divisions. They represent the set of objectives which is immediately below the organizational mission in the hierarchy of objectives.
- *Business objectives.* At this level objectives appertain to particular SBUs or divisions, being only concerned with performance in these respective units. Consequently, they should only appear in companies which participate in multiple businesses. Business objectives are subservient to organizational objectives, representing the planned contribution of each SBU to total company performance.

EXHIBIT 7.1

Finland's Wide-awake Giant

The Finnish conglomerate Nokia is Finland's largest industrial company, with businesses ranging from tissues to telephones, personal computers to rubber boots, and parquet flooring to chemicals. These businesses reflect objectives of market spread, but also of growth, which has been rapid over the past ten years. Major objectives set within SBUs to guide performance are return on capital employed (ROCE) and growth in sales revenue. However, there are major differences in the SBUs. In rubber ROCE is more important than growth, but in telephones growth is more important so as to retain market share in this competitive market. ROCE for the group as a whole is reportedly low, as 12%, but the aim was to achieve 18% by 1988, a level which had previously been achieved in 1982.

Adapted from *Management Today*, July 1987

The range of objectives from which both the above can be selected and established is given in Table 7.1, and discussed below. It has been adapted from work by Greenley[6], where the recommended range resulted from a compilation of types of objective recommended by many writers. Readers wishing to study research surveys that have addressed the frequency of use of these objectives are referred to the articles by Bhatty[7], Grinyer and Norburn[8], Kudla[9], Ringbakk[10], Rue[11] and Shetty[12].

Group 1: directional objectives

Market leadership develops from the understanding of competitors, as discussed in Chapter 4; what is at issue here is the direction to be pursued with regard to competitive standing. Positioning is commonly measured by market share, where objectives are more likely to be set at the SBU level, but will also feature at the operational level in the form of marketing objectives. Here the famous PIMS data base has led to claims by Buzzell *et al.*[13] and Schoeffler *et al.*[14] that higher market share leads to higher profits, although writers such as Anderson and Paine[15], Wensley[16], and Woo[17] have challenged the universality of this relationship. A common-sense argument is that the importance of market share varies from market to market and from industry to industry. Indeed recent research by Prescott *et al.*[18] indicated that the influence of market share on profits is context-specific. Objectives concerning innovation and technological advancements obviously relate product advancements to those of competitors, which are equally applicable at the organizational and business levels. These latter objectives are likely to be qualitative in nature.

Market spread is concerned with the spread of business risk, developing from the understanding of market structures as given in Chapter 5, to represent direc-

Table 7.1 *Range of organizational objectives. (G. E. Greenley,* The Strategic and Operational Planning of Marketing, *© 1986. Reproduced by permission of McGraw-Hill Ltd.)*

Group 1 Directional objectives
  Market leadership, measured by

      competitive position
      degree of innovation
      technological advances

  Market spread, measured by

      number of markets
      number of customer groups
      number of industries
      number of countries

  Customer service, measured by

      product utility
      product quality
      product reliability

Group 2 Performance objectives
  Growth, measured by

      sales revenue
      volume output
      profit margin
      contribution

  Profitability, measured by

      return on capital employed
      return on assets
      profit margin on sales revenue
      return on shareholders' funds

Group 3 Internal objectives
  Efficiency, measured by

      sales on total assets
      stock turnover
      credit period
      liquidity
      department costs on sales

  Personnel, measured by

      employee relations and morale
      personal development
      average employee remuneration
      sales revenue per employee

Group 4 External objectives
  Social responsibility, measured by

      corporate image
      price–profit relationship
      resource utilization
      public activity
      community welfare

tions to be pursued with respect to each of these given measures. While 'number of industries' would be established at the organizational level, the others would clearly be at the SBU level. These objectives can be either quantitative or qualitative. Finally, customer service objectives would be qualitative in nature. While such objectives can be meaningfully set at the organizational level, they are more useful as business objectives where they can be related to specific product lines.

Group 2: performance objectives

All these objectives are quantitative in nature and all can be established at both the organizational and SBU levels. Growth needs to be determined for the total company, with sales revenue and volume output being the most important measures. This gives guidance for the growth to be pursued by each of the SBUs, although the same rate of growth is unlikely to be applicable to each SBU, given the differences likely to be found in their respective industry environments. These differences are also likely to influence the levels of profit margins and contribution that can be realistically achieved, so that these objectives are more situation-specific at the SBU level. However, their establishment at the higher level gives guidance within the hierarchy of objectives.

In the case of profitability objectives the link between the organizational and SBU levels is of major importance. The full range would be established at the higher level to provide the long-range continuity of the aspired levels of company performance. These measures are also important at the SBU level, in order to establish the planned performance of each unit. Again there will be differences in potential performance owing to differences in the respective industry environments. A major problem here is balancing the setting of these SBU-level objectives where there are major differences in SBU potential, while ensuring that they satisfy the overriding higher-level aims.

A final comment on this total group is that they are also of major importance in the setting of objectives in operational planning. All the business functions are able to influence the success of these areas of performance so that effective linkages within the hierarchy are of central importance.

Group 3: internal objectives

Within this group the objectives concerned with efficiency are quantitative in nature while those pertaining to personnel are both quantitative and qualitative. For the former the SBU level is more applicable, where different environments will allow for the achievement of different levels of efficiency. Similarly the levels achieved by other companies operating in these industries can provide guidance for standardizing efficiency. Levels of efficiency to be pursued will largely depend on the degree of autonomy that each SBU has. Where each SBU is only assessed on its performance by measures of growth and profitability then efficiency measures are largely a concern for the internal management of each SBU. However, in general, improvements achieved through these objectives will obviously contribute to the achievement of performance objectives, and may be given more attention at the higher level. These efficiency objectives are also important as a framework for setting operational objectives. The department costs on sales objective is obviously a major parameter for all the operations, but the others can all be related to specific product lines or indeed individual products.

Personnel objectives can be established at both the organizational and SBU levels, and can be both quantitative and qualitative. Employee relations, morale and personal development are central to the performance of individuals, so that initial guidance at the higher level would provide the most value. At the SBU level they are central to creating the working environment of individuals, providing a further framework for additional objectives further down the hierarchy. Average employee remuneration and sales revenue per employee represent the quantitative aims in this subgroup. The nature of these is such that they would be of greatest value at the SBU level, where practices unique to each unit dictate levels to be realistically pursued. However the latter measure is not directly related to the motivation of personnel, but represents aspired levels of achievement for each of the SBUs, based on their respective utilization of human resources.

Group 4: external objectives

Here the focus is on social responsibility, providing specific aims to improve the organization's relationship with society in general. With the exception of the price–profit relationship these are all qualitative objectives. Attention was given to social responsibility in Chapter 6 and these objectives represent the company's intentions in accepting this responsibility. Applicability here is at both the organizational and SBU levels.

Corporate image is important in the demonstration of the acceptance of social responsibility. However, achievements in creating favourable attitudes on the part of members of society also influence performance and operational planning. In the latter corporate image can enhance brand images to be projected for individual products, giving another link through the hierarchy.

The price–profit relationship and resource utilization objectives allow the company to improve its contribution to the welfare of society. While the former is concerned with the equitable share of the value of finished products between customer and supplier, resource utilization relates to effective conversion of inputs into final products by the company. Objectives concerned with public activity and community welfare not only provide additional contributions to society, but can also help to enhance corporate image.

The literature reports several research studies which have attempted to identify whether companies that are more socially responsible than their competitors achieve higher profitability. All were based on companies from the United States. The results are varied in that some have found such a relationship whereas others have not. The two most recent studies, by Aupperle et al.[19] and Abbot and Monsen[20], claim that a relationship between social responsibility and profitability was not identified. However, the methodology of all these studies was fraught with problems of identifying a cause-and-effect relationship. Despite such results the importance of social responsibility is perhaps self-evident on a priori grounds.

Time-scales

One of the characteristics of the hierarchy of objectives listed earlier in the chapter was the period of time to which objectives should relate. It was observed that the higher-level objectives relate to relatively long periods of time, while progression down the hierarchy leads to progressively shorter periods.

While there appear to be no set rules which govern the period of time to which organizational and SBU objectives should be related, writers agree that they must be time-dated. An objective to achieve a growth in sales volume of 20 per cent over a five-year period is clearly very different to the same objective over a one-year period. Some writers suggest standardized time periods for the hierarchy of objectives, as shown in Figure 7.3. Such time-scales may be applicable where industries feature a steady growth, but where there is a long stage of maturity they may be too short, whereas for industries in decline they may be too long. The point is that companies need to establish time periods which are reasonable for their particular situation.

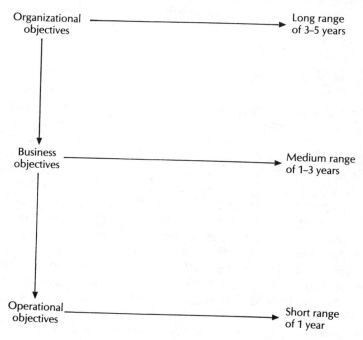

Figure 7.3 *Standardized time periods.*

Once the objectives have been set for the designated time periods, attention must be directed to their future review and revision. One approach is that this is done annually so that the organizational objectives would be presented on, say, a five-year rolling basis. Here the logic is that as each year progresses the firm learns more about the influences of its environments on its businesses. One objection to this approach is that long-range continuity may be lost and that the firm is reacting to short-term changes to make long-range modifications. However, this system does ensure that regular and systematic reviews are made, which relate to the strategic management stage of control as discussed in Chapter 14.

Glueck and Jauch[21] have suggested four major reasons why organizational objectives will need to be changed with time, despite the number of years that are designated as the long-range period:

- The aspirations, values, and expectations of management are likely to change over time, including changes due to the replacement of individual managers. The complexities of these changes will be examined in Chapter 8.
- Life-cycle changes (as discussed in Chapter 5) will lead to major changes in the nature of objectives as opposed to minor modifications to levels of aspired performance.
- An impending crisis is likely to require change, even if this only represents a short-term depression in the growth of the industry life cycle. The severity of the crisis obviously dictates the necessary change.
- The effective exercise of power by specific stakeholder groups, as discussed in Chapter 6.

Magnitude of objectives

In fixing specific values to the quantitative objectives two major features have been well discussed. These features require the setting of values which can be realistically achieved in relation to environmental conditions, but which will also challenge and stretch the capabilities of both individuals and the company to achieve higher levels of performance than are immediately apparent. While the sequence of strategic management stages presented in this book has given the analysis of the environment as preceding the setting of objectives, a reversed sequence would be consistent with increased attention to challenging capabilities. Here the logic is that both organizational and SBU objectives can be set to achieve, for example, a progressive programme of growth without being constrained by environmental forces. If current industries will not allow for this desired growth then the company is 'forced' into investigating potential from other industries. However, the objection to this thinking is that aims must be realistic otherwise they become meaningless.

For most firms the practice is that the objectives will be initially established with values that are realistic, but that an added margin will then be included in order to provide a degree of challenge. Determining the degree of challenge is problematic. If the level is too high then motivation is detrimentally affected, while motivation is achieved through the attainment of objectives and not failure. Also, aiming for high levels of growth leads to the development of higher levels of production capacity. If these planned levels of growth are not achieved the under-utilization of resources, cash-flow problems, and overproduction will result.

Getting the balance right between realism and challenge remains largely a matter of managerial judgement, based on experience of the organization and its environments. Rue and Holland[3] have given some guidelines. The first is to examine past experience of stretching capabilities and its relative success and to use similar margins for future challenges. However, Donaldson[22], for example, has warned against a major reliance on historical performance, based on the obvious problem of merely attempting to perpetuate previous successes. Another guide is to emulate the practice of other companies which also participate in the industry. Here the problem is the comparability of firms despite their common business involvement. The other guide given by Rue and Holland is to extend managerial judgement to include many managers from the structural hierarchy. This allows for a breadth of experience and thinking, but re-emphasizes the reliance placed on judgement for setting the magnitude of quantitative objectives.

EXHIBIT 7.2

Bulmer's Bittersweet Prospects

The British cider manufacturer, Bulmer, had experienced considerable growth in the early 1980s, but increases in excise duty in 1984–5 and increased competition caused a decline in both profits and profitability. Bulmer then changed the focus of its organizational objectives towards market spread to reduce reliance in cider. Previous strategies to pursue this objective had been the acquisition of the distributorship for Perrier (of France) in the UK, and for the French orange drink Orangina. Increased growth in sales volume in this business was also to be a major objective, with a strategy of premium soft drinks for adults. Increased growth in sales volume was also to be sought from its quality wines and spirits businesses, and its pectin business. Pectin is a food additive, which is extracted from apple pulp. However, it represents a different business, with additional opportunities for market spread in supplying other food ingredients to the food industry. Other stated objectives relate to efficiency, market leadership and personnel. The former is an objective related to competitiveness, while technological market leadership is related to both efficiency and competitive advantage. Finally, the stated personnel objective relates to the morale of managers, which they aim to improve through freedom of managerial action.

Adapted from *Management Today*, September 1987

THE NATURE OF ORGANIZATIONAL OBJECTIVES

While the last section was concerned with the range of alternatives from which objectives can be set, attention in this section is directed to two sets of features of objectives which constitute their nature. The first is an exposition of the roles to be played by objectives, reflecting their importance in the total strategic management process. The second set of features are qualities which have been suggested as being consistent with objectives that are likely to be effective within the total strategic management process. Both sets are applicable to both organizational and business objectives, within the context of the structure of the firm.

As a prelude to the discussions of these two sets of features, the major feature of the nature of organizational objectives is highlighted. This is at the core of the strategic management process, having been emphasized over twenty years ago by Simon[23]. The objectives provide constraints on future courses of action, or, in contemporary terminology, they provide constraints for the total process of strategic management. Part of the process must be to ensure that the constraints are not violated, especially in the design of strategy alternatives and their subsequent selection for implementation.

Roles of organizational objectives

The major roles to be performed by objectives can be classified as those relating directly to the process of strategic management and those relating to people, but which will affect the process indirectly.

Roles related directly to strategic management

Environmental orientation. This role provides for such needs as justification for existence, location within society, and the legitimation of its *modus operandi* for the satisfaction of groups of stakeholders. While the products and services which are supplied provide the physical link to the environment, the objectives are a means of establishing and maintaining their viability.

Guide to action. As mentioned above, the role of organizational objectives is to provide the detail of the planned direction, providing a basis for decision-making at other subsequent stages of strategic management.

Hierarchy linkage. From the concept of the hierarchy of objectives as discussed earlier in the chapter, the organizational objectives provide the link between the higher aims of the owners along with those included in the mission, and the lower-level operationally related aims which provide for performance and results.

Co-ordination of decisions. Here the function of objectives is to contribute to co-ordination in that their integration through the hierarchy provides perceived expectations of performance and behaviour. Such co-ordination also provides a vehicle for improved communication at different levels of management and across these levels, while both these advantages can play a part in the avoidance of internal conflicts.

Constraint adaptation. As environmental changes occur many will indicate that the firm will need to adapt or change as a consequence. In such situations the task of the objectives is to provide the initial means of instigating the necessary adaptations, providing the discipline of a process to give consideration to the potential ramifications of environmental changes.

Basis for control. Within the process of strategic management this function is of major importance. Here there are two issues. The first is that the objectives provide a basis for measuring and judging company performance, by comparing actual results with the standards established in the objectives. Both quantitative and qualitative standards are important, while differences between performance and standards can be traced down the hierarchy of objectives. The other issue is that of taking corrective action as a result of any variances. Here the role is to provide the basis for decision-making in the instigation of corrective action. Chapter 14 addresses control procedures in detail.

Roles related to people

Fostering of motivation. As mentioned during the discussions of the establishment of objectives, another task that organizational objectives can perform is to help provide a stimulus for the motivation of personnel. This is achieved through the participation of managers in the establishment of objectives, which can also relate down through the hierarchy to include their own individual objectives. Motivation can also be fostered through the gradual achievement of objectives, where job satisfaction can be experienced as personal efforts are seen to be instrumental in achieving the specified aims. Managerial participation is considered later in this chapter.

Personal challenges. Providing challenges to individuals to extend their abilities to result in higher levels of performance can also be an important part of motivation, although establishing these challenges requires careful consideration. This proposition was originally established by Locke[24], although Latham and Yukl[25] examined empirical evidence available at that time which had addressed this proposition. Here the results indicated that the specification of objectives leads to increased performance, while setting difficult goals that have been previously agreed can lead to increased performance. In the case of organizational objectives there are two issues. First, challenges established at this level necessitate similar challenges at the operational level to give an overall stimulating working environment. Also, this stretching of abilities at this level provides a framework for challenges at the individual level which are consistent with overall company performances.

Integration of personal achievements. This incorporates some of the issues that have already been raised. The point is that, from the focus of the individual observing upwards in the hierarchy of objectives, the need is to be able to identify individual contributions in relation to those of the operations in which the individual works, and, in turn, to be able to relate operational contributions to the overall performance of the SBU or total organization.

Classification of roles

Finally, attention is given to the classification of the roles of objectives given by Johnson and Scholes[26]. They consider that, in simple terms, strategic management consists of the three major stages of strategic analysis, evaluation, and implementation, with objectives playing a different role in these three major stages. At the analysis stage the role is seen as being one of matching the historical achievements of the firm with the expectations of stakeholders for the future. The evaluation stage necessitates the establishment of yardsticks which can be used as a basis for the formulation and selection of strategy, which is seen by them to be a principal role. However, their emphasis is that the importance of objectives varies with the current standing of a particular firm. For example, they are claimed to be more important when the firm is in a state of crisis as opposed to being in a steady state situation. During implementation they also emphasize the roles of control, motivation and co-ordination, although they are also seen to be important guidelines for appraising specific internal projects.

Qualities of objectives

The second set of features are qualities which are meant to be a feature of effective objectives. Several writers have suggested certain features or qualities that organizational objectives should have if they are to fulfil effectively the roles which have been given above. Those given by Pearce and Robinson[27] exemplify those given in the literature:

Acceptable
Perhaps obvious, but they must be acceptable to the personnel involved. Some companies may attempt to exercise excessive top-down management, dictating levels of performance and aspirations which are not seen to be appropriate. Such practice may be more common in large organizations with several SBUs. Although the intention may be to stimulate growth for the good of the organization, individual enthusiasm may be damaged.

Flexible
Here the suggestion is that a balance is needed between flexibility and rigidity. While the modification of objectives based on mere reaction to environmental change would weaken the process, firms do of course need to match their plans to trends in the environment. This relates to the concept of planning time-scales, as discussed earlier in this chapter. Therefore flexibility could be achieved by a five-year rolling plan, although plans for the current period (say, between one and three years) remain fixed.

Measurable
Again this is the argument that objectives should be quantified. Where this is appropriate then the levels must be realistic, capable of measurement, and must be capable of being broken down to shorter periods of time, such as quarters or months. For qualitative objectives the rule is not as appropriate, although precision of definition of the qualities to be pursued helps in later judgements of attainment.

Motivating

This quality has been discussed, so that all that remains to be said is that care must be taken to ensure that motivation is likely to result.

Suitable

This simply means that each level of objectives needs to be consistent with higher levels in the hierarchy. Therefore, the organizational objectives need adequately to reflect intentions stipulated in the mission, while business objectives also need to reflect the latter as well as integrating with those for the total organization. Avoidance of all inconsistencies may not be totally achievable, but their minimization is intended.

Understandable

As part of the total system of communication, objectives are only likely to be effective if they are adequately communicated throughout the structural hierarchy. Some companies place restrictions on the communication of higher levels of objectives, as an aid to the confidentiality of plans and their protection from competitors. However, against this requirement is the need to avoid misunderstanding the aims being pursued at higher levels, which will lead to ineffective performance at lower levels. Explanations may also need to be made of longer-term intentions if, for example, aspired levels of profitability are to be lowered during the medium term in order to pursue a competitive advantage over the long term.

Achievable

While this may also seem obvious it may not always be realized. The previous discussions on the role of challenging and stretching can unintentionally lead to levels being set which will be difficult to achieve. Judgements on getting the 'right' balance, therefore, have added importance. Short-term changes to any of the environmental variables can also result in objectives becoming unachievable. Also, decision-making in setting objectives relates to a future period of time, so that the weaknesses of forecasting that were discussed in Chapter 3, plus other weaknesses of decision-making, can lead to the unintentional setting of inappropriate objectives.

THE PROCESS OF ESTABLISHMENT

In the section which addressed the establishment of organizational objectives the process was perhaps seen to be rational as part of strategic management. The range of objectives would be selected with their respective magnitudes and time-scales, which would develop the incrementation of previous objectives, given certain environmental conditions and resource availability and capability.

The concept of aspirations has also been used in previous discussions, where the desires or wishes of people can influence rational decision-making concerned with the range, magnitude, and timing of objectives. Here the issue is that these desires and wishes may not be rational, being part of the emotional and complex dispositions of these people. While any of the stakeholder groups that were presented in the last chapter are a source of potential influence, those of managers and directors obviously provide the greatest potential. These emotional and irrational influences are complicated by the structure of organizations, with increasing complexity and size exacerbating the opportunity to achieve rational decision-making. Of particular importance in understanding these aspirations are the values and expectations of managers, as well as the power that they are able to exercise in the organization to be able to pursue their own desires and wishes. The latter is very much dependent on the procedures which the firm uses to allow for managerial participation in planning. This total mix of influences on the process of establishing objectives is given in Figure 7.4.

The importance of these dispositional factors is reflected in that they are given fuller treatment in subsequent chapters than this section would allow. However, as will be already apparent, the main issue here is that an understanding of them is essential for a full understanding of the establishment of objectives in modern organizations. Consequently, these influences are examined in Chapters 8 and 13, while the influence of organizational structure is examined in Chapter 9. The rest of this section looks at the major process for establishing objectives. This process has been labelled 'management by objectives' (MBO). Although it helps to explain the establishment of organizational objectives, it is also applicable as a process throughout the hierarchy.

Management by objectives

MBO is both a philosophy and a general approach to management, which is based on the simple precept that objectives are at the core of management practice. The development of this idea into an initial and coherent body of knowledge is generally attributed to the work of Drucker[28] in the 1940s and 1950s. Since that time MBO has received considerable attention in both the literature and in companies, although excessive exposure and pretentious claims from some quarters have led some executives to view MBO with scepticism. However, the principles of MBO are sound and provide a basis for the establishment of objectives which is consistent with the strategic management model.

Another major contributor to MBO thinking, Odiorne[29], has defined MBO as

a process whereby the superior and subordinate managers of an organization jointly identify its common goals, define each individual's major areas of responsibility in terms of the results expected of him, and use these measures as guides for operating the unit and assessing the contribution of each of its members.

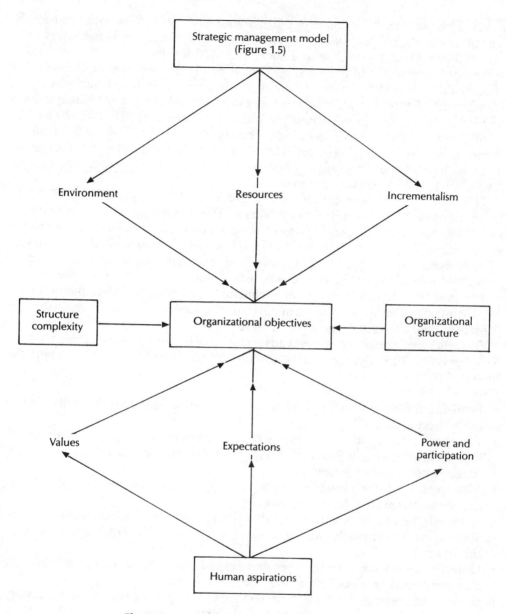

Figure 7.4 *Establishing organizational objectives.*

This definition reflects many of the issues that have already been raised in this chapter, although the inclusion of an MBO system is meant to integrate these issues. The first of these issues is that MBO is designed to work in conjunction with a hierarchy of objectives. This leads to managers participating in the formulation of objectives, with opportunities for participation at both higher and lower levels. This teamwork is central to participation and leads to commitment on the part of managers. Indeed, such a system also allows for operational managers to be involved in goal-setting both at and above the SBU level.

Another issue is that of the integration of all levels of objectives, including those of individuals, as shown in the hierarchy in Figure 7.2. While personal objectives are often difficult to design, it may not always be possible for each manager to have all his objectives incorporated into the hierarchy. However, MBO allows for the identification of these as well as the opportunity of their consideration for incorporation. Indeed this inclusion of personal objectives and the development of consistency with them and those of the organization are seen by Levinson[30], in another classic work, to be a key advantage of MBO.

This leads the definition into responsibility, with all key aspects of all objectives being designated to identified individuals. Here motivation can be fostered, assuming that bona fide participation has been achieved, and commitment to the achievement of results is given an additional boost. This in turn allows for a system of appraising the performance of individual managers, an issue that was propounded by McGregor[31] in another important work.

The final issue here relates to that of control. The system of MBO allows for the establishment of yardsticks, the comparison of actual achievements against these yardsticks, and the instigation of corrective action.

Consolidating the above issues leads to the establishment of the elements of an MBO system. Although there are variations, those given by Stoner[32] provide the basics:

- Ensuring the commitment of all managers at all levels to all the objectives of their direct concern.
- The system starts with initial setting of organizational goals (previous objectives may be used), although these should be subjected to change following the participation of other managers.
- Managers' goals are clearly explained and agreed so that they are able to see their integration into the total hierarchy.
- Although the degree of participation varies enormously, each manager must be allowed to participate and must be able to see that his participation is meaningful.
- Once the objectives have been set and responsibility has been agreed then the managers must be given autonomy to achieve them.
- Reviews of performance must also feature the teamwork that went into establishing the objectives, with the results of these reviews providing inputs to the next round of new objectives.

As a final point on MBO, attention is diverted back to the first paragraph of this subsection. MBO was developed in the 1940s and 1950s, when, as will be remembered from the review of the historical developments of strategic management given in Chapter 1, understanding and development of the discipline was at a low level. Consequently, MBO was, at that time, seen as a major advance, which resulted in its receiving considerable attention. With the progression of under-

standing into the 1980s, resulting in models of strategic managemer
features and advantages of MBO have been subsumed into strategic
However, it is suggested that MBO is not defunct as a result, but th
valuable process to be used within a strategic management framew
valuable capacity of providing a basis for the process of establishir.

FORWARD INTEGRATION

This section is intended to preview the impact of organizational and business objectives on the subsequent stages of strategic management and the associated implications of integration, with the aim of consolidating these issues in preparation for the rest of the book. The other aim is to emphasize the need for the integration of the stages of strategic management, especially where largeness of the company can lead to problems of co-ordination and communication.

Planning strategy

Chapter 9, the first chapter of Part Four, addresses the influences of organizational structure on the formulation of strategy. While the impact of structure on objectives has been discussed above, both structure and objectives can influence the formulation of strategy. Structure necessitates particular strategies for particular SBUs, although it can also represent constraints on developing alternative strategies. Organizational objectives have a major impact on strategy in that the major role of the latter is to provide a means of achieving the former. However, strategy can also influence both structure and objectives. Many other constraints also influence the selection of strategy, some of which may be more important than objectives. This can lead to a modification of the range or magnitude of objectives, that is, to strategy affecting objectives. Also, the selection of a particular strategy may require a different organization of human resources in order to implement it, giving a situation where strategy affects structure (the latter relationship is given more attention in Chapter 9). Figure 7.5 shows graphically the mutual influences described above.

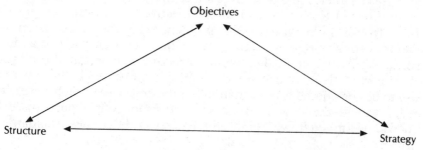

Figure 7.5 *Objectives and planning strategy.*

Implementing strategy

In the implementation of strategy there are three areas where the impact and integration of objectives need to be considered. These are operational strategies, human resource management, and control and effectiveness, each of which is the subject of a chapter in Part Five.

The relationship of organizational and business objectives to operational objectives has been illustrated through the discussions on the hierarchy. Here the point is that the higher-level objectives provide a framework for all the operational objectives, providing demands on the nature of operational objectives to be set. These demands relate to range, magnitude and time-scale. Each operational objective needs to be linked to a higher-level objective, with its magnitude and timing being carefully planned to coincide with these demands, in that their attainment represents the contributions of the operations to total corporate performance. Texts which are concerned with operational planning discuss these linkages in more detail, with that by Greenley[6] showing those for the operational objectives of marketing.

Indeed, the achievement of corporate performance can only occur through these contributions as the implementation of organizational strategy does through operational management. Here there is a particular necessity for specificity and for precision, in order to provide tighter control of results for achievement of performance. However, given the differences in timing it may be necessary to delay the achievement of, for example, growth in sales, where the one-year focus of operational planning provides flexibility within the, say, five-year framework at the higher level. An extension of this point is that operational managers may be frequently required to make decisions on priorities. While the longer-term objective may be to increase market spread, a shorter-term priority may be to build corporate image by improving the range of customer services offered.

The impact of objectives on people has been highlighted at several points in this chapter and all these issues are pertinent to their impact on human resource management. Further discussion at this juncture of the book is inappropriate, as the specific impact and problems of the integration of objectives in relation to the management of human behaviour is better examined after the presentation of the substantive content of Chapter 13.

Issues relating to the strategic management stage of control have also been discussed in this chapter. Here objectives are central in that, quite simply, control activities are directed to the attainment of objectives. However, the practice of control is far from simple, with a major problem being the identification of the environmental variables that are causing differences betwen planned and actual performance. Similarly, the instigation of corrective actions can also be problematic, particularly balancing necessary changes at the strategic and operational levels. Also to be considered is the suitability of the objectives which were actually established. Although the latter are used as yardsticks for control purposes, achieving control will be limited if, with hindsight, it is realised that these standards were inappropriate.

SUMMARY

This chapter has addressed the extension of the organizational mission, by examining the establishment of specific levels of achievement. The resultant organizational objectives give the specific detail of the planned direction.

The first section provided the context for considering these objectives, by discussing the hierarchy of objectives to be found in companies. This was seen to be constituted of objectives concerned with the company and those concerned with individuals. The former ranged from the mission to operational objectives, while the latter ranged from the personal aims of the owners to the aims of operational managers.

The second section tackled the establishment of both organizational and business objectives. A range of objectives was given from which both sets can be established. This range was based on four groups: directional objectives; performance objectives; internal objectives; and external objectives. The section was concluded with the consideration of time-scales and magnitude.

The third section looked at the nature of objectives. This was initially concerned with the various roles that organizational objectives play within strategic management. The other major consideration in this section was a number of qualities of objectives, the presence of which is meant to be indicative of effectiveness.

The penultimate section was concerned with the process of establishment. Major influences on the establishment of objectives were identified. These ranged from variables to be found in the strategic management model, through the organizational structure, to human aspirations. The importance of these influences was highlighted in that they are given greater treatment in other chapters of the book.

The final section was about the forward integration of organizational objectives into the subsequent stages of strategic management. The aim was to consolidate issues of influence that had already been raised and to provide a preview of this influence before proceeding to the remaining chapters.

CHAPTER CASE STUDY ILLUSTRATION:
THE OXFORD INSTRUMENTS GROUP PLC*

Oxford Instruments produces high-technology products for scientific, medical and industrial applications. It is a market leader in superconducting

*Derived from the original case study by E. Newbigging (Copyright © 1984).

magnet systems, but also produces advanced instruments for patient monitoring, materials analysis, and industrial process control. The group is based in the United Kingdom, but has key subsidiaries in West Germany, France, the Netherlands and Switzerland.

Although some of the organizational objectives of Oxford Instruments are specified, many are implied from the case study data. This is perhaps typical of the presentation of many case studies, although it reflects the practice of many companies where several objectives are implied as opposed to being explicitly specified. The following illustration is based on three of the groups of organizational objectives that were given in the chapter, plus a discussion of personal objectives, and a discussion of forward integration.

GROUP 1

Market leadership

A stated objective was to pursue technical leadership which was considered to be essential to success in the industries in which the company participates. Three related objectives were to develop 'next-generation' products by developing the same technology; to develop existing markets with new technology; and to develop new technologies for new businesses. Market leadership for competitive position was also important and in this respect the objective was for incremental product development to secure market position by outperforming competitive products. Combined with technological leadership the group was stated to be making strenuous efforts to attain these leadership objectives.

Market spread

Another major area for setting objectives, with the major stated aim being to achieve a spread of businesses in different and non-interacting markets and geographical areas. However, spread was restricted to markets with growth potential of about 20% per annum. Indeed there is evidence that a market-spread objective had been pursued throughout the company's history. In the early 1970s it had pursued this objective through the strategy of diversification, which included an immediate spread of risk through acquisitions. In the early 1980s the objective was further pursued by the establishment of a subsidiary in the United States and a joint venture in Japan.

Customer service

The only major insight in this area is the aim of achieving high product quality, although this objective is synonymous with the needs and wants that were featured in these industries.

GROUP 2

Growth

A major stated objective was to achieve 'high' growth, although this aim was not quantified in the case study. During the early years of its existence this had been achieved by developing new ideas and markets and developing technologies. However, in the 1970s this aim had been pursued through diversification. The rapid growth that was achieved during the early 1980s also attests to the company's attention to this growth objective. The objective of growth was accelerated by the capital raised from the flotation in 1983, which led to a growth of 68% in sales volume the following year. Finally, growth has become so important that, during the 1980s, the aim was only to develop products, markets or technologies which had the potential of producing high growth.

Profitability

While high growth was a major objective so, too, was a stated objective to achieve high levels of profitability. However, setting this objective had not always been possible in the group's history. At the end of the 1960s it relied on satisfying specific customer requirements, which resulted in unpredictable profits and difficulties in setting these objectives. From 1983 to 1984 the objective of high profits was also boosted by the outcome of the flotation, with 1984 pre-tax profits being more than double those earned in 1983.

GROUP 3

Only implications of the setting of organizational objectives from this group can be identified from the case study. Efficiency objectives are implied in achievement gained in the efficiency of production methods in the early 1980s and in the improvement of premises. The 1983 flotation also had an influence on efficiency, in that borrowings were reduced, while working capital was increased.

Several indications are apparent in the setting of organizational objectives in relation to personnel, in order to enhance employee relations, employee morale, and to achieve personal development. The following are indications of these objectives:

- The ability to attract and keep high-quality staff who are well motivated.
- Turnover of staff was given as being generally low.
- Clearly identified career development objectives for individuals with opportunities for internal promotions.
- Above average salaries with profit sharing and achievement bonus schemes.
- The establishment of a share participation scheme for all personnel.

PERSONAL ASPIRATIONS

Limited, though important, implications are given of the aspirations of the board. The nature of the company and its success since its start-up were closely influenced by the entrepreneurial flair of the founder of the organization, Martin Wood, who aspired to pursue business opportunities with his technical knowledge.

The pursuit of growth is endemic to the thinking and desires of the board for company success. Although high levels of growth were not achieved in the 1970s the goals were retained, with a further reflection of aspirations being the board's desire to retain autonomy by averting a takeover bid. Aspirations for the continued development, growth and success of the group were evident from the decision to become a public limited company, even though this could have eventually led to threats to autonomy.

FORWARD INTEGRATION

The case study illustrates some of the interrelationships of organizational objectives with strategy and structure, as part of the forward integration of the former. Given the objective of growth the major strategy was that of product development and innovation, featuring existing, modified and new technologies, which in turn dictated the organizational structure of the group. Indeed these different approaches to product development led to different types of structure within the subsidiaries:

- Growth from incremental improvements to existing products which were managed by executives within existing companies and development teams.
- Growth from new products based on existing technology, where the structure featured special development teams, as existing teams had experienced difficulty in detaching themselves from existing products.
- Growth from new products in the same market but with different technology, where the company had found it necessary to restructure the organization by bringing in people with the necessary technical expertise.
- Growth from new ventures in new products and markets where new technology is necessary; major changes to structure were found to be of most value, where small companies or SBUs were established to pursue these developments.

In all these situations the point is that there was an interrelationship between objectives, strategy and structure. However, in each situation the common objective of growth had led to different strategy approaches, which required different organizational structures.

REFERENCES

1. Granger, C. H., 'The Hierarchy of Objectives', *Harvard Business Review*, **43**, 3, 1964, 63–74.
2. Urwick, L. F., *Notes of the Theory of Organizations*, American Management Association, New York, 1952.

3. Rue, L. W. and Holland, P. G., *Strategic Management: Concepts and Experiences*, McGraw-Hill, Singapore, 1986.
4. Rowe, A. J., Mason, R. O. and Dickel, K. E., *Strategic Management and Business Policy*, 2nd edn, Addison-Wesley, Reading, MA, 1985.
5. Richards, M. D., *Setting Strategic Goals and Objectives*, West, St Paul, MN, 1986.
6. Greenley, G. E., *The Strategic and Operational Planning of Marketing*, McGraw-Hill, Maidenhead, 1986.
7. Bhatty, E. F., 'Corporate Planning in Medium-sized UK Companies', *Long Range Planning*, **14**, 1, 1981, 65–76.
8. Grinyer, P. H. and Norburn, D., 'Strategic Planning in 21 UK Companies', *Long Range Planning*, **7**, 4, 1974, 80–8.
9. Kudla, R. J., 'Elements of Effective Corporate Planning', *Long Range Planning*, **9**, 4, 1976, 82–93.
10. Ringbakk, K. A., 'Organized Planning in Major US Companies', *Long Range Planning*, **2**, 4, 1969, 46–57.
11. Rue, L. W., 'Tools and Techniques of Long-range Planning', *Long Range Planning*, **7**, 5, 1974, 61–5.
12. Shetty, Y. K., 'New Look at Corporate Goals', *California Management Review*, **22**, 2, 1979, 71–9.
13. Buzzell, R. D., Gale, B. T. and Sulton, R. G. M., 'Market Share — A Key to Profitability', *Harvard Business Review*, **53**, 1, 1975, 97–106.
14. Schoeffler, S., Buzzell, R. D. and Heany, D. F., 'Impact of Strategic Planning on Profit Performance', *Harvard Business Review*, **52**, 2, 1974, 137–45.
15. Anderson, C. R. and Paine, F. T., 'PIMS: A Re-examination', *Academy of Management Review*, **3**, 1978, 602–11.
16. Wensley, R., 'The Market Share Myth', *London Business School Journal*, **6**, 2, 1981, 3–5.
17. Woo, C. Y., 'Market Share Leadership: Does It Pay Off?', *Proceedings of the Academy of Management Conference*, 1981, 7–11.
18. Prescott, J. E., Kohl, A. K. and Venkatraman, N., 'The Market Share – Profitability Relationship', *Strategic Management Journal*, **7**, 1986, 377–94.
19. Aupperle, K. E., Carroll, A. B. and Hatfield, J. D., 'An Empirical Examination of the Relationship between Corporate Social Responsibility and Profitability', *Academy of Management Journal*, **28**, 2, 1985, 446–63.
20. Abbott, W. F. and Monsen, J. R., 'On the Measurement of Corporate Social Responsibility', *Academy of Management Journal*, **22**, 1979, 501–15.
21. Glueck, W. F. and Jauch, L. R., *Business Policy and Strategic Management*, 4th edn, McGraw-Hill, New York, 1984.
22. Donaldson, G., 'Financial Goals and Strategic Consequences', *Harvard Business Review*, **63**, 3, 1985, 57–66.
23. Simon, H. A., 'On the Concept of Organizational Goals', *Administrative Science Quarterly*, **9**, 1, 1964, 1–22.
24. Locke, E., 'Toward a Theory of Task Motivation and Incentives', *Organizational Behaviour and Human Performance*, **3**, 1968, 157–89.
25. Latham, G. P. and Yukl, G. A., 'A Review of Research on the Application of Goal Setting in Organizations', *Academy of Management Journal*, **18**, 4, 1975, 824–45.
26. Johnson, G. and Scholes, K., *Exploring Corporate Strategy*, Prentice Hall, London, 1984.
27. Pearce, J. A. and Robinson, R. B., *Strategic Management*, 2nd edn, Irwin, Homewood, IL, 1985.

28. Drucker, P. F., *The Practice of Management*, Harper and Row, New York, 1954.
29. Odiorne, G., *Management by Objectives: A System of Management Leadership*, Pitman, New York, 1965.
30. Levinson, H., 'Management by Whose Objectives?', *Harvard Business Review*, **48**, 4, 1970, 125–34.
31. McGregor, D., 'An Uneasy Look at Performance Appraisal', *Harvard Business Review*, **35**, 3, 1957, 89–94.
32. Stoner, J. A. F., *Management*, 2nd edn, Prentice Hall, Englewood Cliffs, NJ, 1982.

CHAPTER 8
VALUES AND EXPECTATIONS

This final chapter of Part Three completes the consideration given to the planning of direction. The content of this chapter differs in nature from that of the previous seven, in that it is totally concerned with managerial behaviour. The issues examined influence the utilization of strategic management, although they are not an integral part of the stages in which decision-making is carried out. However, in practice the influences of managerial behaviour are intertwined with these stages, which indeed is also a feature of the other chapters. The aim of this chapter is to give these issues the additional attention that their importance merits.

The chapter is concerned with the human behaviour of managers who participate in strategic management, as opposed to a particular stage of strategic management. This differentiation was initially given in Chapter 1, when the strategic management model was originally introduced, and values and expectations were presented as influences which impinge upon decision-making within the stages of strategic management rather than being part of it.

Also highlighted in Chapter 1 was the point that these issues of human behaviour are as important as the logical stages of the strategic management process. Organizations, regardless of their size, are groups of people working together and it is their behaviour which moulds the nature of organizations and leads to the decisions which are made. While influences of their behaviour in relation to the planning aspects of strategic management are tackled in this chapter, those relating to implementation are the subject of Chapter 13, although in some instances it is inappropriate to adhere strictly to this separation.

The complexity of human behaviour *per se* and many of the consequential problems of its understanding are likely already to be appreciated by the reader. This general field of study applied to companies has been labelled 'organizational behaviour' and is now represented by a large body of literature. A major concern in the preparation of this chapter has been to limit the treatise to that knowledge which is applicable to the model of strategic management, while ensuring that major issues are adequately discussed.

This chapter is entitled 'Values and expectations' because it is these concepts which are taken to be the central features of the influence of human behaviour on planning. However, the content of the chapter is more comprehensive. It is organized into three major sections in order fully to examine managerial values and expectations and their ramifications. In the first section they are examined at the level of the individual manager, although the section is about managerial dispositions as values and expectations, which are discussed alongside other important influences of human behaviour on planning. The second section examines values and expectations at what can be considered the corporate level. This is about the concept of corporate culture, which is the set of values and expectations which are established for the operation of the company rather than being attributed to a particular individual. The last section is concerned with ramifications arising from values and expectations. An important orientation of strategic management is that it seeks to identify changes that are occurring, or are likely to occur, in the environment, as well as instigating consequential changes to the organization. However, a basic trait of human behaviour is to resist change. Consequently, the last section addresses managerial resistance to these changes in relation to values and expectations.

MANAGERIAL DISPOSITIONS

In this section four major features of the influence of human behaviour on planning are considered. These are illustrated in Figure 8.1 and include the core influences of values and expectations, with attitudes and capabilities representing extensions to these influences.

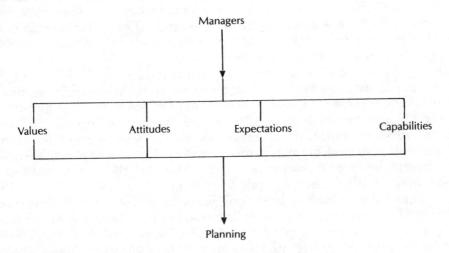

Figure 8.1   *Major influences on planning.*

Values

While the literature exhibits some differences in defining these concepts of human behaviour, Williams[1] has defined values as being cognitions, opinions or beliefs that underlie preference and choice in behaviour. Endemic to this explanation is the past experience of managers which has moulded these cognitions, opinions or beliefs. However, the values which influence their behaviour relative to strategic management are not just those formed while working for their current company. Here Johnson and Scholes[2] have given three major sources for the formation of managerial values:

- External influences of the values of the society and peer groups to which managers belong.
- The nature of the business, with the market situation and product range being of particular importance.
- The company culture, including company age and history, managerial styles practised, and planning and control systems.

It is not just business-related values that are likely to affect behaviour towards planning, but the total gambit of personal values that have been acquired. This leads to an important point, highlighted by writers such as Chang and Campo-Flores[3], which is that executives have difficulty in separating their feelings, emotions and personal preferences from logical analysis when making decisions. The ramifications of human behaviour are just as important as logical stages of decision-making.

Classification of values

Christensen *et al.*[4] have suggested a two-way classification of values, based on an internal/external split. The former set of values is derived from an individual's entrepreneurial flair, personal drive and energy, which induce an approach to planning based on innovative values. The external set are derived from a manager's formal education along with the effect of indoctrination in company policies and planning procedures. These values determine the degree to which a manager becomes a product of the business environment, which may be in opposition to the internal value set. Such a conflict may instigate resistance to the changes that are likely to arise from strategic management, which will be discussed further below.

The work of Guth and Tagiuri[5] found that managers' business values tend to have a particular focus or orientation. For example, a given manager could have an economic orientation towards what is useful and powerful, or a social orientation towards concern for the society. Finally, England[6] investigated the values of managers in five different countries. As might have been expected, many differences were found, although commonly found values were pragmatism, competence, high achievement, and traditional business objectives.

Personal aims

As an end result of the value set of each manager a range of personal aims will be formed. As was seen in Chapter 7 these feature at several levels within the hierarchy of objectives, and can influence the subsequent objectives of the organization.

Although personal aims may be merely 'carried in the heads' of managers in some companies, where MBO is practised managers should be forced to make them explicit just as the performance objectives for specific job functions are specified. While it is perhaps self-evident that managers will devote a high proportion of their executive time to personal aims, problems arise where there is conflict in compatability between these and the objectives of the organization. Saunders[7] claims that the higher the manager is within the hierarchy then the easier it will be for him to pursue self-interest, even to the detriment of the company.

For the purposes of this chapter personal aims can be related to performance, economic security and psychological security. Performance is concerned with achievements in specific jobs functions, but also relates to the specific unit, department or even SBU in which the manager is located. Economic aims are obviously concerned with the total remuneration package, but are also related to the standard of living that can be achieved. A problem here is that financial rewards are often linked to short-term gains as opposed to longer-term objectives. Psychological security can be manifest in several personal aims linked to many issues such as career structure, personal status, job security, rewarding work, belongingness, and sickness and retirement security. Lack of achievement by managers of any of these aims is likely to result in some kind of conflict situation.

Most of the concepts presented in this section are illustrated in Figure 8.2.

Attitudes

While values can be considered to be potential influences on human behaviour, attitudes are concerned with tendencies to behave in particular ways. However, in the literature writers admit to problems in the definition of attitudes and in the differences to be found in proposed definitions. Baron and Byrne[8] have defined attitudes as 'relatively enduring organizations of feelings, beliefs, and behavioural tendencies towards other persons, groups, ideas, or objects'. In context here the concern is with managers' behavioural tendencies towards their participation in planning for strategic management, the constraints that the latter places upon their job functions as a top-down process, and its general level of perceived importance. Chisnall[9] sees the major characteristic of attitudes as being a predisposition or state of readiness to act or react in a particular way to a particular situation.

In simple terms, it can be said that managerial attitudes that are favourable will result in the effective use of strategic management and the acceptance of the changes that it proposes. In practice it is a complex matter to assess the many attitudes of the many managers in the hierarchy, anticipating the likely influence that they may have on strategic management, and assessing their response and related resistance to the organizational changes that would result from the implementation of the proposed planning. This complexity is compounded by the enduring nature of attitudes, which means that, once formed, they can be difficult to change. Consequently, problems in utilizing strategic management are likely to reinforce these adverse attitudes. Methods for assessing attitudes are considered to

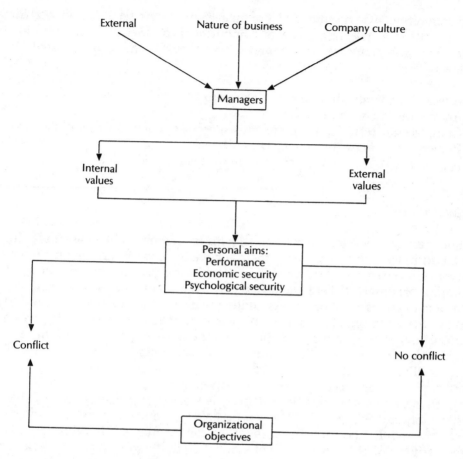

Figure 8.2 *Managerial values.*

be outside the scope of this book, but response and resistance to change are considered below.

Previous researchers have given indications of the attitudes of managers towards planning. Taylor and Irving[10] included reasons why strategic management was introduced into the companies they surveyed. While there was no common reason across their sample, a large proportion said that it was a change in attitude at director level which led to its introduction. This was in contrast to other reasons which 'forced' its introduction, such as increased intensity of competition or worsening environmental conditions. However, once the process is instigated it would appear that attitudes can be changed to appreciate the value of strategic planning, as managers become aware of the advantages that accrue as a consequence; see the research by Higgins and Finn[11] and Al-Bazzaz and Grinyer[12].

At lower levels in the management hierarchy many attitudes relate to support given at the higher levels. In the surveys by both Ames[13] and by Kudla[14] support and commitment from senior levels of management were seen to be of vital importance. Attitudes reflecting a lack of commitment towards planning were investigated by Brown *et al.*[15], who found a tendency for them to be based on the following:

- A lack of understanding of planning.
- An inability to measure results.
- Complacency resulting from previous successes achieved without planning.
- Reluctance to make long-range commitments.
- A tendency to focus on the short term as it is more identifiable.

Expectations

While managers develop their personal aims from their set of values and exhibit a set of attitudes that will underlie their behaviour towards strategic management, they will also perceive the probability of achieving their aims given the resultant planning proposals. Where there is a perceived inconsistency between personal aims and organizational objectives conflict is likely to arise, which is also likely to be the case when organizational strategy is perceived as offering little to promote personal interests. Given the complexity of the range of personal aims to be found in the management hierarchy it is likely that some perceived incongruity will be present. Therefore, if some conflict is to be present, then it presents a potential impediment to the success of strategic management.

Within the literature this field of study is labeled 'expectancy theory'. According to Gray and Starke[16], the theory is based on the outcomes that a person sees as desirable and that person's belief that they can be attained. Expectancy theory is presented within the general field of motivation in the work-place, as these expectations (in the form of personal aims) and the expectations of the likely probabilities that they will be obtained will influence a person's motivation to perform effectively.

This form of influence of human behaviour on strategic management is illustrated in Figure 8.3, which shows the stages explained above, starting with the manager's personal aims and attitudes, and the organizational objectives and strategy. Perceptions precede the formation of expectations, with the latter represented by both personal aims and the assessed probability of their achievement. Resultant motivation then leads to potential influence on the success of strategic management. However, the ability of managers to exert influence will depend on their location within the hierarchy and the power that they have been able to achieve relative to their positions and that of other managers. The simple principle that the higher a manager is in the hierarchy the greater is his ability to pursue personal expectations is probably true. However, current theory on organizational structures helps this understanding, which is followed up in Chapter 9. Sources of personal power are discussed in Chapter 13, in which the issue of expectations is pursued further.

Gray and Starke[16] explain that considerable research has been done to test expectancy theory within the general working environment of managers. How-

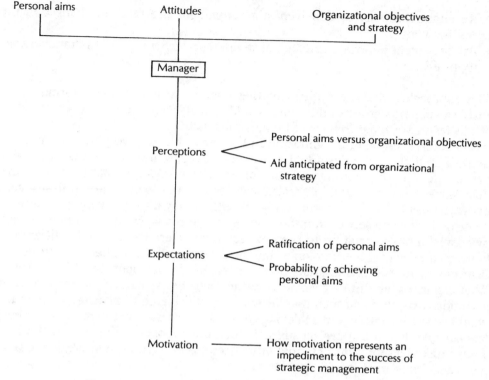

Figure 8.3 *Expectancy theory and strategic management.*

ever, the results indicate that expectations provide only a partial explanation of managerial motivation, which is not surprising given the complexity of human behaviour. Guth and Macmillan[17] used expectancy theory to predict that middle managers will attempt to intervene in decision-making relating to the implementation of strategy if it is perceived that the strategy will detrimentally affect their self-interest. Although their study was limited in that it was based on only 90 middle managers in American companies (but from a 'wide diversity of industries and [of] widely varying size'), the results indicate the ability of managers to influence strategy as a consequence of their expectations. This influence was found, in this sample, to extend from not only being able to delay or reduce the quality of implementation, but also to the possibility of sabotaging its success. Further research is obviously needed to investigate further the extent of such influence.

Capabilities

The issue of managerial capability was examined in Chapter 3 as one of the three areas of the internal audit. In that chapter there were two ways in which it was claimed managerial capability could be examined:

- Resultant company responsiveness to anticipate and react to changes in the environment.
- An assessment of certain managerial attributes which will give resultant capability profiles.

The approaches that were given in that chapter to generating information to enable an understanding of the above would provide an input to the understanding of this feature of the influence of human behaviour.

The interpretation of capabilities can be seen as having two potential ramifications. The first can be described as the actual capabilities of the managers who participate in both planning and control. Here standard approaches of personnel management for individual appraisal can lead to the identification of any gaps between essential skills and current skills, which may lead to changes in employment policies. The second ramification relates to managers' perceptions of their own capabilities in relation to their expectations. Here there may be differences between a manager's perception of his capabilities and his 'actual' capabilities, as determined in the formulation of his personal mangement capability profile. Where a manager thinks that he is better than he is then he is likely to have ambitious expectations, such that he would establish ambitious personal aims and would be fairly confident in achieving them. Where a manager perceives that he is less capable than the appraisal suggests then the opposite is likely to be the case. Both situations represent potential influences on the success of strategic management and necessitate careful consideration.

CORPORATE CULTURE

Wheelen and Hunger[18] have provided the following definition of 'corporate culture'. 'A corporation's culture is the collection of beliefs, expectations and values shared by the corporation's members and transmitted from one generation of employees to another.' While the last section dealt with values and expectations at the individual level, corporate culture addresses them at the corporate or organizational level. However, the culture cannot be merely a compilation of all values and expectations of all managers. The above definition refers to a collection which will be the result of much negotiation and the exercise of power to influence or coerce the acceptance of particular values to the detriment of others. Such influences can stem from individuals, from coalitions of individuals or from formal groups within the structure, such as a particular department or SBU. The resultant shared set of values is likely to be a compromise as far as most managers are concerned, although the resultant set will represent expected norms of behaviour to be followed by members of the managerial hierarchy. While the above definition suggests that the culture is passed on, and indeed culture is endemic to the organizational behaviour of a group of people working together, successive changes in managers and changes in the values and expectations of existing managers mean that the culture will be in a state of flux.

EXHIBIT 8.1

The Importance of being Coloroll

Coloroll is a home furnishings group, with businesses based on wallcoverings, household textiles, and ceramics. The group has achieved tremendous growth, from a turnover of £6 million in 1978 to one of £100 million in 1987. A major contribution to this success are the values and expectations that have been established as the corporate culture by the Chief Executive, John Ashcroft, based on clear individual responsibilities, clear objectives, tight control, and extensive ambition for future growth and success. A major value is gains in market share in all businesses, with full commitment to these gains and aggressive strategies for their achievement. Expectations develop out of the philosophy of thinking like a big company, and the major objective for 1990 is a sales turnover of £250 million. Ashcroft continuously reminds managers about the company's previous successes, to reinforce their commitment to achieving this major objective. He also believes in 'management by walking around', in order to gain information about the company's operations. Performance objectives for managers must be attained by them, and excuses for failure are not readily accepted. However, efficiency and commitment to the company are rewarded with generous working conditions, especially above average pay. Divisional managers are also expected fully to understand their markets, customers, consumers and competitors, as part of Coloroll's culture is based on taking risks in order effectively to satisfy customer and consumer needs.

Adapted from *Management Today*, January 1987

Seven features of this set of shared values and expectations have been identified by Robbins[19]:

- The degree of autonomy given to individuals to exercise responsibility, initiative and innovation.
- The amount of direct supervision that is deemed to be necessary for particular levels of management.
- The type of assistance and 'warmth' that managers provide to their subordinates.
- The ability of employees to identify and relate to the company as a corporate body.
- The degree to which rewards are related to performance as opposed to being set amounts.
- Developing the willingness to be honest and open, which includes interpersonal relationships.
- The degree to which individuals are encouraged to take risks, to be innovative in their thinking, and to be aggressive towards the future development of the company.

While all these features are pertinent to the success of strategic management the first and last are of major importance. Using the phraseology of Cleland and King[20], the culture provides an opportunity clearly to establish a bias towards the importance of strategic management, and particularly towards planning, so that managers come to accept that it is a central and integral part of the way that the company is run. Indeed the importance of strategic management could be established as one of the features of culture, to be added to the list given above.

Corporate culture can also be seen to relate to some of the previous chapters in that the shared set of values and expectations is important. In analysing the environment culture was seen as being part of the internal audit (as given in Chapter 3), within the context of assessing managerial capability, in the sense of assessing the compatibility of managers with the culture. The organizational mission reflects the corporate culture in that the established set of values and expectations influences the formulation of the mission, as given in the mission reason of 'company climate and philosophy' (see Chapter 6). Finally, corporate culture also has an influence on the formulation of organizational objectives in that again the established set of values and expectations influences the range and magnitude of objectives that will be established.

The role of corporate culture

It was said above that the corporate culture will represent expected norms of behaviour to be followed by the members of the managerial hierarchy. For organizations still dominated by the founder the culture provides a vehicle for communicating the expectations of the founder to other employees. Similarly, where a company is run by an autocratic senior management team who feature a 'top-down' style of management, again the role is to convey their expectations. However, where the shared set of values has developed within the company the major role of culture is one of the socialization of managers, particularly those new to the company.

Wheelen and Hunger[18] have listed the major roles to be played by corporate culture:

- It helps to convey a sense of identity for employees.
- It can be used to develop personal commitment to the company.
- In the sense that a company is a social system it helps to instil stability.
- It provides a guide for behaviour as a result of the established behavioural norms.

In this sense the culture can be seen to be very much concerned with the control of individuals, through an indirect process of indoctrination as opposed to a direct process of issuing orders and demanding reports on the completion of those orders. As will perhaps be already apparent, culture can also be used to instil the discipline of strategic management within the managerial hierarchy. Whether this would relate to its introduction or to the desire to develop planning to become more sophisticated, the required dispositions of managers can be promoted through modifications to the culture.

Cleland and King[20] have suggested that it is particularly important when the dispositions of managers can be described as being parochial, in that they tend to base their thinking almost totally on their own backgrounds, their particular functional specialisms, and on 'tunnel vision', where the many complexities of the company are not recognized. Again the point is that the role of culture is an aid to overcoming such parochialism, by extending the thinking of managers to the state necessary for participation in strategic management.

Types of culture

While a company can establish a unique culture in that, at a particular point in time, its set of shared values and expectations will differ from that of other firms, some writers have suggested classifications of broad types of corporate culture. Although the stance taken in this book is that culture is unique to each company, two of these classifications are examined. Deal and Kennedy[21] take a simplistic approach which classifies four generic cultures as illustrated in Figure 8.4, where the classificatory factors are risk and the speed at which feedback is available on the relative success of decision-making. While the labels used are colloquial, the classification is based on a requirement to take into account external environmental factors in developing the culture. Indeed those of importance are likely to vary from industry to industry.

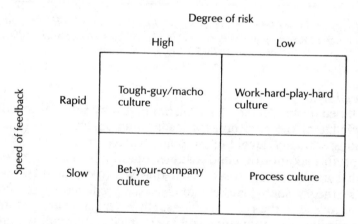

Figure 8.4 *Classification of generic cultures. (L. W. Rue and P. G. Holland,* Strategic Management, © 1986. *Reproduced by permission of the McGraw-Hill Book Co.)*

Miesling and Wolfe[22] also look to the environment in suggesting a classification of approaches to planning, which they advocate as being particularly applicable at the SBU level. This classification is based on the following conditions:

- Beliefs about cause-and-effect relationships in the environment that affect the planning of strategic management.
- Changes that take place in the external environment to reflect environmental stability.

The approach results in four different styles of planning with associated styles of decision-making (see Figure 8.5). The adoption of one of these styles becomes part of the culture in that each depicts the adoption of particular beliefs and values.

Cause-and-effect relationships

	Known	Unknown
Stable	Computational planning style Analytical decision-making	Consensual planning style Intuitive decision-making
Dynamic	Contingency planning style Incremental decision-making	Conceptualized planning style Inspirational decision-making

Environmental change

Figure 8.5 *Classification of planning styles. (Reproduced by permission of the publisher, from 'The Art and Science of Planning at the Business Unit Level' by Miesling and Wolfe,* Management Science, © *1985 TIMS, Rhode Island.)*

Computational style

This style is based on an ideal model of planning using a rational approach, where perfect knowledge of the environment leads to an analysis which can result in decision-making which is devoid of irrational behaviour. It assumes a long-term rationale of profit maximization and assumes that the personal aims of managers coincide with company objectives. Given the two environmental conditions in Figure 8.5, in theory such planning models are predicted to represent reality accurately and to lead to the right decisions. However, in reality it is unlikely that complete knowledge of relationships and guaranteed stability of the environment will be encountered. When firms do believe that they are in this situation of near perfect knowledge, then the culture is orientated to a belief that planning is effective and that the right decisions are made.

Consensual style

Where cause-and-effect relationships are unknown, recourse is made to personal aims, and managerial values, beliefs and expectations. As already mentioned above, negotiation and exercise of power occur between individuals and coalitions until a consensus of opinion is reached between the various managers who are involved with each of the issues to be addressed. However, the obvious major problem of such a style is bias relating to and reliability of the intuitive abilities of the managers concerned. Senior managers must be able to reconcile differences of judgement and be able to understand both the formal and informal processes that feature within the organization. Here the culture needs to establish open rapport between managers, eagerness to address long-range issues, innovative thinking, and procedures for participation.

Contingency style

In this situation firms are seen to have knowledge about the relationships of variables in the environment, although the latter features many changes in its dynamic nature. Here the style needs to avoid reliance on a single plan, but needs to develop a plan with a number of alternative courses of action for each of a number of issues, each of which represents appropriate action if a particular change occurs. Each of these planned courses of action would be contingent on the manifestation of a set of market conditions, where the latter are a number of alternative scenarios which model particular situations (scenario writing was introduced in Chapter 3 as a method of forecasting). Where alternative scenarios are not developed a single plan is produced, which is incrementally modified as time progesses and the ramifications of changes become apparent. Here the culture needs to develop managerial thinking to be creative within scenario writing and to be research-orientated in order to be able to identify changes and their consequential incremental plan modifications.

Conceptualized style

For effective planning this set of environmental conditions obviously represents the most difficult style to develop and utilize. Indeed fixed and rigid plans which quickly become inappropriate as a result of the changed environment challenge the credibility of strategic management. While such conditions present many threats, many opportunities for business development may also be generated. Here the onus on strategic management switches to a process for seeking opportunities, assessing their risks, and appropriate exploitation, as initially discussed in Chapter 3. Here the culture again needs to be geared to incrementalism to allow for the identification of threats and the subsequent modification of plans. Also, creativity and innovation in managerial thinking are even more important if such opportunities are to be exploited.

Changing corporate culture

In so far as culture is a set of values and expectations which is a compromi
complexity of values and expectations across the even more complex augm

of human behaviour within a company, it is inevitable that a firm's culture is difficult both to define and to change. Although the board of directors may be able to model its 'ideal' culture, for many firms this model may be only conceptually held in the minds of these executives. However, this set of values and expectations at the corporate level is clearly as important as those at the individual level. Indeed, writers such as Cleland and King[20] have suggested that it is of major importance in ensuring that strategic management is effective. Therefore, despite the difficulty of the task it is obviously of paramount importance that corporate culture is given consideration, to strive to model the perceived ideal culture as enviomental conditions change and to attempt the pursuit of cultural changes.

MANAGERIAL RESISTANCE TO CHANGE

The various issues of the influence of managerial behaviour on strategic management represent potential managerial resistance to change. There are two forms of change to consider. The first represents changes that can either be threats or opportunities from the environment, but which are likely to necessitate reaction on the part of the firm. The second represents the firm's reaction to the environment, which should be ultimately planned within the stages of strategic management. However, the ability of the firm both to identify and to react to environmental changes, and to instigate momentum for their planned consequental changes to the company will clearly affect the firm's success. The purpose of this section is to examine the nature and ramifications of potential managerial resistance to these changes, as a consequence of their influence.

EXHIBIT 8.2

How to Change Companies

The following comes from the experience of Midland Bank International in France, West Germany, and the United Kingdom in instigating change. Four major areas of change were identified. First, the approach to strategy which must become targeted to specific consumer banking needs. Second, the organizational structure, which in banks has not changed in 50 years, and is very bureaucratic. Change is needed to modify the structure and make it responsive to market requirements. Third, corporate culture needs to be changed, to become less technically-based and more people-orientated. Fourth, a change is needed in the behaviour and attitudes of personnel. Behaviour and attitudes must be modified to focus on customers, and away from current preoccupations with internal problems. It is recognized that change is not easy to achieve; it is not a natural phenomenon that will happen automatically. The process of change needs to be effectively planned and implemented.

Adapted from *Management Today*, April 1987

To recapitulate, these major influences of managerial behaviour are as follows:

- From values, the possibility of goal conflict.
- From expectations, a motivational impediment to successful strategic management.
- From managerial capability, latent ability to react.
- From culture, receptiveness to individual control and indoctrination in the discipline of strategic management.
- From culture, receptiveness to a planning style.

These influences affect both forms of change as mentioned above and both are of obvious importance to successful strategic management.

Environmental change

Ansoff[23] has provided an explanation of the types of resistance that relate to changes that take place in the environment. As a prelude he explains that the consequence of resistance is the incursion of two types of costs. The first of these is the loss of profit, as a result of both resistance and a failure to predict the ramifications of the said changes. The other cost is the expenditure necessary not only to react to the change eventually, but also to take corrective and compensatory action to return profits to their aspired level, as well as make up for lost profits. In most cases the longer the period during which resistance occurs and in which there is inaction then the greater the losses will be, while the consequential changes to be planned in the strategic management become greater and perhaps more radical.

Ansoff[23] suggests that resistance to environmental changes can be explained in three types of management behaviour:

Reactive management

In this type of company, changes in the environment and their ramifications on performance may not be immediately recognized. Initial identification is likely to lead to the application of techniques which have been previously successful in tackling such ramifications, such as marketing aggression, improved efficiency, cost reductions, or reduced output. If these techniques fail to work the environmental change represents a new threat, which will eventually force or trigger the firm to take further decisions to tackle the change. Indeed, the study of these so-called 'trigger points' has been given recent attention in the literature.

In the reactive management behaviour type of company there can be considerable delay in reacting to or considerable resistance to environmental change. Ansoff[23] has suggested that this delay or resistance can extend beyond the rational trigger point and he identifies four contributing factors to this situation:

- A system delay caused by the internal inertia of collecting, analysing and disseminating information pertinent to the environment.

- A verification delay where, even though the ramifications of change have been identified, managers fail to appreciate its real significance or believe that it is merely a quirk in the trend which will eventually 'flatten out'.
- A political delay where, even if the significance of the ramifications is fully realized, personal interests may lead to resistance, such as avoidance of blame, seeking to protect personal span of control, or gaining time in order to seek new employment.
- An unfamiliarity delay where new changes resulting in new managerial challenges represent major decision-making difficulties which challenge the capabilities of both the corporate body and individual managers. Ansoff claims that Western managerial culture is imbued with this type of resistance.

Therefore in this type of management behaviour delays and resistance are based on influences of managerial behaviour, as recapitulated at the beginning of this section. The point to emphasize is that individual values and expectations and corporate culture are influential in causing resistance to change.

Decisive management

In this type of company little, if any, research and monitoring of the environment is carried out. Therefore changes can occur which may be either threats or opportunities, but the company is either unaware of them or is not in a position fully to assess their likely ramifications. However, it tends to be quick in recognizing the build-up of losses as a result of resistance and will quickly respond, but again initially with previously used approaches. If these fail to work then it will also be quick to decide to abandon them in favour of new approaches. Therefore, delay or resistance is reduced in that it reacts quickly to a trigger point, although additional delay and resistance are introduced as its reaction is not based on an understanding of the changes taking place in the environment.

In this type of situation the resultant ability of the firm to avoid resistance to change is totally based on managerial behaviour. Indeed this total philosophy of management which gives little attention to monitoring the environment becomes part of the corporate culture. Little discipline in this respect is imparted to individual managers, while the planning style features inspirational-type decision-making. This means that great reliance is based on managerial capability, even though this capability may be largely intuitive and cavalier in nature. However, resistance to change can be exacerbated by both the values and expectations of individual managers. Uncertainty in the direction of the company and in decision-making can lead to a perception of conflict between personal aims and the perceived objectives of the company. As a result, low expectations lead to reduced motivation, with perceived conflict and low motivation being a recipe for managers to resist change in their working environments.

Planned management

This type of management is based on systematic and logical planning for the future, such as following the model of strategic management that is used in this book. While reactive and decisive management are a result of environmental changes affecting the company, this type is obviously geared to identifying changes before or as they occur. Ramifications can then be taken into account so that all the stages of strategic management, especially objectives and strategies, can be planned, implemented and controlled accordingly.

In theory this may hold but in practice delay and resistance to environmental change can still occur in firms that feature this mode of management. One reason can be the approach used in forecasting. If this is based merely on extrapolations of past patterns into the future then certain changes can influence these trends incrementally over a period of time without being noticed, causing a delay and subsequent resistance before action is taken. This is then similar to reactive management. Changes may only be identified when they are significantly large, at a particular point in time, and provide an obvious visual impact. However, where non-extrapolative techniques of forecasting are used, such as scenario writing (see Chapter 3), much of this resistance can still occur owing to managerial influences. Managers may have difficulty in believing and accepting the forecasts so that scenario predications remain unheeded or are only partially taken into account. A common reaction is to consider that the magnitude of the anticipated change is a result of forecasting error, so that the forecast is 'doctored' downwards. Actual impact will then be only as experienced so that again resistance can be introduced into the planning.

Ansoff[23] also claims that the contributing factors to delay that were pertinent to reactive management can also be applicable in planned management. Systems delay, so he claims, can also feature through some internal inertia, although because the corporate culture is geared up to strategic management there is less chance of it occurring, while its impact is likely to be a lot less than in a reactive management situation. Verification, political and unfamiliarity resistance can all be justified on the premiss that no matter how sophisticated the forecasting it is still based on conjecture and not actual experience. Verification is based on the probability of the occurrence of change, political delay on maintaining the status quo as opposed to reacting to speculation, and unfamiliarity delay on the assumption that the current process of strategic management will be able to accommodate the action needed as a consequence of change. Again it is apparent that delays and resistance are based on influences of managerial behaviour, relating to individual values and expectations and corporate culture.

Organizational change

As mentioned earlier, this is the other form of change, where changes to the organization are necessary as a consequence of environmental changes. These changes should normally be planned within the stages of strategic management.

The creation of momentum for change has been well discussed in a recent article by Dutton and Duncan[24]. They present a model to illustrate the development of momentum that will lead to organizational change, and a range of propositions that relate to the instigation of change. This model has been adapted and is presented in Figure 8.6. The triggering mechanism is as described above (as changes in the external environment) although strictly speaking it should be as an integral part of the strategic management process. The model shows that the momentum for change is generated by two aspects of managerial perception, one concerned with the way managers perceive that organizational change is necessary, and the other being concerned with managers' perception of the possibility that changes can be made. The momentum for change equates to the concept of managerial resistance to change that has been used in the previous discussions. The relationship is that resistance will decrease as the momentum for change increases, while change can be a gradual modification or a major upheaval over a relatively short period of time.

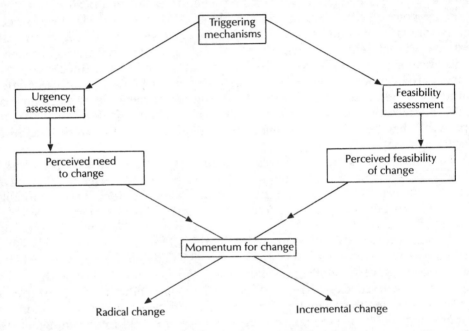

Figure 8.6   *Momentum for organizational change.*

The article* by Dutton and Duncan[24] discusses urgency and feasibility assessments in detail, and they use the label 'strategic issues' to refer to events or changes in the environment which could trigger organizational change. However, it is the range of propositions which arises from their discussions which is important at this juncture, and which reflects on the influences of managerial behaviour.

The first of these propositions is: 'The more decision-makers perceive they understand a strategic issue and perceive that the organization has the capability for dealing with the issue, the greater the momentum for change.' This proposition

*Adapted by permission of John Wiley & Sons Ltd.

is clearly consistent with the influence of values and expectations at both the individual and corporate culture levels. In particular, the expectations of managers concerning whether or not they really understand the need for change and whether they consider that it can be achieved, will partly determine any resistance.

The second proposition is: 'The more a strategic issue is diagnosed by organizational decision-makers as urgent and feasible to resolve, the greater the momentum for change, and the more radical the change outcome.' In fact this is the major thrust of Dutton and Duncan[24]; that it is the process of diagnosing the environment which is the key to increased momentum and reduced resistance. Where this analysis indicates urgency and feasibility then managers have learned that change is necessary. Here the culture is central to indoctrinate managers to accept the importance of diagnosis in the first place and to be receptive to planning orientation.

The third proposition is: 'The more differentiated an organization's belief structure (lower concensus and more complex), the more frequently strategic issue diagnosis will be triggered.' This proposition is a consequence of the complexity of values and expectations and the differences that are to be found between individuals, coalitions and formal groups. While greater differentiation can lead to conflict and difficulty in developing and implanting a culture, the advantage is that different views and different perspectives on situations can result in more innovative and creative thinking, in that a wider range of views are developed, while differences lead to negotiation as the differences are discussed and settled. However, the major point is that the process needs to be controlled in order to result in greater momentum and not greater resistance.

An opposing phenomenon of human behaviour is that of managerial conservatism, which has been the subject of a recent article by Sturdivant et al.[25]. Managers exhibiting the trait of conservatism would feature little innovation and creativity in their thinking, would tend to resist change, and would be moderate and cautious in the actions that they pursue. Although their research was limited in its generalization to a wide population of organizations, the thrust of it is that conservatism, as manifest in resistance to change, may be at the heart of problems confronting companies which are losing their competitive position.

The fourth proposition is: 'The more differentiated an organization's belief structure, the greater the perceived feasibility of change, and the greater the momentum for change.' Following the argument for the third proposition, a controlled internal environment of free-flowing ideas about possible changes will lead to more alternatives being considered, a greater chance that a feasible course of action will be identified and hence greater momentum for and less resistance to change. Again corporate culture is a vehicle for accommodating this type of process, while the personal expectations of managers are likely to be extended in this type of stimulating environment, which in turn will lead to more differentiated thinking.

The fifth proposition is: 'The greater the supply of organizational resources, the less the perception of urgency, the less the perceived need to change and the less the momentum for change.' In the words of Sturdivant et al. a large organization with a continuing supply of resources, particularly built by past success, can lead to 'illusions of invulnerability in the minds of the decision-makers'. These 'illusions' could be featured not only in the minds of individual managers to mould their expectations but could also be featured as a component within the corporate culture. This means that the triggering of change is likely to be delayed until such time as the environmental change causes cost increases, while the results of the diagnosis may be subject to analytical bias or 'doctored' because of this corporate arrogance. In either situation the outcome is likely to be resistance to change.

The sixth and final proposition is: 'The greater the supply of organizational resources, the greater the perceived feasibility of resolving an issue, and the greater the momentum for change.' Here the point is that adequate resources can also have the opposite effect to that in the fifth proposition; that is, to reduce resistance and increase the momentum for organizational change. In companies where the invulnerability syndrome is suppressed, resources can be channelled into the effective collection, analysis and dissemination of information about the environment, and managers can become confident about their ability to solve problems. Confidence and capability are enhanced so that managers are prepared to tackle change and resistance is accordingly reduced. Here the process of diagnosis again needs to mould the corporate culture to give further indoctrination in the overall discipline of strategic management and an associated planning style. In turn the values and expectations of managers will be modified again to reduce the tendency to resist change.

SUMMARY

This is one of the chapters of the book devoted to the human behaviour of managers rather than to integral stages of the strategic management process. Organizations, regardless of their size, are merely groups of people working together and it is their behaviour which moulds the nature of organizations and leads to the decisions which are made.

The central themes of the chapter were values and expectations, which were examined at the individual and corporate levels. The major ramifications of these values and expectations were seen to be pertinent to changes which need to be tackled. These changes are endemic to strategic management, and were classified into those which are identified within the environment and those which need to be made to the organization as a result of the former.

The first section examined four major features of the influence of human behaviour on planning. As well as values and expectations these included managerial attitudes and capabilities. Of central importance to this section were the personal aims of managers, the expectations that they finally set for achievement from the working environment and their expectations of the probability of achieving these aims.

The second section examined values and expectations at the corporate level, which was presented as the concept of corporate culture. This was defined as the collection of beliefs, values, and expectations that are shared by managers to represent those of the firm as opposed to those attributable to a single manager. Several features of corporate culture were given while their link to the values and expectations of individual managers was discussed. The section also tackled the roles that culture can play in a firm and the different types of culture. A major classification of types of culture was based on planning style and associated decision-making. The final concern of this section was the problems associated with changing the culture.

The third and final section was concerned with managerial resistance to change. Here there were two forms of change: those which occur in the environment, and those that are made to the organization as a consequence. Within both of these the focus was on the potential for resistance to change on the part of managers, as a consequence of their values and expectations at both the individual and corporate levels. The section first looked at these influences in relation to environmental change, where Ansoff's three types of management of change were discussed. Attention was then directed to influence in relation to organizational change, where the thrust was based on a model proposed by Dutton and Duncan and a range of associated propositions.

CHAPTER CASE STUDY ILLUSTRATION: HOFFMAN—LA ROCHE V. STANLEY ADAMS*

This case study shows clearly the difference in the values and expectations between the Swiss based Hoffman–La Roche, the world's largest pharmaceutical company, and a previous senior manager in this organization, Stanley Adams. In 1973 Adams considered that Roche was guilty of unfair trading practices, and his feelings were so strong that he decided to act against the interests of his employer by reporting his concerns to the EEC Commissioner for Competition.

At the time of the case study, Swiss-based Roche was considered to be the largest ethical drugs company, although sales figures had never been publicly available. They were based on three SBUs: ethical drugs (two-thirds of the business); bulk vitamins (one-quarter of the business); and aromatics and flavours (the remainder). Roche claimed that most of its sales came from only two products, branded Librium and Valium, which are probably those products of Roche which are best known to the general public.

*Derived from the original case study by Eric Newbigging (Copyright © 1986).

The business practices that Adams perceived, and which led him to act against the interests of Roche, were based on his experience of the bulk vitamins SBU and were reported in the case study as:

- Although it had expanded production on a world-wide basis and had reduced production costs, there appeared to be no intention to pass these savings on to consumers.
- It persuaded smaller producers to stop production and to buy direct from itself; these companies also agreed to sell at the same prices as Roche.
- Where this persuasion failed these companies were then persuaded by Roche to set selling prices the same as Roche's on a world-wide basis.
- It also persuaded other manufacturers to agree to fixed market shares in each market throughout the world.
- It instigated and held regular meetings of producers to achieve complete control of selling prices.

Adams's conclusion was that Roche had mostly eliminated fair competition, but where this had not been achieved it had, with the co-operation of other producers, distorted competition completely.

In 1972 a Free Trade Agreement was established between the EEC and Switzerland, which included the EEC rules on competition. The latter included Articles 85 and 86 of the Treaty of Rome, concerning companies abusing a dominant market position. As a result of Stanley Adams's reporting these practices to the EEC Commission, in 1976 Roche was fined some £250,000 for unfair trading practices under Article 86.

CORPORATE CULTURE OF HOFFMAN–LA ROCHE

The case study discusses several issues which are indicative of Roche's corporate culture. As reported by Adams, the company required employees to be loyal at all times, and to believe that what the company does must be good because their welfare is dependent on the company's welfare. Indeed this aspect of company culture seemed to be common to many Swiss companies. Similarly, Roche normally appointed only Swiss nationals to senior management positions, with Adams's appointment (as a British citizen) being unusual. To communicate their culture the company provided extensive training to new managers, and for senior management this included experience of company practices in all departments. Periodically managers were summoned to headquarters to be indoctrinated in the practice and culture of the company. This included demands to increase turnover, to find new products, and to make more money for the company.

Although Roche operated many overseas subsidiaries, all were tightly controlled from the company headquarters in Switzerland; this control included the imposition of limits on wage payments and strict control of selling prices. However, senior overseas managers were paid half their salary in the country where they worked and the other half in a Swiss bank account, in order to moderate local income tax, as well as demonstrating lower salaries to locally employed managers.

Roche appeared to value the successes of their managers; Adams's success in establishing and developing a Venezuelan subsidiary was rewarded with praise and the offer of a more senior appointment. However, board-level conflict meant that this promotion did not materialize, implying conflict and weak concern for individuals within the culture.

Finally, the major feature of culture that is portrayed in the case was the company's beliefs and values concerning competition. These have already been indicated in relation to its competitive practices, as perceived by Adams. While the world supply of vitamins had exceeded demand, these competitive moves had managed to result in continued price increases, as opposed to price reductions which should have occurred with free market forces. The implication is that the culture valued domination, manipulation, and control of the environment, so that major changes in the latter would be only those instigated by Roche.

VALUES AND EXPECTATIONS OF STANLEY ADAMS

As he was not a Swiss national, Stanley Adams was not imbued with the value of Swiss corporate culture which demands loyalty to the company regardless of the cost to individuals. Indeed, he considered that ruthless suppression of individuals or smaller companies was not only morally wrong, but was also indicative of an incorrect approach to management *per se*.

Adams's dedication to his work, his attitudes to challenging the status quo and the need to be creative in developing alternative approaches contributed to the success of his management of the Venzuelan subsidiary. Within three years of its establishment it had achieved an annual turnover of 6 million Swiss Francs. Adams valued the rewards associated with this performance, including his high salary, salary bonuses, an elegant lifestyle, and the experience of living abroad.

Adams was then returned to headquarters in Basle and was promoted to a higher managerial position as the world product manager for a Roche product range. However, the major vitamin producers operated a collusive oligopoly, and, because of his senior position, he was expected to contribute to its operation. Here there was an immediate conflict in values in that this way of 'doing business' was not consistent with his own personal values. This conflict intensified as he formed the opinion that his employer was aiming to eliminate competition rather than to compete effectively. Also, as he travelled in poor countries he began to realize the effects that were resulting from this approach, including the influence that the controlled supply of drugs had on prices during times of epidemics in these poor countries.

Adams also disapproved of the regular indoctrination meetings for senior managers, where he could not agree with what he perceived as the major value of the culture, that is, to make money regardless of the consequences for others. These conflicts of values became more serious for Adams until he eventually came to the conclusion that he had to take some action. However, this was obviously a major concern as his position and associated remuneration meant that he had come to expect a high standard of living for himself and his family, which would obviously be in jeopardy if such action were taken.

Eventually, his belief in what was right and wrong forced him to take the action of reporting the practices of Roche to the EEC Commissioner for Competition. At this time he was still an employee of Roche, but the EEC Commission guaranteed that it would not reveal the source of its information, although he also planned to leave the organization. By the end of October 1973 he had supplied the necessary information to the Commission, at which time he resigned from Hoffman–La Roche.

POSTSCRIPT

The Adams family moved to Italy, where Stanley established a business as a pig farmer. On New Year's Eve 1974 the family were travelling to Switzerland to visit Mrs Adams's relations. However, the Swiss police arrested him at the border and he was eventually charged with industrial espionage. His identity as the source of the information given to the EEC had obviously been revealed. After three months in custody he was released, but had now to face life without his wife, who had committed suicide because of the prospect of his facing twenty years' imprisonment had he been found guilty.

Adams sued the EEC Commission for damages, his case being that they had been negligent and were in breach of confidence over his disclosures. He was the first person to sue the Commission and in 1985 the European Court awarded him substantial damages.

INTEGRATIVE CASE ILLUSTRATION: PART THREE

The integrative case study provides indications of the directional planning that was done by Plessey at various times over the period of the case. Indications of organizational mission are given, although insufficient information is available to determine a mission statement. Organizational objectives are listed at a particular stage of the company's development, while emphasis on priorities is also given. Indications of values and expectations can also be extracted.

ORGANIZATIONAL MISSION

At the beginning of the case study a statement by the Chairman and Chief Executive of Plessey in 1983 is given. Although this cannot be taken as a bona fide mission statement, it includes many issues that would be included in the mission, such as:

- Increased attention to world-wide marketing.
- Working to improve performance and particularly profitability.
- Maintaining future developments in high-technology areas of business.
- Ensuring that these technological developments are more closely related to the needs of customers.
- Striving to integrate the technology of product design with that of manufacturing to ensure optimum performance.
- Utilization of professionalism in technology, new product development, and manufacturing as major competitive advantages.

In the period between 1977 and this statement (1983) weaknesses of the previous POST (Plessey Objectives, Strategies and Tactics) planning system had become apparent. A major weakness was seen to have been that the mission and objectives were not adequately and meaningfully defined. In particular, the latter were not in a form which could be adequately used to establish strategies for the SBUs, which resulted in problems of determining priorities and allocating resources, as well as failure in establishing operational-level planning as part of routine management.

Consequently, in 1978 the planning process was revised, which gave new direction. It was considered that previously the Company had attempted to serve too many markets with too few resources. The new mission was based on giving priority to high-technology business, with the corporate centre defining the overall direction for development and choosing between SBUs for the allocation of resources. In order to avoid the previous problems, planning guidelines were also issued to the management boards of the SBUs and the trading companies. By 1980 the reduction of markets and products had been achieved, and with its excellence in R&D Plessey was achieving the direction which was needed.

ORGANIZATIONAL OBJECTIVES

The case study refers directly to objectives that were established by Plessey in 1975, and which were reported to shareholders as corporate objectives:

- To maximize earnings per share.
- To become a world-wide enterprise.
- To invest in selected products and markets on a planned basis, choosing opportunities which optimize the use of resources within prescribed fields of business, e.g. telecommunications, electronic systems, and components.
- To sustain an efficient and productive organization, by being competitive in world markets through managing technology, manufacturing and market skills.

These four objectives can be classified using the typology given in Table 7.1. The first belongs to group 2 (performance, profitability); the second and third to group 1 (directional, market spread); and the fourth to group 3 (internal, efficiency).

Compared with the spread given in Table 7.1, these four objectives seem to be somewhat limited, with no objectives directly addressing market leadership, customer service, growth, personnel and social responsibility. One implication is that the four were only a selection of the full range, having been selected to satisfy the target audience of shareholders. However, another implication is that companies are unlikely to have a full range, but will only establish those which are considered to be the most important at a particular point in time. For example, the importance of market spread to Plessey is reflected in the fact that in 1975 they were operating in 136 countries.

However, as already reported above, by 1977 it had been realized that the objectives which had been previously set were neither adequate nor meaningful. Consequently, they had failed to play their correct role in strategic management, with their most crucial weakness being perhaps not providing the framework for determining strategies for the SBUs. Although in 1978 future direction was revised, again as reported above, the case study does not give the organizational objectives that were established as a consequence.

VALUES AND EXPECTATIONS

Several indications are given of the preparedness of Plessey to respond to change over particular periods of time. While these indications are reflective of corporate culture, Plessey participated in industries that feature many changes, which perhaps influenced 'forced' changes.

In 1975 the perceived importance of strategic planning was a feature of the culture in that two planning systems were introduced: POST and STAMP (Strategic and Tactical Asset Management Programme). The aim was to change 'corporate behaviour' so that systematic planning would be used to pursue opportunities and challenge threats from the environment through the internal allocation of resources. This changed behaviour would allay the tendency towards sporadic decision-making in Plessey's planning endeavours. As mentioned above, by 1977 many weaknesses had been identified in these systems, but again the culture was able to support change in order to attempt to remove many of these.

In 1983 changes to the management of the organization were again needed because of intensified environmental trends, and the culture was again important. Effective strategic planning was seen to be the key to survival, but with an emphasis on the continued appraisal of its effectiveness and the involvement of line managers. The resultant revisions were valued as a substantial evolution of POST, giving improved management control of the company's businesses.

In the early 1970s the inference is that perhaps the culture allowed for too much intervention in planning by the main board directors, by interfering with management in the companies, and by their monthly detailed assessment of company results. By 1976 a changed mode of operation had been built into the corporate culture. This involved a new organizational structure with the maximum of delegated authority to each of the managing directors of each of the subsidiary companies that formed this structure. By 1983 this approach was consolidated in that the Chief Executive Office concentrated on group objectives, strategies and policies, with necessary appraisals at the SBU level for consistency and overall performance.

REFERENCES

1. Williams, T. G., *Consumer Behaviour*, West, St Paul, MN, 1982.
2. Johnson, G. and Scholes, K., *Exploring Corporate Strategy*, Prentice Hall, London, 1984.
3. Chang, Y. N. and Campo-Flores, F., *Business Policy and Strategy*, Goodyear, Santa Monica, CA, 1980.
4. Christensen, C. R., Andrews, K. R., Bower, J. L., Hindmarsh, R. G. and Porter, M. E., *Business Policy*, Irwin, Homewood, IL, 1982.
5. Guth, W. D. and Tagiuri, R., 'Personal Values and Corporate Strategy', *Harvard Business Review*, **43**, 5, 1965.
6. England, G. W., 'Managers and Their Value Systems', *Columbia Journal World Business*, **13**, 2, 1978, 35–44.
7. Saunders, C. B., 'Setting Organizational Objectives', *Journal of Business Policy*, **3**, 4, 1973, 13–20.
8. Baron, R. A. and Byrne, D., *Social Psychology: Understanding Human Reaction*, Allyn and Bacon, Boston, 1977.

9. Chisnall, P. M., *Marketing: A Behavioural Approach*, 2nd edn, McGraw-Hill, Maidenhead, 1985.

10. Taylor, B. and Irving, P., 'Organised Planning in Major UK Companies', *Long Range Planning*, **4**, 2, 1971, 10–26.

11. Higgins, J. C. and Finn, R., 'The Organisation and Practice of Corporate Planning in the UK', *Long Range Planning*, **10**, 4, 1977, 88–92.

12. Al-Bazzaz, S. and Grinyer, P. H., 'How Planning Works in Practice', *Long Range Planning*, **13**, 4, 1980, 30–41.

13. Ames, B. C., 'Marketing Planning for Industrial Products', *Harvard Business Review*, **46**, 5, 1968, 100–11.

14. Kudla, R. J., 'Elements of Effective Corporate Planning', *Long Range Planning*, **9**, 4, 1976, 82–93.

15. Brown, J. K., *et al.*, 'Long Range Planning in the USA', *Long Range Planning*, **1**, 3, 1969, 44–51.

16. Gray, J. L. and Starke, F A., *Organizational Behaviour*, 3rd edn, Merrill, Columbus, OH, 1984.

17. Guth, W. D. and Macmillan, I. C., 'Strategy Implementation versus Middle Management Self-interest', *Strategic Management Journal*, **7**, 1986, 313–27.

18. Wheelen, T. L. and Hunger, J. D., *Strategic Management and Business Policy*, 2nd edn, Addison-Wesley, Reading, MA, 1986.

19. Robbins, S. P., *Essentials of Organizational Behaviour*, Prentice Hall, Englewood Cliffs, NJ, 1984.

20. Cleland, D. I. and King, W. R., 'Developing a Planning Culture for More Effective Strategic Planning', *Long Range Planning*, **7**, 3, 1974, 70–4.

21. Deal, T. E. and Kennedy, A. A., *Corporate Cultures*, Addison-Wesley, Reading, MA, 1982.

22. Miesling, P. and Wolfe, J., 'The Art and Science of Planning at the Business Unit Level', *Management Science*, **31**, 6, 1985, 773–81.

23. Ansoff, H. I., *Implanting Strategic Management*, Prentice Hall, Englewood Cliffs, NJ, 1984.

24. Dutton, J. E. and Duncan, R. B., 'The Creation of Momentum for Change through the Process of Strategic Issue Diagnosis', *Strategic Management Journal*, **8**, 3, 1987, 279–95.

25. Sturdivant, F. D., Ginter, J. L. and Saywer, A. G., 'Managers' Conservatism and Corporate Performance', *Strategic Management Journal*, **6**, 1985, 17–38.

Planning Strategy

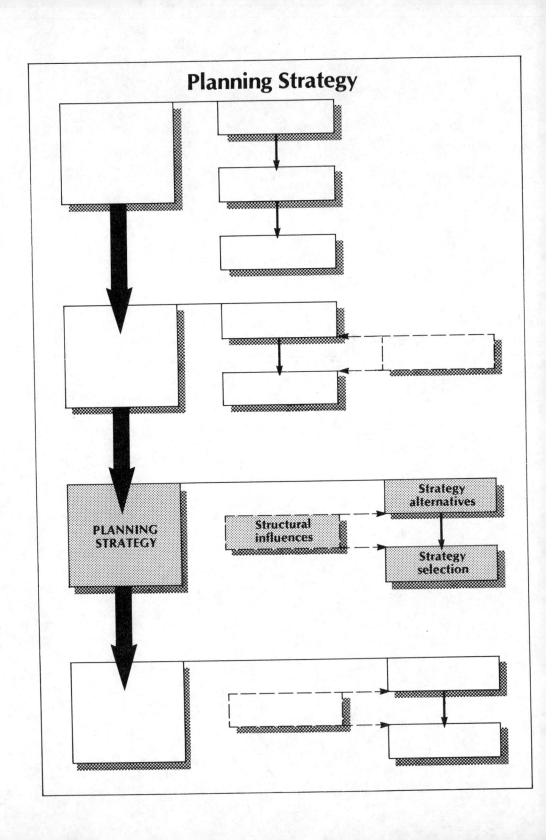

PLANNING
STRATEGY

Structural
influences

Strategy
alternatives

Strategy
selection

PART FOUR
PLANNING STRATEGY

OUTLINE OF PART FOUR

Having planned future direction, attention moves on to the means of pursuing this planned direction. As mentioned in Chapter 1, in simple terms this can be considered in terms of 'how' the organization is to tackle the achievement of this direction. The outcome of this part of strategic management should be planned action that relates to the whole organization. Here there are perhaps two major ramifications. First, the company becomes committed to particular courses of action, the ramifications of which are enduring in nature, as discussed in Chapter 1. Second, the organizational strategy provides a framework for the development of operational strategies. This planning of strategy is presented in three chapters. Chapter 9 addresses the organizational structure, where the issue of structure providing a constraint on strategy is compared with the issue of strategy determining the structure to be developed. In Chapter 10 the various approaches to organizational strategy are examined, as well as the generation of alternative but viable strategies. In Chapter 11 attention is given to the many techniques which can aid decision-making to select the strategy to be pursued from these alternatives.

CHAPTER 9

STRUCTURAL INFLUENCES

This chapter examines the role of structure within strategic management. Particular attention has been given to the relationship between structure and strategy in the literature, which provides the basis for locating structure at this particular juncture in the book. In the model of strategic management used throughout the book structure is given in a 'dashed box'. This means that, although it is an integral part of strategic management, it is not a stage of decision-making within the process. Rather it is seen as impinging on decision-making within the respective stages of the process. The aim of the chapter is to discuss the many issues that relate to structure as part of this impingement on the other stages of strategic management.

Structure is discussed in the organizational behaviour literature as well as in the strategic management literature. While the former takes the focus of the effects of structure on individual and group behaviour and span of control, the strategic management literature tends to focus on the strategy–structure relationship. There are two main issues pertinent to this relationship. The first is that strategy comes first so that the structure is designed in order to accommodate the implementation of strategy. The second issue is that structure is taken to be a constraint on strategy, possibly retarding its planning. Both these issues are tackled in this chapter, although the first issue is more likely to be applicable in the long term and the second issue in the shorter term.

In most textbooks on strategic management the treatment of structure follows that of strategy. This presentation is based on the strategy affecting structure logic. There are several reasons for reversing the presentation of chapters in this book. One of these is the difference in time horizons, as mentioned above. Another reason is that organizational strategy can be applicable at the corporate and SBU structural levels, giving an ordering of strategies similar to the hierarchy of objectives. Indeed increased attention has recently been given to the important differences between corporate-level and business-level strategies. In the final section of Chapter 8 attention was given to links between objectives, structure and strategy. This sequence provides another reason for addressing structure in this order. Also, as will be seen in this chapter, many influences are likely to have an affect on structure, of which strategy is one, so that it is considered important to be aware of the other influences before formally addressing strategy. Finally, for some companies, especially where there are no separate SBUs, the structure can be the major mechanism for integration, so that the structure becomes the company, with personal values and expectations being closely linked with the structure.

This chapter consists of five major sections. The first is concerned with the basic types of structure, while the second examines the major influences on structural design. The third section addresses the matching of structure and strategy, and the fourth is concerned with the effectiveness of structures. The final section is a summary.

BASIC TYPES OF STRUCTURE

While much of the attention to structure in the strategic management literature has been as a vehicle for the implementation of strategy, there are more fundamental roles that an established structure needs to play, which were established in the early management literature. Perhaps the basic function of structure is to provide a process for the division of labour. Regardless of the size of the company the need is simply to spread the total work to be done among the available human resources. Following on from this is the need to establish lines of authority in order to ensure that each of these divisions of work is completed. Therefore the structure allows for the delegation of authority, giving individual managers specific authority for certain parts of the company. Leading on from this point, the lines of delegation also provide channels of communication, so that the structure is not just that of an organization of people, but is also a network for communication between them. The structure is also seen to be a formal process to aid the attainment of objectives. Companies operate through the performance of people and the structure is the organization of the human resources. All these fundamental roles are important in

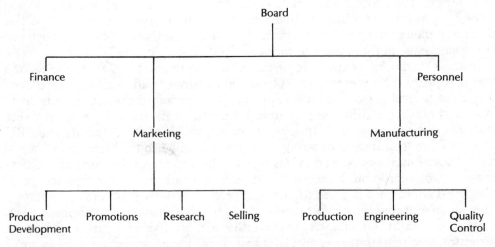

Figure 9.1 *A functional structure.*

looking at basic types of structure and at influences on their modification, as well as influences on strategy.

Initial consideration of structural types was given in Chapter 1, when levels of management were being considered. Here the split was between strategic and operational management, to give a basic split of two levels in the structure. Attention was also given to the structuring of companies into a number of divisions, labelled as 'strategic business units' (SBUs). The latter were again considered in Chapter 5. In this context the approach was that advocated by Ansoff[1], who described distinct segments of environments (or industries) as 'strategic business areas' (SBAs), with SBUs representing a company's structural organization to exploit particular SBAs. Further consideration of SBUs is given below.

In the literature most of the major strategic management texts advocate five basic types of structure, with books by Byars[2], David[3], and Bates and Eldredge[4] being typical. Each of these types is discussed in turn.

Functional structures

Perhaps the simplest type of structure, developed from the principle of division of labour, and is the traditional approach. The approach is to structure the company or areas of responsibility that relate to traditional business functions or operations, such as manufacturing, marketing, finance and personnel. This type of structure is shown in Figure 9.1. This shows a simple split into four departments, with each occupying the same level within the hierarchy, with the head of each department reporting directly to the board. From firm to firm differences will be found not only in the way these functional splits are made, but also in the relative size of each department. For example, some companies have a separate selling function. Relative size will influence the way each of these splits will themselves be structured, with Figure 9.1 showing a typical split, although many variations are to be found.

This type of basic structure tends to be found in firms which take a traditional approach to their business, where they operate in a stable environment which features little change, and where the industry life cycle has experienced a relatively long phase of maturity. It is also found in many small companies where a simple structure reflects the number of people employed and where a more complex structure would be likely to cause problems of communication and control. It also tends to feature in single-business companies where participation in a single SBA or industry does not necessitate an SBU-type structure.

A major advantage of this type is that it allows for specialism of management, as well as allowing managers to concentrate on improving their capabilities to operate in these areas of specialism. However, there are a number of disadvantages to this type of structure. The obverse of specialism is that managers can become too loyal to their department through role identification, so that attitudes may result in conflict between department and organizational objectives (as highlighted in Chapters 7 and 8). Another disadvantage is that as the number of personnel increases each functional department becomes more complex; additional layers of management are introduced into the structural hierarchy, resulting in co-ordination and control difficulties. As size increases it is likely that managers have fewer opportunities to participate in other functions of the business, or indeed merely to appreciate their integration. Again conflict can be the resultant problem. Perhaps the major problem of a structure of this type is that managers, except for the board, can have difficulty in perceiving the totality of the business, resulting in difficulties in the practice of meaningful strategic management.

Divisional structures

According to some writers a division and an SBU are synonymous, which indeed is the approach taken by some companies. However, writers such as David[3] suggest that they can be different concepts in designing an organization's structure, although this is likely to be only applicable in larger firms. Attention here will initially be given to divisionalized structures.

As companies begin to expand, the simple structure based on the business functions tends to be too limiting for the increasing complexity. Particular problems are delegation of authority, communication and co-ordination, and lack of attention to particular products. Therefore the company as a whole may then be split into several divisions, where each division is only concerned with a particular product line. For example, a firm operating in the travel industry may establish four product divisions, as shown in Figue 9.2. Each division represents a unique product line and the nature of the business in each is sufficiently different to warrant a different structure. Indeed each could constitute a separate SBU and operate as a business distinct from the others. Consequently product divisions and SBUs can be synonymous. While this approach offers close control of products, control by the board can be lost as each division needs a high level of autonomy.

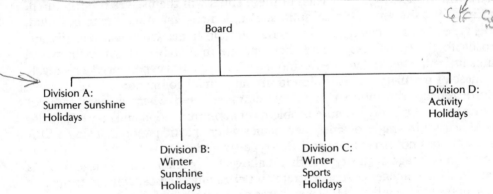

Figure 9.2   *A product-divisional structure.*

Another common form of divisionalization is to form geographic divisions, as shown in Figure 9.3. Here there is no split by products, but the nature of the markets in each geographic area is normally very different, so that different products are likely to be required. Therefore the divisions are established in order to provide concentration on these areas. An important feature here can be the employment of nationals from each of the areas, so that managerial participation is by people who should have a deep understanding of the respective market needs and wants.

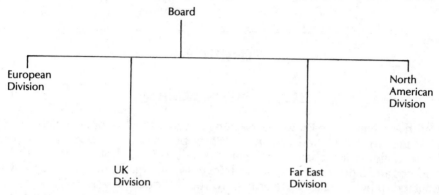

Figure 9.3 *A geographical division structure.*

Another type of divisional structure is based on a customer grouping. For example, a paint manufacturer may have divisions based on households, industrial applications, and marine applications. Here the nature of the market needs and wants is sufficiently different to require a different marketing approach, and these divisions allow for concentration on and development of these requirements. Here each division serves totally different customers, whereas in a product-divisional structure certain divisions may be in competition with each other.

The major advantages of adopting a divisional structure are as follows:

- Delegation of authority can be explicit and accountability can be clearly identified.
- Managers can relate to a division, develop a divisional corporate culture and benefit from successes in the division.
- Managerial and employee motivation can be developed as opposed to managers being 'lost' in a complex and large structure.
- Clearer definition of industries and markets allows for clearer identification of opportunities and strategic management can be more meaningfully applied to each of the divisions.

Major disadvantages of a divisional structure are as follows:

- As described above, functional or operational specialists are required in each division so that duplication of personnel results.
- Separate divisions will incur separate overheads and expenditure, where additional buildings and plant may be needed, while economies of scale in expenditure may be lost.

- Given the delegation of authority highly experienced and qualified senior managers will be needed in each of the divisions, contributing to increased costs.
- Divisionalization normally requires a well-established head office where both functional and senior managers co-ordinate the integration of the divisions, especially group long-range planning through a strategic management system.

EXHIBIT 9.1

How Thistle was Grasped

Scottish and Newcastle Breweries own the chain of Thistle Hotels, which is one of the largest in the United Kingdom. When purchased in 1979 it was a highly diverse nation-wide chain, with many variations in its hotels, with ill-defined standards and a poor public image. Changes in the organizational structure were instigated to help tackle these problems. The first decision was to create a highly centralized organization at company headquarters in Edinburgh to manage the company centrally. However, this structure was not effective, as decision-makers were too remote from the needs of the individual hotels. The structure was then changed through decentralization. This was based on regional directors whose major role was to liaise between hotel general managers and a much smaller headquarters team based in London. Hotel managers were then given responsibility for profits, so that the new structure placed more responsibility on management teams within the regions.

Adapted from *Management Today*, June 1987

SBU structures

As mentioned earlier, product divisions and SBUs can be taken to be the same form of structure, as advocated by writers such as Wheelen and Hunger[5]. In such a case the divisions illustrated in Figure 9.2 would be redesignated as SBUs instead of divisions. However, David[3], for example, outlines the type of organizational structure where SBUs and divisions may be different. Usually this will be in large complex organizations where a breakdown into a relatively small number of clearly identifiable divisions is not possible, probably as a result of many products being offered across a large number of markets. Figure 9.4 illustrates a hypothetical manufacturer of vehicles, where each SBU is based on a unique set of products and markets. Indeed, Leontiades[6], among others, has suggested the existence of several criteria in order to constitute an SBU: it must have a unique mission; an external market focus; identifiable competitors; and control of its own business functions. In Figure 9.4 the complexity of products, markets, and countries is logically structured into the three SBUs, each with its own divisions. However, each SBU has different types of divisions. In SBU 1 they are product divisions, while in SBU 2 they are more closely akin to customer divisions. SBU 3 is clearly split on a geographical basis. However, in all three the products/markets are different, not just between SBUs but also between divisions. Further divisional structuring could also be developed. For example, both the divisions in SBU 2 could be split on a geographic basis, and the SBU 1 divisions could be split by private motorists and fleet owners. Further consideration of this splitting will be given later in the chapter.

The major advantages of SBU structures relate to the delegation of authority, and to the concentration of resources and expertise for the development of business within each respective SBA. Each SBU is autonomous and is able to exploit opportunities related to its SBA, although there will be a strategic management framework in which to operate (consisting of organizational objectives as seen in Chapter 7 and organizational strategy as will be seen in Chapters 10 and 11). However, although each SBU will have its own resources, each will be able to draw on those of the group, while other strengths due to size will also be applicable.

A major ramification of introducing an SBU structure can be resulting problems of integration, co-ordination, and communication, in that an extra level of management has been introduced into the hierarchy. However, the specialization achieved within each SBU should go some way towards compensating for such problems. Another problem can be defining the nature of autonomy that each SBU should have, determining the relative autonomy between SBUs, and defining the role to be played by head office staff, particularly the intervention to be exercised by the board of directors. Another problem can be the abuse of this type of structure, particularly its introduction in smaller firms where such a structure is not really feasible. Here the problem would be manifest in difficulties of co-ordination and integration, but also perhaps in an inadequate spread of resources to support each of the SBUs effectively.

Matrix structures

Matrix organizational structures have been adopted only relatively recently, and current evidence indicates that they are not very widespread. However, they offer several advantages. This type of structure is illustrated in Figure 9.5. This illustration is a combination of a functional and an SBU structure. Rather than organizing the managers in a hierarchy, the arrangement of first-line managers from the board is as shown, where those on the horizontal have equal status with those on the vertical. Other personnel are located within the circles, reporting to both a functional and an SBU manager. For example, a manager in the marketing department may also be responsible to the SBU 1 general manager, while a manager working in personnel may also be responsible to the SBU 3 general manager. In other words, each person past the first level is subject to two channels of command.

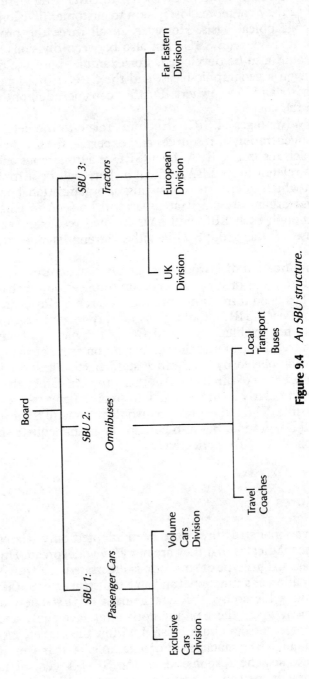

Figure 9.4 *An SBU structure.*

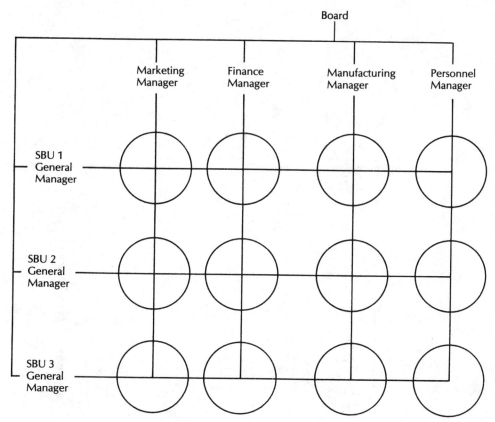

Figure 9.5   *A matrix structure.*

The aim of this type of structure is that it should have the advantages of both a functional and a divisional structure. Hence the SBU orientation allows for focus on and specific attention to business areas and markets, with direct responsibility for their development. Additionally, the functional managers are able to develop their expertise, while concentration of each functional resource is likely to be a greater strength than spreading each across the SBUs.

However, the problem with this type of structure is obviously the potential for conflict as a result of overlapping authority and responsibility. As many managers will have two immediate superiors problems of delegation and leadership may also occur. The other major problem can be a result of competition among the SBUs for the resources of each of the functions. This needs careful control and the establishment of priorities where the capacity of each function may be stretched.

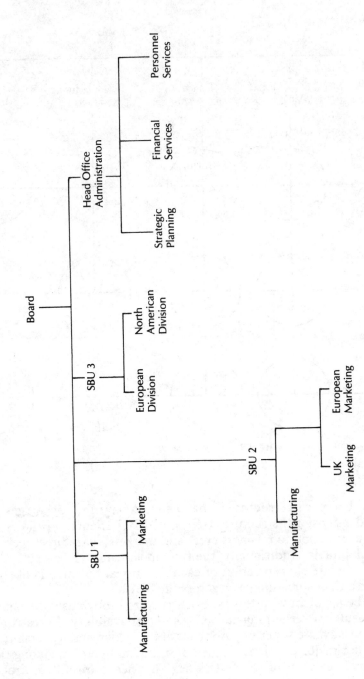

Figure 9.6 *A hybrid structure.*

Hybrid structures

For many organizations, especially large and complex ones, the organizational structure will be a combination of the structures already mentioned. Indeed it seems that most firms have an almost unique structure, modifying it to their particular situation. A type of hybrid structure is shown in Figure 9.6. This is merely meant to show that several alternatives or combinations are possible. The first major split is by the SBUs and some of the functions that are centralized at head office, as well as a department with responsibility for company-wide strategic planning. SBU 1 features a simple functional split, with reliance being placed on head office for the other functions. In SBU 2 manufacturing is from a central responsibility, although marketing has been split on a geographic basis. Here the implication is that other functions would be performed at head office, although if SBU 2 is large then other functions may be brought into the geographic split. SBU 3 is based on two divisions and here a major issue will be the extent of autonomy that each is to have. For large divisions autonomy could be almost total and they could be run as almost separate companies, but with links through the group strategic planning at head office.

INFLUENCES ON STRUCTURAL DESIGN

In the introduction to the section on basic types of structure several factors which can potentially influence a company's structure were mentioned. Other influences on structure will have perhaps been apparent from the explanations of each of the basic types of structure. The aim of this section is to discuss the range of influences that have been identified in the literature.

Most books on strategic management and business policy give several factors that can potentially influence a firm's organizational structure, with that of strategy being seen as the influence which is universally of greatest importance. Indeed, this approach is adopted here with a consideration of the variables providing the bulk of this section, while the next section is concerned with the matching of structure and strategy. However, before this, brief attention is given to the historical development of the study of influences on structure, where external contingencies have also been seen as important influences on structure along with those of strategy.

This body of knowledge has been labelled 'contingency theory', where the organizational structure is seen to be dependent upon the rate of environmental change. Major contributions to this theory have been outlined by Galbraith and Kazanjian[7], starting with the work of Burns and Stalker[8]. This work showed that, in an environment featuring rapid changes in markets and technologies, successful firms rapidly changed their structure as necessary, whereas in stable environments the successful firms were found to have more formalized and permanent structures. These proposals were strengthened by the work of Lawrence and Lorsch[9], who were able to link external contingencies to structure and performance with the proposition that higher performance would be found in companies where the structure is matched to environmental conditions. Of particular importance in contingency theory is the influence of technological change, where changes are seen to be a major cause for firms to modify their structures.

The work of Child[10] is described as challenging contingency theory. This work examined the influence of company size and other internal variables on performance. This developed earlier work by Chandler[11] and reinforced the strategy-structure relationship, in that strategy is the central force that not only results in a firm's performance in a given environment, but also leads to the selection of environments in the first place, and can itself contribute to changes in the environment. However, the nature of these relationships is still not fully understood, leading to writers on strategic management discussing many potential influences on structure. These influences are shown in Figure 9.7, where those in the top half of the illustration are external influences and those in the bottom half are internal influences.

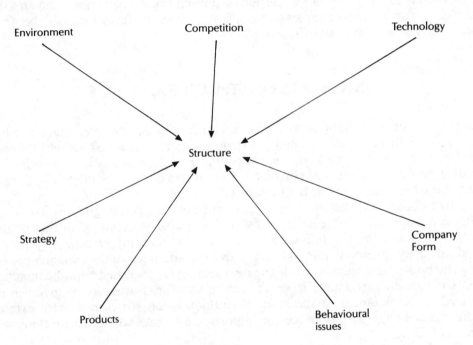

Figure 9.7 *Potential influences on structure.*

Environment

As already mentioned above, it seems that factors from the environment play some part in influencing the nature of a firm's organizational structure. The cause of the influence seems to be change and uncertainty in the environment, where the more dynamic and turbulent the environment the greater the potential for firms to modify their structures. What is not clear is whether this influence is direct or whether the influence is through the process of strategic management with environmental changes affecting strategy which then influences structure. However, most writers concluded that conditions which prevail in the environment have some influence on the make-up of structure.

Mintzberg[12] has attempted to explain the general types of structure that will result from two major features of the external environment. These are the complexity and the dynamism of the environment; Figure 9.8 shows the predictions of the interaction of these two features.* Complexity is given on the vertical axis and is simply classified as either low or high. Similarly, dynamism is also classified according to whether it is at a high or low level. Low complexity means that management can be centralized with little need for splitting the structure into divisions or SBUs. Where there is also low dynamism then standard systems and processes of management can be used which change little with the progression of time, representing a centralized bureaucratic type of structure. However, where low complexity is linked with a high level of dynamism, the centralized management needs to abandon the bureaucratic style in favour of an approach that can identify change and react accordingly. In this context this approach has been labelled 'organic', giving the centralized organic type of structure in the bottom right-hand cell. When the environment features high levels of complexity then several divisions and/or SBUs will be needed, so that the matrix predicts decentralization for both these cells. Low levels of dynamism will again result in bureaucracy, while high levels of dynamism will result in a decentralized organic type of structure, as given in the top right-hand cell.

Competition

Here there are perhaps two major aspects of competition which can potentially influence organizational structure; these have been outlined by Johnson and Scholes[13]. The first is that increased competition is likely to lead to decentralization, so that divisions or SBUs can focus on specific sources of rivalry. Extending this issue, a fuller understanding of rivalry, or indeed an increasing intensity of rivalry, will contribute generally to the complexity of the environment, leading again to decentralization as given in Mintzberg's structural types (Figure 9.8). However, again the issue of strategy needs to be brought into the argument. Intensified competition is also likely to necessitate consideration of changes to strategy and again changes in the latter are likely to require changes in structure.

The other aspect of competition is based on the argument that intensified rivalry will need increased attention to managerial control, in order to retain business and to monitor performance. Here there are ramifications on size of structure, job functions, and focus of plans. The first ramification may require additional managers either to execute such duties or to spread managerial attention across more

*Permission to quote from Henry Mintzberg, *The Structure of Organizations: A Synthesis of the Research*, p. 286, granted by Prentice Hall, Inc., Englewood Cliffs, NJ.

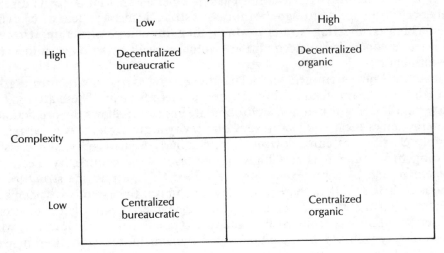

Figure 9.8 *Mintzberg's structural types.*

duties. The second ramification may result in a new level of management, such as the establishment of brand or product managers in the marketing department. The final ramification again relates to the formation of divisions or SBUs, which will allow the opportunity to focus on specific levels of rivalry and challenge their presence accordingly.

Another aspect of competition relates to a strategy followed by some companies, which consists basically of following or imitating actions taken by the leading competitors. Consequently, the formation of divisions by the leading competitor is likely to be initiated by following firms, while the augmentation of personnel to specific job functions may also be followed.

Technology

Research by Woodward[14] in the 1960s and by Gerwin[15] in the 1970s illustrated that the nature of manufacturing technology can have a major impact on structure, although these results are less valid in relation to current developments. However, the potential influence of technology on structure has also been mentioned above in the context of contingency theory, where rapid changes in technology are seen to lead to changes in structure. For example, changes in the technology related to a particular product line may lead to a new division in order fully to utilize the technology to develop product benefits. Alternatively, technological developments in production may allow for centralization of manufacturing across a number of divisions, leading to economies of scale and quality control improvements.

Where the development of technology is largely external to the firm any developments are likely to contribute to the complexity of the environment. This can again be related to Mintzberg's structural types, implying a tendency towards decentralization.

Like the potential influences of the environment and competition, that of technology can also be questioned in relation to either a direct or indirect influence. Technology has already been seen to be important in the formulation of organizational mission and objectives, while changes in technology also mean modifications to strategy which in turn lead back to structure. Again it is likely that the influences caused by technology will be via modifications to strategy.

Strategy

Several of the linkages of structure and strategy have already been outlined. However, as mentioned in the introduction to this chapter, the importance of this relationship and the matching of structure with strategy warrant a separate major section; this follows the present consideration of influences on structural design.

Products

This is the first of the internal influences to be considered. As already seen in the section on basic structures, products provide a major basis for organizing the structure into divisions and SBUs. The example of the firm operating in the travel industry (Figure 9.2) and that in vehicles (Figure 9.4) feature product differences which can be logically arranged into separate divisions and indeed these almost self-explanatory divisions seem to dictate just how the company should be structured. However, at the core of the structuring should be not the products *per se*, but the nature of the needs and wants of the markets that the products seek to serve. Such an understanding was given in Chapter 5. Here the major principle is that this focus is essential to give a marketing orientation to the organization, based on the simple but essential tenet that failure to serve market needs and wants eventually means business failure. Therefore although the structuring may ostensibly be based on products, the true relationship should be market understanding followed by product design, followed by organizational structure.

The potential problem of allowing products to have too great an influence on structure is that the company may evolve a philosophy based on a product/production orientation as opposed to a marketing orientation (see Chapter 6). Here the structure is perceived by personnel to be comprised of separate product identities, each with its own structure of managers and each only concerned with the performance of its respective products. Where this type of situation develops the role of centralized personnel, especially those employed as group planners or marketeers, becomes important. Their task is then to oversee orientations within each product division, as well as establishing the correct orientation to markets across the totality of the company. In some situations it may be that, although the structure has led to this inappropriate orientation, it can only be corrected through a change in the structure, perhaps to a matrix structure, to shift the focus away from the products.

Behavioural issues

Chapter 8 addressed the influence of behavioural issues on strategic management by focusing on managerial values and expectations. The many behavioural issues that were presented as being pertinent to strategic management *per se* are also pertinent to the structuring of the organization. Perhaps the major concern is that decisions on structure can also be influenced by emotional criteria, as well as the criteria that logically need to be taken into account from all the other potential influences, as given in Figure 9.7. A major issue is that resistance to change is also likely to influence modifications to structure, even where strategy demands are strong. The organizational structure can represent many emotional ties for managers in that it gives identification of location and status in the hierarchy, is often used as a basis for allocating company perquisites, defines the domain of a manager's authority, identifies the status of his department, gives location in relation to the board, and can be a source of personal managerial power. Consequently managers often resist structural changes on the assumption that such changes may be detrimental to any of these emotional ties to the status quo.

Alternatively, where managerial values and personal objectives are geared to increasing performance, both personally and for the company, then less resistance to change is likely to be experienced. Here the problem can be one of instigating unnecessary change, with changes to structure being passed off as the approach to pursuing identified opportunities, as opposed to bona fide planning of their exploitation through strategic management. An example of this is the 'empire-building' syndrome, where managers seek to expand that part of the structure for which they are responsible in order to develop personal status and power. Again the argument reverts back to the suitability and compatibility of the structure in relation to the structure being followed.

Company form

This is the last of the potential influences on structure and is concerned with how the unique features of a company influence its structure. Within the literature three major features are generally seen as being important: company history, size and ownership.

Companies with a long history in traditional industries may feature structures that were developed for historical reasons, and which may be typical of other companies in that industry. Also, there may be some resistance to changing job titles and department structures which have been in existence over a relatively long period of time and which have become part of the culture. Associated with this historical development is growth in company size, where growth in the scale of operations has simply necessitated the employment of more people and the structure has been necessarily modified to accommodate these additions. Cannon[16] has proposed five stages of organizational growth which are pertinent to the influence of size on structure.

The first of these is the *entrepreneurial stage*. Decisions are made at the top, few people are needed and their structuring is informal, requiring little formal co-ordination and communication.

The second is the *functional development stage*. As the company grows top management is unable to be involved in all the decisions, so that delegation is needed and the structuring of functional managers allows for this delegation. However, problems of co-ordination and communication can develop within this delegation.

The third stage is *decentralization*. As discussed above, some of these problems are tackled by splitting the structure into a number of divisions, so that size is controlled by establishing manageable areas of the business. The structure has thus developed with growth in size. However, problems can also develop, particularly in relation to the control of the divisions by the board.

The fourth stage is *staff proliferation*. One approach to attempting to overcome these problems is to augment the structure with staff positions, especially to assist top management and the board. These positions do not involve line-management responsibilities, but are advisory and consultative in nature. Although this augmenting of the structure aims to overcome the above mentioned problems, it can also create problems of conflict between staff and line managers.

The final stage is *recentralization*. As companies become very large the structure is often modified to give more control and integration of the divisions by establishing a head office structure. This also facilitates the practice of strategic management, providing responsibility within the structure for long-range direction.

Although the above represent stages that firms tend to go through as they grow, most firms will go through stages in an unpredictable way. The sequence of stages will vary and at a particular point in time the structure is likely to feature aspects of several of these stages. The point that Cannon is making is that company growth tends to develop in stages and that particular stages of growth are likely to have particular influences on structure.

The final feature of company form is that of ownership. In Chapter 6 attention was given to stakeholders, groups of people who have an interest in the company. Where ownership is spread over a large number of people then the board has considerable autonomy and stakeholder influence on structure is unlikely. Where ownership is concentrated, such as with a holding company, or an individual, then stakeholder influence may affect the structure, just as it can affect other aspects of the business.

 ## MATCHING STRATEGY AND STRUCTURE

As already well illustrated in the last section, strategy can have a major influence on structure, either directly as an influence, or indirectly through several of the other influences that were given in Figure 9.7. In the introduction it was argued that, although this relationship has been identified, the reverse can also be found. In this situation the structure is a constraint on the future development of strategy. Much attention has been given to the former by researchers and the overall

EXHIBIT 9.2

Marketing is the Message at McGraw-Hill

McGraw-Hill is an international publishing house based in the United States and with a major presence in Europe. Before 1985 the organization had been structured into divisions based on books, magazines, and statistical services, representing a traditional product structure. In 1985 the structure was dramatically changed and these divisions were abandoned. The new structure was to be focused on markets rather than products, with 19 SBUs which were called 'market focus groups'. Each SBU concentrates on a specific industry, such as construction, transportation, and health care, supplying all products to service publishing needs, which were previously supplied by the separate divisions. The aim of the new structure was to generate new strategies to serve the needs of specific industries, the latter being better understood as a result of this focusing. Indeed, many new products were consequently developed across the SBUs. Before the change to the new structure it was recognized that there would be problems related to its introduction, many being related to managerial resistance to change. However, the commitment of the Chief Executive to the importance of a new structure meant that much of this resistance could be overcome.

Adapted from *Fortune,* 16 February 1986

outcome of these results is discussed after attention is given to the constraining influences of structure. However, debates about matching strategy and structure continue in the literature, although the relevance of each relationship to organizational types has not been established.

Structure constrains strategy

Research by Hax and Majluf[17] has shown how structure can constrain strategy. Where a proposed new strategy requires major changes to structure resistance to change may make the strategy less attractive. As will be seen in Chapter 11, many criteria are used for selecting the strategy to be adopted, of which this type of change is but one. From company to company the relative importance of these criteria will vary when making the selection, but where resistance is sufficiently high then it may be a determining variable to avoid such change, so that the structure has the effect of constraining strategy selection. This resistance is likely to be higher when the cost of structural change is high, despite the potential benefits to be gained by the proposed strategy. This point has been discussed by Baligh and Burton[18] in the context of systematic cost–benefit analysis indicating a non-viable structural change. However, where emotional resistance is high the cost argument may be used regardless of the logic of the cost–benefit analysis results.

Hall and Saias[19] have noted the impact that structure can have in moulding the perceptions of managers, given its importance in providing identification of an individual's location and status. Managers who are 'locked into' particular divisions or SBUs perceive strategic issues in relation to this structure, while the total approach that is taken to strategic planning is likely to be administered in relation to the structure. Again the inference is that structure affects strategy formulation.

Bobbit and Ford[20] have suggested that the relationship perceived by managers is dependent on managerial style. *Re*active decision-makers are likely to believe that structure follows strategy, which itself has been influenced by environmental changes. However, *pro*active decision-makers are likely to seek to retain a stable structure and select strategies which are likely to be consistent with this stability. This gives the proposition that the direction of the relationship is unlikely to be universal.

On the basis of these arguments, and given the potential influences on structure as discussed previously, it seems that the complexity of company situations and their tremendous differences means that the design of the structure of any company is likely to be situation-specific, where the situation relates to the complexity of these variables at a particular point in time.

Structure follows strategy

This relationship was founded on the most famous work on structure, and the one which is most documented and referred to, that by Chandler[11]. Indeed Glueck and Jauch[21] claim that, since this pioneering work of Chandler, the dominant viewpoint has been that strategy is the independent variable, while structure is the dependent variable; that is structure follows strategy. Several other hypotheses were also generated from this work:

- Complex structures are a result of the concentration of several basic strategies.
- Structure is moulded by the growth element of strategies (see Chapter 10).
- Strategies tend to develop incrementally so that changes to structure also tend to occur incrementally.
- Organizations tend to avoid structural change until the existing structure leads to the inefficient execution of a new strategy.

Despite the importance of this work several limitations need to be appreciated. First, the work was published over 20 years ago, based on data collected in earlier years, and business environments have obviously changed greatly since that time. Second, the work was based on only 70 companies, which at the time were among the largest in the United States.

Research to investigate the relationship in Europe was carried out by Channon[22] in the United Kingdom and Pooley-Dyas[23] in France. Both found a real association between increasing reliance on diversification strategies and movements towards multidivisionalization, although there were some differences by country. However, both claim that a diversification strategy alone is not sufficient to lead to a change in structure, but is likely to be linked with increased competitiveness. However, overall there was support for the structure-follows-strategy relationship. Later work by Mansfield *et al.*[24] also identified an association between diversification and movements by firms to modify their structures and to adopt a divisionalization approach.

As with the conclusion arrived at in the last section, it seems that there is insufficient evidence to give an adequate understanding of the structure–strategy relationship. Indeed, in reality it is likely, as already indicated, that the complexities of both the internal and external environments are such that a simple relationship is not an adequate explanation. The relative importance of each of the potential influences on structure that were examined previously is likely to vary from organization to organization, while in a single organization they are likely to vary with the passage of time. For the latter, changes in the total business environment are likely to lead to a shift in the relative importance of these influences. Additionally, the passage of time will also feature changes in the values and expectations of managers, while individuals will leave the company and new managers will be employed; both changes are more than likely to contribute to the relative importance of influences on the structure.

EFFECTIVENESS OF STRUCTURE

Once the many issues that have been discussed in this chapter have been appraised and modifications to the structure have been completed, then the issue of the likely effectiveness of the new structure becomes pertinent. However, many of the changes that will be made are likely to be incremental in nature so that the effectiveness to be achieved is built on the former structural base. Also to be considered is whether or not some of the smaller incremental changes should be implemented, in that minor changes may do little to improve effectiveness. At another extreme is the type of organization which makes many changes, appearing to be in an almost continuous state of reorganization. This approach can almost be built into the corporate culture, although Byars[2] makes the point that changes in structure cannot compensate for an inappropriate strategy, poor product offerings, or having the wrong people in key managerial positions.

In assessing the appropriateness of a structure, Drucker[25] has suggested that an effective structure is the simplest 'that will do the job well' and that will avoid the problems which it does not create. While this type of explanation may appear too idealistic, the implication is that there are no ideal structural formats for particular types of company or for particular types of environmental situation. In determining whether or not it has the right structure a particular company is faced with trying to 'fit' a structure, from the range available, with the relative forces created by the potential influences that are likely to mould the structure (Figure 9.7). Indeed most writers on strategic management, such as

Byars[2], observe that both researchers and practising managers seem to support this lack of standard structures for standard situations, so that firms inevitably face problems not only in the operation of a particular structure but also in its selection, modification, and in assessing its effectiveness.

A simple guide to action is to say that the structure should be modified when the strategy is changed or when there is a failure to achieve objectives. Both types of change obviously relate to effectiveness, although the latter is concerned with the effectiveness of the structure in relation to performance. While a change in structure may need to follow poor performance there are, of course, many variables within the complexity of a firm's total business environment which affect performance, of which structure is but one. Therefore, changing structure merely to counteract poor performance is unlikely to achieve the desired effect; though a careful analysis may well indicate otherwise. The situation is likely to be that a combination of factors has brought about poor performance and that any change in structure is needed as a consequence of modifications to these factors, such as a need for greater penetration into existing markets or for diversification into new markets. Chapter 14 is concerned with the control of strategic management *per se* and also with its effectiveness. Further attention will, therefore, be given to these issues in that chapter.

Drucker[25] has suggested several symptoms that are indicative of an ineffective organizational structure. These are offered below as giving indications of possible problems, although again they are not meant to be a panacea for assessing and solving structural problems. Again these guides are offered in the context of aiming to achieve the 'right fit' of structure in relation to potential influences.

The first symptom suggested by Drucker is the existence of *many levels of management*. Drucker suggests that this is probably the most common and most serious symptom of an ineffective structure, where excessive levels are introduced in the hierarchy. However, the problem is to identify the difference between what is excessive and the levels of management that are actually needed to support the divisional and SBU structure that is required for pursuing the business. The balance is between having too many levels which can cause problems of co-ordination and communication, and not having an adequate structure to be able effectively to pursue the business in the selected SBAs. Determining the correct number of levels remains largely judgemental, although comparisons with other firms may give guidance.

Drucker's second symptom is *too many meetings* attended by too many people. While meetings obviously have an important role for co-ordination and communication, the point that Drucker is making is that structuring may force too many meetings, or that the administrative systems needed to support the structure require too many meetings in order to effect co-ordination across the structure. Here the point is that the meetings may detract from the job functions of managers, as well as possibly causing excessive conflicts during their execution. Again determining just what is too many and where they cause the structure to become ineffective remains largely judgemental.

The third symptom is *procedural problems*. Here the claim is that ineffectiveness is often reflected in an over-reliance on procedures to be followed by managers, which can detract from managerial motivation and which can contribute to inter-departmental conflict. Although the establishment of set procedures is clearly an aid to effective management, the issue is again that of magnitude, but again it is a matter of judgement as to what represents adequate procedures and what constitutes a system that is likely to cause problems.

Finally, Drucker establishes the simple tenet that an effective structure will direct the attention of key managers to *key issues*. An ineffective structure will have the opposite effect. To avoid this symptom careful monitoring is obviously needed across the organization, in order to define the job functions of managers, their areas of responsibility, and the reporting to be done to higher levels.

As mentioned earlier, the effectiveness of the structure is part of the overall effectiveness of strategic management, which is to be tackled in Chapter 14. As the symptoms described above are largely judgemental in nature it is important that decisions on structure are made within the overall context of control, so that such decisions are consistent with the total process of strategic management.

SUMMARY

In this, the first chapter of Part Four, attention has been given to structure in relation to organizational strategy. The initial attention in the chapter was to the basic types of structure that can be selected, which are functional structures, divisional structures, SBU structures, matrix structures, and hybrid structures. Although these (except the last) provide standard structural types most firms will adapt these to their own situation, so that most end up with a hybrid form.

The next section examined the range of influences that are likely to affect the design of the structure. These were seen to be owing to the environment, competition, technology, strategy, products, behavioural issues, and company form. Important within these influences is the work which has been done in the area of contingency theory, as well as the work which has examined the strategy–structure relationship.

The third section addressed the matching of strategy and structure. Here two major relationships were examined. The first was that structure provides a constraint on strategy, where strategy is selected in order to support the existing organizational structure. The other relationship is that structure follows strategy, so that strategy is the independent variable while structure is dependent on strategy. However, the conclusion here is that there is insufficient evidence to give an adequate understanding of the strategy–structure relationship.

The final section tackled the assessment of the effectiveness of an organization's structure. Here the problem is one of determining just how much the structure has contributed to company performance, against the assumption that modifications should only be made in order to improve performance. A number of purported symptoms of an ineffective structure were examined, although these provide only limited guidance.

CHAPTER CASE STUDY ILLUSTRATION:
CLUB MEDITERRANÉE (A)*

Club Med is a French company whose business is based on vacation villages for tourists, who pay a fixed sum to go on holiday for a fixed period of time. All the facilities are provided in the village. They are particularly orientated to sports activities. Although the villages are located on five continents they predominate in Europe, while French tourists are their largest group of customers.

At the time of the case study the company had experienced considerable growth, with sales having more than tripled over a six-year period. This level of sales had been achieved through an expansion of the number of villages to 90, and the company was planning further growth over the following three years with the introduction of a further 20 villages. This growth was causing problems in relation to the organizational structure. Pressures on the structure were exacerbated in that the activities provided were many, including swimming, tennis, sailing, water-skiing, windsurfing, archery, gymnastics, snorkelling, deep-sea diving, horse-riding, yoga, golf, boating, soccer, excursions and skiing. The last named was confined to a few winter resorts, although the other villages were concerned with summer holidays.

1981 STRUCTURE

At this time the structure was largely a functional one with the director-level appointments as given in Figure 9.9. These were essentially centralized head office appointments for the running and administration of the company, although the MD of Operations had responsibility for the administration of the villages. However the structure was essentially based on centralization. A major observation is the direct span of control of the CEO, where nine senior directors reported directly to him, although much of the management of the company was through the Management Committee which was comprised of all these executives.

The structure below the MD of Operations was largely a matrix structure. One of the axes was comprised of a number of country managers, while the other axis was comprised of product managers, where each was responsible for a particular group of services that were supplied in the villages. However, this structure consisted of eight product managers and sixteen country managers, all of which reported directly to the MD of Operations.

*This case study illustration is based on the original case, 'Club Méditerranée (A)', prepared by Professor Jacques Horovitz as a basis for class discussion. Copyright 1981 by IMEDE, Lausanne, Switzerland. All rights reserved. Summarized by permission. IMEDE declines all responsibility for errors or inaccuracies in the summary.

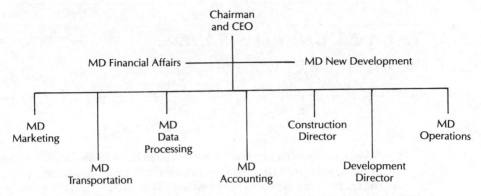

Figure 9.9   *Senior management structure, Club Méditerranée, 1981.*

PROBLEMS WITH THE STRUCTURE

Several of the potential influences on structure that were given in the present chapter had had an effect on this structure, so that several problems were now seen to be affecting the effectiveness of it. Despite the attention given in the literature to the influence of strategy on structure, in this case, at that particular time, it seems that organizational objectives were having a greater influence on the demands being placed on structure. The major objectives were:

- Continued growth by doubling capacity every five years.
- Continued innovation to avoid a traditional hotel offering, with many activities that satisfy changing customer needs.
- Continued internationalization of structure, employees and business philosophy.
- Increased productivity through standardization and internal efficiency.
- To keep the concept of 'a village protected as much as possible from the outside world'.

Other influences which had caused problems within the structure can be classified as follows:

Environmental

It was considered that the company had insufficient understanding of the requirements of its customers, due partly to ineffective co-ordination between the marketing and operations functions. Thus modification to the structure would be needed in order to improve this co-ordination and enhance customer orientation, by improving the sporting and other holiday facilities on offer.

Products

As an extension of the above, the service products themselves had not been sufficiently adapted to changing customer needs, especially when they had expanded into other countries. Again it was considered that the structure had exacerbated this poor adaptation. Of particular importance was the employment of the people who provide the services directly to customers, by providing instruction and organization in customers' participation in the various sports. Previously they had been mostly recruited in France for all Club Med villages, although the increased internationalization of the company meant that different nationals should be employed as an essential part of the service product being offered.

Behavioural issues

A previous problem in the structure had been overcome by a reorganization to the structure given above. Previously responsibility for operations had been divided between five area managers rather than there being a managing director of operations with overall control. This had previously resulted in each area manager attempting to attract better resources to his respective area, which had caused acrimony in the company and which was obviously not conducive to effective management.

However, the current structure, based on centralization, was also causing problems of co-ordination and communication with the many people who now worked for Club Med. Fast growth meant that systems that were used in previous years could no longer cope with the volume of people employed, so that again the structure needed to be modified accordingly.

Company form

The stage of growth that Club Med had now reached had led to this highly centralized form. However, the sheer size of the company meant that each MD had a large span of control, so that this centralization of decision-making had put tremendous strain on the directors. For example, the Managing Director of Operations had reporting to him 90 chiefs of villages, eight product managers, and 16 country managers. The structure was obviously seen to be in need of modification in order to decentralize decision-making and to improve the effectiveness of the span of control.

Also arising from this situation was the problem of an overload of information attached to the many issues that were to be considered by each director. Again a modification to the structure would have allowed for more effective communication of information, fuller consideration of issues by the appropriate level of management, and resultant improvements in managerial effectiveness over both the short and long term.

REFERENCES

1. Ansoff, H. I., *Implanting Strategic Management*, Prentice Hall, Englewood Cliffs, NJ, 1984.
2. Byars, L. L., *Strategic Management*, Harper and Row, New York, 1984.

3. David, F. R., *Fundamentals of Strategic Management*, Merrill, Columbus, OH, 1986.
4. Bates, D. L. and Eldredge, D. L., *Strategy and Policy*, 2nd edn, Brown, Dubuque, OH, 1984.
5. Wheelen, T. L. and Hunger, J. D., *Strategic Management and Business Policy*, 2nd edn, Addison-Wesley, Reading, MA, 1986.
6. Leontiades, M., 'A Diagmatic Framework for Planning', *Strategic Mangement Journal*, **4**, 1, 1983, 11–26.
7. Galbraith, J. R. and Kazanjian, R. K., *Strategy Implementation*, 2nd edn, West, St Paul, MN, 1986.
8. Burns, T. and Stalker, G. M., *The Management of Innovation*, Tavistock, London, 1961.
9. Lawrence, P. and Lorsch, J., *Organization and Environment*, Harvard University Press, Boston, 1967.
10. Child, J., 'Managerial and Organizational Factors Associated with Company Performance', *Journals of Management Studies*, **11**, 1974, 175–89 and **12**, 1975, 12–27.
11. Chandler, A. D., *Strategy and Structure*, MIT Press, Cambridge, MA, 1962.
12. Mintzberg, H., *The Structure of Organizations: A Synthesis of the Research*, Prentice Hall, Englewood Cliffs, NJ, 1979.
13. Johnson, G. and Scholes, K., *Exploring Corporate Strategy*, Prentice Hall, London, 1984.
14. Woodward, J., *Industrial Organization: Theory and Practice*, Oxford University Press, London, 1965.
15. Gerwin, D., 'Relationships between Structure and Technology at the Organizational and Job Levels', *Journal of Management Studies*, **16**, 1979, 70–9.
16. Cannon, J. T., *Business Strategy and Policy*, Harcourt, Brace and World, New York, 1968.
17. Hax, A. and Majluf, N., 'Organization Design: A Case Study on Matching Strategy and Structure', *Journal of Business Strategy*, **4**, 2, 1983, 72–86.
18. Baligh, H. H. and Burton, R. M., 'Marketing in Moderation — the Marketing Concept and the Organization's Structure', *Long Range Planning*, **12**, 2, 1979, 92–6.
19. Hall, D. J. and Saias, M. A., 'Strategy Follows Structure', *Strategic Management Journal*, **1**, 1980, 149–63.
20. Bobbitt, H. R. and Ford, J. D., 'Decision-Maker Choice as a Determinant of Organizational Structure', *Academy of Management Review*, **5**, 1980, 13–23.
21. Glueck, W. F. and Jauch, L. R., *Business Policy and Strategic Management*, 4th edn, McGraw-Hill, New York, 1984.
22. Channon, D. F., *The Strategy and Structure of British Enterprise*, Macmillan, London, 1973.
23. Pooley-Dyas, G., *The Strategy and Structure of French Enterprise*, Harvard Business School, Cambridge, MA, 1972.
24. Mansfield, R., Todd D. and Wheeler, J., 'Structural Implications of the Company-Customer Relationship', *Journal of Management Studies*, **17**, 1, 1980, 19–33.
25. Drucker, P., *Management: Tasks, Responsibilities, and Practices*, Harper and Row, New York, 1974.

CHAPTER 10
STRATEGY ALTERNATIVES

Following the discussion of the relationship between strategy and structure in the last chapter, this chapter moves on to consider strategy alternatives — 'how' the organization might achieve its direction as specified in the mission and objectives (Chapters 6 and 7 respectively). The focus of this stage of strategic management is the requirement to generate different alternative strategies, as reflected in this chapter, although the process of selection is tackled in Chapter 11. As with objectives, strategy alternatives need to be generated at the organizational and business levels, resulting in organizational strategy alternatives and business strategy alternatives.

In the preceeding chapters several references were made to the concept of organizational strategy. In Chapter 1 strategy was introduced as being 'how' objectives are to be achieved. It was also mentioned that attention to strategy needs to be at several levels in a company, particularly at the organizational, SBU and functional levels.

In Chapter 7 attention was given to the interrelationship of objectives, structure and strategy, where it was said that, depending on a particular firm's situation, each of these aspects of strategic management has the potential of influencing the others. It is necessary to re-examine these issues in this chapter, but within the context of generating alternative strategies. The theme of a cause-and-effect relationship between strategy and structure was pursued further in Chapter 9 and these discussions also help in the understanding of the generation of alternative strategies.

While the presentation of this book is based on the assumption that all stages and aspects of strategic management are of equal importance, strategy is the stage which is perhaps the *force majeure* of strategic management. Indeed the literature currently appears to be giving strategy the major attention. The reason for it being the *force majeure* was implied in the outline of Part Four; that it provides the foundation for action that relates to the whole organization. By selecting and establishing an organizational strategy the firm becomes committed to this action, the ramifications of which are enduring in nature. Also, decisions made at this stage provide the framework for functional strategies, which need to be planned at the operational management level and which relate to shorter time periods.

The subject-matter of this chapter is divided into six sections. The first section is an overview of the concept of strategy. The second section looks at the major influences on the formulation of strategy alternatives, while the third tackles managerial participation in the process. The fourth section examines the major classifications of strategy alternatives to be found in the literature. The penultimate section addresses organizational strategy alternatives and the last section business strategy alternatives.

OVERVIEW OF STRATEGY

While the presentation of strategy alternatives and the process of selection are presented in separate chapters, in practice the generation of the alternatives and a subsequent selection are part of the same process. Viable alternatives can only be generated within the context of the current environment and previous decisions which relate to ongoing stages of strategy management. The first stage in this chapter is to give an overview of this process. However, the initial attention in this section is given to an understanding of the concept of strategy.

Understanding strategy

The concept of 'strategy' in relation to business has been discussed by Evered[1]. Strategy comes from the Greek word *strategos* — *stratos* meaning 'army' and *agein* meaning to 'lead'. Thus in the business context it simply means leading the total organization. Within the strategic planning framework it means leading the organization to pursue its mission and objectives.

However, several changes in meaning have occurred, which have been highlighted by Evered[1]. Initially leading an army referred to a role, as a general in command of an army. It later came to mean 'the art of a general', and here Evered emphasizes the importance of psychological and behavioural skills related to the role. By the time of Pericles (450 BC) it came to mean managerial skills, while by the time of Alexander (330 BC) it referred to the skill of employing forces to overcome opposition. The former is an example of strategy in the political administration sense, while the latter is an example in the military sense. Of particular importance here are the connotations of behaviour issues associated with strategy, which, as already discussed, seem to have received limited attention in the literature.

As the literature on strategy related to business developed much interpretation of 'what strategy is' developed, resulting in much confusion both in the literature and in firms. The label 'corporate strategy' was adopted fairly early in the development of the literature, but additional confusion arose with the term 'corporate planning', and later with the concept of 'strategic planning'. Indeed, 'corporate strategy' developed a *broad* meaning and a *narrow* meaning. In a relatively early though well-respected book, Andrews[2] defined corporate strategy as 'the pattern of decisions in a company that determines and reveals its objectives, purposes or goals, produces the principal policies and plans for achieving those goals, and defines the range of businesses the company is to pursue'. Here the 'broad' meaning is that corporate strategy incorporates both objectives and their means of attainment (given as principal policies and plans). However, the 'narrow' meaning is that corporate strategy consists of only the means of attainment of established objectives, with the latter being separate from strategy issues. In other words, objectives can be seen as 'what' is to be achieved and strategy as 'how' they are to be achieved. It will already be evident to the reader that this latter approach has been adopted in this book, although the concept of organizational strategy is used as the company-wide strategy, as introduced in Chapter 1. Here the aim is to alleviate confusion, but to also incorporate the different levels of strategy needed in companies. These issues will, of course, be discussed in more detail later in this chapter.

Review of the process

It has already been said that in the literature most attention has been given to strategy rather than to other aspects of strategic management. In the introduction to this chapter it was said that strategy is the *force majeure* of strategic management. However, despite the importance of strategy it still needs to be presented relative to the importance of the rest of strategic management, an issue which is now addressed.

Chang and Campo-Flores[3] see the process of strategy formulation as consisting of two phases: the preliminary and formulation phases. The latter is concerned with considering alternatives and final selection. These aspects will be considered later in this chapter and in Chapter 11. The preliminary phase would normally involve the following considerations:

Objectives and mission
As the main purpose of strategy is to realize these the suggestion is that they should be reviewed at this stage. In theory considerable attention should already have been given, although there are two major reasons for their review. First, a number of years may have elapsed since they were established as a long-term trend to be pursued, and although the mission is likely to remain unchanged specific levels of magnitude of certain organizational objectives may require modification.

The second reason relates to the ongoing nature of management, and particularly to changes in the general environment and specific markets, as well as the actions of competitors. However at this stage it is important that the true meaning of the mission is carried forward to be fully realized when formulating strategy. Again a time-lag can result in managers merely forgetting the thrust of this mission, but the real value of ratification at this stage is the discipline of systematically integrating all stages of strategic management. Central to the ratification process are the basics of the mission: what business are we in, what should we be in, and what should we not be in?

Ongoing strategies

The starting point is obviously current strategies and the trend in those used previously in that, for many organizations, changes in strategy tend to be incremental. However, a danger can be reliance on previous strategies which have proved to be successful, as changes in the business environment are likely to mean that they may no longer be feasible. Despite this it may be that, even in the preliminary phase, current strategies do not need to be changed. However, the important issue is to get a balance between essential change and avoidance of change that is likely to lead to inconsistencies in long-range planning. Fuller attention will be given to these issues in Chapter 11.

Assumptions and issues

Although analysis of the environment (see Part Two) will produce much information about trends concerning the environment, markets and competitors, a full understanding is unlikely to be achieved, so that a range of assumptions will need to be made. Such assumptions could include forecasted growth in GNP, pending political decisions, a maturity of the size of certain markets, or the adoption of certain marketing tactics by competitors. The stage of making assumptions from the information produced at the analysis stage is part of the conversion process of 'raw' knowledge into its utilization. Although many of these assumptions will be based on value judgements, they must be specified in the strategic plan so that their reasonableness can be compared to reality at a later stage. Assumptions will also be needed about managerial values and expectations and about the organizational structure. Although it may be reasonable to assume that values and expectations will not change, the issues that were raised in Chapter 8 mean that such an assumption may not be valid, particularly if radical changes to strategy are a possibility. Similarly a static organizational structure may be assumed, although a major structural change may be needed before the strategy selection process can proceed.

Contingencies

At the time of formulation a particular strategy may be adequate given the analysis of the environment and the objectives to be pursued. In some industries the environment may be fairly stable, so that little change to the strategy may be anticipated over the period of the plan. However, in a dynamic environment where major changes are probable, then a range of contingency strategies may be needed. For example, forecasts may be indicative of high market growth which would require a particular strategy. However, a range of contingency strategies would give alternative strategies that would need to be adopted, should actual growth be at lower levels. In the preliminary phase the need is merely to identify the possibility that contingency strategies may need to be incorporated into the final strategy selection process.

INFLUENCES ON STRATEGY

In this section attention is given to influences that are likely to mould the strategy to be selected. As this consideration comes before strategy formulation, these influences are the ones that are likely to dictate or mould the strategy to be chosen. Consequently they should be explicated at this stage. Other considerations can be used as criteria for the actual selection process, but these will be addressed in Chapter 11.

Table 10.1 *Major influences on strategy formulation.*

Opportunity orientation
Competence and resources
Environmental threats
Managerial values and aspirations
Obligations to society
Strategy and organizational personality

A range of preselection influences has been given by Thompson and Strickland[4], which are used as the basis for the rest of this section. These influences are summarized in Table 10.1.

Opportunity orientation

The concept of opportunity was examined in Chapter 3 in relation to the analysis of the environment. While an environmental opportunity may exist it may not be convertible into a company opportunity. Potential growth in certain industries may be outside the scope of the organizational mission, or an opportunity for growth from an export market may be suitable but the company may not have the resources for its exploitation.

At this stage of strategic management the need is to reconcile and validate environmental opportunities with the internal analysis of the company (also examined in Chapter 3); here the magnitude of opportunities obviously influences the selection of strategies. However, although the analysis may have been based on sound research methodology, assessing the full ramifications of opportunities largely remains a process of managerial judgement.

Competence and resources

Although resources may not be immediately available, competences of the firm may be indicative of the acquisition of additional resources. This could be either an external acquisition, or an internal acquisition from other divisions or SBUs.

Analysis of competences was examined as part of the internal audit in Chapter 3; the three areas of organizational capability were resources, operations and managerial capability. Distinctive competences of a company as competitive advantages were also discussed in Chapter 6, in that they are very much taken into account in the formulation of the mission statement. Here the issue is that, although resources may be a limiting influence, distinctive competences will instigate opportunity exploitation. Consequently judgements about the quality of these competences will need to be compared with judgements about resource availability.

Environmental threats

While strategies may be planned to exploit opportunities, threats provide two major types of impediment. First, they may be threats which are likely to cause difficulty in implementing the continuation of a strategy, or a new strategy to pursue a new opportunity. Examples here would be adverse economic trends, changing consumer expectations, or enhanced competitive marketing activity. Second, they may be severe threats, so that the company needs drastically to modify direction by adopting a defensive strategy to counter them. An example here would be a technological development by a major competitor that will make existing products obsolete, or a sudden and drastic increase in raw materials costs.

Again the identification of threats is part of the environmental analysis, as outlined in Chapter 3. However, the problem is the identification of such threats, which is often difficult with conventional forecasting techniques. Although scenario writing may be of help, their identification may still be largely a process of value judgement. However, Thompson and Strickland[4] suggest that managers have a tendency to react to threats rather than attempting to predict them, which is part of managerial resistance to change as discussed in Chapter 8. This being the case, there is certainly a major need to consider such influences at this stage, in order to avoid shorter-term 'forced' modifications to strategy.

Managerial values and aspirations

Chapter 8 discussed fully the influences and ramifications of managerial values and expectations in relation to strategic management. Before establishing strategy it is important to reaffirm the potential of these influences in the formulation process. While systematic and logical processes of decision-making may be employed, it is inevitable that emotional and irrational processes will also be included, again as within the range discussed in Chapter 8.

Of particular importance is the almost inevitable situation that managers will have their own preconceived ideas about what the strategy ought to be. While their personal experiences of the success or otherwise of previous strategies will affect this preconception, personal aspirations are likely to be of particular importance in this normative assessment of preferred strategy.

Obligations to society

The company's overall approach to accepting its responsibility to contribute to the satisfaction of the needs of society in general has been tackled as part of the organizational mission (Chapter 6). Although the company may have committed itself to a general obligation to protect and improve the welfare of society, adopting particular strategies is likely to result in more specific influences on particular aspects of society.

Therefore at this stage of preselection the range of public interests that are most likely to be affected by strategy need to be explicated. These were examined in Chapter 6 under the broad headings of quality of life, human resource management, and corporate power. Consequently, if social responsibility has been accepted in the mission, then a potential infringement of social welfare should be a major influence on strategy decision-making.

Strategy and organization personality

The final preselection influence that needs to be explicated relates to the concept of corporate culture, as discussed in Chapter 8. As the shared set of corporate values and expectations, as opposed to those of individuals, part of the influence of culture is to provide a guide for behaviour, which includes establishing a strategy. For example, in Chapter 8 Miesling and Wolfe's[5] classification of planning styles was examined, where each classification would mould the type of strategy to be developed. Strategy personality can be viewed as being a refinement of corporate culture. A firm may have a tendency to adopt aggressive strategies, or steady-growth strategies, or merely to follow developments initiated by competitors. This would be the strategy personality, and would constitute a level of expectation within the broader corporate culture.

PARTICIPATION IN STRATEGY FORMULATION

Before generating strategy alternatives and completing the selection process, a major consideration is the participation of various managers from different levels in the hierarchy. The issue of participation was initially addressed in Chapter 1. Here it was pointed out that tremendous variation is to be found in companies in relation to the job titles of managers who are required to participate in the formulation of strategy. Variations in managers' abilities and attitudes will also affect their willingness to contribute effectively.

McGlashan and Singleton[6] have made the general claim that as many managers as possible from many levels of the hierarchy should be encouraged to participate in the formulation and selection of strategy. Although this may be ideologically beneficial it is unlikely to be practical, except in relatively small companies with only a single business. Again attention is diverted to Chapter 1, where some general indications of participation by the board, the managing director, senior managers and a specialized department were discussed in relation to different levels of strategy. However, a major consideration is whether the board of directors should lead the development of strategy, or whether this should be delegated to senior management. A major consideration will be the structure of SBUs and divisions and the resultant necessity for a hierarchy of strategies. Here it may be difficult for the board to appreciate the business environment in all SBUs, so that delegation may be more effective. However, the board still has the advantage of being able to provide the *Gestalt* company understanding, due to the very position of its members in the structural hierarchy. Regardless of the arrangements made, the continued commitment of the board to the importance of the need for appropriate strategies and their effective implementation is essential to the success of strategic management *per se*.

Although companies do exhibit variation in the way they manage the strategy formulation process, with differences in resultant participation, McLellan and Kelly[7] have identified four major ways in which participation tends to be organized.

Bottom-up approach

This approach is described as being initiated at the business-unit level. Managers within each SBU are organized to develop a business-level strategy for each of the SBUs. Arrangements are also made for developing operational strategies for each of the SBUs, which key into their respective business level strategies. The overall organizational strategy then results as a combination of each of the SBU strategies.

The advantage of this approach is that the managers who participate in formulating each respective business-level strategy are experienced and conversant in their particular SBUs, and therefore should be suitably qualified to participate. Similarly, they can involve operational managers, to ensure the integration of the business-level strategy with the respective operational strategies. However the problem with this approach can be that the organizational strategy, as a resultant combination, lacks overall direction. The logic and systematic planning of direction to be gained from strategic management may be lost, with the resultant compilation strategy offering little to achieve organizational mission and objectives.

Top-down approach

In this approach participation is limited to senior management or directors; strategy is seen to be the exclusive province of the top of the hierarchy. Consequently strategy is influenced by the aspirations, values and expectations of a limited number of executives. The advantage of this approach is that the role of strategic management in providing systematic overall company direction can be established, and inconsistencies or conflicts at the business level can be removed. Less participation means that agreement and unification are likely to be easier to achieve. The finalized logic of the unified plan can then be passed down as a framework for the development of the operational plans, where the role of each will be logically defined.

The disadvantage is the lost creativity and entrepreneurial flair which can be exhibited by many managers and not just those located at the top of the hierarchy. Participation also encourages motivation and enthusiasm, so that involvement by operational-level managers in higher-level plans is likely to improve their performance at the operational level. Another disadvantage would be the loss of participation and development of strategies at the business level, where a restrictive higher-level plan from above could stifle the generation of innovative ideas in the SBUs.

Interactive approach

This approach is quite distinct from the bottom-up and top-down with its interchange both upwards and downwards, with open negotiation and exchange between different levels of management. This allows for a maximum amount of participation by different levels of managers. Therefore organizational, business and operational strategies may go through different stages of modification and refinement, as each is allowed to influence the other before finalization. The major advantage is that a richness of creative and innovative ideas can be encouraged, while many opportunities are available to ensure that the different levels of strategy can be fully integrated. The major problem is that of controlling the process and it must be implemented carefully. Many managers are obviously going to be involved, many interests will be pursued and conflict between SBUs for the allocation of resources may be generated.

Semi-autonomous approach

The last of the four approaches relies on different methods of formulation at the organizational and business levels. The latter are given considerable autonomy to develop their own strategies, which are given approval at the organizational level with little alteration. Consequently participation by the majority of managers would be in a business-level strategy. The organizational strategy would be mostly concerned with overall future direction and in particular selecting new businesses to pursue. Decisions here would lead to the establishment of new SBUs or modifications to the scope of some of the existing SBUs. However such changes would not be on a regular basis, so that the semi-autonomy of the SBUs could be maintained. Participation at this higher level would be restricted to senior managers, or to corporate staff employed solely in a planning capacity.

CLASSIFICATION OF ALTERNATIVES

To the student of strategic management it may be confusing to find that there is a wide variation in the way the writers of textbooks advocate that companies should generate alternative strategies. Indeed this variation in advice on how to develop the 'best' strategy has led to much confusion, not only for students but also for managers. Despite this variation, all the writers have the same aim, which is to provide an approach that will allow for the generation of alternative strategies (that could be used to pursue the organizational mission and objectives), from which the optimum strategy can be selected. The generation of alternatives is tackled in the remainder of this chapter, while strategy selection is the subject of Chapter 11.

One cause of confusion is the need to take into account the structuring of companies into a number of SBUs, an issue initially raised in Chapter 1. The consequences are effects on the stages of strategic management. In Chapter 7 it was seen that objectives may need to be set at the organizational level, the business level, and the operational level. Similarly, where there are a number of SBUs, strategies also need to be established at the organizational, business and operational levels. Organizational and business level strategies are examined in this chapter and although differentiating between the two has caused confusion,

Table 10.2 *Four major classifications of strategy alternatives.*

Ansoff's alternatives
- Ansoff[8]
- Bowman and Asch[9]
- Johnson and Scholes[10]
- Luffman *et al.*[11]
- Pearce and Robinson[12]

Porter's alternatives
- Porter[13]
- Aaker[14]
- Christensen *et al.*[15]
- Rue and Holland[16]
- Wheelen and Hunger[17]

Growth alternatives
- Aaker[14]
- Chang and Campo-Flores[3]
- Glueck and Jauch[18]
- Harvey[19]
- McGlashan and Singleton[6]
- Rue and Holland[16]
- Wheelen and Hunger[17]

Level-of-business alternatives
- Aaker[14]
- Higgins[20]
- Rue and Holland[16]
- Thompson and Strickland[4]
- Wheelen and Hunger[17]

Coventry University

Lanchester Library
Tel 02476 887575

Borrowed Items 13/10/2010 11:58
XXXXXXXXXXXXX3702

Item Title	Due Date
3800100543252	
* The strategy pathfinder	20/10/2010
38001003229956	
* Exploring corporate strategy	03/11/2010
38001001449226	
* Strategic management	03/11/2010
38001005271196	
* All about Six Sigma	03/11/2010

Amount Outstanding : £7.00

* Indicates items borrowed today
Thankyou
www.coventry.ac.uk

attempts are made in this chapter to reduce this confusion. Operational strategies are examined in Chapter 12.

Although there is variation in the alternatives given by the writers they can be combined as four general classifications of alternatives. The remainder of this section examines these four classifications, while the next two sections are concerned with the approaches for generating alternatives that are to be adopted in this book. These classifications are summarized in Table 10.2, which gives examples of authors whose recommendations fall within each classification.

EXHIBIT 10.1

Geest Rationalization

The Geest Group is based on fresh fruit and vegetables, and is well known to the general public for its bananas. The development of the company after the Second World War resulted in the following businesses:

- Growing and importing fruit and vegetables, including bananas.
- Wholesaling fruit and vegetables.
- Shipping and transportation.
- Physical distribution in the United Kingdom.
- Manufacturing boxes for garden bulbs.
- Mechanical handling and agricultural equipment.
- Food processing and manufacture.
- Grape growing and wine-making.
- Computer services.

However, these businesses were rationalized, with a new mission based on being a marketing organization and not a prime producer. Consequently many businesses were sold, leaving four businesses: bananas; other fresh fruit and vegetables; prepared foods; and horticulture. Here much synergy is achieved across the businesses, through common distribution services and common outlets. Geest continuously looks for new businesses in the food industries, having examined some 1,500 potential acquisitions in recent years.

Adapted from *Management Today*, April 1987

Ansoff's alternatives

In a relatively early work of the 1960s Ansoff[8] proposed four major components to be considered in establishing organizational strategy, but labelled as 'corporate strategy'. This approach has certainly had a major impact on the development of strategic management and has provided a basis for much later thinking.

The first of these components is *product-market scope*. As an extension of the broad definition of the company's business that was given in the mission statement, this component specifically defines the separate businesses in which the company is to participate. Each product-market scope can be considered as a separate SBU in that the requirements of customers in each market are different, while the products needed to serve each scope are consequently also different.

Having determined the scopes or SBUs in which to participate, the next component is concerned with how growth is to be pursued. Ansoff originally gave the alternatives of market penetration, market development, product development, and diversification, which he presented in a *growth vector* matrix as shown in Figure 10.1. The meaning of each of these alternatives will be given later in the chapter.

Products Markets	Present	New
Present	Market penetration	Product development
New	Market development	Diversification

Figure 10.1 *Ansoff's growth vector matrix. (H. I. Ansoff,* Corporate Strategy, *Penguin Books,* © 1987. Reproduced by permission.)

The third component is *competitive advantage*. In pursuing the selected growth alternatives attention is directed to how the company can develop strengths to overcome rivalry to be found in the product-market scopes.

The final component, *synergy*, is concerned with how the firm will consolidate its strengths. Ansoff used the 2+2 = 5 concept, where the combined results of individual strengths produce a *force majeure* greater than where each strength is allowed to operate independently.

The writers given under this classification in Table 10.2 advocate that strategy should be largely based on the alternatives as given in the growth vector matrix. Bowman and Asch[9] and Johnson and Scholes[10] advocate the four growth alternatives of Ansoff, but add a strategy of no growth and of withdrawal from a product-market scope. The alternative of no growth is labelled 'consolidation', while those of divestment, liquidation or selling out are used for the alternative of withdrawal. Luffman *et al.*[11] and Pearce and Robinson[12] also include consolidation and divestment, along with the alternative of achieving growth by vertical or horizontal integration. Further attention is given to these alternatives in the next section.

Porter's alternatives

Attention to the Porter[15] approach to strategy has already been given in Chapter 4. In this approach strategy is based on how the company is to compete in the marketplace. Three broad generic strategies are proposed, based on cost leadership, differentiation, and focus. Although these were explained in Chapter 4, they are outlined again for convenience.

The first strategy is *cost leadership*. The aim is simply to achieve lower costs than competitors, but without reducing comparable product quality and benefit offerings. This is equivalent to Ansoff's component of competitive advantage, allowing for relatively greater returns and more power in the marketplace.

The second is *differentiation*. This generic strategy is based on achieving industry-wide recognition of different and superior products and services compared to those of other suppliers. Achieving differentiation is likely to result in insulation against competitive rivalry due to resultant customer loyalty, with this resultant competitive advantage leading to increased returns.

The final generic strategy, *focus*, is concerned with selecting only certain markets in which to participate, rather than attempting to satisfy all customer needs. Although this is perhaps similar to Ansoff's product-market scope component, it is more equivalent to servicing particular groups of customers' needs within particular SBUs. It is therefore more concerned with operational marketing strategy (see Chapter 12).

Although this classification is cited by the writers mentioned in Table 10.2, it is generally advocated within the context of a hierarchy of strategies within organizations. Consequently Aaker[14], Rue and Holland[16] and Wheelen and Hunger[17] see Porter's generic strategies as being applicable at the business level of strategy formulation. This means that product-market scopes are selected at the organizational level, while at the business level attention is directed internally into each SBU, with Porter's generic strategies being pertinent to this attention.

Growth alternatives

All the writers given in this classification in Table 10.2 advocate that alternatives for strategy are based on a company's desire and ability to grow. Consequently, alternatives are offered as growth strategies, or as stability strategies where the objective is not to achieve growth. Another alternative is a set of defensive strategies, to be considered by a company when even stability is not appropriate. This could be caused by particularly poor company performance, or by intensive competitive aggression.

A major confusion among these texts is the variation in labels used for the three major alternatives of growth, stability and defence. Additionally there are some differences to be found in definitions. While the alternative growth strategies largely follow Ansoff's growth vector matrix, variations are also to be found in the alternatives that each writer offers.

As in the previous classification Aaker[14], Rue and Holland[16] and Wheelen and Hunger[17] give these alternatives within the context of a hierarchy of strategies. Aaker gives these as business-level strategy alternatives, although Rue and Holland present them as organizational-level strategy alternatives. Wheelen and Hunger, however, give some of the alternatives as being applicable at one level and the others at the other level.

Level-of-business alternatives

In this approach there is more agreement among the writers; three major levels of strategy seem to be appropriate, as already established in this book:

- *Organizational level strategy*. Appertaining to the company in total, but sometimes labelled 'corporate strategy.'
- *Business level strategy*. Appertaining to particular SBUs or divisions, where each SBU has its own business strategy.
- *Operational level strategy*. Appertaining to each of the individual business functions of each of the SBUs. Generally involving strategies concerned with finance, marketing, production, research and development, and personnel.

However, the major confusion seems to be locating where each of these particular strategy alternatives is to be in the hierarchy, as reflected in the above discussions. The approach adopted in this book attempts to overcome this by differentiating between the major considerations to be made at the organizational and business levels in order to establish the respective strategies. The appropriate alternatives are then described as a consequence. Those for organizational-level strategies are presented in the next section and those for business-level strategies are given thereafter.

ORGANIZATIONAL STRATEGY ALTERNATIVES

As a consequence of the direction to be pursued as given in the organizational mission and objectives, broad strategy alternatives can be classified as being concerned with either growth, stability, or defence. However, at this level all three classifications address the number of product-market scopes or SBUs for future participation, in relation to current SBUs.

For companies in a single business the broad alternatives at this level are:

- *Growth.* Expanding company size by participating in additional SBUs. Decisions are needed on the number of additional SBUs, and on a time-scale over which they can be acquired, in relation to resource availability.
- *Stability.* The decision of no change where the chosen alternative is to remain as a single business. Therefore at this level growth is not to be pursued. However, as will be seen later, growth can still be pursued within the business, through the selection of a growth strategy at the business level.
- *Defence.* Where environmental conditions will allow for neither growth nor stability the company may be forced into defending its single business against, say, competitive forces. For the single-business company this is obviously a critical strategy as failure will mean failure of the company.

For companies that already participate in several SBUs the broad alternatives at this level are:

- *Growth.* Here the decision concerns the number and nature of SBUs that could be acquired within the scope of the mission. Again such decisions are within the context of the resources needed for such expansion.
- *Stability.* Again the decision of no change, where it is considered to be appropriate neither to enter new SBUs nor to abandon any of those already acquired.
- *Defence.* Where the multi-business firm is forced into this situation the strategy may be to attempt to retain a presence in current SBUs, or sell some of them.

Within each of these classifications there are a number of alternative strategies that could be adopted. These are summarized in Table 10.3 and explained in detail in the rest of this section.

Table 10.3   *Organizational strategy alternatives.*

Growth
- Related diversification
- Unrelated diversification
- Backward integration
- Forward integration

Stability
- Holding
- Harvesting

Defence
- Turnaround
- Divestment
- Liquidation

Growth

In the original Ansoff growth vector matrix diversification was classified as being a strategy of launching new products into new markets. As this strategy takes the firm away from its current areas of experience then diversification represents a new business and a new SBU. Related diversification is where there is, however, still a 'common thread' relating the new SBU to the existing businesses, such as technology or managerial skills. For example, the holiday company mentioned in Figure 9.2 may diversify into leisure theme parks, where the management skills related to leisure would provide the common thread, although the products would be different as would the market needs and wants to be served.

Unrelated or conglomerate diversification is where there is no common thread, with the new SBU being an opportunity which is totally outside the scope of existing businesses. An example of this form of diversification would be the holiday company forming an SBU to exploit the market for computer software.

The other two alternatives for growth at the organizational level are based on integration, where the company seeks to grow by going after different businesses in the same industry. Backward integration is where an SBU is established to supply products which are currently inputs into an existing SBU. Backward integration for the holiday company would be entering the air-travel business and also supplying air travel to other holiday companies. This is clearly a different business to the holidays themselves, being different products and markets. Forward integration is where an SBU is established to cut out a third party between it and the final consumer. Forward integration for the holiday firm would be the establishment of a retailing SBU to supply their holidays, and those of other companies, to the general public. Again the business is different and growth would be achieved through a retailing business as opposed to production business.

If any of these alternatives are to be followed then also to be considered is the way in which they will be achieved. While any of these growth alternatives may be tackled by the internal development of resources and personnel, the firm may wish to look for external involvement. An acquisition is the purchase of a company that is already established in the new SBU, so that the acquired company provides the basis for the new SBU. An alternative to an acquisition is a merger, where two companies form into a single organization and combine their SBUs. Another way is the setting up of a joint venture; that is, collaborating with another company. Here the companies remain separate, but one will provide, say, technological expertise while the other provides, say, managerial expertise. Shared experience allows each company the opportunity for growth, while the sharing of profits is generally predetermined.

Stability

At the organizational level a stability strategy implies that the company is satisfied with its performance and direction. Therefore the decision is not to enter new SBUs. This means that sales volume and profitability in existing SBUs are satisfactory and that further growth into additional SBUs may be deemed to be too risky. Indeed, if substantial growth is being achieved to satisfy stakeholder expectations, there is likely to be little desire to achieve further growth.

The alternatives given in Table 10.3 are those most suggested by writers in the literature. Holding at this level simply means allowing the company to continue at its current rate of development through any growth that is being achieved within each SBU. This will be established in the business-level objectives and the business strategy will be determined accordingly.

When a company is achieving satisfactory performance through domination of the marketplace it may wish to take advantage of this power and generate cash for future business expansion. This alternative has been labelled a 'harvesting strategy' and is normally associated with cost-cutting and possibly price increases to generate these extra profits. At this level the concern is one of deciding whether this strategy is appropriate to only one or several SBUs. However, use of the cash is generally predetermined (such as future diversification), as harvesting may result in only short-term gains.

Defence

As already mentioned, where the company is unable to pursue growth or stability, then this strategy can be followed. Often called 'retrenchment', it consists of three alternatives, as shown in Table 10.3. At this level all three are applicable to multi-business firms, but they are likely to be specific to particular SBUs.

When a turnaround strategy is adopted the company attempts to better its competitive standing in order to improve performance. This is done through improvements to current operations, particularly through higher efficiency. For the single-business company this would relate to the total company, but where there are several SBUs then it is likely to be relevant to a particular number. Divestment is a strategy of selling off an SBU. This may be necessary if the competitive environment of the SBU no longer allows for effective performance, or if the SBU no longer fits into the mission. Liquidation strategy involves disbanding an SBU, with the sale of assets in order to generate cash. For multibusiness companies both strategies provide capital for future investment, while for a single SBU company it will, of course, result in the dissolution of the company.

Synergy

Finally, there is an additional feature of organizational strategy that needs to be addressed. This is the concept of synergy, as mentioned in the previous section. As outlined in that section synergy is a feature of strategy that is concerned with the consolidation of strengths. Ansoff[8] originally identified four major sources of synergy as follows:

- *Sales synergy*. This is where many products can use the same distribution channels and where combined sales personnel can sell many products effectively.
- *Operating synergy*. This is the combined strength of spreading many overheads across several products, the higher utilization of facilities and personnel, and the advantages of common learning curves.

- *Investment synergy*. Here strength is achieved by planning capital investment to ensure joint use of production plant and shared R&D.
- *Management synergy*. This is achieved where managerial skills, expertise, and knowledge can be shared among SBUs to enhance management within each.

EXHIBIT 10.2

Europe's Takeover Kings

A recent report has outlined some acquisitions by some of Europe's major companies. These represent strategy decisions at the organizational level as new SBUs, or horizontal integration in existing SBUs as business-level strategies.

- Générale Occidentale, the Paris based holding company, acquired France's second largest book publisher, Presses de la Cité. However, their bid for La Cinq TV station failed.
- Bolloré Technologies Industries of France acquired SCAC, a French transportation services company.
- The British-based conglomerate, Hanson Trust, acquired the Imperial Group in a billion-pound takeover. The Imperial Group was itself a conglomerate, with major SBUs in tobacco, brewing, hotels and food.
- In Italy the electronics company, Olivetti, acquired the German typewriter company, Triumph-Adler. In France they purchased major stakes in auto-parts manufacturer, Valeo; frozen fish producer, Davigel; and clothing retailer, Yves Saint-Laurent.
- Acquisitions have also been made by the Italian food company, Ferruzzi. A major acquisition was the European cornstarch operations of the American company, CPC International. They also acquired a large stake in Beghin-Say, France's largest producer of sugar.

Adapted from *Fortune*, 20 July 1987

BUSINESS STRATEGY ALTERNATIVES

As a result of decisions made at the organizational strategy level the following choices are now available:

- No change in the number of SBUs or remaining a single business.
- Additional SBUs may now feature in the organization.
- Some SBUs may have been removed from the organization.
- Some SBUs may have been designated for stability.
- Some SBUs may have been designated for turnaround.

The process for arriving at the selection of the organizational level strategy is presented in Chapter 11. The aim at the business level is to develop a strategy for each of the SBUs, to determine how each SBU is to proceed into the future. Therefore the focus is within each SBU, rather than across all SBUs as at the organizational strategy level.

Apart from the SBUs which have already been designated for stability or turnaround, the broad strategy alternatives within each of the other SBUs are also based on a choice of growth, stability or defence. The alternatives that are available at the business strategy level are summarized in Table 10.4. These are applicable to either a single-business company or to each of the SBUs of a multi-business company. Here the growth alternatives are different to those that were applicable at the organizational level. However the stability alternatives have the same labels that were used at the higher level, while defence at the business level is restricted to a strategy of turnaround.

Table 10.4   *Business strategy alternatives*

Growth
- Market penetration
- Horizontal integration
- Market development
- Product development

Stability
- Holding
- Harvesting

Defence
- Turnaround

Before attention is given to each of these alternatives there is an additional feature of business strategy that needs to be addressed: competitive advantage, which was mentioned earlier in the chapter. In principle, this is simply to develop strengths to overcome competitive rivalry. In practice these strengths will be developed through the operational strategies (see Chapter 12), with the marketing strategy playing a central role. Of particular importance is competitive dominance by the building of market share, the development of superior products as perceived by customers, and expertise in the effectiveness of marketing communications. Also to be considered are Porter's[13] generic competitive strategies of cost leadership, differentiation, and focus. Again, where these are to be adopted as part of the business strategy the implication is for their implementation through the operational strategies.

Growth

As shown in Table 10.4 there are four major choices that can be considered when it has been decided to pursue growth within a particular SBU. Although all operate internally within an SBU each will lead to growth in a different way. Three of these choices are from the growth vector matrix previously considered.

Market penetration

This strategy alternative means that the SBU continues to participate in the same markets, offering the same products. Growth is achieved by gaining a larger share of the markets with these existing products. In other words growth is by winning additional business to the detriment of competitors, by penetrating further into the volume of sales that constitutes these markets. As a business level strategy this is the alternative with the lowest risk, as there is previous experience of the markets and as there is to be no investment in new products.

Horizontal integration

This is the third type of integration strategy, the other two types having been classified as organizational level strategies. As with market penetration, growth in the SBU is achieved by gaining additional market share. However, this is done not by internal development but by buying market share through the acquisition of a competitive company or a competitor's SBU. Consequently market share is obtained instantly as the new market share is merely added to the existing market share. Here the risk is obviously greater than that associated with market penetration, in that additional resources and personnel must be absorbed into the current base. However, the augmented SBU is still to operate in the same markets with similar product offerings.

Market development

In this strategy alternative, SBU growth is achieved by moving into new markets with existing products. This alternative is normally chosen when products feature state-of-the-art technology and are continuing to satisfy customer needs, but are nevertheless in markets where little growth can be expected. Here the implication is that expenditure on marketing promotions in current markets is likely to have only a marginal influence on sales, so that the same expenditure is likely to have a greater impact in new markets. However, the level of risk is greater than that associated with the former alternatives. There is, first of all, the problem of market knowledge and associated buyer behaviour. Additionally there is the problem of identifying likely competitive reactions. Finally, there is the problem of the acceptance of established products in new markets. Differences in markets, such as culture differences, may mean that some product modification needs to be made before the launch, in order to achieve consumer acceptance.

Product development

In this final alternative for SBU growth the approach is to remain in existing markets but to introduce additional products. Such a strategy is based on the assumption that the total market will be shared among all products in the market, so that additional products will yield additional sales and market share. This strategy is particularly relevant in markets where product switching is a feature of buyer behaviour, such as in most confectionery markets. Similarly, low brand loyalty would support such a strategy, as would an industry where product life cycles tend to be of a short duration. The risk associated with this alternative is perhaps different from that of market development, rather than greater or less. Given that the SBU is to continue its focus on existing markets then the risk is obviously less. However, new products need to be developed so that risk is obviously related to development costs, launch costs, and the period of time associated with break even. However, for certain market types it may be that greater risk is associated with a failure to launch new products. Where product life cycles are short then failure to follow critical lead times will add to the risk. Similarly, failure to match competitors' additional product introductions will add to risk in markets where brand switching and low brand loyalty are a feature of buyer behaviour.

Stability

As reinforced at the beginning of this section, a stability strategy at the business level may have been designated at the organizational level. Or it may be an alternative that will be arrived at as a business level decision. In either case the implication is that the current performance of the SBU is deemed to be satisfactory.

A holding strategy means that the aim for the SBU is not to achieve growth in any of the ways explained above. The aim is to retain current market share, although any growth in market size would result in growth in volume sales. However, the point is that additional resources or efforts are not expended beyond current levels. This means that operational strategies continue as previously implemented and at previous levels of expenditure.

A harvesting strategy, as previously explained, is concerned with generating cash rather than gaining growth in sales volume. Where SBU performance is satisfactory and where there is domination of competitors in the market place, then this power is used to harvest cash from the business activities of the SBU. At this level of strategy the concern is with generating the cash as opposed to determining where it is to be used for future investment in the organization. Achieving the implementation of this alternative again comes about through the operational strategies, where decisions need to be made to achieve cost-cutting and price manipulation in order to achieve higher levels of profits.

Defence

At the business strategy level the only alternative is a turnaround strategy, as shown in Table 10.4. As mentioned previously, this strategy for a particular SBU may have already been designated at the organizational level, or it may be selected at the business level. The aim is to improve competitive standing in order to change SBU performance from a level which is not satisfactory to one which will satisfy business level objectives set at a higher level of performance. This is achieved through the operational strategies, as discussed in Chapter 11. To reinforce the point, improved efficiency needs to be achieved from all the operations. Once this has been achieved the aim is likely to be to convert this strategy into one of the growth alternatives, with market penetration being the one which is likely to be initially applicable.

SUMMARY

This chapter has examined the range of alternatives that are available to a company when planning its strategy. The focus has been on strategy alternatives at both the organizational and business levels. Attention has not been given to the selection of alternatives, which is the subject of the next chapter.

The first section of the chapter was an overview of the concept of strategy. It looked at the meaning of the concept and reviewed the process of strategy formulation.

The next section examined major influences on the formulation of strategy alternatives. These were opportunities; competence and resources; environmental threats; managerial values and aspirations; obligations to society; and strategy and organizational personality.

The third section addressed the issue of managerial participation in strategy formulation. Four major orientations to participation were identified: the bottom-up approach; the top-down approach; the interactive approach; and the semi-autonomous approach.

The next section examined the major classifications of strategy alternatives that appear in the literature. This led to the final two sections of the chapter, which present the strategy alternatives advocated in this book.

The first of these are organizational strategy alternatives, which were classified into those concerned with growth, stability, and defence. For growth there are four alternatives, two each based on diversification and integration. The alternatives for stability are holding and harvesting, while those for defence are turnaround, divestment, and liquidation.

The final section was based on business strategy alternatives, which are also classified into alternatives for growth, stability, and defence. Business strategy alternatives for growth are market penetration; horizontal integration; market development; and product development. The alternatives for stability at this level are holding and harvesting, although for defence the only alternative is a turnaround strategy.

CHAPTER CASE STUDY ILLUSTRATION:
THE VOLVO GROUP*

By 1972 the Volvo Group had become the largest industrial organization in Scandinavia (based on sales), representing 8% of all Swedish exports. Although passenger cars produced half the company's sales revenue, in relation to the other world-wide manufacturers of cars Volvo was quite small. The case study describes major strategic moves of Volvo between 1972 and 1979.

At the time the case study was written the Volvo Group was organized into the following SBUs:

- Passenger cars.
- Trucks and buses.
- Tractors.
- Construction equipment.
- Forest machinery.
- Marine, industrial and aircraft engines.
- Leisure products.

During this period attempts were made to achieve growth at both the business and organizational levels. The business level strategies followed for passenger cars and for trucks/buses were given particular attention in the case study.

PASSENGER CARS SBU

Before 1972 Volvo had only been involved in producing large saloon cars, namely the Volvo 240 series. Product development was achieved by acquisition of the Dutch car manufacturer, DAF. By 1976 Volvo owned 75% of DAF. At the time DAF produced only one range of small cars, known as the 66 range.

During 1976 Volvo launched a new car, the Volvo 343, as a result of the acquisition. This was a medium-sized three-door hatchback, which had been designed to bridge the gap between the larger 240 series and the small 66 series. This product development strategy at the business level also enhanced its marketing strategy at the operational level, by now providing participation in three market segments (see Chapter 12).

---

*Derived from the original case study by W. M. B. Steele. Copyright © 1979 by Cranfield Institute of Technology.

The acquisition to achieve this business level strategy featured high costs beyond the initial expenditure of acquisition. The DAF operations resulted in major losses in 1975 and 1976, while the 343 launch suffered from poor supplies of components and from an expensive image in the marketplace. By 1978 the Dutch Government agreed to invest in Volvo's Dutch company in order for it to survive, but a cost to Volvo was that the Government's ownership rose from 25% to 40%. Further costs resulted from this strategy, when, in 1978, Volvo was forced to relaunch the 343 range as a result of the poor sales achieved by the original launch.

PASSENGER CARS AND TRUCKS/BUSES SBUs

In May 1977 a planned merger between Volvo and the other major Swedish vehicle manufacturer, SAAB-Scania, was announced. SAAB-Scania was also organized into passenger cars and trucks/buses SBUs, but the merger would make the new organization the largest industrial company in Sweden. These enlarged SBUs would allow for rationalization of production, the achievement of economies of scale, an overall reduction in costs, and an increased challenge to international competitors. An immediate business level strategy of market penetration would also, of course, be achieved with their combined market shares. Both companies were achieving profits from their respective trucks/buses SBUs and both could be classified as cash cows (see Chapter 11). However, both the passenger cars SBUs were currently not profitable and could be classified as problem children. Indeed, the new trucks/buses SBU would be the third largest producer in the world.

However, major influences prevailed over the future of the new strategy, as the merger plan had to be approved by major stakeholder groups, namely shareholders, workers' representatives, and the Swedish Government. By August 1977 talks had broken down and the planned merger was abandoned. Here the influences emanated from internal stakeholders in SAAB-Scania. Initially managers in the truck division could see little advantage in the merger. This was followed by resistance from management in the cars SBU, based on perceived difficulties of amalgamating the two product lines, It was anticipated that SAAB's front-wheel drive cars would be difficult to integrate into a product line with Volvo's rear-wheel drive cars. This resistance led to a split of opinion over the merger by the SAAB-Scania board and hence the breakdown of talks.

POTENTIAL GROWTH STRATEGIES

In early 1978 an announcement was made that Volvo and the Norwegian Government had agreed a possible reorganization of Volvo into a joint Swedish–Norwegian company. The Norwegian Government would supply major capital investment, which would allow for potential growth which could otherwise not be achieved. As far as strategies were concerned there would be three major ramifications:

- Growth from product development in the cars SBU by producing new models in Norway.
- The development of aluminium and plastic components for automobiles to enhance existing cars, but also to allow for backward integration into the component industry as an organizational level growth strategy.
- An organizational growth strategy of diversification, through the establishment of an oil company which would be granted North Sea exploration rights.

However, there was also the possibility that a partial divestment of part of one of the SBUs would be necessary: the subsidiary which manufactured Swedish military aircraft engines would need to be excluded from the agreement for security reasons.

After the announcement there was much resistance to the proposed agreement, which was eventually to lead to its breakdown. This resistance also meant, of course, that these new growth strategies could not be implemented. Initially the opposition political parties in Norway were against it, while a poll of business leaders showed that they also opposed the proposed investment.

By January 1979 the Volvo board were forced to abandon this potential for growth because of the influence of Volvo's major stakeholders. Less than two-thirds of the shareholders supported the proposal, which was insufficient for the agreement to go ahead. Several reasons were given by the shareholders for this lack of support. A major concern was that the strategy of diversification into the oil industry represented too high a risk. It was also anticipated that insufficient capital would be supplied by the Norwegian Government, while some of the capital to pursue these strategies would be diverted to Norway, diluting the investment and possibly reducing future divided payments.

REFERENCES

1. Evered, R., 'So What's Strategy?', *Long Range Planning*, **16**, 3, 1983, 57–72.
2. Andrews, K. R., *The Concept of Corporate Strategy*, Irwin, Homewood, IL, 1970.
3. Chang, Y. N. and Campo-Flores, F., *Business Policy and Strategy*, Goodyear, Santa Monica, CA, 1980.
4. Thompson, A. A. and Strickland, A. J., *Strategy Formulation and Implementation*, Business Publications, Plano, Texas, 1983.
5. Miesling, P. and Wolfe, J., 'The Art and Science of Planning at the Business Level', *Management Science*, **31**, 6, 1985, 773–81.
6. McGlashan, R. and Singleton, T., *Strategic Management*, Merrill, Columbus, OH, 1987.
7. McLellan, R. and Kelly, G., 'Business Policy Formulation: Understanding the Process', *Journal of General Management*, **6**, 1, 1980, 38–47.
8. Ansoff, H. I., *Corporate Strategy*, McGraw-Hill, New York, 1965.
9. Bowman, C. and Asch, D., *Strategic Management*, Macmillan, Basingstoke, 1987.

10. Johnson, G. and Scholes, K., *Exploring Corporate Strategy*, Prentice Hall, London 1984.
11. Luffman, G., Sanderson, S., Lea, E. and Kenny, B., *Business Policy: an Analytical Introduction*, Blackwell, Oxford, 1987.
12. Pearce, J. A. and Robinson, R. B., *Strategic Management*, Irwin, Homewood, IL, 1985.
13. Porter, M. E., *Competitive Strategy*, Macmillan, New York, 1980.
14. Aaker, D. A., *Strategic Market Management*, Wiley, New York, 1984.
15. Christensen, C. R., Andrews, K. R., Bower, J. L., Hammermesh, R. G. and Porter, M. E., *Business Policy*, Irwin, Homewood, IL, 1982.
16. Rue, L. W. and Holland, P. G., *Strategic Management*, McGraw-Hill, New York, 1986.
17. Wheelen, T. L. and Hunger, J. D., *Strategic Management and Business Policy*, Addison-Wesley, Reading, MA, 1986.
18. Glueck, W.F. and Jauch, L. R., *Business Policy and Strategic Management*, McGraw-Hill, New York, 1984.
19. Harvey, D. F., *Strategic Management*, Merrill, Columbus, OH, 1982.
20. Higgins, J. M., *Organizational Policy and Strategic Management*, Dryden, New York, 1983.

CHAPTER 11

STRATEGY SELECTION

This chapter is the culmination of our consideration of the planning of strategy. This is a decision-making stage within the model of strategic management adopted in the book, in which the most appropriate organizational and business level strategies for the future are selected. While many firms will not be in a position to select new strategies at either level on an annual basis, a systematic approach to strategic management will still involve the consideration of alternatives. At this stage it should be noted that the literature is perhaps less adequate in addressing strategy selection than other stages of strategic management, with management judgement playing a major role in the process.

In common with other strategic management books, the approach taken in this chapter is to present a number of evaluative criteria and techniques that can be used to select appropriate strategies from potential alternatives, as discussed in Chapter 10. Like the previous chapter the presentation is orientated to organizational and business levels of strategy, differentiating between single- and multi-business companies.

Although the focus is on selection, in practice selection is likely to be limited for many firms, for two major reasons. First, for most firms major changes to strategy are unlikely to occur on a regular basis over a relatively short period of time — say, less than five years. Rather changes tend to be incremental, with major changes of diversification or acquisitions being feasible only at particular times. Second, many of the alternatives mentioned in Chapter 10 may not be feasible — lack of resources may rule out integrative, diversification or product development strategies even before they can be considered as alternatives.

Another practical reality needs to be mentioned before examining the selection process. This is the issue that the process cannot guarantee that the 'right' or most appropriate strategy will be selected for the attainment of the objectives set. Selection is not an exact analytical process, many unknown variables can have an influence and the value judgements of managers at particular points in time are also pertinent.

A final point to be made in this introduction relates to the development of evaluative criteria and techniques in the strategic management literature. These have been largely in isolation from investment decision-making that is part of the financial literature, even though this is concerned with the allocation of resources to future developments. This point will be returned to later in the chapter.

This chapter is divided into seven sections. The first recaps on references that have already been made to selection in previous chapters, while the second addresses managerial attitudes to risk in the context of strategy selection. The third section examines selection at the organizational level and the fourth at the business level. The last three sections are concerned with the selection process. These relate to the components of analysis, comparison and selection. The Appendix to the chapter looks at certain selection techniques.

RECAPITULATION

In several places in the previous chapters it has been said that the particular issue being discussed is pertinent to strategy selection. These issues are summarized below:

- *Chapter 1*. As part of the understanding of the nature of management *per se*, the logical stages of decision-making were introduced in Figure 1.1. Referring to this figure, this chapter on strategy selection addresses stage 3, 'evaluate alternative decisions', and stage 4, 'select appropriate decision'.
- *Chapter 3*. Here several issues were given as being pertinent to strategy selection. The first of these is the financial audit where four major issues influence selection: capital budgeting; attainment of funds; the financial mix of the capital structure; and dividend allocation *vis-à-vis* the retention of funds. The second is the respective capabilities of each of the operations or business functions (such as manufacturing and marketing) in that these capabilities will affect strategy implementation. The third is a need to adopt new technology as a competitive advantage with strategy providing a basis for this adoption. The fourth is the overall organizational capability to exploit specific opportunities or overcome particular threats.
- *Chapter 6*. Here the major issue was that the company should be socially responsible in selecting its strategies. This means that strategies should not be detrimental to the general welfare of society.
- *Chapter 7*. One of the major roles of objectives is to provide a basis for decision-making in the selection of strategies. This tenet is applicable at both the organizational and business levels. Although the objectives represent what the strategy needs to attain, the chapter also discussed the opposite relationship where, because of other influences, the chosen strategy may not be suitable for the full attainment of the objectives.
- *Chapter 9*. In this chapter a major issue was the relationship of strategy to structure. One possibility is that the structure of the organization can be a constraint on the selection of strategy. However, the other possibility is that the structure is dependent on the chosen strategies.
- *Chapter 10*. This chapter referred to the need to consider contingency strategies

to be implemented as a consequence of the occurrence of certain environmental conditions.

From the range of influences on strategy selection already identified, it will already be apparent that the selection process is complex; indeed, many other criteria need to be included in the process, which are discussed later in the chapter. As these influences are from both the external and internal environments of companies, writers such as McGlashan and Singleton[1] have emphasized that the selection process is situation-specific, in that the unique situation of each company will mean that the mix and relative importance of these influences will be unique to each company.

In Chapter 10 three major levels of strategy were identified, with the alternatives available at the organizational and business levels having been presented. It follows, therefore, that strategy selection also needs to be discussed at these levels, which is indeed the approach to be taken. The logic of the flow of the process of selection at these two levels of strategy is shown in Figure 11.1, with Figure 11.1(a) referring to organizational level strategy and Figure 11.1(b) referring to business level strategy.

In Figure 11.1(a) the word 'portfolio' refers to the range of SBUs. The process is concerned with assessing the ability of the current portfolio to achieve the organizational objectives and with the evaluation of alternative portfolios. The process in Figure 11.1(b) is concerned with assessing the ability of the current business strategy to achieve the business objectives and with the evaluation of alternative business strategies.

ATTITUDES TO RISK

In Chapter 8 attention was given to managerial resistance to change as a result of strategic management decision-making. Change was discussed as that ensuing from the environment and from within the organization. The latter was discussed in the light of a model proposed by Dutton and Duncan[2], where the momentum to instigate change was triggered from managers' perceptions of the need for change and their perceptions of the feasibility for change to occur.

At the stage of selecting from the alternative strategies that could be pursued, this process of either resistance to or acceptance of change is pertinent. Also affecting this resistance to change is the amount of risk which is seen to be attached to each of the strategy alternatives, where risk is defined as the chance of incurring loss or damage. Readers of this book will be aware that in business it is never possible to eliminate risk totally. Given the many variables in the environment and the situation of making current decisions about future action, an element of risk is inevitable. However, the point is that attempts must be made to define the risks involved with identified strategy alternatives. While attempts can be made at quantifying risk there will still be an associated subjective element.

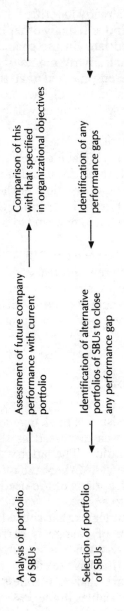

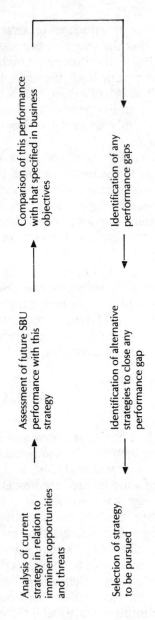

(a) Organizational level strategy selection

Analysis of portfolio of SBUs → Assessment of future company performance with current portfolio → Comparison of this with that specified in organizational objectives

↓

Selection of portfolio of SBUs → Identification of alternative portfolios of SBUs to close any performance gap → Identification of any performance gaps

(b) Business level strategy selection

Analysis of current strategy in relation to imminent opportunities and threats → Assessment of future SBU performance with this strategy → Comparison of this performance with that specified in business objectives

↓

Selection of strategy to be pursued → Identification of alternative strategies to close any performance gap → Identification of any performance gaps

Figure 11.1 *The process of strategy selection.*

EXHIBIT 11.1

Moët Vuitton's Strategy Selection

The selection of strategy for the merger of the two famous French companies, Louis Vuitton and Moët Hennessy, happened over a short period of time, because the companies found that they had similar philosophies within their missions. The rationale for the selection was based on the following:

- Increased size would allow for greater strength, while combining the companies would lead to synergy effects.
- The businesses of each company were complementary, giving growth at the organizational level as opposed to the business level.
- The different businesses also complemented each other financially, as each had a different financial structure and cash requirements.
- Geographical spread of risk was also achieved, as, although both were strong in Europe, Vuitton had been successful in Japan while Moët Hennessy had been strong in the United States.
- The portfolio of SBUs would now be widely spread in terms of products, geographical distribution, retail and wholesale operations, and customer groups.

Adapted from *Management Today*, November 1987

Quantitative assessment

Methods from the financial literature are available for quantifying risk. However, they have been poorly integrated with the strategic management literature, as noted in the introduction to this chapter, and as cited by writers such as Gale and Branch[3].

Decision trees and the discounted cash-flow approach are described in relevant texts such as that by Drury[4]. The capital asset pricing model (CAPM) has also been advocated within the context of strategy selection by writers such as Wensley[5] and Wheelen and Hunger[6]. A detailed explanation of CAPM is outside the scope of this book, but, briefly, it is a method of linking the level of risk involved with a particular alternative to expected returns. The method does have its limitations, however, one of which is the assumption that risk aversion will prevail. Because of the managerial behaviour associated with strategy selection, risk aversion may not be fully followed. Indeed, in some situations the qualitative aspect of selection may lead to a higher-risk alternative being selected. The discussion will return to financial appraisals later in the chapter.

Qualitative assessment

Managers can be classified in a continuum between being strongly risk-averse and eager to take risks. While taking lower-level risks may be deemed to be prudent management, willingness to take greater risks may present the company with greater opportunities. At the organizational strategy level diversification represents a greater potential risk than integration or stability strategies, in that new markets and products need to be handled. However, diversification means greater opportunities for growth than from traditional markets, assuming acceptable competitive and life-cycle conditions.

Where managers' values and expectations result in a tendency to accept and take risk then the resultant strategy selection will tend towards offensive- as opposed to defensive-type alternatives. Therefore, at the organizational level diversification would be preferred, while at the business level preferred alternatives would be market and product development. Such managers are also likely to value growth, innovative ideas for product modifications and internal operations, early entry into new markets, the development of company strengths, and little association with past strategies.

However, the need to take risk in strategy selection may be forced onto managers. Pressures may come from the external environment. Maturity in the life cycle of currently served industries and markets can be a major source, as well as changes in customers' requirements and buyer behaviour. However, in principle, pressure to take additional risk may come from any of the groups of external stakeholders that were mentioned in Chapter 6. Pressures may also be internal. Owners may require a greater return on their shareholdings, requiring, say, diversification to achieve higher levels of profits. Pressure may come from the board of directors for greater growth at both the organizational and business levels. Here the implication would again be for greater attention to diversification and market/product development if required growth cannot be achieved from existing SBUs and markets. Similarly, pressure may be instigated at the business level, where a desire to improve the performance of a particular SBU may lead to a necessity for greater risk to pursue additional opportunities.

STRATEGY SELECTION: ORGANIZATIONAL LEVEL

The process of strategy selection at the organizational level was outlined in Figure 11.1, within the context of a general process of selection. Figure 11.1(a) of that figure has been modified in Figure 11.2, in order to focus on strategy selection at this level. This presentation is based on three major components: analysis, comparison and selection. Put simply, this model suggests an analysis of the outcome of a strategy of continuing in current SBUs, a comparison of likely performance as a result of this strategy with aspirations specified in the objectives, and the selection of a portfolio of SBUs for the future as a result of this comparison.

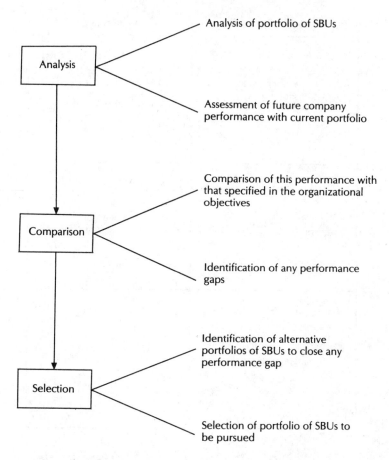

Figure 11.2   *Strategy selection: organizational level.*

Although in practice all three major components are of equal importance in the decision-making process, analysis is given most attention in the literature. This attention has been particularly dominated by the development of portfolio analysis models. Here the literature features explanations of new models as they have been developed, their application into particular situations and resultant claims as to importance, and critiques of their value and applicability.

The different focuses given in Chapter 10 for single- and multi-business companies in the generation of alternatives are also applicable in the selection process, as illustrated in Figure 11.3. Hence the single-business company is faced with either retaining the status quo, with the possibility of a focus on survival, or developing into other SBUs. However, the multi-business organization is faced with selection decisions concerning expansion of the number of SBUs, retaining the status quo, or changing the mix of SBUs.

	Single-business	Multi-business
Growth	Develop into additional SBUs	Expansion of the SBU portfolio
Stability	Remain a single business	Retention of existing portfolio
Defence	Survival in the single business	Retention of some SBUs, abandonment of others

Figure 11.3 *Organizational strategy selection: single- and multi-business.*

While attention is given to the three major components of analysis, comparison, and selection later in this chapter, these three components are also applicable in the process of strategy selection at the business level. Therefore, these components are examined after an outline of the strategy selection process at the business level.

STRATEGY SELECTION: BUSINESS LEVEL

The process of strategy selection at the business level was originally outlined in Figure 11.1(b). This has been modified in Figure 11.4. Again the process is based on the three major components of analysis, comparison, and selection, although the focus is internal to each SBU.

Depending on decisions made at the organizational level, strategies to be selected at the business level will be either for existing SBUs or for new SBUs. There will be no difference between single- or multi-business companies, as the choice is within and related to a single SBU and is not across a range of SBUs.

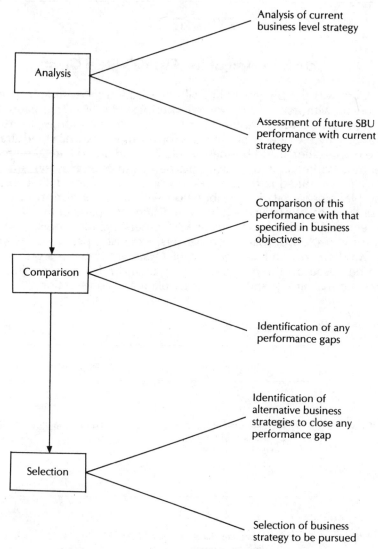

Figure 11.4 *Strategy selection: business level.*

Where the focus is different is in the nature of each SBU, which will be either an existing one or new one. These different focuses and selection alternatives are illustrated in Figure 11.5, based on the broad alternatives of growth, stability and defence. For existing SBUs the choice is across all three alternatives of growth, stability, and defence, as discussed in Chapter 10. However, for new SBUs the focus is obviously on establishing participation in the business. Therefore, the emphasis is on establishing market share and continued growth. This applies to new SBU entry through the company's own internal activities, as well as entry achieved through the acquisition of another firm. Although in the case of the latter

EXHIBIT 11.2

Shock Treatment for Austria's Steel Giant

Voest-Alpine was the biggest industrial organization in Austria, a state-owned conglomerate with steel at the core of its business. By 1985 the organization had made huge losses and the entire board of directors was forced to resign. The major task facing the new board was the formulation of turnaround strategies at both the organizational and business levels. The old board had taken many risks to enter new markets and to diversify into new businesses. However, many of the diversifications resulted in huge losses, owing to, it is claimed, little expertise in strategic planning. Similarly, collaboration with a Japanese firm in electronics failed, as did a collaborative venture with a steel company in the United States. With steel being Voest-Alpine's major SBU, others included tools, springs, metal garden furniture, ships, road crash barriers, exhaust pipes, wire, steel bridges, vehicle windscreens, and microelectronic systems. The turnaround strategies were to be based on three main SBUs; steel and related processing, finished products and machinery, and engineering plant and construction.

Adapted from *Business*, July 1986

	Existing SBUs	New SBUs
Growth	Increase market share or proceed with new developments	Establish market share
Stability	Retain market share (holding) or generate cash (harvesting)	
Defence	Only turnaround	

Figure 11.5 *Business strategy selection: existing and new SBUs.*

some market share will have already been gained by the acquired firm, it still needs to be retained and increased within the new organizational structure.

The next three sections of this chapter examine the major components of analysis, comparison and selection.

THE ANALYSIS COMPONENT OF SELECTION

There are three major areas of consideration for the analysis of the current SBU portfolio and business strategies, and for an assessment of their likely future performance. These are experience from previous and current strategies, the environment, and portfolio analysis models.

Previous and current strategies

The continuation of past and current strategies into the future seems to be a preferred action, following analysis, for several reasons. Where managers have seen that past strategies have been successful there is a great temptation to assume that they will also be successful in the future. Alternatively, managers may consider that it is unwise to change a 'winning formula'. These types of reason relate to the earlier discussions in this chapter about managerial resistance to change and willingness to accept risk. Writers such as Mintzberg[7] have discussed this reliance on past strategies and have suggested that company culture also tends to support past strategies. Therefore, in some companies it may be necessary to bring new executives into the structure in order to initiate change, especially at the organizational level.

For some companies it may be that changes in the business environment occur slowly and over a relatively long period of time. Therefore, organizational strategy change may be infrequent, while business strategies may also require infrequent changes. Thus strategy changes occur incrementally over a long period of time. Indeed Quinn[8] has suggested that, for many organizations, a process of logical incrementalism has been the approach used to develop strategy. However, this process also includes the firm becoming more sophisticated in the selection of strategies to be used in relation to environmental changes.

Despite the above issues, internal constraints may mean that the company is unable to move away from its current strategies. Organizational structure, which was examined in depth in Chapter 9 and recapitulated in the first section of this chapter, can be one such constraint. Another obvious constraint is that of the availability of finance in order actually to implement other strategy alternatives. Lack of finance may mean that stability is the only alternative, or where certain alternatives are predicted to yield unacceptable rates of return again stability may be the only feasible alternative. The importance of financial issues is addressed again at several points in the selection process.

The environment

Readers will recall that the three chapters of Part Two were concerned with analysing the total environment of companies. Consequently the whole of the analysis is applicable at this stage in order to forecast the suitability of the current portfolio of SBUs, given identified environmental opportunities, and to forecast the likely future performance of the business strategies of each SBU. The major issue from the strategic audits is the ability of the current strategy to exploit important opportunities for growth and/or to overcome any serious threats. From the appraisal of competitors the major issue is obviously that of their ability to render any current strategies obsolete. Changes in rivalry are central to the need for change and can clearly force a change in either level of strategy, even where there is internal managerial resistance to change.

The major issue from the chapter on market structures is that of industry and market life cycles. Here the tenet is that different strategies, at both levels, are likely to be needed for different stages of industry and market life cycles. At the organizational level the issue is one of the balance of the stages of the life cycles of the industries to which each SBU relates. Ansoff[9] has shown two extremes of balance, which have been adapted as illustrated in Figure 11.6. The company participating in industries 1, 2 and 3 is obviously facing a problem of decline in SBUs, so that the mix of SBUs obviously needs to be urgently addressed. However, the company participating in industries 4, 5 and 6 faces a more balanced range of life cycles, with future changes in SBUs needed to reflect the pattern of life-cycle positions. At the business level the issue is that of the stage of the particular industry to which the SBU relates. If the industry is in a growth phase then it represents an opportunity for the expansion of market share, through the adoption of business level growth strategy alternatives. However, the maturity and decline phases clearly do not offer such opportunities, so that stability or defence will be forced into such SBUs.

Portfolio analysis models

Many models have been developed and prescribed and although each is different they all adopt a similar format. The basis of the models is a matrix designed from two axes, although different factors are used to define the axes. In each model each SBU or product is defined in terms of the two factors, so that each can be located in the matrix. The analysis can be carried out at the organizational level by locating the range of SBUs in the matrix, or at the business level by locating the products of a single SBU in the matrix.

The major portfolio analysis models have been listed in Table 11.1, which includes the factors that each model uses to design the matrix. Of these models the Boston Consulting Group matrix and General Electric's planning grid are the most popular. These are explained in detail in the Appendix to this chapter. Detailed explanations of the other models have been given by Abell and Hammond[10], Hofer and Schendel[11], Day[12], and Wind and Mahajan[13]. In addition there

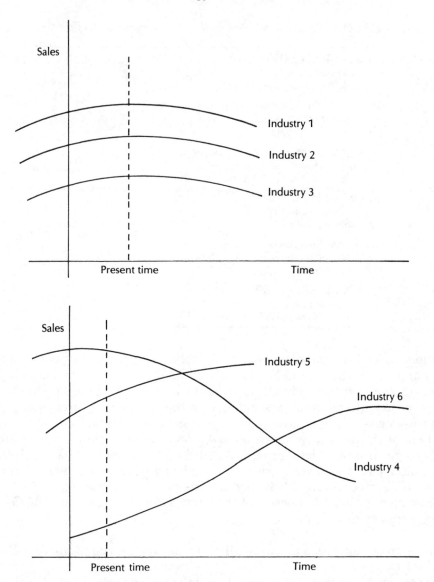

Figure 11.6 *Balancing industry life cycles.* (*H. I. Ansoff,* Implanting Strategic Managment, © *1984. Reproduced by permission of Prentice Hall Ltd.*)

has been much commentary on these models and controversy has developed about their application, with articles by Coate[14], Naylor[15], and Walker[16] being prime examples.

Although these portfolio models are valuable in the total selection process, some have been propounded as being the panacea for all organizational problems of strategy selection. However, in this chapter they are presented as aids to decision-making in strategy selection, within the total process of analysis, comparison and

Table 11.1 *Factors in the design of major portfolio analysis models.*

Boston Consulting Group matrix
- business growth rate
- relative competitive position

General Electric's planning grid
- industry attractiveness
- business strength

Royal Dutch/Shell's directional policy matrix[17]
- business sector prospects
- business unit's competitive capabilities

Arthur D. Little matrix[18]
- industry maturity
- competitive position

Hofer's portfolio matrix[19]
- stage of product/market evolution
- competitive position

Pearce's selection matrix[20]
- purpose of the strategy
- approach to achieve the purpose

selection. Indeed several weaknesses of portfolio analysis models have been identified. For example, Sheth and Frazier[21] claim that they are not adequately linked to objectives and that they provide solutions to selection which are often either too general or too difficult to implement. Part of the controversy surrounding the use of portfolio analysis is that they cause problems for companies in their strategy selection rather than providing an aid to selection. A discussion of this controversy has been given by Giddens-Emig[22]. As Abel and Hammond[10] have pointed out, the formulation of strategy is within a complexity of environmental variables, so that portfolio models can only be partial aims to decision-making.

The major specific weaknesses of the Boston Consulting Group (BCG) model have been given as follows:

- The four-cell approach is too simplistic to classify the complexity of SBUs and products.
- The assumptions that high business growth and high relative market share lead to high profitability and cash generation may not hold.
- Only two variables from a complexity of environmental variables are used for classification.
- Suggested strategies of, say, divestment may lead to lost business as effective product management may result in a continued contribution of cash.

The major weaknesses of the General Electric model have been given as follows:

- Subjectivity in the establishment of the factors, which can lead to justification of previously held views on selection.

- Although multiple variables are used there are still other environmental variables that can influence the classification.
- In defining industry attractiveness there is a problem of defining current attractiveness and that for the long-term future.
- Major influences from competitive activity can easily be 'hidden' within the classification factors.

THE COMPARISON COMPONENT OF SELECTION

The next stage of the selection process is to compare the performance likely to be achieved from the continuation of the current strategies with the levels of performance specified in the objectives. This stage is also applicable at both the organizational and business levels.

It will be recalled from Chapter 7 that objectives which can be established at both the organizational and business levels were presented in four groups related to direction, performance, and the internal and external environments. Some of these are quantitative in nature while the others are qualitative objectives. Comparison of likely company performance from current strategies with that given in the performance objectives is by a technique known as 'performance gap analysis'. The influence of current strategies on the other objectives is generally assessed by the technique of scenario writing.

Performance gap analysis

This method requires the plotting of forecasted performance from the current strategy with that specified in the objectives, over time. The analysis is applicable at both the organizational and business levels. As an example the performance objective of sales revenue growth is used in Figure 11.7, in which three possible situations are depicted.

In Figure 11.7(a) the forecast is that sales to be generated from the existing strategy will be sufficient to meet sales required by the objective. Therefore a performance gap has not been identified. Indeed, the prediction is that from year 3 onwards the strategy will generate more sales than required. This higher level of performance will need to be addressed. One outcome would be to assume that the forecast will be inaccurate, and to subject it to further annual analysis. Another alternative would be to revise the objectives upwards in order to pursue the maximum potential from this strategy. However, such a revision needs to be compatible with the other stages of strategic management.

In Figure 11.7(b) the forecast of performance is adequate until sometime in year 3, from which point the performance gap widens as the current strategy becomes less and less appropriate. Clearly the gap needs to be overcome if the objective is to be achieved. Similarly, in Figure 11.7(c) the forecast is for an obvious gap in performance between sales to be generated by the strategy and sales specified in

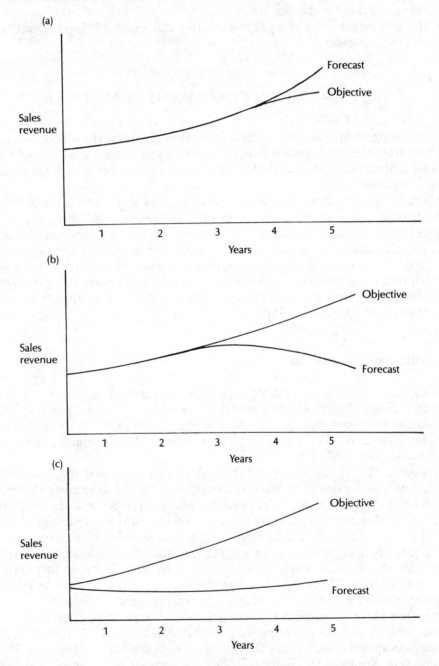

Figure 11.7 *Performance gap analysis.*

the objectives. Indeed, as the years progress a widening gap is predicted. For such a situation to arise immediately during the first year is perhaps unlikely, in that the objective for this year is obviously unrealistic. Such a situation could only be tolerated where the availability of resources allows for the pursuit of high growth. However, such a gap allows for a discussion of the principles for tackling identified performance gaps.

One alternative to overcoming a performance gap is simply to revise the objective until it equates with the forecast. Here the justification is that objectives should be realistic and that the forecast is a prediction of reality. However, such an approach may be inconsistent with the aspirations for company growth and with other reasons for establishing these levels within the objective (as examined in Chapter 7). Indeed the gap is indicative of an inadequate strategy producing only mediocre returns, which then forces the company to consider alternatives.

The other alternative is, of course, to tackle the gap with the aim of closing it. Figure 11.8 illustrates how this can be done. It shows a performance gap of the type identified in Figure 11.7(c), with the extremes being the objective line for the next five years and the forecast of performance over this period from the current strategy. One possibility is to overcome the gap with business level growth strategies, as given in Chapter 10. It may be that the entire gap can be closed with internal strategies of market penetration, market development, or product development, or with the external strategy of horizontal integration. However, Figure 11.8 shows a situation where only part of the gap has been closed in this way, which is labelled the 'expansion gap'. At this level the alternatives are either to continue to attempt to close the remaining gap, or to resort again to revising the

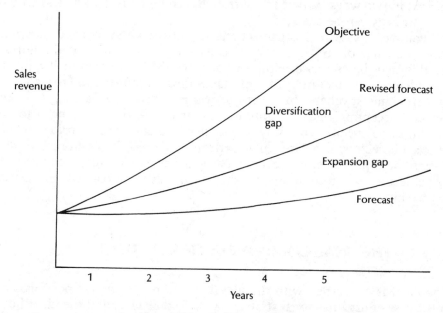

Figure 11.8 *Tackling performance gaps.*

objective downwards, but to the level of the revised forecasts. Again the justification is that of ensuring that the objectives are realistic. However, the remaining gap can be tackled through organizational level growth strategies. In the literature this gap has been labelled the 'diversification gap', although, as was seen in Chapter 10, the strategies that can be used to tackle this gap are based on integration as well as diversification. The point is that in order to overcome this final gap growth cannot be fully achieved from existing businesses and therefore there is a need to move into other businesses.

The philosophy behind this type of analysis is that the company is being forced into stretching performance to achieve higher levels of growth. Indeed it illustrates the principle of setting high levels in the objectives in order purposely to generate gaps which will necessitate addressing alternative strategies.

Scenario writing

Scenario writing was introduced in Chapter 3 as a method for forecasting technological, social and political trends. The method is concerned with the construction of a number of possible outcomes which allow for deductions about the future. Therefore for each of the other objectives the approach is to construct its outcome as, say, achievement, marginal failure, or gross failure, as the result of the current strategy. For the other quantitative objectives this is equivalent to performance gap analysis, while for the qualitative objectives it will result in judgemental assessments of their likely achievement.

As with performance gap analysis, predicted inability to achieve these objectives can be tackled in two ways. Either the objectives can be revised to be less ambitious, or the strategy can be changed.

Where a company has several organizational objectives with predicted gaps and failure, then a change of strategy may not solve all gaps or anticipated failures. Similarly, this may be the case within a particular SBU. Therefore it will be necessary to determine a hierarchy of importance for achievement and to trade off some objectives against others. In effect this will be a process of aiming to close some gaps and accepting that the ambition of some objectives may need to be reduced. While the specific company situation will dictate the priorities to be placed on each objective, it is likely that performance objectives will receive the highest ratings of importance. However, at particular points in time it may be that directional objectives will be of more importance, in order to spread risk or pursue market leadership.

THE FINAL COMPONENT OF SELECTION

This component is concerned with the identification of alternative portfolios of SBUs in the case of organizational strategy (as in Figure 11.2) and the identification of alternative business strategies in the case of business level strategy (Figure

11.4). The final stage is the selection of the strategies to be pursued at each level. The previous components of analysis and comparison will have given indications of possibile alternatives, but the aim is to be exhaustive in examining other alternatives as given in Chapter 10. In finalizing the selection of strategies the considerations are the appropriateness of alternatives with the rest of the stages of strategic management, termed strategic fit, timing implications, and a financial appraisal.

Strategic fit

Future strategies must be consistent with future direction, purpose and philosophy, as expounded in the organizational mission. New alternatives obviously need particular attention, especially where diversification is a possibility, to ensure that the 'fit' is consistent with the overall vision for the future.

While environmental analysis has been used as an input throughout strategic management, the general business environment, the competitive situation, and market structure conditions represent the framework which will ultimately determine whether or not any of the alternatives are feasible. Given the many variables to be found in the environment that can influence this feasibility, the final decision remains judgemental, despite the guidance given by the analytical tools presented in this chapter.

Two final considerations to determine strategic fit are the organizational structure and managers' attitudes to risk. As both these constraints have already been well addressed, the requirement here is merely to locate them in context. In the case of structure, the concern is that either it may be a constraint, or essential changes to structure following changes to strategy will need to be carefully implemented. Managerial resistance to change may suppress innovative thinking to select strategies not previously followed. The aim is a balance between creativity of thinking, to generate alternatives, and disciplined decision-making within an analytical framework.

Timing

There are several aspects of timing that are applicable to strategy selection. A major concern of many managers is that decisions made today represent long-term commitment to market participation and financial expenditure. No matter how rigorous the analysis of the environment the information used is from past and current situations, with forecasting into the future being very much concerned with uncertainty. However, the point is that a lack of analysis means increased uncertainty, while, with the passing of time, more knowledge is incrementally gained about the environment.

An aspect of timing has already been raised in the section on analysis, which addressed the balancing of portfolios in relation to their respective industry life cycles. Here the implication for selection is a balance of portfolio life cycles at the organizational level and at the business level the identification of an opportunity or a threat as a consequence of the current phase of the life cycle. For firms with a single product in an SBU the product life cycle is also applicable.

Another aspect of timing relates to the urgency associated with the need to change a strategy. Often urgency is caused by competitive activity. At the organizational level diversification may need to be rapid in order to beat a competitor's entry, or to avoid the creation of barriers to entry by existing competitors. Similarly, the stength of rivalry may be indicative of stability strategies, or may force the company into a defensive strategy. At the business level changing strength and competitors' relative market share will have a major influence on the feasibility of the individual growth strategies.

Yet another aspect of timing is the lead time which will prevail from the time when a strategy is adopted until it begins to have an affect on company performance. At the business level this impact may occur after a relatively short period of time, although product development necessitates longer periods. At the organizational level diversification is likely to require the longest lead time, especially when the strategy is implemented with current resources. However, the lead time will be considerably reduced when diversification is achieved by acquisition.

A final aspect of timing relates to the generation of cash flow over the future period, plus the creation of profits with time. Both need to relate to the required performance as stated in the organizational objectives.

Financial appraisals

Mention has already been made on a number of occasions of the role of financial appraisals in strategy selection. Descriptions of relevant techniques are considered to be outside the scope of this book, but details are to be found in the financial literature.

The first part of the appraisal is the availability of funds in order to finance potential strategy alternatives. For alternatives such as stability strategies or market penetration, funding may simply represent current expenditure, but the implementation of other alternatives will require capital investment. Here the raising of capital may be internal, from new loans, or from new share capital. In the case of internal funding, portfolio analysis provides indications of the availability of investment funds generated from one SBU or product for use in another SBU or product. From here a funds flow forecast will be eventually produced. This is a forecast which compares the sources of funds which are to be used for future strategies with the use or application of these funds in the implementation of these strategies.

The appraisal can also incorporate standard techniques of capital investment appraisal. The poor integration of these techniques with the strategic management literature has already been noted. Research by Barwise et al.[23,24] has investigated this isolated development of the study of investment decisions by both disciplines. The implication is that standard techniques of investment appraisal should be used in conjunction with the techniques of strategic management, particularly taking into account behavioural issues. These techniques of investment appraisal are usually taken to be payback and breakeven analysis, profitability analysis as return on investment or capital employed, discounted cash flow, and the capital asset pricing model.

The other major aspect of the appraisal is to anticipate the likely affects of the financing of strategy alternatives on the rest of the company. Of immediate concern will be influences on liquidity and working capital. Predictions should also be made of future asset utilization, changes in capital structure, and the allocation and spread of capital between SBUs and/or divisions.

SUMMARY

This chapter examined the process of strategy selection at both the organizational and business levels.

Various references were made to strategy selection throughout the previous chapters, and the chapter began by recapitulating these issues. The second section discussed the issue of managerial attitudes to risk within the context of strategy selection, again developing from several issues of attitudes which were discussed in the preceding chapters.

The next two sections gave a framework of the selection process at the organizational and business levels, respectively. Here the common features of the process were given as the components of analysis, comparison and selection.

In tackling the analysis component, three major areas of consideration were identified. These were previous and current strategies, the environment, and portfolio analysis models. Two of the most popular portfolio analysis models are explained in detail in the Appendix to this chapter.

The comparison component is based on performance gap analysis and scenario writing. In the selection component organizational and business level strategies are selected from alternatives which can potentially close any identified gaps between performance as specified in the objectives and that anticipated from current strategies. The major considerations were given as strategic fit, timing and financial appraisals.

APPENDIX

THE BOSTON CONSULTING GROUP MATRIX

This model of analysis can be used for either SBUs or for individual products. Therefore, it is applicable at the organizational and business levels. Analysis is based on two variables which both classify the nature of each SBU or product and indicate the appropriate strategy to be followed:

- *Relative competitive position.* This is market share, but measured in relation to the largest competitor. It is assumed that a relatively high market share will generate high profit margins, resulting in the generation of large cash flows by the SBU or product.
- *Business growth rate.* The higher the growth rate the easier it is to generate cash and increase market share. Such cash generation allows for further investment to produce further growth. However, high levels of growth also require investment into the SBU or product in order to finance the growth.

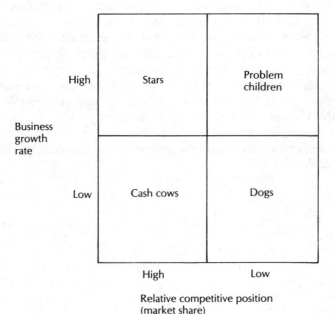

Figure 11.9 *The basic BGC matrix.* (Adapted by permission of the Boston Consulting Group.)

These two variables form the basis of the basic BCG matrix, illustrated in Figure 11.9. Each SBU or product is classified into one of the quadrants according to how it measures up against the two variables in qualitative terms:

- *Cash cows*. These SBUs or products are high earners of cash as they have high market shares, while low growth means that they do not absorb cash. These are the main generators of cash for the company and provide a basis for future investment.
- *Dogs*. Those classified in this quadrant generate little cash as they have low market shares. They also require the investment of cash if they are to grow, as the business shows little growth, and expansion can only come about through gaining market share from competitors. Indeed, cash flow is likely to be negative.
- *Problem children*. Here a low market share means that low levels of cash are generated, although they are classified as being in a growth business. However, in order to take advantage of this growth and to increase market share cash must be invested.
- *Stars*. High market share means that these SBUs or products generate high levels of cash, while still exhibiting good growth potential. However, they also absorb cash in order to pursue this growth.

For the range of SBUs or for the products within a particular SBU, the full analysis is achieved by quantifying the axes. From information gathered in the analysis of the environment, each SBU or product is then classified within the respective quadrant. The axes are quantified as follows:

- *Relative competitive position*. This is plotted on a logarithmic scale as a ratio of the company's market share to that of its largest competitor. The split between high and low is arbitrarily set in relation to rivalry within the industry.
- *Business growth rate*. This is a linear scale where growth is a percentage relative to the industry and the split between high and low is again arbitrarily set at a level appropriate to the industry.

These scales are shown in Figure 11.10, where 10 per cent is the split between high and low growth rates and 1.5 is the split between high and low relative market share. In this figure six SBUs are illustrated by the circles A, B, C, D, E, and F. The area of each of these circles represents the current sales volume of each of the respective SBUs.

The shaded circles for each of the SBUs represent the forecasted future sales volume and their positions represent their forecasted positions in the matrix at this future point in time. As a result of this analysis the following strategies are indicative for each of the SBUs. SBU A is a star business with increasing sales and heading towards becoming a cash cow. Therefore any of the business-level growth strategies could be pursued. However, market share is declining so that market penetration also needs to be considered. The obvious implication for SBU B is a divestment strategy, selected at the organizational level. SBU C is a problem child becoming a star. Again an emphasis on business level growth strategies and perhaps acquisition to give

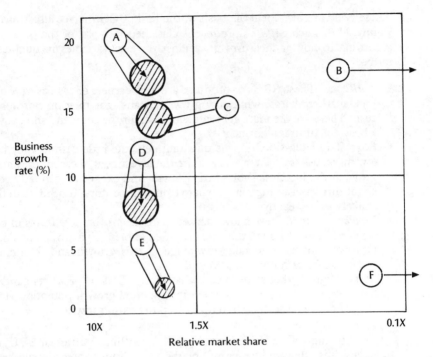

Figure 11.10   *BCG analysis. (Adapted, with permission, from G. S. Day, 'Diagnosing the Product Portfolio', Journal of Marketing, April 1977, page 34).*

horizontal integration are indicated. For SBU D stability is indicated. Alternatives are holding to retain relative market share, or to 'harvest the new cash cow' and generate cash for future investment. SBU E is still a cash cow, but the trend is towards its becoming a dog. Consequently a turnaround strategy may be appropriate to retain the cash cow status. SBU F is an SBU for which a turnaround strategy is not feasible and therefore liquidation or divestment are the feasible alternatives.

As well as giving indications for specific strategies, the BCG matrix can be used to identify the balance of the relative nature of all the SBUs. This can then be used as guidance for participation in existing and future SBUs, as part of organizational strategy selection.

The example given in Figure 11.11 shows a portfolio that can be considered to be out of balance. Of all the SBUs, only F is a cash cow, although its sales volume is relatively small compared to the others, while its market share may be declining. SBUs A, B, and C are problems, with only A having potential for becoming a star, even though its sales volume is relatively low. Finally, D and E have a doubtful future.

There are several implications for the mix of these SBUs if a balance is to be obtained. The major implication is that SBUs as stars and cash cows should be sought, in order to give growth for the future. Only SBU A provides a prospect from the existing portfolio, so that additional SBUs are likely to come from diversification or integration. However, there may be a

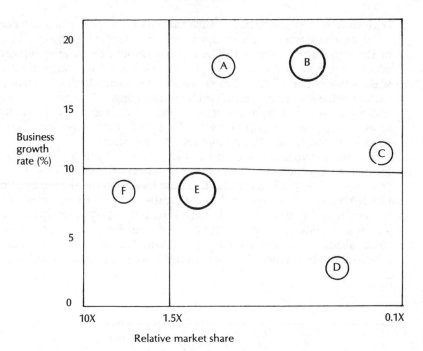

Figure 11.11 *Balancing SBUs in the BCG matrix. (Adapted with permission of Pergamon Press, from B. Hedley, 'Strategy and the Business Portfolio', Long Range Planning, February 1977, page 12.)*

problem of finance, as currently only SBU F is available for harvesting cash for future investments. For A and B a turnaround strategy may be a possibility, but for C and D divestment and liquidation are likely to be the only alternatives. Thus the analysis has clearly indicated a need to change the mix of the portfolio at the organizational level of strategy.

GENERAL ELECTRIC'S PLANNING GRID

The basis of this model is similar to that of the BCG model, in that a matrix is used with two axes to classify and analyse either SBUs or products. However, rather than using two variables for the matrix, the GE approach uses two multiple factors, labelled 'industry attractiveness' and 'business strength'. Another difference is that the matrix or grid is composed of nine cells rather than four. These two factors are compounded of several variables. Industry attractiveness is composed of market growth; industry size and profitability; competition; industry cycles; economies of scale; and general environmental variables. Business strength is composed of market share; profit margins; production capacity and efficiency; marketing expertise; technological capability; and managerial capability.

In order to calculate a value for each of the factors, each variable needs to be assigned a weighting and a rating. For industry attractiveness a weighting is given to each of the variables such that those variables which are deemed to be more important to the company are given higher weightings. The sum of the weights must equal 1. The ratings measure the relative importance allocated to each of the variables in representing industry attractiveness. A scale between 1 and 5 can be used, where 5 represents high importance. For each variable a score is determined by multiplying the weight by the rating, and a total score for industry attractiveness is arrived at by adding up the scores. This gives a composite score for industry attractiveness. The same process is used to calculate a score for business strength.

The basic matrix is illustrated in Figure 11.12. Each SBU or product is located within the matrix by using the scores calculated for industry attractiveness and business strength. Those located in the shaded areas of the top left-hand side of the grid are indicative of growth potential. This is because they feature either high or medium business strength in an industry which is considered to be attractive for growth. Alternatively, those located in the shaded areas of the bottom right-hand side of the grid are indicative of a no-growth situation. Business strength is considered to be only medium

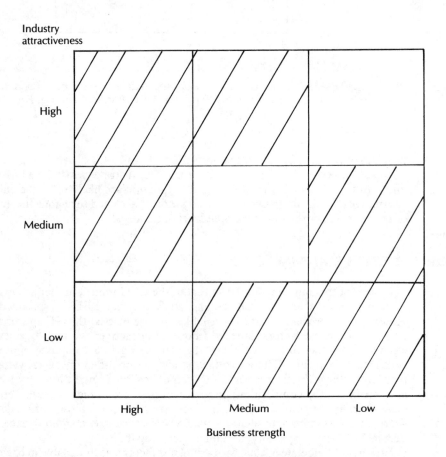

Figure 11.12   *The basic GE grid.*

or low, while the industry features little attractiveness. Businesses here are likely to continue to generate earnings, but the implication is that additional investment cannot be justified. Those appearing in the unshaded areas in the middle of the grid could be either growth or no-growth opportunities. Here other aspects of the selection process would be needed in order to identify the potential for growth.

The analysis can be extended by representing the SBUs or products in the grid in terms of sales volume. This approach is shown in Figure 11.13. The total area of the circle for each SBU is proportional to the size of the industry measured in sales volume. The shaded segment of each circle represents the market share of the SBU. For individual products the total

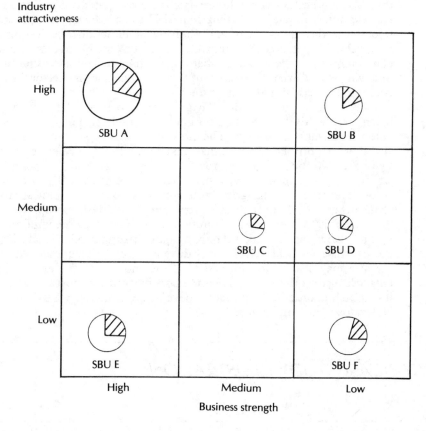

Figure 11.13   *GE grid analysis. (Adapted with permission, from C. W. Hofer and D. Schendel,* Strategy Formulation, *copyright 1978 by West Publishing Company. All rights reserved.)*

circle would represent market size and the shaded segment the product's market share.

As a result of the analysis and classification depicted in Figure 11.13 the following strategies are indicated for each of the SBUs.

Growth is the obvious strategy for SBU A given its location in the grid, the relatively large size of the industry and its established market share. Investment is therefore indicated in order to exploit this opportunity. In the case of SBU B, although the industry is relatively attractive and large, business strength and market share are poor. A holding strategy would continue the achievement of earnings, but a turnaround strategy is also possible with the aim of moving the SBU into the left-hand side of the grid. SBU C shows medium strength and attractiveness that could go either way in the grid. However, the industry is relatively small, and it seems to be moving towards the low/low sector. Consequently, holding is probably the best alternative. In the case of SBU D, although business strength is low the industry is still attractive. However, if it is not feasible to improve strength then the implication is for harvesting the cash that the SBU generates. Although the company has strength in SBU E the industry has little attraction. However, the industry is relatively large so that harvesting may be a viable proposition. Alternatively, it may be possible to pursue market penetration to increase market share, to be followed by harvesting in the following year. Given the location of SBU F in the low/low sector the likely choice in this case would be divestment.

Like the BCG matrix, the GE grid can also be used to identify the balance of the SBUs, to be used for guidance in selecting new SBUs as part of the organizational strategy. The illustration already given in Figure 11.13 also shows a portfolio of SBUs that can be considered to be out of balance. Only SBU A appears in the growth area of the grid and, although it is strong, it is not supported by other SBUs. Three of the SBUs are located across the centre of the grid, with only B showing any indications for achieving growth. In the case of D harvesting seems most appropriate, while divestment is the only feasible solution for F. Therefore the implication is that a balance can be achieved only by participating in additional SBUs in the growths cells, achieved either by diversification or integration. Although the aim may also be to move SBUs B, C and E into the growth areas, balanced against this alternative is the possibility of the short-term harvesting of cash in order to help finance developments into new SBUs that will be located in growth sectors.

CHAPTER CASE STUDY ILLUSTRATION:
OLIVETTI & CO. SpA*

Olivetti had been a family-owned Italian company in the typewriter business. By 1976 the company had changed in several major ways. It was no

*This case study illustration is based on the original case, 'Building alliances (B) – Ing. C. Olivetti & Co. SpA', prepared by Research Associate, Juliet Taylor, under the direction of Professor George Taucher, as a basis for class discussion. Copyright 1986 by IMEDE, Lausanne, Switzerland. All rights reserved. Summarized by permission. IMEDE declines all responsibility for errors or inaccuracies in the summary.

longer run by the family and was now only partly owned by them; it was one of Italy's largest companies; it had diversified into several businesses; it was now seriously undercapitalized.

During the 1950s and 1960s growth had been achieved through organizational and business level strategies. At the organizational level the following SBUs seem to have been established:

- Typewriters.
- Teleprinters and teletype machines.
- Office furniture and filing cabinets.
- Adding machines and calculators.

At the business level growth had been achieved through market penetration in Italy, and through market development with the establishment of 22 sales branches throughout the world. Entry into the United States had been through the acquisition of the Underwood Company, a prestigious office machinery manufacturer, in 1960. This strategy was successful, resulting in large increases in sales volume and in market share. However, the costs associated with the selection of these strategies were high. By 1960 the company was in an alarming state of indebtedness, which was exacerbated by the acquisition of Underwood. The latter had been almost bankrupt when taken over and it took four years to achieve a successful turnaround strategy. Other costs of the acquisition were increased investment and increased administrative problems.

Growth continued through the 1960s and into the 1970s. However, the period featured massive funding problems in order to sustain these selected strategies. The debt situation had worsened and increased loans and reinvested profits were no longer sufficient to sustain the company growth aimed for from these strategies. The Olivetti family had sold almost half its stock to a consortium, but by 1978 it seemed that the company would end up bankrupt, or that control would be taken by the Italian Government.

THE NEW ERA

In 1978 an Italian industrialist with a substantial personal fortune, Carlo de Benedetti, invested several trillion lire in Olivetti and became the Vice Chairman and Chief Executive Officer. This provided the impetus for a turnaround strategy for the whole company. The case study also explains the personal influences that de Benedetti was to have on the selection of strategies and in their implementation for future success. These included his leadership qualities, his foresight and vision for future direction, his appraisal of important environmental issues and his attitude towards risk within the context of pursuing opportunities.

Within the typewriter SBU technological developments had led to electronic machines to replace manual typewriters. De Benedetti quickly introduced this product development strategy. Indeed his willingness to take risks in its selection accelerated the product line launch, beating competitors, including IBM, to the marketplace by several months. This eventually led to Olivetti becoming the world's number one typewriter company, ahead of IBM. However the cost of this strategy was again increased debt, due to retooling for production and increased R&D costs.

The successful turnaround of the company allowed Olivetti to raise new capital in Italy. R&D could forge ahead, although expenditure was to be tightly controlled. Technological developments were also sought through joint ventures with a number of American high-technology companies. In 1982 a major joint venture was set up with the American company Docutel, a manufacturer of automatic bank teller machines. This would allow Docutel the strategy of diversification into the office industry, and would allow Olivetti the strategies of market penetration and development in the banking industry for all its SBUs. However, the venture led to large losses, which again exacerbated Olivetti's recent history of indebtedness.

During the 1980s Olivetti remained in the same SBUs although the greatest proportion of its business continued to come from typewriters. Consequently, organizational level strategy remained largely unchanged. At the business level, within the SBUs, product development continued to be the major strategy as major technological advances were made within the industries. With the development of computers the trend was to computer-based office information systems. Word processors were to start making electronic typewriters obsolete, while personal computers began to replace traditional adding machines and calculators. Olivetti was able to apply this new technology to its products, thus achieving a continued product development strategy. By 1982 Olivetti's personal computer product line could be considered to be a new SBU, hence a new organizational strategy was in place. Olivetti's success in selecting this strategy was reflected in the fact that it became a leading European manufacturer of data-processing equipment (excluding mainframe computers). However, within this business it was not terribly successful in pursuing market development, as sales in world-wide markets were poor, and as it was unable to penetrate the American market.

INTEGRATIVE CASE ILLUSTRATION: PART FOUR

The integrative case study provides illustrations of strategy decisions taken by Plessey at both the organizational and business levels. The case study is concerned with the strategies that were selected and their ramifications, which particularly show changes in SBUs. Structural changes are also illustrated in relation to the strategy changes. This illustration is presented over three major time periods.

1971–3

The case study reports that, at the beginning of this period, the main weakness of Plessey was a lack of foresight in strategic thinking. It was stated that the company was entering the 1970s with the wrong product mix, inadequate acquisitions criteria, and an organizational structure not suited to its management style.

At this time the organizational strategy was based on participation in 24 SBUs, organized into nine divisions as follows:

- Telecommunications.
- Communications and marine.
- Consumer electronics.
- Contract and supply.
- Dynamics.
- Electrical components.
- Electronic subdivisions.
- Industrial electronics.
- Radar.

The organizational structure had recently been changed in order to support this strategy, with recentralization at the top of the managerial hierarchy, aimed at closer control of the company. The structure was based on autonomous SBUs, with the general manager of each SBU carrying full profit responsibility. Each division had a managing director; all reported to the Managing Director of the Plessey Group. This structure also defined accountability, allowing each division to pursue its own future through its respective SBUs and within the context of group resources.

1974–9

At the beginning of this period the organizational strategy was based on the nine divisions and 24 SBUs mentioned in the last section. The POST planning programme utilized portfolio analysis to segment the company's products and markets, to compare them with those of competitors, and to identify threats and opportunities. A large number of 'dead dogs' were identified, which led to a better understanding of cash flows, investment priorities, and market conditions. The product mix was consequently rationalized to remove these 'dead dogs'. This strategy of participating in nine product divisions was also situated within a structure which allowed for participation in 136 countries.

Within the telecommunications SBU the major business strategy followed was that of product development. This was an essential strategy as a result of changes in technology and was to involve a modernization of UK telecommunications from electromechanical systems to electronic systems. The latter was to be based on the digital System X. A ramification for Plessey was that this strategy of product development required a major conversion of production processes from a labour-intensive process producing electromechanical switching systems, into a capital-intensive process to produce electronic systems. The other major ramification for Plessey was that System X would also be produced by GEC and STC, although it would be totally marketed by British Telecom.

At the organizational strategy level a diversification into consumer electronics was proving to be unsuccessful. This strategy had been achieved through the acquisition of a company named Garrard. The new SBU was making a loss and attempts were made to implant a successful turnaround strategy. In the event this strategy was not successful, which led to a decision to disinvest, which was carried out in 1979.

During 1976 managerial appointments were made at a senior level, which changed the structure and the organizational strategy. The latter was now to be based on a number of product-based subsidiaries with world-wide product management responsibility. This was obviously a different basis to the previous strategy, which was a number of product divisions and a number of overseas divisions. The first of these subsidiaries was established as Plessey Electronic Systems Ltd. Later in 1976 an additional diversification strategy was adopted. This was to establish an SBU in the hydraulics industry.

By 1977 revisions had been made to overcome weaknesses to their planning system. As a result several criteria were established for the selection of future strategies:

- To compete in world markets where there are opportunities for industry or market dominance.
- To plan to achieve a balanced portfolio, avoiding over-reliance on particular markets, technologies or expertise.
- To base future investment decisions on achieving this balanced portfolio, using internal funds for routine operations and external funds for acquisitions.
- To provide technological support for all operations at an international level.

As a consequence of using these criteria in a new approach to planning strategy, the decisions made in 1978 identified a fragmentation of effort across the company. Attempts were being made to serve too many markets with too few resources. Under the guidance of the board, strategies to be followed would now be selective. With an emphasis on high-technology in the mission, the divestment of 18 SBUs was to follow.

1980–3

Plessey entered the 1980s with a much simpler structure, as a result of its divestment strategies. Indeed, as mentioned above, in the previous 2½ years, 18 businesses had been divested. It was considered that Plessey now had a balanced portfolio and extensive product development strategies were being pursued at the business level.

By 1983 the move to base the company on product-based subsidiaries had been completed. There were now three such subsidiaries, which encompassed 26 SBUs. As well as the headquarters structure, which was comprised of group services and corporate staff, the organizational structure was completed with four overseas divisions.

Therefore the organizational strategy was to participate in these SBUs, structured in the subsidiaries as follows:

- *Telecommunications and Office Systems.* Seven SBUs consisting of controls; major systems; circuits; office systems; communications systems; public networks; and telecommunications.
- *Electronic Systems.* Ten SBUs consisting of communications systems; avionics; defence systems; military communications; radio systems; security products; displays and sensors; marine equipment; and radar equipment.
- *Engineering and Components.* Nine SBUs consisting of plastics; aerospace; connectors; microwave equipment; optoelectronics; semiconductors; switches and wire-wound devices; processing and memory systems; and computer peripherals.

Throughout the early 1980s other strategies were also selected. In 1982 Plessey became the first British company to enter the public exchange market of the United States, through the acquisition of the American company Stromberg Carlson. In 1983 it formed a joint venture with the American company Scientific Atlanta, thus diversifying into satellite and cable communications equipment. The narrower product mix meant that Plessey's R&D function could now be given more specific direction, and advances could be focused on product development in defined SBUs. Joint ventures were also used to acquire new technologies, for example, with the American company Andersen Laboratories, which was in the business of advanced signal processing devices for defence and telecommunications technology.

REFERENCES

1. McGlashan, R. and Singleton, T., *Strategic Management*, Merrill, Columbus, OH, 1987.
2. Dutton, J. E. and Duncan, R. B., 'The Creation and Momentum for Change through the Process of Strategic Issue Diagnosis', *Strategic Management Journal*, **8**, 3, 1987, 279–95.
3. Gale, B. T. and Branch, B., 'Allocating Capital more Effectively', *Sloan Management Review*, **29**, 1, 1987, 21–31.
4. Drury, C., *Management and Cost Accounting*, Van Nostrand, Wokingham, 1985.
5. Wensley, R., 'Strategic Marketing: Betas, Boxes, or Basics', *Journal of Marketing*, **45**, 1981, 173–82.
6. Wheelen, T. L. and Hunger, J. D., *Strategic Management and Business Policy*, Addison-Wesley, Reading, MA, 1986.
7. Mintzberg, H., 'Patterns in Strategy Formulation', *Management Science*, **24**, 9, 1978, 935–45.
8. Quinn, J. B., 'Strategic Change: Logical Incrementalism', *Sloan Management Review*, **20**, 1, 1978, 7–11.
9. Ansoff, H. I., *Implanting Strategic Management*, Prentice Hall, Englewood Cliffs, NJ, 1984.
10. Abell, D. F. and Hammond, J. S., *Strategic Market Planning: Problems and Analytical Approaches*, Prentice Hall, Englewood Cliffs, NJ, 1979.
11. Hofer, C. and Schendel, D., *Strategy Formulation: Analytical Concepts*, West, St Paul, MN, 1978.
12. Day, G. S., 'Diagnosing the Product Portfolio', *Journal of Marketing*, **41**, 1977, 29–38.
13. Wind, Y. and Mahajan, V., 'Designing Product and Business Portfolios', *Harvard Business Review*, **59**, 1, 1981, 155–65.
14. Coate, M. B., 'Pitfalls of Portfolio Planning', *Long Range Planning*, **16**, 3, 1983, 47–56.
15. Naylor, T. H., 'The Strategy Matrix', *Managerial Planning*, **31**, 4, 1983, 4–9.
16. Walker, R. F., 'Portfolio Analysis in Practice', *Long Range Planning*, **17**, 3, 1984, 63–71.
17. Robinson, S., Hitchens, R. E. and Wade, D. P., 'The Directional Policy Matrix', *Long Range Planning*, **11**, 13, 1978, 8–15.
18. Naylor, T. H., *Corporate Planning Models*, Addison-Wesley, Reading, MA, 1979.
19. Hofer, C. W., *Conceptual Concepts for Formulating Corporate and Business Strategies*, Intercollegiate Case Clearing House, Boston, MA, 1977.
20. Pearce, J. A., 'Selecting among Alternative Grand Strategies', *California Management Review*, **14**, 3, 1983, 23–31.
21. Sheth, J. N. and Frazier, G. L., 'A Margin-Return Model for Strategic Market Planning', *Journal of Marketing*, **47**, 1983, 100–9.
22. Giddens-Emig, K., 'Portfolio Planning: A Concept in Controversy', *Managerial Planning*, **32**, 3, 1983, 4–14.
23. Barwise, T. P., Marsh, P. R. and Wensley, J. R. C., 'Strategic Investment Decisions', *Research in Marketing*, **9**, 1987, 1–57.
24. Barwise, T. P., Marsh, P. R., Thomas, K. and Wensley, J. R. C., 'Managing Strategic Investment Decisions', *Proceedings of the British Academy of Management Conference*, September 1987.

Implementing Strategy

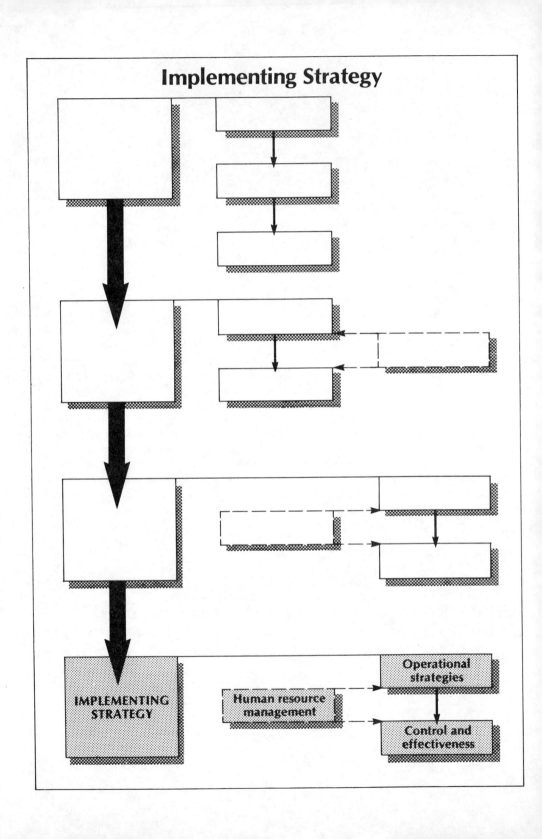

IMPLEMENTING
STRATEGY

Human resource
management

Operational
strategies

Control and
effectiveness

PART FIVE

IMPLEMENTING STRATEGY

OUTLINE OF PART FIVE

This final part of the book completes the strategic management process. While Part Four addressed the planning of strategy in order to pursue the direction planned in Part Three, this final part addresses the implementation of strategy. Implementation is presented as consisting of three major aspects, which are each tackled in a single chapter. First, the implementation of strategy is achieved through the performance of the individual business functions or operations. Central to operational management are operational strategies, so that the latter are the subject of Chapter 12. The second feature is that implementation is achieved through the people located at different levels within the organizational structure. Consequently Chapter 13 is about human resource management within the context of strategic management. The final feature of Part Five is controlling the implementation of strategy to achieve the planned direction and appraising its effectiveness. Consequently Chapter 14 is concerned with control and effectiveness.

CHAPTER 12   OPERATIONAL STRATEGIES
CHAPTER 13   HUMAN RESOURCE MANAGEMENT
CHAPTER 14   CONTROL AND EFFECTIVENESS

CHAPTER 12

OPERATIONAL STRATEGIES

This chapter tackles the first feature of implementation, the carrying-out of organizational and business strategies through operational management in general, and operational strategies in particular. The chapter links the formal stages of strategic management through a formal framework of hierarchies of objectives and strategies. This is in contrast to Chapter 13, which looks at the less formal process of implementation through people. Five major operational strategies are discussed. While each of these strategies has a unique role to play, all need to be closely integrated for effective strategic management. Each of the five operational strategies is presented as a number of broad issues. However, the detail behind each of these broad issues is beyond the scope of this book. This does not mean that these details are less important than the higher-level strategies. Rather it is a case of having different, albeit important, roles to play within the total company.

In this chapter attention is given to the core of operational management. In Chapter 1 the latter was defined as being concerned with the management of the individual business functions or operations, that is, with the role that each has to play in the organization. Central to each of these operations is strategy at the operational level of management, or a range of operational strategies relating to marketing, R&D, production, finance and personnel.

As mentioned in the introduction to Part Five, organizational and business level strategies are implemented through the performance of operational management. Operational strategies are not only central to this level of management, but relate directly to the higher levels of strategy. This represents a hierarchy of strategies within organizations, similar to the hierarchy of objectives discussed in Part Three.

While this chapter addresses major issues of each of the above mentioned operational strategies, it does not represent a detailed treatise on the operations. Readers of this book will be aware of the detailed literature pertaining to each of these management disciplines. Rather the aim is to highlight those issues of operational strategies which are important within the context of strategic management in general, and those which are particularly important to the implementation of organizational and business strategies. Indeed the planning of direction and strategy as part of the strategic management process provides a framework for all activities to be carried out at the operational level of management.

This chapter is structured into eight sections. The first section examines the nature of operational management by comparing it to strategic management. The second is an overview of implementation and reflects on some issues from Chapters 13 and 14 as well as on operational strategy issues. The next five sections address operational strategies concerned with marketing, R&D, production, finance, and personnel, respectively. The final section looks at the integration of these operational strategies.

THE NATURE OF OPERATIONAL MANAGEMENT

In Chapter 1 brief mention was given to operational management but within the context of explaining the role of strategic management. Although strategic management can be considered to be superior to operational management in the sense that it provides a framework for the latter, it is not superior in the sense of being more important *per se*. Rather it is largely a difference in the roles that each has to play in an organization, with both being important and complementing each other. First, attention is given to these differences; this is followed by an outline of operational management.

Role differences

Major role differences between these two forms of management have been put forward by Greenley[1], developed from those given by Glueck and Jauch[2]. These have been adapted and are given in Table 12.1. The first group of differences shows the overall difference in nature. Operational management is concerned with the short term and develops out of the planning framework set for the company in the strategic management process. As already established above, at this level each function is addressed in its entirety, but within a framework relating, for example, R&D to the rest of the organization. While long-range decisions will commit the firm to capital expenditure and market participation which will be difficult to change, operational decisions can be changed or modified.

The second group of differences shows the dependence of operational management on the higher level, with a functional as opposed to corporate-wide orientation. Senior managers in operations are inevitably trained and experienced in particular professions, and their values and expectations are strongly influenced by the values and norms established by their respective professions. Because of the difference in the relevant time periods the relative success of operational objectives and strategies is immediately apparent. However, this is also partly due to their different roles, with those at the operational level having a more specific function in the control process (see Chapter 14).

Role difference no. 8 in Table 12.1 indicates that the directional nature of strategic management needs to look at innovations and new areas of business. At the lower level, and especially in the short term, the focus is on the continuation of

Table 12.1 *Role differences between strategic and operational management.*

Strategic management	Operational management
1. Overall long-range company direction	1. Day-to-day performance and results.
2. Long-range framework for the company.	2. Only one stage in the company's development.
3. Decisions have an enduring effect.	3. Decisions can be changed or modified.
4. Corporate orientation to match company to its environment.	4. Functional and professional orientation.
5. Identification of new objectives and strategies.	5. Objectives derived from those at higher levels.
6. Objectives and strategies evaluated with a corporate perspective.	6. Objectives are subdivided into specific goals.
7. Relevance of objectives and strategies only in the long term.	7. Relevance of objectives and strategies immediately apparent.
8. New areas and innovations can be investigated.	8. Continuance of current areas of business.
9. Issues may be abstract, deferrable and unfamiliar.	9. Issues are normally immediate, concrete and familiar.

current directions, unless the strategic management framework dictates new and innovative thrusts for the next period of time. The final difference shows that operational management is generally concerned with the familiarity of existing business, decisions which need to be made immediately, and with issues that generally do not feature abstract aspects.

An outline of operational management

In Chapter 1 the nature of management *per se* was examined, using principles expounded by writers such as Stoner[3] and Ansoff and Brandenburg[4]. The major implication here is that the three major functions of operational management are also planning, implementation and control. Chapter 1 also presented the logical stages of decision-making and again the implication is that these stages are also applicable in operational management. Therefore, in principle the nature of operational management is similar, but, because of the different roles, the nature of its constituent parts is very much different.

As a result of the above a more comprehensive outline of the nature of operational management can be given. Although these stages can be considered to be common across all the operations, from marketing to personnel, there will obviously be vast differences in the way they are applied to each of the operations. For companies consisting of several divisions or SBUs it is likely that operational management will be separate for each unit. However, some operations may be shared as head-office functions, as illustrated in Chapter 9.

Analysis of the environment

As decisions need to be made in operational management information needs to be gathered for all functions, although vast differences in the type of information needed are apparent. For example, in marketing detailed knowledge is needed about individual markets, of the type discussed in Chapter 5. In personnel information needed includes knowledge about labour markets, internal and external employee relations, and employment legislation. However, the different nature of the decisions at this level means that the analysis of the environment of each of the operations is obviously different from the analysis of the macro-environment needed for strategic management.

Such is the importance of information at all levels of management that a recent development in some companies (and in the literature) is to see information as a resource, which needs systematically to be collected and disseminated throughout the managerial hierarchy. This has led to the concept of management information systems, which has become a discipline in its own right in the literature, and a process in some companies to pursue this aim of integrated information collection and dissemination. Readers interested in management information systems are referred to the books by Higgins[5] and Thierauf[6].

Planning

For each of the operations the general principle is to determine what needs to be planned in order to implement the organizational and business strategies. As discussed in Chapter 7, objectives need to be set at the operational level within each SBU. Normally they will be labelled with the particular function to which they apply, such as marketing objectives or R&D objectives. However, the role of these objectives is different. At this level they are more concerned with specific performance and control within each SBU, as opposed to the directional orientation of the higher-level objectives. Pearce and Robinson[7] have emphasized the importance of integrating them with the higher levels, and ensuring that they are specific, measurable and time-dated.

From here the next stage is to plan the operational strategies, as discussed in this chapter. Using the terminology of Chapter 10, an operational strategy is the means for attaining a respective set of operational objectives for a particular SBU. Again objectives are 'what' is to be achieved and a strategy is 'how' they are to be achieved. At the operational level the 'how' relates to a range of broad issues for each of the operations. Implementation of the higher-level strategies is achieved in that they provide the basis for selecting these operational issues, working on the basis of 'what each of the operations needs to do as a consequence of the higher-level strategies'. Figure 12.1 attempts to show this relationship. The double-headed arrows represent the operational objectives and strategies providing implementation for those at the higher levels, with the latter providing a framework for the planning of the former.

Implementation and control

In the proceeding months after the completion of the planning of the operational strategies the plans are turned into activities. In other words, production of the various products within each SBU takes place, marketing activities will take place, finance will be allocated and controlled, personnel will be managed, and R&D will continue. However, the point is that these activities develop out of operational planning, which in turn is within a strategic planning framework, resulting in implementation of the organizational and business strategies. Finally, control of the implementation of the operational strategies is synonymous with control of the implementation of organizational and business strategies. Control is the subject of Chapter 14.

AN OVERVIEW OF IMPLEMENTATION

The aim of this section is to provide an understanding of the major issues that relate to the implementation of strategy as discussed in Chapters 10 and 11. As mentioned in the introduction to Part Five, implementation necessitates the development of operational strategies, effective human resource management, the control of activities, and an appraisal of the effectiveness of strategies.

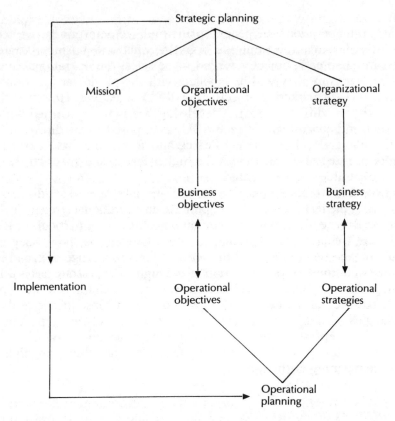

Figure 12.1 *Relating operational planning to strategic planning.*

The central issue is that the company needs to move from the planning of organizational/business objectives and strategies into action. It is this transition which is at the core of developing activities for successful implementation. Rue and Holland[8] have suggested a range of major issues for this transition into implementation.

Operational issues

As already established in this chapter, these issues need to be addressed and resolved for effective implementation. More attention is obviously given to these issues in the following sections on the different operational strategies.

Structural issues

The importance of organizational structure in the overall strategic management process was discussed in Chapter 9. These influences of structure on strategy are also effective at the operational level, and in turn influence implementation. Therefore at this point it is suggested that the major issues of Chapter 9 should be reviewed. Of particular importance will be the way the departments in which each of the operations takes place are structured, and the relative status of the head of each department in the total hierarchical structure.

Integration of operations

Although this chapter tackles the operational strategies separately, in practice they are obviously not implemented in isolation. Indeed for effective implementation full integration of the operations is essential. Although in theory this may seem like a simple concept, in practice many conflicts and problems of co-ordination can arise. Both are couched in behavioural aspects, many of which were examined in Chapter 8 as managerial values and expectations. However, despite the good intentions of managers to ensure integration, problems of co-ordination between the operations can still occur. This will be particularly prevalent in large organizations with a complex structure of several SBUs or divisions, or where some of the operations are centralized in a head office. Further attention is given to integration in the last section of this chapter.

Leadership and commitment

For successful strategy implementation managers throughout the hierarchy need to be committed to the strategies, while leadership needs to be apparent from above to inspire such commitment. However, a major concern is that strategy does, of course, impinge on all personnel and therefore inspiring commitment in all personnel through leadership can be problematic. As discussed in Chapter 8, the many differences to be found in values and expectations will influence the importance that personnel will attach to the strategies presented to them. In turn this will influence their commitment to implementation. The situation will be exacerbated by the fact that many people will not have had the opportunity to participate in the planning of strategy, which tends to lessen commitment. Issues of leadership, commitment and participation are given further consideration in Chapter 13.

Reward systems

As a consequence of the above, implementation obviously necessitates attention to managerial motivation and associated reward systems. Pecuniary rewards for effective implementation in the marketing and production operations can be easily arranged by relating individual performance to sales volume and production output, respectively. However, this type of reward is less easy in the other operations. Having said this, non-pecuniary rewards are also important. These rewards relate particularly to values and expectations, as discussed in Chapter 8, with the realization of expectations being central. Participation by management in the initial planning is also relevant here, as the satisfaction of being part of both planning and implementation can be a rewarding experience. Reward systems will be given further attention in Chapter 13.

Control of actions

The control stage of strategic management consists of two aspects. The first is control of performance, aiming to achieve the objectives established at respective levels. The other feature is control of the activities that arise as a result of the operational strategies. The process is continuous and should lead to modifications of activities in order to correct the course of action for the achievement of objectives. Therefore control is very much part of implementation and a major issue in the transition from planning to action. As already mentioned, the subject of control is given full attention in Chapter 14.

Communicating higher-level strategies

Here the tenet is that, for effective implementation, there needs to be clear communication of the nature of organizational and business objectives and strategies, as well as explanations of why they are necessary. Although the above is a straightforward statement, clear communication may not always be achieved. This may be as a result of poor communication on the part of senior management, or restricted communication which has been purposely designed. Such restriction may be to avoid access by competitors, or to avoid communicating strategies which are likely to be unpopular and which may suffer from sabotage in their implementation. There may also be situations where the release of information may raise the expectations of stakeholders about future performance, and where such an effect is deemed to be inappropriate. Further attention is given to communication in Chapter 13.

MARKETING STRATEGY

Much attention has been given to marketing strategy in the literature. Examples of this attention are the books by Cravens[9] and Jain[10], and articles by Boxer and Wensley[11], Greenley[12], and Walker and Ruekert[13]. There are perhaps several reasons for this attention. One is the considerable attention given to the marketing orientation of organizations *per se* and to the important role that marketing strategy has been given in this orientation. Another reason is that this strategy follows in the hierarchy of strategies as already developed. As operational strategies are within a particular SBU, the marketing strategy is concerned with how the firm is to tackle the markets of the SBU. Hence there is a logical progression of strategies, which is perhaps intuitively more appealing than for the other operational strategies. In explaining marketing strategy writers have given broad statements of meaning, such as 'crucial and central issues to the use of marketing', 'the broad means for achieving marketing objectives', and 'the deployment of major marketing forces'. All these statements are consistent with strategy being the 'how' of operational management. However, there have been differences of opinion as to what constitutes the central issues, broad means, or major forces of marketing strategy. Greenley[12] has suggested five classifications of broad issues, which are given in Figure 12.2 and are discussed below.

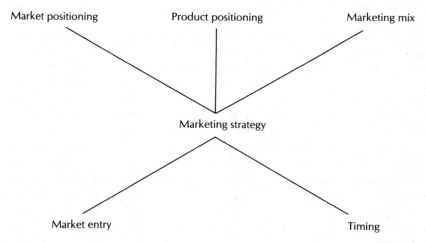

Figure 12.2 *Broad issues of marketing strategy.*

Market positioning

As a consequence of the strategy established at the business level, the marketing strategy now needs to address the question of how the firm is to tackle the market of the particular SBU or product-market scope. In Chapter 5 it was seen that markets are heterogeneous in nature. Although there is a common need across all customers of a market, different groups of consumers exhibit different requirements. This is the concept of market segmentation, and Chapter 5 explained the various bases which can give rise to market segmentation. For most markets several of these bases can be sensibly used for segmentation purposes. The first part of market positioning is deciding which form of market segmentation to adopt. Decisions are then made about which segments to participate in. Broad alternatives are to participate in one segment, several segments, or all segments. The selection made will be the firm's market positioning in the SBU.

Product positioning

Attention is now directed to each of the segments in which the company is positioned. Achieving an understanding of the buyer behaviour of customers, as discussed in Chapter 5, will now lead to decisions on product positioning. Here there are two issues. The first is the number of products to locate in the segment, which will be as a result of buyer behaviour, segment size and competitive presence. The second issue is determining the overall nature of each of these products. At this stage of marketing strategy development the nature refers to broad product specification and USPs (unique selling propositions).

Marketing mix

Much of the marketing literature addresses the detail of the functions of marketing operations, which are generally organized around the four Ps of product, place, price and promotion. For different companies operating in different markets the four Ps have different relative degrees of importance. Consequently, firms use these functions in different ways, or they mix them differently to give a particular marketing mix for a particular market. Therefore this issue of marketing strategy is to determine how the four Ps are to be utilized, or the relative degree of reliance that is to be placed on each. The detail to be attached to each of the four Ps is generally referred to as 'marketing tactics'. Books on general marketing and those on specific functions, such as advertising, give considerable attention to tactical issues.

Market entry

In Chapter 10 it was explained that moving into a new SBU could be achieved by internal development, an acquisition, a merger, or by collaboration. While the decision in this context is made at the organizational strategy level, similar decisions need to be made relative to the operational level concerning entry, re-entry, positioning or repositioning in particular market segments. Market positioning could be extended by obtaining the expertise for entry into new segments from external sources, which could also provide additional products for enhanced product positioning. Alternatively it may be that changes to positioning could be achieved internally. The R&D and production functions may have the capability of developing new products for this positioning, while the marketing department may have the expertise needed in these segments.

Timing

In Chapter 11 several issues of timing were identified as important in the selection of both organizational and business strategies. Most of these issues also have a bearing on the development of marketing strategy. For example, a decline in the industry life cycle of an SBU is indicative of a likely need to spread market positioning or to enhance product positioning. Changes to the marketing mix will also be necessary in the decline phase. Similarly, urgency identified at the higher level may instigate a quick increase in the number of segments for participation, which may suggest either collaboration or an acquisition for an early entry into a new segment. However, timing also relates to when particular marketing tactics should be executed. Timing may simply relate to seasonal trends of the industry. Alternatively tactics may follow relevant indicators from the external environment. These can range through the many external variables that were identified in the strategic audit in Chapter 3, such as economic indicators, industry trends, or specific events such as a trade exhibition. Alternatively the external indicator may be chosen as competitors. The timing of tactics may be to be first to carry out, or to be early but following the first competitor, or to take a laggard position by being one of the last competitors to make tactical changes.

Hierarchy of strategies

Having explained marketing strategy a hierarchy of strategies can now be illustrated. This expands the point, made earlier in this section, that marketing strategy closely follows higher-level strategies, with a logical progression which is perhaps intuitively more appealing than for the other operational strategies.

This hierarchy is outlined in Figure 12.3. In this example diversification and market penetration have been selected for the illustration. In the case of diversification unfamiliarity would certainly be of major concern in selecting the number of segments to enter initially and the method of entry. Unfamiliarity with the new SBU would also be a major concern in formulating tactics. The business strategy of growth by market penetration could be achieved by several marketing strategy alternatives. It could be through market positioning by progressively expanding into additional segments, or through product positioning by placing several products in the initial segments to capture more customers in these segments. Alternatively, it could be achieved through initial participation in a limited number of segments with a limited number of products, but with effective tactics to achieve high market share in these segments.

R&D STRATEGY

Central to research and development strategy are changes which may need to be made as a consequence of the higher-level strategies. As mentioned in Chapter 3 in the section on appraising operations capability, R&D is concerned with advancing the technology of both products and their production processes. The first issue to be tackled is whether or not future higher-level strategies are indicative of a necessary change to the directions currently being taken in R&D. If change is

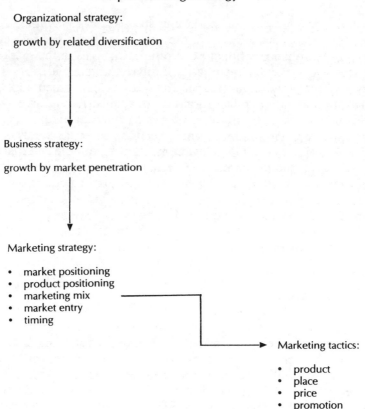

Figure 12.3   *A hierarchy of strategies.*

EXHIBIT 12.1

Norsk Data's Mini Miracle

Norsk Data of Norway is reported to be the fourth largest supplier of mini-computers in Europe. In competing with the large mainframe manufacturers, Norsk developed a particular marketing strategy based on market and product positioning. Its major market segment was customers who did not need the computing power of a mainframe, while still having several applications requiring extensive data processing. These requirements would be satisfied with one or two networked minis and a cluster of terminals. The markets it chose to serve were Government departments and medium-sized companies. Product positioning in these segments was to offer a 'package' of both hardware and software, often tailor-made to customer needs. Its competitors offered standard computers but not the software.

Adapted from *Management Today*, May 1987

necessary then it will relate to the focus of future R&D, the division of effort between products and production, and its relationship to that of competitors.

The importance of R&D obviously varies from industry to industry, with the nature of the industry of each SBU dictating the importance of R&D strategy to a particular company. However, the importance of R&D strategy is also a function of the support of senior management and their integration of R&D into the strategy hierarchy (see a recent article by Brownlie[14] for a relevant discussion). For some companies R&D may be available from external institutions. Here the issue is one of either 'buying in' this expertise or merely using external sources to augment in-house activities. Regardless of the source of R&D, writers such as Capon and Glazer[15] and Hayes and Abernathy[16] have suggested that the basis of R&D strategy should be the premiss that technology is a major asset. As such it needs to be effectively deployed through the process of R&D.

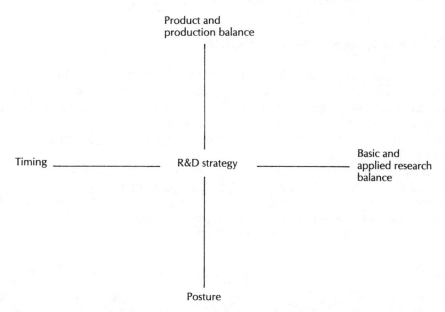

Figure 12.4   *Broad issues of R&D strategy.*

While there is a lack of agreement in the literature as to the broad issues which should constitute R&D strategy, those given in Figure 12.4 are the most commonly cited.

Product and production balance

The basic but essential decision on how R&D should be split between these two requirements is a major issue. The decision will result in an allocation of both expenditure and effort, where the latter relates to creative work and man-hours.

The strategy chosen could obviously be concentration on products, concentration on production, or some kind of split between the two.

The choice will be partly determined by the nature of the industry. High-technology products will obviously need considerable attention to their future development, although their production is also likely to be high-technology in nature. However, mass production of components or low-tech products will benefit more from concentration on production processes. There are obviously close links between this issue of R&D strategy and marketing and production strategies. For the former the link will be with product positioning in relation to relevant market segments, as well as with developing consumer benefits within the marketing mix. The link with production strategy will be the major issue of how to manufacture most efficiently. This issue will be raised again later in this chapter. However, more efficient production can also lead to improved consumer benefits of product quality, reliability and better value.

Basic and applied research balance

Basic research involves pure scientific research with no apparent and immediate commercial application. Applied research, however, relates directly to the requirements of organizational and business strategies. Product development, for example, would favour direct applied research, whereas a turnaround strategy would require, at least in the short term, applications directly into improved production efficiency.

Basic research requires a long-term financial commitment which carries high risk, and which may have no future benefit or an extremely long payback period. However, the potential advantage is the development of 'breakthrough' products which can give tremendous competitive advantages.

Posture

Here the decision is between taking an offensive and a defensive competitive posture towards the utilization of R&D for technological advancements. In the former the approach will be to lead the industry in making technological advantages, related to either products or production. The aim is to introduce these advantages before competitors in order to gain competitive advantages in the marketplace. With a defensive posture the company merely follows and copies advances in technology which have already been introduced by competitors. The posture selected will clearly be a result of the established higher-level strategies. Growth strategies will be conducive to an offensive posture, stability to a defensive posture, whereas turnaround could result in either orientation.

Timing

Many R&D projects are necessarily scheduled over long periods of time. This issue of strategy is concerned with defining these periods, and assigning priorities to particular projects. These decisions will result from the timing constraints that have already been addressed in the strategic management process. The major issues of timing were examined in Chapter 11 as part of strategy selection, which will also determine these timing issues of R&D strategy.

EXHIBIT 12.2

Sitting Pretty

The French company L'Oréal is one of the world's four leading cosmetics companies; it also has a pharmaceuticals division. At the operational level the cosmetics division has a reputation for using aggressive marketing tactics, but is also successful in new product launches. A major success was the timely launch of their suntan lotion, Ambre Solaire, in 1936, the summer after the French government's decision to grant paid vacations to workers. A recent successful launch was L'Oréal Styling Mousse, following five years' extensive R&D. However, its commitment to R&D is claimed to be the major reason for its success. In cosmetics this amounted to 3.4% of sales turnover in 1987, and is said to be the highest in the industry. The headquarters R&D function employs 1,000 researchers, and new products are extensively tested in their 300-seat hair salon, where they are applied to the hair of thousands of French women.

Adapted from *Business,* January 1987

PRODUCTION STRATEGY

As a broad definition, production is the process of converting inputs into value-enhanced output, where the latter is directed at satisfying needs and wants of consumers. While production is often only associated with the manufacture of physical goods, it also includes the production of services. In the case of an output of physical goods the inputs can be raw materials, components, people and machines. In the case of services machines and supporting physical products can be included, but the bulk of the input is the knowledge and skills of the people who perform the services.

The process of production is generally split into two major functions: systems design and operations planning. The former starts with products specified in the marketing strategy and works through the design of the production capabilities that are needed in terms of plant, equipment, factory layout and work methods. Operations planning is concerned with the day-to-day planning and control of current production over the full range of products or services.

The core theme of production strategy is the efficiency of production processes and the ramifications of this efficiency on costs and consumer benefits. However, Wheelwright and Hayes[17] have pointed out that many companies are orientated to traditional production processes, so that attitudinal changes may be essential to implement changes in production strategy. Most writers in the literature give the broad issues which are highlighted in Figure 12.5 as the components of production strategy.

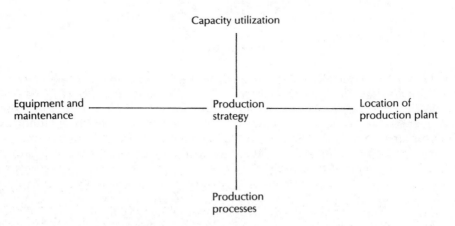

Figure 12.5   *Broad issues of production strategy.*

Capacity utilization

There are two elements to the issue of production capacity. The first is deciding how capacity requirements will change in the future, while the second is how the capacity will be utilized. The first of these will be a result of objectives and strategies that have been planned at both the organizational and business levels. Growth may quickly absorb current capacity in the medium term and therefore additional capacity would be required. On the other hand, stability or defence may mean under-utilization of production resources, leading to shorter production shifts, idle plant and laid-off employees. Also to be considered in the assessment of capacity is the mix of capacity requirements between particular products and product lines of the SBUs. Although an overall increase in capacity may be needed this could be a result of diversification and a requirement for different capacity. Unfortunately this may also be associated with a necessary reduction in capacity in another SBU. Approaches to increasing capacity can be through an incremental build-up, by planned capital investment in new plant, by acquiring or merging with another producer, or by collaboration with another producer.

Attention in this strategy is then directed to utilization of the capacity. A first decision here is the allocation of capacity to specific products or product lines, although this allocation will be controlled during scheduling as part of operations planning. The other decision is to address the volume of output to be produced per unit time. While most production processes will work at a constant level of output, demand from the marketplace is likely to exhibit seasonal fluctuations. Here the strategy decision is between a high and a low level of capacity utilization. If the former is adopted then excess production will take place at particular times of the year, which will need to go into stockholding. Where the strategy is to utilize capacity at a low level the higher levels of demand are usually obtained by subcontracting to other producers. Indeed this may become a strategy in itself; obtaining most, if not all, production output for a number of products from another company.

Location of production plant

Here the issue is how the company is to locate production output in relation to the geographic markets that it serves. Locating new plant alongside old on the same site is likely to achieve economies of scale in production, whereas locating new plant on other sites is likely to incur higher production costs and overheads. However, where markets are spread throughout the country, or throughout several countries, then the ongoing benefits of locating production capacity on different sites within these markets are likely to exceed the costs to be incurred. Indeed for companies which establish globalization as part of their organizational objectives a geographical spread of production capacity as a strategy is consistent with this aim.

Such location does, however, need to be the subject of a careful appraisal. Once established it cannot be relocated in the short term. Extensive capital investment is likely to be needed, and the break-even point may be several years ahead. Location decisions are based on many criteria, including long-run market demand, availability of labour, availability of inputs, capital expenditure, and the efficiency of distribution channels to several markets.

Production processes

Within this component of production strategy there are several issues to consider, among them:

- The basic technology to adopt.
- Speed of adoption of new technology.
- Quality of production equipment to employ.
- Flexibility needed in the process.
- Levels of quality control of the production output.

Here there are many links with other operational strategies. The technology of production was seen earlier in this chapter to be the province of R&D strategy, although its adoption as a process is a decision of production strategy.

Wheelwright and Hayes[17] emphasize that early adoption of technological advances can result in competitive advantages. These can be as either direct consumer benefits or as improvements to internal efficiency. Aligned to this decision is that of the quality of production equipment. Higher specifications may mean higher capital investment, but also greater reliability and a longer life. However, the last point again needs to be related to technological advances which may quickly make current plant obsolete. Perhaps of overriding importance is the quality of production output and quality control processes. The ultimate judge of quality is the consumer, so that this process needs to be closely planned with marketing strategy.

Equipment and maintenance

The two major issues here are the scheduling of essential maintenance of production equipment and plant, and establishing a programme for the replacement of plant. Both are obviously essential to retaining both internal efficiency and quality of finished output. While such activities necessitate production 'downtime' and lost output, they are nevertheless essential activities, representing controlled 'downtime' as opposed to lost production through breakdowns or unacceptable output quality.

FINANCIAL STRATEGY

Financial issues have been examined in several chapters of this book; notably in Chapter 3 as part of the operations capability analysis and in Chapter 11 as part of the strategy selection process. Financial strategy is obviously at the core of the organization, to provide capital for the implementation of the higher-level strategies.

Readers of this book will be aware of the vast literature in the fields of finance and accounting. This probably exceeds in size the literature for each of the other operations, including marketing. Given the size of this literature and the importance of courses in finance and accounting in both undergraduate and postgraduate programmes, the aim of this section is merely to outline basic issues of financial strategy. Most writers seem to give the broad issues of financial strategy as shown in Figure 12.6.

Capital structure

This is the issue of the permanent financing of an organization, represented by preference shares, equity (ordinary shares, retained earnings and capital reserves), and long-term debt. A major part of the strategy is the balancing of the mix of these elements of the structure, and determining how higher-level strategies are likely to affect this mix. Of particular importance to the structure is the relation-

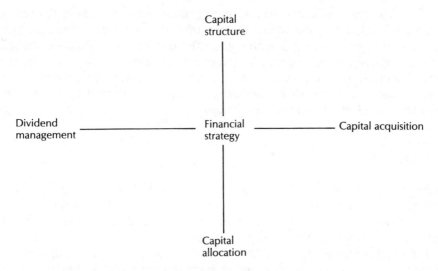

Figure 12.6 *Broad issues of financial strategy.*

ship between debt or loan capital and equity, known as 'gearing' or 'leverage'. This is generally calculated as a ratio, so that a long-term trend can be established and an acceptable level established as part of the strategy. The degree of leverage which a firm elects to insert into its capital structure has been addressed, for example, by Sandberg *et al.*[18]. Chang and Campo-Flores[19] suggest that capital structure strategy should be planned on the basis of simplicity, safety and flexibility, although these decisions do need to be supportive of the higher-level strategies.

Capital acquisition

Several approaches can be taken to the acquisition of capital, which can be either as an internal source, as further loan capital, or as additional share capital. Capital acquisition is needed, of course, for funding organization and business strategies, being particularly important for growth strategies.

An initial consideration is simply between internal and external acquisition. With the exception of diversification, product development and turnaround strategies, it may be that other alternatives can be funded internally. For some large conglomerates it may be that all alternatives can be funded internally, while for small firms even market penetration may require additional loans.

Where long-term debt is to be increased, then the concern is the resultant change in gearing, as a major criterion against which the decision needs to be made. Hence the cost to be borne is not just the price of borrowing but the change in leverage and associated increased vulnerability. Where external acquisition is to be through additional share capital, then the value of shareholders' funds and capital employed will change, as will performance measures based on these (see

Chapter 14). However, over the long term the aim is that investment of this capital in the higher-level strategies will, of course, increase earnings to improve performance. Also to be considered is a change in the mix of ownership and any influence on the relative power of stakeholder groups. If new ownership is to be spread then share capital may be preferred to additional loan capital. However, if autonomy is a major objective then loan capital may be preferred to an increase in power of the shareholder stakeholder group.

Capital allocation

Here the strategy is concerned with how acquired capital is to be allocated among the SBUs. If the organization is able to raise all the capital demanded by the planned direction of all SBUs then there will be no problem of allocation. Each SBU will be able to pursue its business strategies.

Such an ideal situation may not prevail on two counts. First, the organizational strategy may require new directions which require high levels of funding, resulting in investment being reduced at the business level in preference for these higher-level requirements. Second, the organization may be unable to acquire sufficient capital to cover the needs of all SBUs. Therefore priorities will need to be attached to opportunities identified across the SBUs. Those designated for growth, on the other hand, may be allocated additional capital in order to initiate that growth, regardless of opportunities being missed elsewhere. Another issue in the allocation of capital is that of timing. Depending on industry life cycles and levels of competitiveness in individual SBUs, it may be possible to defer funding in one SBU without loss of market share. Preference could then be given to another SBU where it is deemed that funding needs are more immediate.

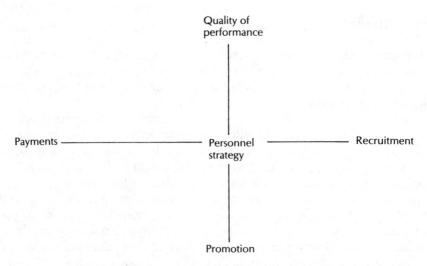

Figure 12.7 *Broad issues of personnel strategy.*

Dividend management

The issue of dividend management relates closely to the issue of capital acquisition. As net profit is either retained for investment or paid out as a dividend, an increase in the former means a reduction in dividend payments. Therefore, it is necessary to determine the mix between the two. Although a lower dividend means a lower return on the investment of the owners, there are also advantages to this. Where profits are retained for investment it may not be necessary to increase loan capital or to raise share capital. The former will have a favourable effect on gearing, while the latter will retain the current concentration of ownership. Forgoing current dividends for capital investment should lead to longer-term growth and higher dividends in the future. However, in finalizing this issue of strategy attention also needs to be paid to the current demands of shareholders, and their collective power as a stakeholder group.

PERSONNEL STRATEGY

Regardless of the level of sophistication in the planning of direction and strategy, the implementation of the latter is dependent on the performance of people. Indeed the overall effectiveness of strategic management is dependent on the behaviour of people in the organization. Consequently, strategies need to be developed in order to control and monitor human performance. Human behaviour is discussed at several points in this book. Of particular importance was the attention to values and expectations in Chapter 8. Of similar importance is the attention given to the management of people, which is the subject of Chapter 13.

In common with other areas of management studies, variation is to be found in the usage of terminology. For example, Guest[20] has emphasized that the terms 'personnel management' and 'human resource management' are used interchangeably. Some of these variations will be tackled below. The broad issues of personnel strategy to be examined are given in Figure 12.7.

Quality of performance

This issue is concerned with how to appraise the quality of the performance of individuals throughout the organization. In considering this aspect of controlling performance, separate attention normally needs to be given to managerial staff and blue-collar employees. For the latter the strategy is likely to be to link performance to production output through some form of productivity arrangement. The strategy may relate to individual performance or to a collective performance. Participation by employees in formulating this issue of strategy is normally through the process labelled 'collective bargaining' (as part of industrial relations), which is also the vehicle for negotiating other conditions of employment.

For managerial staff this type of appraisal is generally not suitable, so that another strategy will need to be developed. Given the complexity of managerial roles and their wide variation in nature across organizations, realistic appraisal schemes can be difficult to establish. Of particular importance to the context of this book is the integration of human resources into strategic management. Indeed, Guest[20] has also emphasized that one of the ways in which human resource management and personnel management have been differentiated is by claiming that the former is concerned with this integration into strategic management. Further attention will be devoted to these issues in Chapter 13.

Recruitment

This issue of personnel strategy is concerned with how the company is to plan for the quantity of future human resources, within different classifications of jobs. Attention again needs to be devoted to both blue-collar and managerial staff. This planning process has traditionally been called 'manpower planning', with Bowey[21], for example, defining it in terms of co-ordinating the requirements for and the availability of different types of employee.

This issue of strategy needs to give particular attention to the qualities, values, expectations and behavioural traits of the type of people that it would prefer to employ in different job functions. In Chapter 8 the importance of corporate culture was discussed. As far as recruitment is concerned the culture will provide an overall framework, in that people will be selected who are seen to fit into the requirements of the culture. For managerial staff this consistency with corporate culture is of particular importance. Included here would be the consistency of management style as adopted by the company and that of individual managers. Potential conflict in management styles could be potentially disastrous for the effective implementation of strategies. Again meriting special attention, in this aspect of managerial recruitment, are the attitudes of new managers to the importance of the process of strategic management *per se*, in relation to the importance specified by the company.

Promotion

In considering the internal promotion of personnel, in relation to the appointment of new employees, again a split in strategy is likely between that for blue-collar employees and that for managerial employees. For the former the strategy to be adopted will result from collective bargaining, as part of the industrial relations process. For managers the strategy needs to balance the relative advantages of internal promotion against external appointments. The advantages of the former include perpetuating the corporate culture, rewarding individual effort, providing a basis for motivation, and providing a continuity of managerial participation in the long-range development of the company. Advantages of external appointments include the influx of new experience, the addition of different expertise, a different perspective on managerial thinking, and a new element of competitiveness within the managerial hierarchy. Indeed, the adoption of some of the organizational and business strategies given in Chapter 10 may necessitate the influx of new managers.

Payments

Having utilized a range of human resources, the strategy must now tackle the issue of how they will be rewarded. This tends to be a large area of study in the literature devoted to personnel management. Again a split between blue-collar and managerial employees seems to be followed. For the former a mechanism of free collective bargaining is again likely to be in operation, with perhaps national wage scales being part of the strategy. For managers the complexity and diversity of job functions mean that this issue of strategy can again be complex. Perhaps the major split in the approach is either to have different salary scales for different levels of management or to have a free system of negotiation. Further consideration will be given to managerial rewards in Chapter 13.

INTEGRATING OPERATIONAL STRATEGIES

It will already be apparent that close integration of the operational strategies will be necessary for the effective implementation of the higher-level strategies. Although the total systematic approach to strategic management fosters this form of integration, there are several general principles that are worth highlighting. While integration is necessary for effective implementation, a lack of it can also lead to managerial conflicts between the operations, which should clearly be avoided.

Recent attention has been given to the integration of operations in the literature. Particular attention has been given to the integration of marketing and technology, given the obvious impact of technology on the nature of many products. Examples of articles here are those by Capon and Glazer[15], Nystrom[22] and Ruekert and Walker[23]. General principles for the integration of operations have been set out by Rue and Holland[8] and are discussed below.

Capability analysis

A careful consideration of the strengths and weaknesses of each of the functions can indicate potential conflicts. For example, a production weakness of little flexibility in manufacturing could cause conflicts with the marketing department where it is seen as reducing consumer selection. Information to understand this feature of integration is available from the operations capability appraisal in the strategic audit (Chapter 3).

Trade-offs

Here the principle of integration is based on managers' recognizing that all functions, incuding their own, are likely to feature strengths and weakness. The aim is interfunctional recognition and acceptance that they provide constraints to current operations. The aim is then to work as a team to overcome weaknesses and build on strengths, regardless of the operations to which they relate.

Communication

As already mentioned in this chapter, a major issue is the communication of higher-level strategies. The clearer this communication the more likely it will be that the role of each of the operations will be understood, both within the total strategic management process and in relation to the other operations.

Participation

Following on from the last point, participation in the process would normally enhance communication with the potential of lessening conflict. Also, participation will give a deeper understanding of objectives being pursued and the strategies being used. Again the principle is that such participation will help avoid conflict and will promote integration.

Multifunctional experience

Some companies experiment with a broadening of the experience of operational managers. For particular periods of time managers will be encouraged, or indeed required, to work in other operations in order to experience the working of the relevant departments and the problems that arise. Here the principle is that an appreciation of the other operations will help avoid conflicts and will foster integration.

Co-ordination

Closer co-ordination, in theory, will result in closer integration. Indeed the whole of the strategic management process is orientated to co-ordination. However, specific stages are particularly associated with co-ordination. Management by objectives through the hierarchy of objectives is one such stage, as was seen in Chapter 7. Of similar importance are the subjects of Chapters 13 and 14: human resource management, and control.

SUMMARY

This chapter has examined operational strategies within the context of strategic management. The first section looked at the overall nature of operational management by comparing it to strategic management. The next section presented a general overview of implementation, outlining the links between the planning of strategy and carrying it out.

The next five sections examined each of the major operational strategies: marketing; R&D; production; finance; and personnel. The major issues of a marketing operational strategy were given as market and product positioning; the marketing mix; timing; and market entry. R&D operational strategy issues were presented as product and production balance; basic and applied research balance; posture; and timing. In the case of production the operational strategy issues of capacity utilization; location of production plant; production processes; and equipment and maintenance were examined. The broad issues of a financial strategy — capital structure; capital acquisition; capital allocation; and dividend management — were discussed. Finally, personnel operational strategy issues — quality of performance; recruitment; promotion; and payments — were presented.

The final section of the chapter looked at the integration of operational strategies. Although several aspects of integration had been raised in the chapter, this section presented six general principles for the integration of operations.

CHAPTER CASE STUDY ILLUSTRATION:
LEVI STRAUSS AND COMPANY*

Levi Strauss had gained about one-third of the world market for jeans by 1981, making it the world's largest manufacturer. It was also a major company in the world apparel industry. In Europe it had production facilities in Belgium, France, Italy, the Netherlands, Norway, Sweden, Switzerland and the United Kingdom.

This case study deals with several issues of operational strategies which were applicable in Europe. The company had been established in the United States in the 1850s by Levi Strauss, a Bavarian immigrant. The case study claims that the company's success is partly explained by its marketing expertise, in particular an ability to identify and respond quickly to new markets. In addition it made opportunities through approaches to market segmentation and subsequent market positioning.

*Derived from the original case study by Neil H. Snyder. Copyright © 1981.

As the apparel markets in the United States became saturated with suppliers in the early 1980s, Levi's was looking for greater growth of sales in Western Europe. Countries such as Austria, Belgium, Italy, Switzerland, the United Kingdom and West Germany were seen as being of particular importance. Operational strategies were central to this growth, with particular reliance on marketing strategy.

MARKETING STRATEGY

Consumer perception of the Levi's product had changed drastically over the years, from originally being a work garment, and a teenage fad in the 1950s, to a fashion product in the 1970s and 1980s. The company's marketing orientation had been partly responsible for the latter, but had also led to market segmentation. In the jeans market its market positioning strategy was based on fashion conscious people between 20 and 39. Product positioning was based on high-quality products. However, for Europe they were also positioned in a number of other markets, namely sportswear, youthwear and womenswear.

There were several major features of its marketing mix strategy. A major strength was obviously wide acceptance of the Levi's brand name image, and the resultant achievement of high brand loyalty. A wide range of products was offered, in order to accommodate shifts in consumer preferences. Also, quality of product was linked to reasonable prices. Although distribution had been mostly through department stores, the strategy was to develop into more specialized clothing outlets. Levi's used advanced computer systems to define trends and to anticipate changes in demand. The latter was particularly important for stock control, resulting in an efficient delivery and stock-control service to retail customers. Media advertising was also an important element of the mix strategy, to promote quality linked with style and fashion.

R&D STRATEGY

The case study claims that this is one of Levi's most important competitive advantages. R&D related to products investigated new fabrics, new garments, and improvements in the functional performance of products. R&D was also concerned with improving automated and semi-automated production equipment. Here the aim was to continue as the industry leader in efficient manufacturing techniques. Strength in R&D was reinforced through close liaison with the corporate marketing research department. Identified trends in fashion, consumer attitudes, and retail point-of-sale trends, for example, were all closely integrated with R&D operations.

PRODUCTION STRATEGY

Little is given in the case study on production strategy, except for production plant location. As already indicated, this was based on globalization to reflect the company's total business. Production and distribution centres were located in North America, Latin America, Asia and Europe. In Europe there was also a wide spread of locations in Belgium, France, Italy, the Netherlands, Norway, Sweden, Switzerland and the United Kingdom.

PERSONNEL STRATEGY

Some implications of their personnel strategy are given in the case study. Traditionally the apparel industry employs relatively high levels of unskilled and semi-skilled workers. Consequently wage levels are among the lowest of all manufacturing industries. Levi's payment strategy reflected these industry norms. The company also had a strategy of production location in local areas of low labour cost, providing another feature of personnel strategy.

The case study also implies concerns for quality of performance by personnel. All production and distribution centres were reported as having strong community relations programmes, with all employees being encouraged to be socially concerned and active. To support this Levi's contributed 3% of after-tax profits to pursuing social responsibility.

REFERENCES

1. Greenley, G. E., 'The Relationship of Strategic and Marketing Plans', *European Journal of Operational Research*, **27**, 1, 1986, 17–24.
2. Glueck, W. F. and Jauch, L. R., *Business Policy and Strategic Management*, McGraw-Hill, New York, 1984.
3. Stoner, J. A. F., *Management*, Prentice Hall, Englewood Cliffs, NJ, 1982.
4. Ansoff, H. I. and Brandenburg, R. G., 'The Design of Optimal Business Planning Systems', *Kommunikation*, **3**, 4, 1967, 163–88.
5. Higgins, J. C., *Information Systems for Planning and Control*, Arnold, London, 1976.
6. Thierauf, R. J., *Decision Support Systems for Effective Planning and Control*, Prentice Hall, Englewoods Cliffs, NJ, 1982.
7. Pearce, J. A. and Robinson, R. B., *Strategic Management*, 2nd edn, Irwin, Homewood, IL, 1985.
8. Rue, L. W. and Holland, P. G., *Strategic Management: Concepts and Experiences*, McGraw-Hill, New York, 1986.
9. Cravens, D. W., *Strategic Marketing*, Irwin, Homewood, IL, 1982.
10. Jain, S. C., *Marketing Planning and Strategy*, 2nd edn, South-Western, Cincinnati, OH, 1985.
11. Boxer, P. J. and Wensley, J. R. C., 'The Need for Middle-out Development of Marketing Strategy', *Journal of Management Studies*, **23**, 2, 1986, 189–204.
12. Greenley, G. E., 'An Understanding of Marketing Strategy', *European Journal of Marketing*, **18**, 6, 1984, 90–103.
13. Walker, O. C. and Ruekert, R. W., 'Marketing's Role in the Implementation of Business Strategies', *Journal of Marketing*, **51**, 1987, 15–33.

14. Brownlie, D. T., 'The Strategic Management of Technology', *European Journal of Marketing*, **21**, 9, 1987, 45–65.
15. Capon, N. and Glazer, R., 'Marketing and Technology: A Strategic Coalignment', *Journal of Marketing*, **51**, 1987, 1–14.
16. Hayes, R. H. and Abernathy, W. J., 'Managing Our Way to Economic Decline', *Harvard Business Review*, July–August 1980.
17. Wheelwright, S. C. and Hayes, R. H., 'Competing through Manufacturing', *Harvard Business Review*, **63**, 1, 1985, 99–109.
18. Sandberg, C. M., Lewellen, W. G. and Stanley, K. L., 'Financial Strategy: Planning and Managing the Corporate Leverage Position', *Strategic Management Journal*, **8**, 1987, 15–24.
19. Chang, Y. N. and Campo-Flores, F., *Business Policy and Strategy*, Goodyear, Santa Monica, CA, 1980.
20. Guest, D. E., 'Human Resource Management and Industrial Relations', *Journal of Management Studies*, **24**, 5, 1987, 503–21.
21. Bowey, A. M., *A Guide to Manpower Planning*, Macmillan, London, 1974.
22. Nystrom, H., 'Product Development Strategy: An Integration of Technology and Marketing', *Journal of Product Innovation Management*, **2**, 1, 1985, 25–33.
23. Ruekert, R. W. and Walker, O. C., 'Interactions between Marketing and R&D Departments in Implementing Different Business Strategies', *Strategic Management Journal*, **8**, 1987, 233–48.

CHAPTER 13
HUMAN RESOURCE MANAGEMENT

This chapter builds on the issues of the human behaviour of managers that have already been presented in the previous chapters. Indeed, the issues that relate to implementation do, of necessity, link back to those of planning. As will be recalled from the introduction to Part Five, human resource management appears in a dashed box in the model of strategic management used in this book. This means that, although it is an integral part of the model, it is not a stage of the strategic management decision-making process. Rather it represents a set of influences on decision-making (see Chapter 1). Discussions on behavioural issues within the strategic management literature have been derived from two different literatures. These are the traditional literature on general management and the developing literature encompassing the study of organizational behaviour. Although this chapter raises and explains the central issues pertinent to the implementation of strategy, further study of these issues should also incorporate these two literatures.

In the introduction to Part Five it was said that a feature of implementation is that it is achieved through people, located at different levels within the organizational structure. This chapter contrasts with the last chapter. In Chapter 12 the linkages of the formal stages of strategic management with operational management were addressed. In this chapter attention is given to the less formal issues of the human behaviour of managers in strategy implementation. The focus of the chapter is on the management of this behaviour, in order to achieve effective strategic management.

Readers will be aware of the many issues of the human behaviour of managers which have already been raised throughout the previous chapters. Indeed Chapter 8 was totally concerned with behaviour, focusing on values and expectations. In that chapter a broad split was made between behaviour associated with planning and that associated with implementation. Also, it was said that Chapter 8 was about planning issues whereas Chapter 13 would be about implementation issues. While this is true, generally speaking, behavioural issues between the two are often difficult to separate, given their close association.

Another feature of this chapter is that managers are viewed as a resource, as reflected in the chapter title. While the phrase 'human resource management' has slipped into common usage in both the literature and organizations, the point is that people provide the ability and the initiatives for company success. Indeed, a company is basically a group of people and its success is largely dependent upon its people.

Five major sections constitute this chapter, with the first giving an outline of the concept of human resource management. The second section looks at leadership within the context of implementation, and is followed by a section on managerial participation. The fourth section examines the management of change as a result of strategic management, while the final section looks at the integration of operations.

AN OUTLINE

Generally speaking, relatively little attention has been given in the literature to human behaviour within the context of strategic management. Lyles and Lenz[1] have noted the lack of attention in strategic planning, claiming that its study is at a very early stage of development. Little research has been done which directly centres on behavioural problems during the planning process. However, Taylor[2] has made some relatively early claims about human behaviour during the implementation of plans. He suggested that the major issues are resistance to change, motivation, cognitive limitations, and blocks to innovation.

The label 'human resource management' (HRM) has come into popular usage in both the literature and in firms. However, through its usage several different meanings have become attached to it, as identified by Guest[3]. Some authors use it merely as a synonym 'personnel management', but one which is more fashionable than the latter; the text by Wheelen and Hunger[4] is an example.

Another use of the label 'human resource management' is to distinguish it from the traditional function of personnel management. Here Guest[3] suggests that the difference is that HRM is concerned with the integration of human resources into strategic management. Such a view could be taken to mean all human resources in a company, including all managers in the hierarchy and all blue-collar workers in the company. While such an interpretation may be suitable for a specialist text on HRM, it is taken to be too wide a perspective for this book. Consequently, the focus on HRM in this chapter is on managers within the hierarchy who will be instrumental in the implementation of strategy. Although, as yet, there is no consolidated theory of HRM, Guest[3] suggests four main dimensions of HRM; these will be useful in developing the chapter:

- It will be concerned with integration.
- It will foster commitment from individuals to the success of the company.
- It will allow for flexibility and adaptability in the 'handling' of people during implementation.
- It will foster the development of a quality orientation in the performance of individuals, departments and the overall organization.

In Chapter 12 several issues were raised that are central in the transition from planning to implementation. Some of these are pertinent to HRM. These were the integration of operations, leadership and commitment, reward systems, and the communication of higher-level strategies. These issues will also be useful in developing the understanding of HRM to be developed in this chapter.

Problems of implementation

Given the complexity of human behaviour it is not surprising that firms experience problems in the transition from planning to implementation. An appreciation of these problems also provides a basis for this chapter on HRM. Abell and Hammond[5] have mentioned a range of problems that can arise because of human behaviour, but which relate to planning. However, these problems are also relevant to implementation and are therefore pertinent here:

- Planning can become a ritual rather than a systematic process.
- Divisions can develop between managers who participate in different levels of planning.
- Communication may be purposely made ineffective.
- Plans may be developed in order to pursue self-interest.
- Strategies may be merely projections of current strategies with little consideration of alternatives.
- Plans may be largely or partly ignored when day-to-day actions are carried out.

On the other hand, Pekar[6] has described a range of problems that can arise because of human behaviour during the implementation of strategy:

- Managers may be unwilling to accept techniques and processes with which they are not familiar.
- Developing communications problems between operations.
- A lack of competent managers in key positions.
- A lack of understanding and experience in strategic management.
- Poor senior manager commitment to the total strategic management process.
- Poor communication down the managerial hierarchy of objectives to be pursued and strategies to be used, with little justification of the rationale being used.

Approach to human resource management

In developing a structure to explain HRM within the context of strategy implementation all the issues discussed in this section were taken into account. The result was the structure shown in Figure 13.1, which is based on four major components.

The first of these is leadership and delegation, which needs to be exercised throughout the managerial hierarchy to achieve implementation. The second

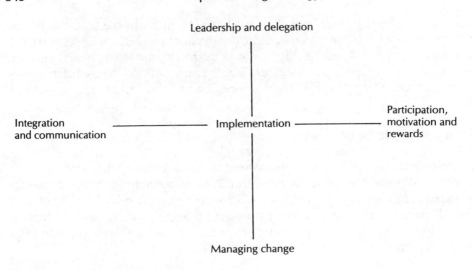

Figure 13.1 *Structure to explain human resource management.*

component is concerned with the managers themselves. Attention first needs to be given to their participation in implementation, which will relate to previous participation in planning. Following participation is the motivation of managers to perform effectively in their participation in implementation. This motivation is obviously central to the management of these human resources, as is the other consideration in this component, rewards that are to be made for effective participation.

The third component centres on the need to ensure that HRM incorporates the change that is instigated by strategic management. Here attention will be given to managers' perceptions of change, the use of power to effect change, and essential personal commitment for effective implementation. The final component concentrates on integration and communication, which are issues that permeate across the problems that were listed earlier in this section.

LEADERSHIP AND DELEGATION

Leadership

As a starting point to implementation, leadership is concerned with influencing people to carry out particular activities, while delegation is concerned with the formal direction of people to carry out these activities. Although a manager will be able to delegate tasks because of his position within the organization, his ability to effect that delegation will be largely determined by his leadership skills.

Books on both general management and organizational behaviour have given attention to leadership. Examples of the latter are those by Buchanan and Huczynski[7] and Gray and Starke[8]. Stoner[9] has defined leadership as a process that will

---

EXHIBIT 13.1

Norsk Data's Democratic Management

Norsk Data of Norway is reported to be the fourth largest supplier of mini-computers in Europe. It is reported to have a philosophy of not dictating decisions to its managers from the top, having decentralization of decision-making from headquarters, with the aim of practising democracy within its management. With this approach Norsk have achieved high levels of growth in both sales and profitability. Leadership has derived from the President, Rolf Skår. It is said that his commitment and leadership have played a major role in the company achieving its position in Europe. He was also responsible for establishing a corporate culture, and for communicating it to stakeholders. This is based on delegation, shared values, being part of a team, creating an environment for participation, and aiming to be ahead of competitors.

Adapted from *Management Today*, May 1987

---

allow a manager to influence and direct the activities of personnel. He also says that the quality of leadership is based on the traits or personal characteristics of managers, including behavioural patterns that are common to effective leaders, and on the environment in which the leadership is to be performed. Watson[10] claims that outstanding companies are distinguished by the way leadership is practised to make the work of individuals both meaningful and effective.

In contrast, delegation is generally defined in terms of assigning formal authority to individuals to carry out specific activities. Influence is not needed in delegation as the manager has the right to take action as defined in the delegated tasks, and to have it accepted by others. However, delegation without leadership is unlikely to be effective (see below).

While subordinates will be required to operate within a framework of delegation, they will look to their senior managers for inspiration, commitment to planned objectives and strategies, and for confidence in the future, which will affect their motivation to fulfil their work obligations. Given the importance of the decisions to be established in strategic management, leadership from the very top of the organization clearly needs to expound commitment to these decisions, while providing inspiration and confidence in the future. This needs to be associated with a determination that the subsequent operational management will be successful in achieving implementation. While this may seem obvious, it is not always achieved in practice. Indeed the practice of effective leadership is a complex process. Wright and Taylor[11] have suggested that it takes place at three levels in a company (see Figure 13.2):

- At the micro level, which involves the behaviour of managers in influencing people.

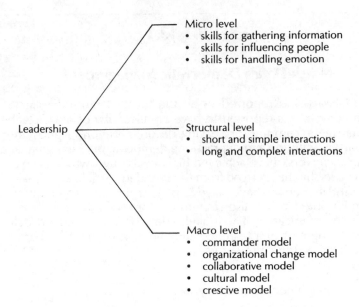

Figure 13.2   *Levels of leadership.*

- At the structure level, which explains how the micro level operates.
- At the macro level, which is concerned with the overall interaction of managers with their subordinates.

Micro-level leadership

At this level Wright and Taylor[11] are concerned with the skills that individual managers need for leadership. These they group into those required for information gathering, for influencing the behaviour of individuals, and for the handling of emotion.

Within the context of strategic management, information is concerned with finding out how well employees understand the requirements of strategic management, the progress of the implementation of strategies, and feedback on performance being achieved. Indeed systems for gaining this information should be part of the control process, which is examined in the Chapter 14.

Influencing skills are concerned with getting employees to achieve satisfactory levels of personal performance. Here there are several skills that will need to be used in particular situations, some of which will be more appropriate to particular individuals. One skill is the ability to give a direct order and have it accepted. Another is the ability to use threats or criticism, while requesting people to perform in a particular way and providing them with rewarding recognition are other skills. These skills are obviously of particular importance in the implementation of strategy through the operations, often being triggered by the control process.

Handling emotion has perhaps been given insufficient attention in the literature, given that emotion affects human behaviour in organizations just as it does in other human endeavours. Part of leadership is raising emotional levels so that employees become more enthusiastic about the demands of strategic management and more confident in tackling them. However, managers will also be required, in the words of Wright and Taylor, 'to defuse emotional situations'. Such situations could feature frustration, resentment, anger, or even fear, as a result of the demands of strategic management. These are perhaps more difficult to handle as such concerns obviously need to be allayed before enthusiasm can be tackled. While the skills for influencing behaviour as mentioned above can also be used here, sympathetic understanding and encouragement also need to be achieved through careful explanations of the issues of strategic management.

Structural-level leadership

As mentioned above, this level is concerned with how the micro level operates, and with the way managers interact with their subordinates. Interactions may be short and quite simple, or much more complex and spread over a longer period of time. A routine order which is readily understood and accepted is an example of the former. However, the presentation of the framework for the operation of a department from the strategic plan would be a complex form of structural-level leadership.

While shorter interactions require little preparation and would be based on discussions, complex interactions require careful preparation. Indeed large organizations with complex strategic management will often have conferences, seminars, and workshops in order to lead employees through their long-term plans, and to expound individual responsibilities. Although the planning of interactions is essential for these types of situation, interaction related to day-to-day performance requires an informal approach. Indeed outside of the formal reporting of performance in relation to the strategic plan, this represents part of the working relationship between any manager and the people who report to him.

Macro-level leadership

This level has traditionally been referred to as the 'leadership style' of a company. Although several classifications of style have been given, that by Bourgeois and Brodwin[12] relates to the implementation of strategy. They identify five different styles:

- *Commander model.* Strategy is formulated at the top of the company and is merely passed down the hierarchy with orders to implement it.
- *Organizational change model.* Again strategy is formulated at the top, but the company is modified to implement it, particularly with changes to the organizational structure.
- *Collaborative model.* Senior managers are involved in the formulation of strategy in order to achieve their commitment to implementation.
- *Cultural model.* Middle and lower-level managers are also involved in strategy formulation, aiming for wider commitment to subsequent implementation.

- *Crescive model.* The aim here is to encourage a culture where all managers can freely participate in strategy formulation and implementation, but with guidance from the top.

In each of these classifications the style of leadership is obviously different and therefore the impact on individuals will also vary. Although the models become more democratic the implication of the writers is that the crescive model is not necessarily better than the commander model. They merely represent different styles, each of which may be more appropriate in certain types of organizations.

Delegation

In the introduction to this section it was said that delegation is generally defined in terms of assigning formal authority to individuals to carry out specific activities (see Stoner[9]). Authority is delegated through the hierarchical structure and in the case of strategic management will operate through the SBUs. In essence the senior managers of each SBU have been delegated authority to implement their respective business strategies in pursuit of their respective business objectives. Similarly, senior managers within each of the operations are delegated authority to carry out their respective operational strategies in pursuit of their respective operational objectives.

As authority is progressively delegated down the hierarchy its acceptance is also associated with responsibility and accountability. Responsibility is generally defined in terms of the obligations that a manager has to his company as a consequence of the authority delegated to him. In other words, not only has he the right to take action, but he is obliged to carry out the action. Accountability is generally defined in terms of being answerable to the company for the effective discharge of responsibilities. Managers are therefore accountable for the decisions that they are allowed to make, the actions that follow and the results that ensue. Accountability also implies that individuals are judged by their superiors.

Consequently, as highlighted earlier, delegation is concerned with formal direction, whereas leadership is concerned with the less formal influence of employees. However, both clearly have a place in the implementation of strategy. Delegation provides the structure through which human resources can be marshalled for implementation, while leadership plays the role of ensuring that the management of these resources can be maintained.

PARTICIPATION

In this section attention is given to the second component of Figure 13.1. The central feature of this component is the participation of managers in implementation, which will relate to previous participation in planning. Of equal importance is the motivation of managers to perform effectively in their participation, and the rewards that they receive for effective participation. These features of participation are shown in Figure 13.3.

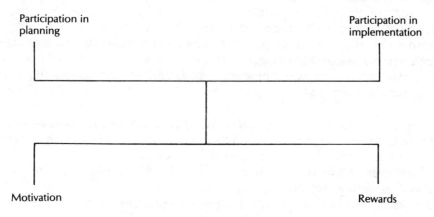

Figure 13.3   *Features of participation.*

Managerial participation

The issue of participation has already been addressed at two junctures in the book. Earlier in this chapter attention was given to leadership style, where participation in both strategy formulation and implementation was included. Indeed, participation was central to the alternative styles of leadership given. In Chapter 10 fuller attention was given to participation in strategy formulation, within the context of developing strategy alternatives. Of particular importance here was the involvement of particular managers within the hierarchy in both the organizational and business level strategies.

Thus participation in the implementation of strategies relates to participation in their formulation. Involvement in the latter should provide commitment to implementation, in that managers feel that they have become part of the process. This association will be related closely to motivation and the rewards for participation, which will be returned to later in this section.

Kloeze, Molencamp, and Roelofs[13] have suggested that participation needs to be explained in terms of degree and direction. The degree of participation explains the amount of involvement that individual managers will have in both formulation and implementation. This will be partly determined by the way authority is delegated, but will also be determined by how influential the participation is allowed to be. In other words, whether the managers are truly allowed to be involved and are allowed to make decisions, or whether they are merely allowed to have some input which is not fully incorporated into decision-making. The latter can be called 'pseudo-participation'.

The direction of participation explains the actual areas of strategic management in which managers are allowed to participate. While previous discussions have emphasized the value of broadening managers' participation during planning, the constraints placed on such participation by the organizational structure will limit an individual manager's actual participation. Where there are many managers in the structure then the constraint will be even greater, given the difficulty of developing a system to allow many managers to participate. However, effort needed to overcome such constraints should be compared with the value to be gained from wider participation.

Overcoming this logistics problem can be tackled by addressing four major issues (see Dickson[14]):

- Pursuing interaction among managers by arranging for them to meet.
- Communicating information and different points of view as a two-way process, both up and down the organizational structure.
- The degree to which the influence of individuals should be allowed to have an effect on strategy formulation or implementation.
- The actual effect that managers are able to exert in relation to their individual positions and delegated authority.

Motivation

Like leadership, the motivation of individuals in organizations has been given considerable attention in the organizational behaviour literature; examples are the books by Steers[15] and by Gibson et al.[16].

Issues of strategic management have been seen at several junctures in this book to influence managerial motivation. Earlier in this chapter leadership was seen to be a major influence on motivation, providing encouragement to fulfil work obligations effectively. In Chapter 7 the role of objectives in managerial motivation was discussed. In Chapter 8 expectancy theory was introduced in the context of managerial values and expectations, but as part of the general theory of motivation in the work-place.

A major theme of motivation is that there are many theories which attempt to explain what motivates managers and why. Consequently, a simple explanation of motivation is not appropriate. However, Gibson et al.[16] have suggested some common features of the theories. Motivation is concerned with the forces acting on or within individuals to initiate and direct their behaviour. Motivation of specific individuals is inferred from their behaviour and resultant performance, but is directed by goals or objectives that are seen to be important to them. Factors affecting motivation may be either physiological, psychological or environmental. Differences in the theories of motivation explain these issues in different ways. Readers interested in these are referred to the above-mentioned texts.

As in participation, motivation needs to be achieved in both the formulation and implementation of strategy. Motivation in the former will largely be achieved through processes already explained. Initial impetus will be through matching individuals' objectives with those of the organization. The framework of the strategic management plan will provide the general environmental factors, while leadership, delegation and participation represent other influences on behaviour towards performing effectively in strategy formulation.

Motivation in the implementation of strategy requires a different focus. Strategy is carried out, as already established, through the implementation of organizational strategies, related to the functional departments of the organizational structure. Therefore the orientation of managers is towards the implementation of the strategies of their respective departments. Within each department particular duties will be delegated to each manager, so that the work required to complete the respective operational strategy will be related to individual managers' job functions. Consequently motivation for each individual will be based on the personal need to perform effectively in a particular job function. However, although individuals will be motivated by this intrinsic value within the job function, they will also be motivated by rewards.

Rewards for effective participation

Reward systems related to the implementation of operational strategies were discussed in Chapter 12. There it was said that concentration on pecuniary rewards to the exclusion of non-pecuniary rewards will not be appropriate, as the latter are of extreme importance. Again considerable attention has been given to the motivational values of various reward and punishment systems for managers. A concise account in relation to strategy has been given by Galbraith and Kazanjian[17].

Pecuniary rewards

Traditional approaches have been based on paying managers sums in addition to salary, based on current sales turnover or profits. However, the argument against this approach is that it directs effort to short-term gains, whereas effort in strategic management does, of course, need to be directed towards issues which are unlikely to have immediate effect in the short term.

To overcome this problem rewards need to be related to performance levels over several years. Although simple in principle, developing formulae which take into account the issues that are likely to affect performance over a long period is rather complex. However, these rewards can be related to business level objectives, although determining the relative contribution of managers to their achievement is also difficult. Similarly, obtaining compatible measures across several SBUs can result in problems of perceived acceptability on the part of managers. Work on devising pecuniary rewards relevant to strategic issues has been completed by Rappaport[18].

Non-pecuniary rewards

These can be generally classed as those concerned with fulfilment of personal needs, and those that involve tangible incentives. The latter generally relate to status relative to position in the hierarchy. Things such as size of office, furniture, car, health insurance, and expense accounts fall into this category. They can perhaps be split into those rewards that demonstrate the relative success of the manager, and those which increase standard of living but not through salary payments.

Rewards based on fulfilment of personal needs can be combined with the system of management by objectives, as introduced in Chapter 7. This can be related to a provision for allowing managers to realize their values and expectations (Chapter 8). Consequently, the principle is that turning these into personal objectives, related to those of the organization, and subsequently achieving them, becomes a reward in itself. Such an experience should then contribute to further motivation, and eagerness to participate in future strategy formulation and participation.

While positive motivation and associated rewards are obviously aimed at improving the performance of managers, they can also place undue pressure on managers, so that some may suffer from stress. Recent attention has been given to occupational stress in the literature, although it has been found to have different meanings to different people. Several definitions have been offered, but within the context of strategic management stress means that individual managers feel themselves suffering from tension and anxiety as a result of excessive psychological, and perhaps physical, demands. Major research has been carried out by Cooper[19,20], who suggests several sources of stress:

EXHIBIT 13.2

Virgin's New-found Modesty

The Virgin Group is based on three SBUs: music; communications; and retail/-property. In the business and financial community the group is seen as being largely managed by its Chairman, Richard Branson, and overreliant on his business skills. Elsewhere it is claimed that this is not the case. Indeed, Branson's major skill is seen to be his ability to delegate responsibility and, although he is a creative entrepreneur, he readily allows other people to manage new projects that he has initiated. This is well illustrated in both music and communications. Both have managing directors who have been given the responsibility for planning future direction, with little interference from Branson. Indeed he is quoted as saying that for a chairman the art of delegation is of major importance, finding the right managers and coming up with ideas for new ventures. Within the group there is an informal management style, little centralization, an emphasis on internal promotion, and motivation by incentive and share option schemes. Personnel work in small groups, have pleasant surroundings and are allowed to dress as they feel comfortable.

Adapted from *Management Today*, March 1988

- Factors intrinsic to the job.
- Role in the organization.
- Career development.
- Relationships at work.
- Organizational structure and climate.
- Home–work interface.
- Redundancy.

While the constraint of space precludes a full discussion of these sources of stress, it is perhaps evident to the reader that they pertain to managers participating in strategic management. The importance of the issues to be addressed provides potential for initiating any of these sources, while participation could be avoided by certain managers if they thought that they could be put into a stressful situation as a consequence.

MANAGING CHANGE

The third component of Figure 13.1 to explain HRM within the context of strategy implementation has been labelled 'managing change'. This component consists of the instigation of change as required by strategic management, and the role of power in managing change. The treatment given in this section to these two issues is summarized in Figure 13.4.

Consequences of change in both the environment and in organizations have been mentioned in a number of the previous chapters. Orientating companies to change has been a major developing theme in the literature. For example, a major text by Ansoff[21], which has been frequently quoted in previous chapters, is very much focused on the orientation of firms to change through the use of the process of strategic management. Within the organizational behaviour literature there has been similar attention to orientation to change. Beer[22], for example, addresses the field of organizational development, which is that part of the organizational behaviour literature which addresses change in organizations.

Instigating change

Like most of the issues related to the human behaviour of managers that are addressed in this chapter, the issue of their reaction to change has been referred to in previous chapters. In Chapter 3 managerial capability was examined in relation to the responsiveness of the company to change. A major concern here was managers' perceptions of their own capabilities and any differences between these perceptions and their actual capabilities. In Chapter 8 attention was given to managerial resistance to change as part of their values and expectations. Of particular importance here was the initiation of the momentum for change, with increased momentum reducing resistance. This theme was extended in Chapter 11. Here

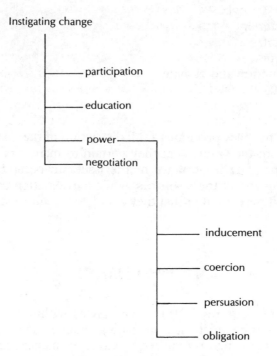

Figure 13.4 *Managing change.*

managerial attitudes toward risk were examined, where risk attached to change will also affect resistance. Managerial attitudes will vary between eagerness to take risks to pursue opportunities and a strong aversion to risk.

In instigating change the aim is obviously to avoid managerial resistance. Bowman and Asch[23] have suggested several ways that change can be approached.

As discussed in the last section, the acceptability of change will be partly dependent on *participation* in the decision-making leading up to the proposed change. However, degree and direction of participation by individual managers need to be carefully considered. The planning of participation over a long period of time, to create internal acceptance of change for increased organizational effectiveness, is part of the field of organizational development, as mentioned above.

Another factor on which acceptance of change may depend is *education*. By education Bowman and Asch mean that changes which must occur, as a result of strategic management, are explained to those who will be affected by them. The assumption is made that if the logic, rationale and justification for change are explained, then it will be readily accepted. This assumes that the recipients will agree with the explanation given and will accept the justification. However, differences in values and expectations mean that acceptance will not always be fully achieved. Therefore, although education does have a place in instigating change, it needs to be used in conjunction with participation and other ways of approaching change.

Manipulation of people — the use of *power* — to accept change is also often needed to reduce resistance. As mentioned earlier, power is given fuller consideration later in this section.

Where there is strong resistance to change, then senior management may be unable realistically to 'force' change through education or manipulation. In these situations *negotiation* will be needed in order to address the proposed changes and their ramifications. Negotiation assumes that although there are differences between the parties, there is some common ground from which agreement can be achieved. Here there may need to be some modification of, say, strategies in order to avoid resistance, or some compensation for managers who present the greatest resistance, because of the impact that they are likely to experience. The latter can range from training to give more competence in handling change to the provision of additional resources to accommodate change.

In practice companies which tackle their futures through the process of strategic management will also develop these ways of instigating change as part of their management style and corporate culture. Indeed the importance of integrating these behavioural issues into the field of organizational development has been reflected in the literature. An interesting case study of the management of change, which is situation-specific to a major British clothing company, has been well discussed by Johnson[24].

Power

Many definitions of power have appeared in the management literature. Weber[25] has defined it as 'the possibility of imposing one's will upon the behaviour of other people'. While managers may have the authority (through delegation) to implement change, they must be able to exercise this authority and convince others that decisions made and changes proposed are worthy of acceptance. Therefore the instigation of change may need to be achieved through the use of power, by exerting influence to modify the behaviour and attitudes of the people who are to be affected by the proposed changes.

While the traditional literature on general management has given much attention to the sources from which managers are able to gain their power and use it, specific attention has also been given to power utilization in the context of the implementation of strategic decisions. A major contribution here is the book by MacMillan and Jones[26], and much of the following discussion of power is drawn from this source.

The outcome of the use of power is manipulation. In this context it is manipulation of people to accept changes resulting from strategic management which may otherwise be resisted. MacMillan and Jones[26] specify four means of manipulating people through the use of power:

- *Inducement*. Those who show resistance are persuaded by the promise of a reward to accept change. Rewards offered for persuasion could be promotion, increased status or increased salary.

- *Coercion*. Resistance to change is challenged by the threat of the imposition of an unfavourable situation if change is not accepted. Coercion could be attempted by a threat of demotion, reduction in status, or even the termination of employment.
- *Persuasion*. Resistance to change is countered by discussing and arguing the case for change and eventually convincing doubtful managers that change is necessary. Neither threats nor rewards are used to manipulate the people concerned.
- *Obligation*. Here the manipulation is also based on discussions and arguments in favour of the case for change. Although the initial resistance is abated and change is accepted, the managers will still not necessarily be in agreement with the proposed changes. Arguments would be couched in terms of what is good for the future of the company as a whole, so that individuals feel obliged to accept proposals, even though they may not fully support them.

While the above represent the means of using power, sources of power have also been given attention in the literature. These sources of power are generally classified into those that relate to the company and those that relate to individuals as personal power. Within the context of strategy MacMillan and Jones[26] claim that the former is of major importance. However, personal power can arise from personality traits, such as natural powers of leadership, a charismatic personality, or finding it easy to 'get on' with people. Personal power can also be derived from an individual's particular situation, such as particular knowledge, a particular stakeholding in the company, or a reputation for a successful style of management.

MacMillan and Jones[26] give four sources of power that relate to the company: The first is *the use of authority*. The ultimate power of any manager lies in the authority delegated to him. Pfeffer[27] has called this 'legitimized power', in that the organization allows a manager to induce, coerce, persuade, and obligate people, within his control, to accept decisions made within his realm of delegation. Thus each manager has his position within the hierarchy as a source of power. At the top of the organization the power is greatest. However, even here there is potential for the undermining of power by stakeholder groups, particularly from the ownership of the company.

The second source of power is control over and *possession of resources*. While they do not give examples, some are particularly relevant to the instigation of change. Control over financial resources is perhaps an obvious example, with managers who have control over large budgets being in a particularly strong position. Similarly, managers with responsibility for large departments with large numbers of people can use this resource as a source of power, by using these people to support and promote proposed changes.

Information is also considered as a resource and constitutes a source of power. While some managers may resist the change planned in new strategies, it is likely that they will not have access to all the information about the total environment that was used to formulate these new strategies. Without this information they may find it difficult to make their case successfully against change. Thus power lies in access to information.

Resources may also be related to particular operations of the company. If it is dedicated to marketing orientation, through the organizational mission, then the marketing function will be seen as being of extreme importance by the board, giving senior marketing managers power to influence change. Similarly an organization which is R&D-led will impart similar power to the R&D function.

The third source of power lies in *control of alternatives*. While there may be some resistance to changes likely to result from planned strategies, the avoidance of these changes would necessitate the abandonment of the strategies. However, if the logic of strategy selection, as presented in Chapter 11, indicates that other alternatives are not feasible (for whatever reason), then power to instigate these changes lies in the logic of the selection process. In this situation opponents to change will have little or no power where feasible alternatives are not available.

The fourth source of power lies in *leveraging existing influence*. Resistance to change can be perhaps overcome by exerting power through people who already have influence over those people who are resisting. For example, directors may be able to use their departmental managers to convince individuals in their respective departments to accept planned change. Again, chairman of key committees may be able to exert power to overcome opposition, or existing procedures for generating participation may represent an opportunity to convert opposition into acceptance.

INTEGRATION AND COMMUNICATION

This is the final component of Figure 13.1 to explain HRM within the context of strategy implementation. During implementation the planned organizational and business strategies become fragmented as they are pursued through the operational strategies. Indeed encouraging delegation and participation only adds to implementation being completed as a series of separate parts. Although leadership will help to consolidate these parts into a unified effort, attention to integration is still needed.

In this section the two major issues of integration are taken as being the co-ordination of effort across the organizational structure and the identification and control of conflict between individuals and departments. These issues will be addressed as problems of integration, both vertically and horizontally, within the organizational structure.

For effective implementation of strategy attention also needs to be given to the effective use of communication. In simple terms communication can be considered as the two-way transfer of information. As readers will be aware, communication across organizational structures is often ineffective. Communication has also been given considerable attention in the organizational behaviour literature, as it is both fundamental and essential to all managerial activities at all levels of management. The issue of communication will also be included as part of both vertical and horizontal integration (see Figure 13.5).

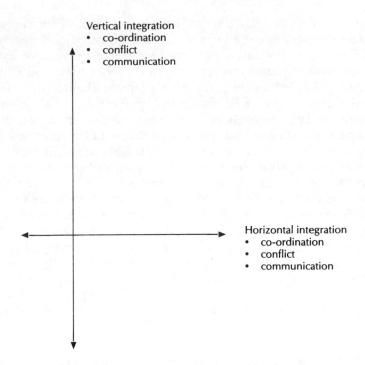

Vertical integration
• co-ordination
• conflict
• communication

Horizontal integration
• co-ordination
• conflict
• communication

Figure 13.5   *Vertical and horizontal integration.*

Vertical integration

An initial problem here is the integration of strategic management issues into management activities throughout the management hierarchy. While a major thrust of all books on strategic management is that the process needs to be integrated into corporate management, writers such as Ansoff[21], King[28], and Naylor[29] give this form of integration particular attention.

Indeed, the whole logic of the strategic management process (as used in this book and as originally given in Figure 1.5) is meant to provide integration. The logic of the stages should give co-ordination between them and provide a basis for communication. Of particular importance is integration in companies which feature several SBUs. However, again the process provides a basis for integration by co-ordinating strategies and objectives at the business level with those at the higher level. Also, as presented in previous chapters, the establishment of both objectives and strategies in hierarchies provides further opportunities for integration. Certainly a major aim is the co-ordination of both these aspects of management at the interfaces between the various levels of management. Similarly, the formal establishment of a hierarchy for each should enhance communication, while giving managers the opportunity to relate to specific objectives and strategies should go towards the avoidance of conflict.

Alongside these hierarchies is, of course, the hierarchy of managers or the organizational structure. As was seen in Chapter 9, this structure represents the official and formal chain of command. Not only does it represent the framework for the delegation of authority, but it also provides a basis for integration and communication. For the former the structure is the whole basis around which the issues of HRM revolve for the implementation of strategy. As a vehicle of communication it provides a channel for downward communication of expectations, and a channel for upward communication of the relative success of implementation. However, although the structure provides these formal channels of communication, their efficiency will be dependent on the managers who use them. Behavioural issues such as attitudes, motivation and leadership will certainly affect the efficiency of these channels. Similarly, the effectiveness of information systems will also influence these channels. This process was originally introduced in Chapter 3, which was concerned with the collection, analysis and dissemination of information.

Horizontal integration

This form of integration is needed at both the SBU level and the operational level. Although integration at the SBU level generally has more focus during planning than during implementation, at the operational level the major onus is on implementation.

Aspects of horizontal integration were introduced in Chapter 12, as part of the explanation of operational strategies. There it was claimed that, in practice, integration of the implementation of operational strategies is not always straightforward, even though in principle full integration is essential. Problems of co-ordination and conflict are couched in behavioural issues of HRM, most being linked to values and expectations. Even despite good intentions of managers to ensure integration, problems of co-ordination during the implementation of operations still occur, which can result in conflict.

Where the organization is structured into a number of SBUs, problems of integration can be compounded. Where the operations are particular to any given SBU, integration of their implementation is largely limited to that SBU. However, if certain operational departments serve a number of SBUs, conflict can arise as each SBU vies for the resources of these departments. Similar problems can arise if a number of operations are provided on a group basis. Conflicts can arise as each SBU attempts to get a higher production-capacity allocation, for example, or a greater share of the resources devoted to market research.

However, probably the greatest concern for integration relates to the implementation of operational strategies for a particular SBU. Because of the different objectives, strategies and managerial dispositions to be found within each of the operations, problems of co-ordination, communication and conflict can result. These problems can certainly be caused by legitimate difficulties of co-ordinating the different tasks to be performed by each of the strategies. However, many problems will be a result of the behaviour of managers, in that their different expectations result in a conflict of interests. In Chapter 12 general principles for the integration of operations were given from the text by Rue and Holland[30]. These were analysis of the capabilities of each of the operations; interfunctional recognition of strengths and weaknesses; striving for clearer communications; continued participation; managers gaining experience in other functions; and closer co-ordination.

SUMMARY

In this chapter attention was given to issues of the human behaviour of managers in relation to the implementation of strategy. The chapter started with an examination of the different meanings of HRM and problems of transition from the planning of strategy to its implementation.

The first major component of HRM within the context of strategy implementation was given as leadership and delegation. Leadership is concerned with influencing people to behave in particular ways, whereas delegation is the formal direction to carry out particular activities. Leadership was explained in terms of micro, structural, and macro levels, whereas delegation was explained in terms of authority.

The second component revolves around participation. First, managerial participation in implementation was related to that in planning. This was followed by a discussion of the motivation of managers within participation. Here a major feature was the many factors, physiological, psychological, or environmental, that can affect motivation. This component also included discussions of pecuniary and non-pecuniary rewards for managers.

The third component was based on the management of change resulting from strategic management. Ways of instigating change were suggested, ranging from managerial participation in its original formulation to 'forced' changes through the manipulation of managers. The latter issue was explored further as the process of power. The means of manipulation to exercise power and sources of power were covered.

The final component of HRM involved integration and communication. In the former a split was made between vertical integration within the organizational structure, and horizontal integration across particular levels of the structure. The major issues of integration, co-ordination and conflict were tackled both vertically and horizontally. The issue of communication was tackled in the same way.

CHAPTER CASE STUDY ILLUSTRATION:
HABITAT–MOTHERCARE*

This British-based retailing group also operates in the United States and Europe. Mothercare is well known in many European countries, while Habitat is particularly associated with France and Belgium. The case study describes the success of the group, which has been based on the vision, dynamism and leadership skills of Sir Terence Conran.

Sir Terence Conran is the founder of the group; as it has developed and achieved rapid growth in recent years the major force behind this success has been Sir Terence's abilities. His philosophy for the business has been based on the following principles:

- Several identifiable SBUs involved in speciality retailing.
- The establishment of autonomy within each SBU with delegated responsibility.
- A strong central organization providing marketing, product design, retailing systems, and financial services.

Delegation is very much within the organizational structure, allowing for managerial participation and motivation. However, the role of the central organization has been defined, which will allow for the participation of personnel with specialized skills in the key areas of planning and implementation. The skills of design and marketing are repeatedly emphasized throughout the case study as being of central importance to the group.

The leadership skills of Conran were very much seen as being central to the performance of Habitat–Mothercare. His influence is described as being 'quiet but involved'. Leadership through consultation with managers is a major feature, so that he seems to provide strong and reliable leadership, while at the same time allowing managers to participate effectively. This style of leadership was also said to be the major reason for the successful takeover of Mothercare by Habitat, even though the former was a much larger company. Indeed this leadership style was effective in amalgamating the two different corporate cultures – Mothercare was described as being systems-driven, while Habitat was design- and marketing-driven.

Like Habitat, Mothercare had been founded and developed by a dynamic leader, Selim Zilkha. Both were said to have similar leadership styles, being autocratic and approachable. Both were said to be at the centre of their organizations, stamping their own attitudes and values on their businesses. Conran was involved in new product development, but also got involved in approving designs and even negotiating with some suppliers. Both were said

*Derived from the original case study by C. M. Clarke-Hill. Copyright © 1986.

to be generalists with a *Gestalt* approach to business, although Conran was said to be the entrepreneur.

Thus although this approach allows for delegation, it is still the principles of Conran, especially related to design, which permeate through the management of the group. The case study claims that the company is made up of very professional management teams, in both the SBUs and in the central organization. Responsibility is delegated to the operating companies to prepare their own design and marketing briefs, for both the products to be sold and store layout. The Design Group then implements these briefs. Therefore although the central design organization may be said to have considerable power as a result of Conran's principles, the process of delegation into the operating companies tempers this power.

Aspects of managerial participation have already been implied above. Another indication in the case study comes from comments about the retail outlets that have been acquired by the group. The initial approach explained is that little is done physically to change the stores, but the emphasis is on personnel. Here Conran provides motivation and the leadership required to improve performance. In France he changed salary structures by linking them to store performance and not to the retail price index. However, the emphasis in participation is on efficient management.

The involvement of Sir Terence in the management of change as a consequence of acquisitions and growth was also explained as having been at a high level and of major importance. It was claimed that the merger had changed management style, as previously exercised at Habitat, away from entrepreneurship to an orientation of shareholder satisfaction. Growth and its resultant changes had also caused several managerial problems. The major problem claimed was that management resources were stretched to the limit, with the resultant ramifications to be expected from such a stressful managerial situation. In France performance dropped drastically in the early 1980s. In 1982 the French Government made major changes to its economic policies. As a result, trading conditions and the retailing environment changed drastically, and the group's performance in France declined accordingly. Consequently management change was needed within the group, which was again instigated and implemented through the business principles of Sir Terence Conran.

REFERENCES

1. Lyles, M. A. and Lenz, R. T., 'Managing the Planning Process: A Field Study of the Human Side of Planning', *Strategic Management Journal*, **3**, 1982, 105–18.
2. Taylor, R., 'Psychological Aspects of Planning', *Long Range Planning*, **9**, 2, 1976, 66–74.
3. Guest, D. E., 'Human Resource Management', *Journal of Management Studies*, **24**, 5, 1987, 503–21.
4. Wheelen, T. L. and Hunger, J. D., *Strategic Management and Business Policy*, 2nd edn, Addison-Wesley, Reading, MA, 1986.

5. Abell, D. F. and Hammond, J. S., *Strategic Market Planning: Problems and Analytical Approaches*, Prentice Hall, Englewood Cliffs, NJ, 1979.
6. Pekar, P. P., 'Planning: A Guide to Implementation' *Managerial Planning*, **20**, 1980, 3–6.
7. Buchanan, D. A. and Huczynski, A. A., *Organizational Behaviour*, Prentice Hall, London, 1985.
8. Gray, J. L. and Starke, F. A., *Organizational Behaviour: Concepts and Applications*, 3rd edn, Bell & Howell, Columbus, OH, 1984.
9. Stoner, J. A. F., *Management*, 2nd edn, Prentice Hall, Englewood Cliffs, NJ, 1982.
10. Watson, C. M., 'Leadership, Management, and the Seven Keys', *Business Horizons*, March–April 1983, 8–13.
11. Wright, P. L. and Taylor, D. S., 'The Interpersonal Skills of Leadership', *Leadership and Organisational Development Journal*, **2**, 2, 1981, 6–12 and **2**, 3, 1981, 2–6.
12. Bourgeois, L. J. and Brodwin, D. R., 'Strategic Implementation: Five Approaches to an Elusive Phenomenon', *Strategic Management Journal*, **5**, 1984, 241–64.
13. Kloeze, H. J., Molencamp A. and Roelofs, R. J. W., 'Strategic Planning and Participation: A Contradiction in Terms?', *Long Range Planning*, **13**, 5, 1980, 10–20.
14. Dickson, J. W., 'Participation as an Interaction, Communication and Influence Process', *Personnel Review*, **12**, 1, 1983, 17–22.
15. Steers, R. M., *Introduction to Organizational Behaviour*, 2nd edn, Scott Foresman, Glenview, IL, 1984.
16. Gibson, J. L., Ivancevich, J. M. and Donnelly, J. H., *Organizations: Behaviour, Structure and Processes*, Business Publications, Plano, Texas, 1985.
17. Galbraith, J. R. and Kazanjian, R. K., *Strategy Implementation: Structure, Systems and Process*, 2nd edn, West, St Paul, MN, 1986.
18. Rappaport, A., 'Selecting Strategies that Create Shareholder Value', *Harvard Business Review*, May–June, 1981, 139–49.
19. Cooper, C. L., *The Stress Check*, Prentice Hall, Englewood Cliffs, NJ, 1981.
20. Cooper, C. L., 'Stress in the Workplace: Recent Research Evidence', *British Academy of Management Conference*, Warwick, September 1987.
21. Ansoff, H. I., *Implanting Strategic Management*, Prentice Hall, Englewood Cliffs, NJ, 1984.
22. Beer, M., *Organization Change and Development*, Scott Foresman, Glenview, IL, 1980.
23. Bowman, C. and Asch, D., *Strategic Management*, Macmillan, London, 1987.
24. Johnson, G., 'Managing Strategic Change — the Role of Strategic Formulae' in McGee, J. and Thomas H. (eds), *Strategic Management Research*, Wiley, Chichester, 1986.
25. Weber, M., *Bureaucracy*, Wiley, New York, 1969.
26. MacMillan, I. C. and Jones, P. E., *Strategy Formulation; Power and Politics*, 2nd edn, West, St Paul, MN, 1986.
27. Pfeffer, J., *Power in Organizations*, Pitman, Marshfield, MA, 1981.
28. King, W. R., 'Implementing Strategic Plans through Strategic Program Evaluation', *Omega*, **8**, 2, 1980, 173–81.
29. Naylor, T. H., 'How to Integrate Strategic Planning into Your Management Process', *Long Range Planning*, **14**, 5, 1981, 56–61.
30. Rue, L. W. and Holland, P. G., *Strategic Management: Concepts and Experiences*, McGraw-Hill, New York, 1986.

CHAPTER 14

CONTROL AND EFFECTIVENESS

Chapter 14 looks at the final aspect of implementation that was outlined in the introduction to Part Five. Within the model of strategic management adopted for this book this is the last stage. As will be explained in the chapter, this stage also provides a loop in the process back to the analysis of the environment, reflecting the cyclical and ongoing nature of the strategic management. In addition, there are other links from control into other stages of strategic management, some of which will already be apparent. The stage of control has a joint function. First, through analysis, it provides information for understanding the process. Second, it is the instigator of further managerial action. In contrast, assessments of effectiveness attempt to appraise and improve the value of strategic management.

As the previous chapters have progressively explained the process of strategic management, implications of control have been mentioned. As the final stage of strategic management, control is concerned with attempting to ensure that 'things don't go wrong' during the implementation of strategies. However, as part of the process, analysis required to effect control also provides an information input to the strategic audit. Therefore it is not a final stage but a link to provide a continuous process into the next phase of strategic management.

In Chapter 1 it was said that control is about identifying the need to take corrective action, related to the implementation of current strategies, and to allow for the modification of future plans. These roles will obviously be explored further in this chapter. The major basis for control is the objectives which have been established at both the organizational and business levels, as discussed in Chapter 7.

Control activities can also be applied directly to strategy implementation and due attention is given to these activities in this chapter. In Chapter 12 it was said that control of the implementation of operational strategies necessarily relates to control of higher-level strategies, so that again there are links to previous chapters. Similarly, there are links to Chapter 13, which addressed human resource management. Here part of micro-level leadership was concerned with information gathering for control purposes.

The other focus of this chapter is on the resulting effectiveness of strategic management. In Chapter 1 this was explained as being concerned with longer-term decisions aimed at improving the value of strategic management. If time, resources and effort are to be put into strategic management then its effectiveness as a process should be assessed.

This chapter is structured into six main sections. In the first section a framework for control is established. The next three sections address the control of objectives, profits and strategies respectively. The fifth section looks at the concept of effectiveness, while problems of control are examined in the sixth section.

THE FRAMEWORK FOR CONTROL

Despite its relative importance in the strategic management process, control has been given relatively little attention in the literature. Most books devote a single chapter to control, and attention in journals has been limited. However, three books have been identified which are devoted to control: those by Anthony and Dearden[1], Lorange et al.[2] and Newman[3]. The framework for control provides a system for attempting to ensure that 'things don't go wrong' during the implementation of strategies. During implementation control should be continously exercised through application of the framework. The basis of this application is the achievement of organizational and business objectives, with profits being extracted for separate attention. However, control can also be exercised directly on strategies, without using objectives as a basis.

The framework for control is conceptually easy to explain, although in practice the many complex issues of implementation mean that many problems in 'ensuring that things don't go wrong' can arise. Higgins[4] has suggested a framework for control which is depicted in Figure 14.1 and is explained as follows:

Standards of performance. The first stage is the establishment of standards or norms against which actual performance will be compared. These standards should be both quantitative and qualitative in nature, and will be generally represented by the set of organizational and business objectives. However, qualitative standards will also be represented by planned strategies.

Establishment of tolerances. A discussion of the magnitude of objectives was given in Chapter 7. This stage involves specifying and the deviances in actual performance from the standard that will be accepted or tolerated. Part of these tolerances will relate to forecasting error, but the establishment of tolerances is particularly concerned with the triggering of action.

Measurement of actual performance. This stage involves the use of techniques which can be used to measure actual performance for control purposes. Relevant techniques will be presented in the next three major sections of the chapter.

Comparison of standards with performance. For quantitative measures this may be quite straightforward, although a particular problem can be comparing like with like. For qualitative standards comparisons are mostly based on value judgements, so that they feature much subjectivity.

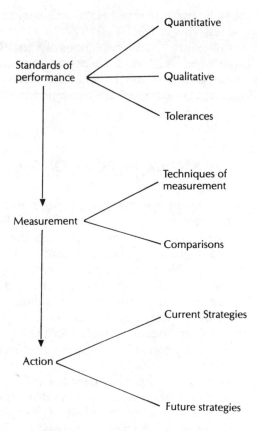

Figure 14.1   *The control framework.*

Current Action. Where performance is not being achieved corrective action may need to be taken to modify existing strategies. Current action is likely to be limited to operational and business strategies, but with more emphasis on the former.

Future Action. While current action is to avoid unsatisfactory performance in the near future, the aim of this action is to learn from the past, by using the generated knowledge as an input to future strategic management decision-making.

These stages are applicable to the discussions on the control of objectives, profits, and strategies that follow in the next three sections. The above framework is also consistent with control issues raised in earlier chapters: in particular the process of measurement and feedback as the loop back into the internal strategic audit, and the importance of control information within the wider management information system. In addition, the stage of comparison is clearly dependent on micro-level leadership, as presented in the discussion of human resource management in Chapter 13.

As control relates closely to objectives, it follows that a hierarchy of control can be established, running parallel to the hierarchies of objectives and strategies.

Strategic control is given by Hofer and Schendel[5] as the type of control to be used at the organizational level of objectives and control. However at the next level 'strategic control' is again the label used for business objectives and strategies. At the operational level operational control focuses on the respective objectives and strategies across the operational functions. The final level is tactical control, aimed at 'ensuring that things don't go wrong' with the implementation of the functional tactics.

EXHIBIT 14.1

Volkswagen Regains Some Beetle Magic

The West German car manufacturer, Volkswagen, had, in the 1960s, the largest-selling small car in the United States, in the form of the Beetle. However, due to several factors, VW lost control of its position in the 1970s, with cheaper Japanese cars taking over their market share. During the 1980s VW's control of its performance in the United States was regained. In 1985 its position in the market rose from 22nd in earlier years to eighth, as measured in a major survey of buyer satisfaction. This was largely achieved with the Golf, which was gaining a reputation in the United States for quality, as it already had achieved in Europe. In 1985 the magazine *Motor Trend* named the Golf 'car of the year'. The Jetta became even more popular in the United States than in Europe, with sales expanding by 120% in 1985.

Adapted from *Fortune*, 31 March 1986

CONTROL OF OBJECTIVES

Developing from the discussion above about hierarchies, it follows that strategic management control must focus on both organizational and business objectives. However, as discussed in Chapter 7, the types of objective to be established at both levels are derived from a common range of types. Consequently, the techniques of measurement for control at both levels are the same. The difference lies in the interpretation of the comparisons and the consequential action to be taken at each level.

In Chapter 7 it was also seen that the range of objectives is split between quantitative and qualitative objectives. Here there is a difference between techniques for comparison, so that treatment of these two has been separated in this section. However before looking at these techniques attention is given to the main reasons why it is important to exercise control of the implementation of strategies, which are apparent from previous chapters.

The first reason is environmental change: a company has little or no control over the vast number of environmental factors presented in Part Two. As these factors represent potential influences on the attainment of objectives, control is needed to monitor changes in these factors and to take corrective action when their influence is felt.

The second reason is delegation: although delegation should be within a process of human resource management (see Chapter 13) problems may arise in its effectiveness. Therefore control is needed to ensure that authority is being exercised to pursue the attainment of objectives.

The third reason is company complexity: a complex organizational structure can also contribute to detrimental influences on the success of achieving objectives. Issues raised in Chapter 9 show how hierarchical structures can develop in complexity, while any cause-and-effect relationship in the strategy–structure relationship needs to be controlled.

The fourth reason is managerial mistakes: as well as being affected by irrational human behaviour in the marketplace, the success of objectives will be affected by the irrational human behaviour of managers. Many of these issues were addressed in Chapter 8. Thus mistakes of judgement or in systematic decision-making can be made in the analysis, planning or implementation stages of strategic management. Control is therefore clearly needed both to identify and correct mistakes.

Quantitative control

Major techniques of quantitative control are given in Figure 14.2 and are explained below.

Variance analysis
In this technique standards given in the objectives are simply compared to actual results and any differences or variances are identified. The technique is particularly relevant to growth and market spread objectives, although the latter can be only at a simple level of analysis.

As an example, the objective for sales revenue growth can be taken at either the organizational or business level. As the total volume of sales quoted in the objective will be related to a number of years, this figure needs to be broken down and related to shorter periods of time, generally into monthly sales targets. The latter then become standards of performance, as illustrated in the control framework. Actual volumes of sales revenue achieved per month are then compared to those given as standard targets, as illustrated in Table 14.1. In this example a cumulative negative variance has clearly developed, which, if not corrected, means that the sales objective will not be achieved by the end of the year. The cause or causes of the monthly negative variances obviously need to be identified. Here the answers are likely to lie in control being carried out at the operational level, where the causes are likely to be operational strategies. As a consequence of the analysis of cause, the following remedial action could be taken: action to correct the cause or causes of the variance; action to compensate for the variance or shortfall in sales; in

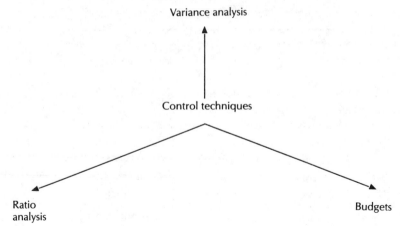

Figure 14.2 *Techniques for quantitative control.*

this example, it has accumulated for £70,000 by the end of April; and action to input the results of this analysis into the strategic audit as part of the next round of planning direction.

Table 14.1 *Variance analysis.*

Sales revenue (£000)	January	February	March	April
Monthly target	100	120	110	120
Cumulative target	100	220	330	450
Monthly actual	80	100	90	110
Cumulative actual	80	180	270	380
Monthly variance	20	20	20	10
Cumulative variance	20	40	60	70

Ratio analysis

As profitability ratios are to be considered later, this analysis is concerned with efficiency objectives and some of the personnel objectives. The technique is to relate the measurement to be controlled to a particular base, with the resulting ratios providing the basis for a technique of control. Ratios which were suggested in Chapter 7 as a basis for some objectives are detailed in Table 14.2. In addition there are several other ratios that can be used for control purposes, including gearing or leverage, and working capital.

These ratios are generally calculated annually and the actual results are compared to the standards that were established in the objectives. Again differences between planned and actual levels are identified and again further analysis is concerned with identifying the cause of any differences. Similarly, this analysis should instigate remedial action. As well as comparing actual ratios with standards given in the objectives, two other standards can be used. The first of these is trends in the value of each of the ratios that the company has achieved over a number of years. Here the aim is to identify either favourable or unfavourable trends in

Table 14.2 *Efficiency and personnel ratios.*

Asset utilization	=	$\dfrac{\text{Sales revenue}}{\text{Total assets}}$
Stock turnover	=	$\dfrac{\text{Sales revenue}}{\text{Stocks}}$
Credit period	=	$\dfrac{\text{Value of debtors} \times 365}{\text{Sales}}$
Liquidity	=	$\dfrac{\text{Current assets}}{\text{Current liabilities}}$
Average (mean) employee remuneration	=	$\dfrac{\text{Total wage bill}}{\text{Number of employees}}$
Sales revenue per employee	=	$\dfrac{\text{Sales revenue}}{\text{Number of employees}}$

performance, or a comparison of current performance relative to that in previous years. The other standard is average values of ratios across the industry in which the company participates. Here the aim is obviously to identify good, average or poor performance relative to competitors. These standards are available from publishers who supply business information as a service to companies, for example the ICC Information Group Ltd.[6]. Although these comparisons should also have been made at the stage of setting the objectives, they can also be of value at the control stage, to enhance the analysis of the causes of performance as reflected in the actual ratios.

Budgets

Readers will be aware that budgets are widely used in finance and accounting. Also, as noted in Chapter 1, budgeting provided an early basis for systematic management, being a forerunner of the current process of strategic management. However, budgets remain an important technique of control in strategic management, although they have wider importance in general financial management.

For this section, which excludes profitability objectives, the technique relates to market spread and growth objectives. Budgeting is important because it is a process of defining all the company's future plans in financial terms. Therefore it gives a full breakdown of anticipated variable and fixed costs, forecasts of sales revenue to be aimed for, and projections of profits to be earned. The final stage of budgeting should be a master budget, which provides a projected balance sheet for the forthcoming period. While in the traditional accounting sense budgets are generally seen as a device for limiting expenditure, as part of strategic management they provide a basis for resource allocation, which can then be used as a technique for control.

For the purposes of strategic management, Pearce and Robinson[7] have classified budgets into capital, sales, and expenditure budgets. Capital budgets are concerned with the allocation of financial resources to the SBUs and/or divisions and to the strategies which are to be implemented. Acquisition of capital and decisions on allocation have already been mentioned in Chapters 11 and 12.

Sales budgets include a forecast of sales revenue and relate directly to sales growth objectives. In some companies this budget will also include costs directly associated with selling, which, when subtracted from revenue figures, give the contribution provided by marketing operations. When only revenue figures are included in this budget then the format is similar to that already given in Table 14.1.

Expenditure budgets provide details of anticipated costs involved in the implementation of operational strategies. Therefore they are generally linked directly to marketing, production and the others, being particularly concerned with the control of departmental costs.

To use budgets as a technique of control the approach is again to compare actual levels with the planned levels given in the budgets. Where variances are identified analysis of causes is again needed. Corrective action must then be taken as a consequence, within the three areas of action mentioned above in the section on variance analysis.

Qualitative control

Several objectives are qualitative in nature: those addressing market leadership (excluding market share); customer service; social responsibility; and some personnel objectives. Here the progression of the achievement of these objectives cannot be based on straightforward comparisons of figures, but is based on the value judgement of managers. In other words, managers must mentally compare their understanding of what has been achieved with the original intentions behind the setting of these qualitative objectives. Here the problem is obviously subjectivity in appraising success, so that recognized and standardized judgement across the company needs to be aimed for.

In order to aim for this standardization of judgement, Glueck and Jauch[8] have suggested three broad criteria:

Consistency

Is what is being achieved consistent with the intentions which were originally established in the objectives? For example, if the company wanted to appear more socially responsible and to improve its image or reputation relative to competitors, can it be realistically said that this has been achieved? Judgement also needs to be made about the consistency of objectives with each other. Being more competitive, for example, may not be consistent with being more socially responsible.

Appropriateness
This criterion diverts judgement to the appropriateness or suitability of intentions that were originally set in the objectives, as well as the suitability of what has been achieved. As the general business environment changes, the ability of the company to achieve market leadership, for example, may change, or more attention and resources may need to be devoted to the personal development of personnel. Also to be considered is the suitability of time periods to which these objectives relate. Current failure to achieve desired intentions may not mean that the objectives are inappropriate, but it may mean that a longer period of time is necessary for their attainment.

Workability
If value judgement suggests that there are variances between planned and actual levels of achievement, then it may be that the latter is realistic and that planned levels were not workable. Although the cause may have been changes in the environment, it could be that the objectives were too ambitious. Alternatively it may be that the objectives could have been worked had additional resources and managerial attention been made available. Therefore part of the judgement needs to be this assessment of just how realistic these qualitative measures are.

CONTROL OF PROFIT

In this section specific attention is given to the control of profits and to profitability. Although this control could have been covered in the last section, its obvious importance merits special attention. The two techniques used for control are budgets and ratio analysis, as discussed in the last section. Profits as an absolute value would be controlled through budgets, whereas profitability as a relative value would be controlled through ratio analysis.

Budgets

As explained in the last section, budgets give a full breakdown of anticipated variable and fixed costs, forecasts of sales revenue to be aimed for, and projections of profits to be earned. Therefore, within the context of this section, budgets provide a focused control technique, by allowing for comparisons of the value of actual profits achieved with planned values given in the budget. Again variances can be identified, analysis carried out of the cause of any variances, and corrective action taken.

Tighter control can be achieved by having several budgets that focus on the control of profits, following the hierarchies of objectives, strategies, and control. At the top would be the master budget for the whole organization, which would be split at the next level into budgets for each SBU and/or division. Thus control can be specifically related to each business area. This also means that each SBU will be accountable for its own profit or loss. This relates to the accountant's concept of profit and cost centres. At the next level in the hierarchy budgets can be prepared for individual product lines and/or individual markets. This gives even tighter control in that poor profit performance can be related specifically to where it has been initiated. Action can then be specifically directed to operational strategies and accountability can be identified with particular departments and/or managers.

In order for this technique of budgetary control to be effective there must be an effective system of integration and communication, as discussed in Chapter 13. Detailed information on sales and costs needs to be communicated both vertically and horizontally, to ensure that accurate measures can be made at the product and market levels. Adequate reporting of variances to managers within the hierarchy who have specific responsibility is also needed, in order to allow them to instigate necessary analysis. However, when this analysis is carried out with the aim of identifying causes, there may be resistance from some personnel to providing necessary information. Such resistance stems from the behavioural issues of human resource management (see Chapter 13), but is likely to be related to a concern about being blamed for any variances. Finally, necessary change as a result of the analysis of variances may be resisted, again for the reasons that were discussed in Chapter 13 under the heading of 'Managing change'. This may be overcome by encouraging participation in the planning of remedial action. However, given the importance of profits it may be necessary to exert power over the behaviour of some personnel in order to execute essential actions.

Ratio analysis

These ratios relate directly to the profitability objectives that were presented in Chapter 7. Like the ratios given in the last section, those discussed here relate profits to a base in order to give relative values of profitability. Books on financial management generally commence their treatment of profitability ratios with an overall profitability equation as follows, where profit is before taxation:

$$\text{Profitability} \quad = \frac{\text{Profit}}{\text{Total assets}} = \frac{\text{Profit}}{\text{Sales}} \times \frac{\text{Sales}}{\text{Total assets}}$$

The ratios that were given as objectives are listed in Table 14.3, where again profit is before tax. As will be noticed, each of the ratios measures profitability on a different basis:

- Return on capital employed measures profit in relation to the capital of shareholders' funds and the long-term loans used to generate the profit.
- Return on assets measures profit against the total of fixed, intangible and intermediate assets that were utilized to generate the profit.
- Profit margin is an expression of the proportion of sales revenue that has been achieved as profit.

- Return on shareholders' funds relates profit to the sum of share capital, reserves, and the profit and loss account balance.

Table 14.3 *Major profitability ratios.*

Return on capital employed	=	$\dfrac{\text{Profit}}{\text{Capital employed}}$
Return on assets	=	$\dfrac{\text{Profit}}{\text{Total assets}}$
Profit margin	=	$\dfrac{\text{Profit}}{\text{Sales revenue}}$
Return on shareholders' funds	=	$\dfrac{\text{Profit}}{\text{Total funds}}$

A major problem in using these ratios is comparing like with like, which is especially important with intercompany comparisons. Different definitions of the four denominators are used by different companies and by different authors. For example, Bishop[9] has given 11 variations on the theme of 'return on capital employed', all of which can be labelled as such but would give a different value. Therefore when comparing ratios it is essential to ensure that they have been determined with a common base.

As in the previous discussion on ratio analysis, control is again by comparing actual ratios with the standards given in the objectives. Also the technique is to identify variances, followed by an analysis of the cause of these variances, and culminating in remedial action. As well as comparing the actual variances to the objectives, the former can be compared to historical trends and to industry norms. Industry norms are seen to be particularly important in the financial literature. Direct comparisons are made with firms in the same industry, or they can be made with other firms of a similar size or similar sales turnover. Even though companies participate in the same industry they can still feature many differences in their nature, which may affect the validity of comparisons. These differences could include:

- Variations in size and capital structure.
- Relative intensity of capital and labour.
- Production efficiency and economies of scale.
- Trends in previous performance and profitability.
- Financial support from a parent company.
- Nature of organizational objectives and strategies.

Despite such differences the aim is still to identify good, average, or poor performance relative to other organizations. These comparisons also provide league tables of the relative performance of different industries, based again on these profitability ratios. Therefore it is also possible to make comparisons of performance on an interindustry basis.

Control charts

This is a technique which is of value in comparing and controlling profitability ratios on a historical trend basis. It is derived from statistical techniques for measuring dispersion of data. A control chart is constructed as shown in Figure 14.3, where a different chart would be needed for each of the profitability ratios. The chart gives a plot of the actual ratio for certain points in time, the ongoing trend, and shows changes in this ratio with time. The centre line represents the standard for comparison given in the objective, while the control limits represent acceptable tolerances. Although the objective line in this example is constant, indicating a stability requirement for this measure of profitability, it would obviously show an upward trend where growth of profitability is an objective.

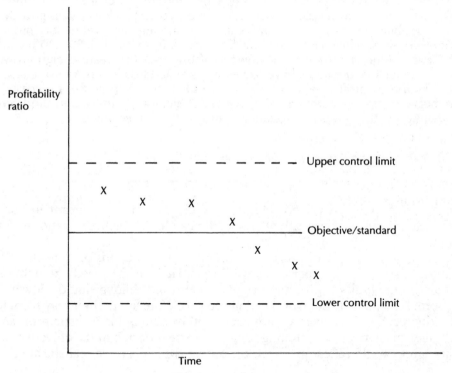

Figure 14.3 *Profitability control.*

All the calculated values of the ratios given in Figure 14.3 are within the control limits, so that acceptable control can be considered to have been achieved. Despite this situation the plot shows a downward trend of profitability, albeit within the control limits. In this case it is the early identification of downward trends which is important. The advantage here is that analysis and remedial action following the identification of the trend can be initiated before it approaches the lower limit. The issue of the time periods to which decision-making relates also needs to be considered. For example, increases in assets would result in a lowering of the value

---

EXHIBIT 14.2

Rising far above Intercompany Rivalries

Unigate is a British-based food group, although about a quarter of its sales and profits are generated from non-food businesses. In previous years a large proportion of its sales had been from its milk business, which in 1987 still accounted for about 30% of turnover. A problem of control for Unigate is that this market is in long-term decline, exacerbated by the general public's health consciousness and the high fat content of milk. Sales increased during the first half of 1987 but problems of control resulted in a fall in profits. However, the board's confidence in its ability to regain profit growth in the future led it to increase the dividend payment. Control of performance since 1982 resulted in profit margins nearly doubling, high annual increases in pre-tax profits despite a lower sales growth, a near doubling of return on capital employed, and a general reduction in debt. Control over strategy has led to a milking of cash from the milk SBU, to provide for a move into both food and non-food businesses that feature high growth opportunities. Acquisitions have played a major part in this control, with a large proportion of profits being used for diversification, such as the purchase of Wincanton car-hire company, the Giltspur exhibition business, and the lateral expansion of the company's restaurant chain in the United States.

Adapted from the *Guardian*, 17 November 1987

---

of ratios in the current period. However, such investment is meant to increase profits earned in future years, which would mean higher values of ratios in future periods.

The use of these control charts over relatively long periods of time also allows for consideration of the upper and lower limits. Here an aim may be to tighten the tolerance of the limits to give more rigorous control. While raising the lower limit may seem reasonable to control shortfalls, lowering the upper limit may seem to be restricting profits. However, as companies will be aiming for realistic profitability (including an element of stretching) this should be reflected in the objective, while higher limits would reflect profit maximization, which is not a realistic aim.

CONTROL OF STRATEGIES

As a result of the previous control techniques it may be that modifications to strategies are necessary. In other words control of objectives can lead to indirect control of strategies. However, direct control of strategies can also be carried out. As an additional form of control it can provide valuable guidance for the future, enhancing the techniques explained above.

This form of control is qualitative, being based on the value judgement of managers. Again the problem is one of subjectivity, although some attempts have been made in the literature to develop techniques to improve objectivity.

Strategy evaluation

The techniques which attempt to increase objectivity have developed from the early work of Tilles[10], where the aim was to provide an approach to the evaluation of strategy. This work suggested six criteria for evaluating strategy. In the literature these criteria are generally recommended for the control of existing strategies, or to be applied to strategies which are currently being implemented. This is in contrast to the evaluation of potential strategy alternatives for the future, as discussed in Chapter 10.

The first criterion suggested by Tilles is whether the strategy is internally consistent. This relates the strategy to those at other levels, the objectives being pursued, and the overriding mission. However, a strategy of growth, for example, may be inconsistent with an objective to retain autonomy or to increase profitability.

The second criterion is whether the strategy is consistent with the environment. Although the environment may have been adequately analysed at the formulation stage, variables may have changed significantly since its inception. Although external variables are of major concern, internal changes may also be applicable within this form of control.

The third criterion is whether the strategy is appropriate in view of the available resources? Although these will originally have been planned they also need to be assessed during implementation. The evaluation will include the availability of resources during implementation and their adequacy to allow for effective use. Emphasis is on exploitation of resources, but is also on constraints as a result of inadequate resources.

The fourth criterion is whether the strategy involves an acceptable degree of risk. Here the principle is again that the situation may have changed from the time when the strategy was originally formulated. While the establishment of strategies should contribute significantly to risk reduction, this aspect of control focuses on whether or not this is being achieved. Also to be considered is the extent, if any, of change of managers' attitudes towards risk as a consequence of strategy implementation.

The fifth criterion is whether the strategy has an appropriate time horizon. Although objectives and strategies should be specified for certain periods of time, they are, of course, reviewed on a regular basis. Therefore, this part of strategy evaluation is part of that review process. Some strategies may be appropriate beyond originally perceived periods of time, while others may need to be changed earlier. As mentioned in Chapter 11, larger periods of time relate to higher-level strategies.

The sixth and last criterion is whether the strategy is workable. Here Tilles advises looking for evidence to indicate that the strategy is appropriate. Although quantitative measures provide some evidence (as discussed earlier), these point not only to the strategy but also to the skills of the managers in using the strategy. Therefore the capabilities of managers also need to be evaluated in relation to the implementation of this strategy, following that discussed in the internal audit in Chapter 3.

Writers such as Learned[11] and Argenti[12] have built on this evaluation, adding questions such as whether in reality the strategy is appropriate to key managers' values and expectations; whether it is providing a clear stimulus to organizational effort and commitment; whether the strategy is really contributing to opportunity exploitation; and whether managers and other personnel are clearly relating to the strategy and understanding its impact. Other writers have proposed similar approaches to strategy evaluation, although perhaps adding little to that already given. An example here is the approach of Rumelt[13].

Motivation to evaluate

Some writers have suggested the necessity to ensure that managers are motivated to carry out this type of evaluation of strategies. Indeed this is likely to be easily achieved if managers perceive a possibility of strategy failure, and if their rewards are based on the attainment of objectives. However, this is a negative way of looking at the importance of control. The implication is that managers should be motivated to see implementation and control as being of equal importance and part of the same process.

In Chapter 13 attention was given to motivation and associated rewards within the strategic management process. While an emphasis was placed on motivation towards long-run issues in that chapter, within the context of control Hrebiniak and Joyce[14] have emphasized the need to balance control between both long- and short-run issues. The problem is seen as being one of motivating managers to ensure the integration of long- and short-run issues.

To achieve this they suggest that rewards should be based not just on performance, but also on the ability of managers to demonstrate that they can evaluate and control both long- and short-run issues of strategy. In Chapter 13 both pecuniary and non-pecuniary rewards were discussed, where the latter were split between tangible incentives and self-fulfilment. For the purposes of motivating, self-fulfilment can be a strong influence to execute this type of control. Alternatively it may be necessary formally to include control into the reward system that is developed for the total process of strategic management.

The control audit

While auditing was presented in Part Two as a stage for the analysis of the environment, the technique of auditing is also appropriate as part of control. In the introduction to this chapter it was said that results from control provide inputs into this analysis for the next phase of strategic management. Indeed this completes the cycle of strategic management, in that auditing as part of control links up with auditing as part of environmental analysis. Therefore although auditing is given a role in both analysis and control, it can also be perceived as being part of the same interconnecting process.

As a technique of control the audit is largely qualitative in nature. Although it relies mostly on the value judgement of managers, results from the analysis of the quantitative techniques that have been discussed in the chapter can also be utilized. The overall aim of this technique is a broad appraisal of the success of strategic management over the previous period of time. While the previous techniques aim to appraise specific areas, the audit aims to provide an overall understanding.

For control purposes the audit generally consists of a range of questions to be addressed. These would follow a format similar to that given in Table 14.4. Although these questions are given in three groups, the answer are all indicative of the relative success of the strategies that have been used. In addition the answers are also indicative of the capabilities of managers to utilize the process of strategic management. Therefore the technique requires impartiality in its use, or ideally it should be carried out by independent auditors. For some companies this may necessitate outside auditors from a management consultancy firm.

Table 14.4   *A control audit.*

Objectives
1. Were the qualitative and quantitative organizational objectives satisfactorily achieved?
2. Were they found to be appropriate to the environmental conditions across the SBUs?
3. Were the qualitative and quantitative business objectives satisfactorily achieved?
4. Did the business objectives contribute satisfactorily to the higher-level objectives?
5. Were the business objectives found to be appropriate within each SBU?

Strategies
1. Was the organizational strategy a success in allowing for the achievement of the organizational objectives?
2. Did the organizational strategy support the pursuit of the mission?
3. Were the business strategies successful in allowing for the achievement of business objectives?
4. Did each business strategy support the higher level strategy and the pursual of the mission?

Mission
1. Is the mission being satisfactorily fulfilled?
2. If not, to what extent is progress being made for fulfilment?
3. Was the mission appropriate for the previous period?
4. Could it have been widened, or indeed should it have been narrowed?

EFFECTIVENESS

For some companies strategic management will be fully integrated into the corporate culture. For other companies it may be only partially utilized, while others may have only experimented with the process. Regardless of the reliance placed on strategic management, some assessment of its value to managers and its effectiveness as a process is likely to be needed.

The common way in strategic management textbooks is to present the process which should result in the company achieving particular end results which represent its performance. If this performance is consistent with the end results/performance as planned in the objectives, then the implication is that the strategic management process was effective. However, as will be readily appreciated by readers, many factors are likely to have influenced the end results achieved, of which strategic management is but one. This has led writers such as Dyson and Foster[15] and King[16] to address effectiveness by examining the nature of the process rather than end results. These two approaches to assessing value and effectiveness are discussed below. Another way of assessing effectiveness is simply to make the assumption that it is of value. Here it is assumed that strategic management *per se* will lead to many benefits for the company, so that regardless of any direct influence on performance the process will be of value. The range of benefits likely to result from the use of strategic management are examined later in this section.

The end-results approach

As mentioned above, the logic of this approach can be summarized as: the performance and end results were consistent with those specified in planned objectives and a systematic approach to strategic management was taken, therefore the process can be considered to be effective. However, the flaw in the logic is that other factors will also have had an influence on the company's end results, so that establishing a cause-and-effect relationship is extremely problematic.

Despite this problem many researchers have attempted to identify this relationship by investigating samples of companies. These surveys are based on researching the association between the level of sophistication of strategic planning used and the overall level of results achieved as company performance. Examinations of these surveys have been carried out by Greenley[17], Shrader *et al.*[18] and Armstrong[19]. Greenley concluded, from the surveys that he examined, that the data are far from conclusive in establishing whether or not sophistication of planning affects performance. Consequently it cannot be concluded that such an approach would be a reliable measure of effectiveness. However, the examination also identified methodological weaknesses across these surveys:

- Little commonality in the definition of terms used.
- Evidence of subjectivity in the definition of terms used.
- General weakness in not identifying other variables that could also have affected end results.
- Evidence of bias in methodological rigour.
- Wide variation in reporting the statistical significance of the results.

Armstrong[19] also concluded that there are serious research problems to be found across the studies. However, he does claim that, on balance, the results do reflect the value of strategic planning. The examination by Shrader *et al.* was a more extensive study than the other two. Again the conclusion was that no clear systematic relationship between formal long-range planning and organizational performance could be identified.

The overall conclusion from these investigations is that research into the effect of strategic management on end results is far from conclusive. A cause-and-effect relationship between the level of sophistication of strategic planning and end results has not been identified from these surveys. Therefore the results do not allow one to claim that the effectiveness of strategic management is necessarily reflected in end results.

The multidimensional approach

As mentioned earlier, this approach is concerned with assessing effectiveness through an appraisal of the nature of the process as opposed to drawing implications from the end results. The major method developed here comes from the work of Dyson and Foster[15,20]. Their method is based on a range of 13 attributes, the presence of which is taken to indicate effectiveness. The result of a particular assessment gives a profile of 13 scores, which is used as a guide to describe overall effectiveness. The 13 attributes are as follows:

- Clear statement of objectives.
- Integration of the planning function.
- Catalytic action of planning.
- Richness of formulation.
- Depth of evaluation.
- Treatment of uncertainty.
- Resources planned for implementation.
- Adequate data.
- Iteration to allow for control.
- Explicit assumptions.
- Quantification of appropriate objectives.
- Control measures.
- Feasibility of implementation.

Several problems are apparent from the use of this method. First, there is the problem of determining the nature of the attributes which actually represent effectiveness, given the problem of relating the process to performance or end results. Second, as the identification of these attributes is not immediately apparent, then there is the problem of knowing whether or not the established set of attributes is complete and adequate. The third problem is getting acceptance between the managers of a company of the relationship of the attributes of effectiveness, as well as agreement between companies. A fourth problem is getting common acceptance of a necessity to weight the attributes to represent their relative degrees of importance. The final problem is, even if such attributes can potentially reflect effectiveness, will the process produce the desired results? As companies are in business to achieve certain end results, defined in their objectives, then the argument reverts back to the tenet that the means for these end results can only be effective if it produces the required end results or performance.

As little empirical testing of this method has been carried out, little has been achieved to overcome these problems. Consequently the method has not been established as a reliable measure of effectiveness. However, it does give valuable guidance about the level of sophistication of strategic management adoption by companies, in relation to logical and systematic normative models given in the literature.

The assumption approach

As outlined earlier, this approach to effectiveness is merely to assume that strategic management *per se* will lead to many benefits for the company, so that, regardless of any direct influence on performance, the process will be of value. Greenley[17] has presented a range of benefits that are likely to result from the utilization of strategic planning. These are split between those that the company intends to accrue to it through the use of strategic planning, and those that merely result as a consequence of using strategic planning. The former are labelled 'potential advantages', while the latter are labelled 'intrinsic values'; both are obviously applicable to the overall strategic management process.

Potential advantages
Those given in the literature have been either advocated by certain managers, or prescribed by certain writers. In both cases they are classified into process advantages and advantages pertaining to personnel. Examples of process advantages cited by Greenley[17] are:

- An objective view of management problems.
- Minimization of effects of adverse conditions.
- More effective allocation of time and resources.
- Less time and resources need be devoted to correcting erroneous and *ad hoc* decisions.
- The creation of a framework for internal communications.
- The provision of a basis for creating competitive advantage.

Examples cited of advantages pertaining to personnel are:

- The integration of the behaviour of personnel.
- The provision of a basis for the clarification of individual responsibilities.
- The encouragement of forward thinking in personnel.

- The stimulation of a co-operative, integrated and enthusiastic approach to tackling problems and opportunities.
- The fostering of a favourable attitude towards change.
- The instilment of increased discipline and formality to operational management.

Intrinsic values

Here there are three groups of values that are considered to result merely as a consequence of utilizing strategic planning. These values relate to the general external environment, markets, and the internal environment: an example of the first is the benefit of risk reduction as a contribution to security of investment; an example of the second is improved assessments of changes in customer requirements; while an example of the third is the resulting internal co-ordination of business functions.

Although some of the above have been reported by managers, there is currently insufficient empirical evidence to substantiate the claim that these advantages and values will be realized by all companies. Therefore it is not reasonable to assume that strategic management will be effective merely because a company uses it, even though the above can be argued strongly on a priori grounds.

PROBLEMS OF CONTROL

In this last section of the chapter attention is given to problems of control. Those given below are from three major textbooks, whose writers suggest that they are key problems to be identified. Although each of these is of major importance, in practice it is likely that other problems of control may also arise.

Harvey[21] cites three major problems of control. The first of these is the *invalid reporting of data*. As will be appreciated from the previous sections of this chapter, control is based on much analysis, which requires valid and reliable information for its completion. Problems can arise in obtaining information, both internal and external, and in its communication through the organizational structure. Invalid information can lead to inaccurate analysis, which in turn can lead to inappropriate action.

The second is *contradictory reporting of data*. One contradiction may be as a result of inconsistency of objectives, as already mentioned earlier. Another common problem is contradiction in information collected for control. Different assessments of competitors' market shares, for example, often yield different results. Internally generated information, such as product costings, may also show some variation or major differences over various periods of time.

The third is *resistance to controls*. In the ideal world all managers and employees would be motivated to pay due care and attention to the use of control techniques. However, following general managerial resistance to change, as discussed in Chapter 13, it would not be surprising for a company to experience some resistance to using control techniques. This could be due to concern that the results of the analysis may blame certain individuals for 'things having gone wrong'. Alternatively, they may be seen as an additional task to the individual's job specification, or they may be seen as being of little value and detractors from implementation activities.

Bates and Eldredge[22] also cite three major problems. The first of these lies in the *excessive authority of a controller*. In some organizations it may be practice to designate a manager to handle control, or to appoint a staff manager to take the responsibility. While such a move has a clear advantage of designating responsibility for the important process of control, Bates and Eldredge suggest that it can also be problematic. Although the controller would have authority in matters to do with control, he would not have line decision-making responsibilities. Therefore, conflict may arise within the hierarchy, particularly if the controller usurps the job functions of other managers.

The second stems from the *abuse of budgets*. Here Bates and Eldredge suggest that problems can arise in the formulation of budgets, as managers obviously know that they are to be partly judged on their fulfilment. Therefore the tendency may be to set budgets at artificially low levels, so that actual results will appear to reflect better performance. As budgets are based on forecasts this can also be a basis for abuse. Normal forecasting error can be a reliable excuse for poor performance or it may give rise to the argument that the budget is invalid.

The third concerns *rewards and punishments*. Where managers are to be personally rewarded for improved performance in certain objectives it is obvious that their efforts in the control process will be in this direction. Indeed, this would be part of planned motivational activity. However the potential problem is insufficient attention to other areas of control. Although such a problem can perhaps be countered through the delegation of responsibilities, the point is that managerial attention to control needs to be monitored.

Finally, we consider the major problems raised by Wheelen and Hunger[23]. The first is *short-term orientation*. Despite the focus of strategic management on the long run, many managers find it easier to focus on short-term issues. This is a phenomenon that has been raised at several junctures in this book, but the claim here is that control of immediate results may be seen as being of overriding importance, compared to the control of long-term trends in performance. This is not to say that short-term performance is not important, as clearly it is, but what is important is a balance of control over both time horizons.

The other major problem cited by Wheelen and Hunger is *goal displacement*. This problem arises when the process of control is perceived as being more important than the objectives or end results that are the subject of the control. In other words, the objectives or goals are displaced by their means of achievement, which are replaced in the order of things as being of more importance. Wheelen and Hunger give two major causes of problems, which they name 'behaviour substitution' and 'suboptimization'. The former they relate to both quantifiable and qualitative objectives. As quantitative objectives are easier to measure, the tendency may be to divert control behaviour to these objectives to the detriment of qualitative objectives. Suboptimization is seen to cause potential problems as a result of splitting the company into SBUs and/or departments with recognizable domains of responsibility. Managers within each area are primarily concerned with controlling the areas in which they are personally located and they may have little concern for other SBUs and/or divisions. Therefore the concern is that, although the division of the structure into units of recognizable responsibility is meant to impove organizational efficiency, it may also lead to problems of control.

SUMMARY

This has been the last of three chapters addressing the implementation of strategy, where attention has been given to control and effectiveness.

In the first section a framework for control was presented, based on standards of performance, measurement and action. The second section then examined control of objectives. This section commenced with a ratification of the importance of control, followed by attention to quantitative and qualitative control. Three techniques for quantitative control were explained: variance analysis; budgets; and ratio analysis. Qualitative control was seen to be based on the value judgements of managers. Three broad criteria were discussed which should help to standardize judgement: consistency, appropriateness; and workability.

The third section tackled the control of profit. Budgets were discussed as the major technique for controlling profits. To control profitability, ratio analysis was suggested as the major technique. The main profitability ratios were given and the use of control charts was discussed.

The fourth section was concerned with direct control of strategies. Approaches advocated in the literature are largely qualitative, relying on the value judgement of managers. The approach to control through strategy evaluation was discussed, in the form of a series of critical questions to be posed about the value of strategies. The next issue of this section was the motivation of managers to carry out this type of control. Finally, the technique of control audits was examined, which links into strategic audits as part of the analysis of the environment (see Part Two).

The final section of this chapter focused on the effectiveness of strategic management as a process. This concept was first examined from the point of view of end results or performance. A multidimensional approach to effectiveness was then discussed, where the nature of the process, rather than end results, is seen to be important. Finally, the assumption approach is based on the premiss that the use of strategic management *per se* will lead to many benefits for the company.

CHAPTER CASE STUDY ILLUSTRATION: TARMAC PLC*

Tarmac is a British-based organization with six SBUs, concerned with quarry products; construction; building products; housing; oil and industrial products; and property. Growth and performance increased dramatically in the 1970s and 1980s, and the case study illustrates the importance of control in this performance.

For the period from 1974–84, sales revenue increased by 330% (from £300 million to £1,300 million), profit increased by 547% (from £17 million to £110 million), with the latter increasing at an annual average of 27% over the last five years. Growth at the organizational strategy level in the late 1960s and early 1970s had been achieved through diversification. However, the above growth to 1984 had been achieved at the business strategy level, within each of the SBUs.

The case study suggests that a major cause of this performance was the company's considerable attention to control and the tightness of measurement and consequential action. Indeed corporate management seems to have been dominated by control activity. That given in the case study is discussed below, in sections that parallel those given in the chapter.

FRAMEWORK FOR CONTROL

Co-ordinating the six SBUs is a major role of corporate headquarters, with the chief executive functions being at the centre. These major functions were given as:

- Reviewing and sanctioning budgets.
- Monthly monitoring of performance against budget.
- Sanctioning capital expenditure proposals.
- Controlling the development of strategy.
- Managing Tarmac's relationship with the financial community.

Control is very much at the centre of the organization, with commitment from the MD to ensure that procedures are used effectively. However, in order to motivate managers within the SBUs to accept the importance of control, detail relating to the SBUs is decentralized to the units. The philosophy is that the company wants the chief executives of each SBU to feel that they have control over the costs of their respective inputs and the value of their outputs.

*Derived from the original case study by A. Campbell. (Copyright © 1986 by the London Business School.)

In November of each year the chief executive agrees a comprehensive budget for each of the SBUs for the following year. This is very much a 'bottom-up' exercise, with the SBUs determining and proposing their own strategies and budgets. Standards of performance are not dictated from HQ, but they are then negotiated for acceptability at the organizational level of performance. However, the aim is to achieve personal commitment by the management team of each SBU to their respective budgets and strategies, which Tarmac considers can only be achieved by full participation.

The mechanism for control is a divisional executive committee for each of the SBUs. These committees meet monthly to measure performance against the standards given in the respective budgets and to plan the implementation of consequential action. Commitment to these committees is required from both corporate headquarters personnel and the management team of each SBU.

CONTROL OF OBJECTIVES

Given the importance of budgets to Tarmac and the reliance which is placed on them, the case study gives little mention of the role of objectives. It is claimed that little use is made of broad quantitative objectives. However, objectives are established related to profitability, which focus on a year-on-year growth in the volume of profits, and maintenance of, or improvements to, profitability ratios. Broad directional objectives are also established for the group. These are developed from an understanding of the future developments of the SBUs, so that again the aim is to avoid the imposition of 'top-down' pressure. Again the emphasis is on control from corporate headquarters.

Perhaps a weakness of this control is its focus on the short term through annual budgets, and its neglect of the longer term through objectives. The emphasis is on current profit and not that in future years. However, it is claimed that this weakness is partly offset by the attitudes of SBU chief executives, who are likely to remain in place over a number of years. Their commitment to yearly increases in performance will likely result in a long-term improvement in performance.

CONTROL OF PROFITS

As already mentioned, control of SBU profits is central to the total process of control at Tarmac. However, achievement of budgets is required and underperformance is unacceptable. In addition each year's performance is expected to be better than the previous year's. Therefore the management team of each SBU is under obligation to achieve profitable growth each and every year. This requirement for profitable growth is seen to be important in encouraging the identification and development of new opportunities. This performance measurement of profits, as part of the total control process, is also used for the appraisal and evaluation of the respective management teams.

CONTROL OF STRATEGIES

As outlined earlier, each of the SBUs is required to formulate its own strategies. Indeed strategy establishment is focused on the SBUs and there is no strategic plan for the whole group at the organizational level. Without such a plan the main link from central headquarters to the SBUs remains the respective budgets. Again the mechanism for control is the divisional executive committees. These meetings allow for the evaluation of strategies in meeting budget standards. Personnel from headquarters are given the opportunity to influence decision-making about strategy, and to instigate action to correct performance. Therefore, as one senior manager said 'the Centre keeps control of the development of strategy', reflecting the organizational level requirement for control, while delegating strategy instigation and formulation to the respective SBUs. The aim is to allow the SBU chief executives to feel as though they are completely in charge of their businesses, and to recognize that HQ will give them the opportunity to forge ahead with their own initiated strategies.

INTEGRATIVE CASE ILLUSTRATION: PART FIVE

Issues relating to operational strategies, human resource management, and control are to be found in the Plessey case study. Together they illustrate problems of implementation, following the issues of strategy formulation that were examined in Part Four. This illustration also shows that there were differences in Plessey's approach to implementation over time.

OPERATIONAL STRATEGIES

In his annual review at the end of 1983, the Chairman and Chief Executive of Plessey emphasized the importance of operational strategies for future improvements to their competitiveness. R&D, marketing, and manufacturing were specified as being of particular importance.

In 1971 the company had developed strengths in production strategy, particularly in quality and cost control. However, marketing strategy at this time was almost non-existent, being simply based on establishing and maintaining contacts in relevant Government departments. With the introduction of the POST (Plessey Objectives, Strategy and Tactics) system in 1975, marketing began to play an important role. Indeed, marketing analysis and thinking were central to the whole system, enabling management to start establishing objectives, formulating strategies, and implementing tactics. A major outcome was the identification of many market segments and several 'dead dogs'. Many of the latter were eventually eliminated to improve performance.

Although the POST system provided an initial and major movement towards systematic strategic management, by 1977 many weaknesses had been identified. One of these weaknesses concerned operational strategies. The claim was that there had been a failure on the part of many managers to integrate the planning of these strategies into their day-to-day management activity. Although changes made to their planning in 1977 were designed to improve the overall effectiveness of the system, the aim was also to achieve more integration of the operations.

The importance of R&D to Plessey's SBUs has been a recurrent theme throughout these illustrations. R&D expenditure had increased 3.6 times between 1974 and 1983. However by this time about 75% of this funding was provided by its customers.

HUMAN RESOURCE MANAGEMENT

During the 1970s Plessey had a Corporate Service Department, established as a headquarters function at the organizational level. Its role was to advise management within the SBUs, although there was no direct participation and authority was not directly delegated to the function. If management within the SBUs would not accept this advice, then the Corporate Service Department could attempt to force its recommendations on the SBUs, through the power of the Plessey board of directors. This system was opposed by several managers in the SBUs. It was perceived as being an interference with responsibility, when authority had been previously delegated to certain managers for certain SBUs. Conflict clearly resulted, which would also have affected commitment and motivation. This was perhaps reflected in 1974 in a failed Anglo-French joint-venture in telecommunications. Part of the cause of failure was claimed to be the inability of Plessey's management adequately to identify and develop new strategic opportunities.

Changes to the organizational structure in 1976 also influenced human resource management. This change was to base the company on a number of product-based subsidiaries, with world-wide product management responsibility. This meant that the managing directors of the subsidiaries were delegated total authority for their respective subsidiaries. Although remedial action and advice were not available from headquarters, this change motivated higher levels of commitment, which was reflected in fewer problems and enhanced performance.

Indications are also given in the case study of the leadership styles of the Chairman and CEO, Sir John Clark, and his brother, Michael Clark, who was Deputy Chairman and CEO. Although Sir John had great expectations for the future of Plessey, he was said to be 'possessive and paternalistic' of the company. It was also claimed that he was very demanding of the senior managers, with high expectations of personal and company performance. However, motivational and participation incentives were encouraged, with the managing directors of subsidiaries being able to earn a performance bonus of up to 50% of their salaries. It was said that Michael Clark was perhaps a more demanding leader, who was reported as believing in placing high demands on managers, while recognizing that he was not an easy person to work for.

CONTROL

The introduction of the POST system in 1977 was not only to instigate systematic planning into the future, but also to achieve the control which is associated with this planning. It was considered to be essential to make managers appreciate that planning is an essential tool of business management. The aim was to co-ordinate and control relationships between objectives, strategies and tactics, which had not been achieved in the past. Prior to this, in 1976, the establishment of the Chief Executive Office was also concerned with control. Here the control issue was one of aiming for closer liaison between the divisions and of achieving more direct responsibilities at the top of the structure.

Monitoring for control was by the main board, the Chief Executive Office, and the divisional managing directors. The main board reviewed all results in detail across the total organization at the end of each month. The Chief Executive Office personnel made detailed comparisons of results, and were also concerned with detailed action relating to specific problems and remedial measures. Divisional managing directors held monthly meetings with their senior management for control purposes. Further monthly meetings were also held at lower levels within each division's hierarchy, again aimed at effecting control.

For 1978–9 it was reported that Plessey had a stronger balance sheet than in previous years, with total debt considerably reduced. However, their return on capital employed (ROCE) for the year was 22%, compared to industry norms of 25–27%. At the end of 1980 ROCE had risen to 27%, as a result of major increases in sales, profits and profit margins. Internal rationalization had improved efficiency, while divestments had also contributed to improved performance. At the end of 1981 record profits were recorded, so that ROCE was 29% for the year. Despite the economic recession and other detrimental environmental influences, the management of Plessey was exhibiting improved performance. For 1982 there were again major gains in profit, although it was noted that half these profits came from a build-up of cash generated by mature products. Despite this position, ROCE for the year had stabilized at 28%.

REFERENCES

1. Anthony, R. N. and Dearden, J., *Management Control Systems*, Irwin, Homewood, IL, 1980.
2. Lorange, P., Scott Morton, M. F. and Ghoshal, S., *Strategic Control*, West, St Paul, MN, 1986.
3. Newman, W. H., *Constructive Control: Design and Use of Control Systems*, Prentice Hall, Englewood Cliffs, NJ, 1975.
4. Higgins, J. M., *Organizational Policy and Strategic Mangement*, 2nd edn, Dryden, New York, 1983.
5. Hofer, C. W. and Schendel, D., *Strategy Formulation: Analytical Concepts*, West, St Paul, MN, 1978.
6. *Industrial Performance Analysis*, 1987–88 edn, ICC Business Publications, London, 1987.
7. Pearce, J. A. and Robinson, R. B., *Strategic Management*, 2nd edn, Irwin, Homewood, IL, 1985.
8. Glueck, W. F. and Jauch, L. R., *Business Policy and Strategic Management*, 4th edn, McGraw-Hill, New York, 1984.
9. Bishop, E. B., 'ROCE as a Tool for Planning and Control', *Long Range Planning*, **2**, 4, 1969, 80–7.
10. Tilles, S., 'How to Evaluate Corporate Strategy', *Harvard Business Review*, **41**, 4, 1963, 111–21.
11. Learned, E. P., *Business Policy: Text and Cases*, Irwin, Homewood, IL, 1969.
12. Argenti, J., *Systematic Corporate Planning*, Wiley, New York, 1974.
13. Rumelt, R., 'The Evaluation of Business Strategy' in W. F. Glueck (ed.), *Business Policy and Strategic Management*, McGraw-Hill, New York, 1984.

14. Hrebiniak, L. G. and Joyce, W. F., *Implementing Strategy*, Macmillan, New York, 1984.
15. Dyson, R. G. and Foster, M. J., 'Effectiveness in Strategic Planning', *European Journal of Operational Research*, **5**, 3, 1980, 163–70.
16. King, W. R., 'Evaluating the Effectiveness of Your Planning', *Managerial Planning*, **33**, 2, 1984, 4–9.
17. Greenley, G. E., 'Does Strategic Planning Improve Company Performance?', *Long Range Planning*, **19**, 2, 1986, 101–9.
18. Shrader, C. B., Taylor, L. and Dalton, D. R., 'Strategic Planning and Organizational Performance: A Critical Appraisal', *Journal of Management*, **10**, 2, 1984, 149–71.
19. Armstrong, J. S., 'The Value of Formal Planning for Strategic Decisions', *Strategic Management Journal*, **3**, 1982, 100–11.
20. Dyson, R. G. and Foster, M. J., 'The Relationship of Participation and Effectiveness in Strategic Planning', *Strategic Management Journal*, **3**, 1, 1982, 77–88.
21. Harvey, D. F., *Strategic Management*, Merrill, Columbus, OH, 1982.
22. Bates, D. L. and Eldredge, D. L., *Strategy and Policy*, 2nd edn, Brown, Dubuque, OH, 1980.
23. Wheelen, T. L. and Hunger, J. D., *Strategic Management and Business Policy*, 2nd edn, Addison-Wesley, Reading, MA, 1986.

Name Index

Subject Index

Coventry University